The Essentials of

Intermediate Astrology

NATIONAL COUNCIL for GEOCOSMIC RESEARCH

Essentials of Intermediate Astrology

ISBN 0-9648415-0-9

Printed in the USA. Designed by M.B. Downing, Charts courtesy AIR Software

a dedication to

Charles Emerson and **Neil Michelson**

-whose combined efforts established and nurtured NCGR

Table of Contents

Foreword

by Robert Hand

As the Chairman of the National Council for Geocosmic Research, I am pleased to introduce this set of writings.

These should prove to be a significant step forward in the realization of one of NCGR's fundamental goals, the improvement of astrological education in modern times. Too often an astrologer's education consists simply of what he or she can glean at astrology conferences, reading miscellaneous books on miscellaneous topics, or astrology articles in magazines. Even when an astrologer does receive systematic training, it is quite often based on the methods of a single teacher. And regardless of how good a single teacher may be, all students are different and need to put together their own astrological toolbox based on a wide variety of sources and opinions.

Most texts in astrology are either aimed at the beginner, and therefore only cover what is deemed by the author to be suitable for a beginner; or the more advanced books cover a single topic area, often exhaustively, but not in such a way as to give the student an overview of the material that he or she needs to master astrology beyond the elementary level. This is not to be viewed as a criticism of such texts. It is simply by way of pointing out a need.

The text in this book is intended to fill that need. Its material was inspired by the Level II curriculum of the NCGR educational program. However, its usefulness is not in any way limited solely to students participating in that program. The articles contain precisely the overview of the techniques and tools that are needed for students who have gotten the basics of astrology down. This material is what comes next. It is considered that a student who has mastered this material, has a basic technical mastery of modern astrology. This is not to say that such a student does not still have to learn the processes of interacting with clients, or developing the skills that he or she might need in a specialized practice. But the material in this book should be mastered before further training. The precise place of this book in the education of an astrologer can be best made clear by filling the reader in on something of the history and purposes of the National Council for Geocosmic Research.

The NCGR was founded in 1972. It was originally started by a group of astrologers, doctors and researchers for the purpose of systematically investigating the lore and literature of astrology. It was also founded in the hope that something could be done to elevate the level of astrological training and education.

Through the '70s NCGR grew from its base in New York City and attracted some of the best astrologers from around the country to its membership until it became a genuine national organization with chapters and members all over the country. In the year 1980, members of NCGR representing all of the local chapters assembled in Princeton, NJ to meet and design a comprehensive and systematic educational program in astrology that would train astrologers and give them an overview of the field, not merely the personal preferences of a single teacher.

The program was designed to increase the knowledge possessed by astrologers of astrology itself so as to include a broader range of techniques, methods, and ways of approaching astrology. The program was designed so that it would go beyond the minimum needed to practice on a day-to-day level, but was designed so that astrologers who had gone through it would have larger collection of material from which to select their tools. This would allow new astrologers to do astrology in the way most appropriate to themselves and their clients. For this reason the NCGR curriculum goes beyond the normal basics of modern astrology and trains students in a variety of modern astrological schools including conventional modern Western astrology as well Cosmobiology, Uranian astrology, sidereal astrology and a variety of other modern techniques that have proved very useful but which tend to get left out of textbooks.

The design of the curriculum is based on a four year course of instruction at a university. It is divided into four levels. Level I is basic modern astrology. Level II is designed to introduce the student to a variety of technical methods that should be at least examined by anyone intending to become a practicing astrologer or researcher. Level III introduces more advanced methods and schools, and begins to prepare the student for independent work and also for counseling. Level IV is the final preparation for being an astrologer consisting of more advanced counseling and research methods, depending upon whether the student aims at being a counselor, teacher, or researcher.

Since the NCGR curriculum has been put in place, considerable progress has been made. Many cities now have complete courses of instruction certifying students in all four levels of the program, and quite a number of students have taken the national exams in all four levels. It is safe to say that the NCGR Level IV graduates are among the best informed and trained persons ever to embark on an astrological career. But it has still been difficult for students who are not near large cities where the curriculum is taught to get training in it. The ideal solution will probably be some kind of correspondence course where each student will work by mail, fax, or phone with a tutor from materials prepared by NCGR However before we can do that, we need to remedy the lack of texts which deal with the various levels of student in the NCGR program. We hope that this text is the first in a series of such texts which will allow students either to prepare themselves in their own individually chosen programs of astrological study, or to study within the context of a regular NCGR program. So, equally, whether you are a general reader interested in the material or a student involved in an NCGR curriculum program, we invite you to join us in the study of this material and together we can all move toward an astrological community that is better trained in astrology and in its proper uses. ✹

Acknowledgement

Alphee Lavoie

In putting this book together there are so many people to thank, as this publication has only been made possible by a group effort.

So first of all a hearty "thank you" goes to all of the authors who willingly contributed the chapters that make up this book. Additionally, I particularly want to extend my gratitude to some other people.

A generous "thank you" to Lorraine Welsh for editing the material for this book and offering her professional expertise in writing and publishing; to Mary Downing for all of her assistance and putting up with all those "last minute" pressures; to Michael Munkasey for technical advising and editing; and to my wife, Carol Lavoie, for editing and taking care of all the little details from start to finish. To all of us who worked on this book, may we all join hands and take a well deserved bow! ✺

—Alphee Lavoie

EDITOR'S COMMENTS

by Lorraine Welsh

This project has been a labor of love and a testimony of faith for everyone involved with it.

It started with Alphee Lavoie's vision and followed through with the NCGR Board of Directors' giving approval to proceed. All of the talented astrologers who contributed articles did so without pay, and even went so far as to turn over copyright privileges to NCGR as well. AND, in a supreme sacrifice, they allowed this book's editors to change spelling, capitalization, punctuation – even words – without a whimper, in order to conform to style. (The only exception is in Diana Rosenberg's listing for "Fixed Stars;" the format just didn't lend itself to change.) Without this superb cooperation we would never have completed this project in the desired time frame.

You will notice throughout that we have tried to maintain a simple style so as not to confuse the reader. For example, we spell "ascendant" without a capital letter; we use AM and PM for times just as your computer software does; and so on. Simple matters, but at least you don't have to shift mind gears from one article to another.

Except when it comes to charts. Here we have allowed each author to choose the chart system of his or her choice. Koch and Placidus were the popular choices. Eventually, you may want to convert the data into the system you use, but at least while reading the article you'll need to follow the author's choice in order to make sense of the arguments presented.

The editing process is complicated. It involves more than just proof-reading for spelling and punctuation errors. It requires the editor to have enough knowledge of the subject to be able to understand even the most obscure point, or to see to it that it be rewritten in clearer language. Any changes to the original text are made with the author's concurrence and in the author's own words so that the style does not change. Sometimes this requires a bit of haggling back and forth, although the authors of this book were all accomplished communicators and were agreeable to any suggestions for further clarification of minor points. Many thanks to them for making this an easy editing project.

One of the most overlooked ingredients – or perhaps the most taken-for-granted – is the work of the book designer and production director. Here, in Mary Downing, the NCGR has a jewel. Like the editor, the designer must also understand the material so as to place charts, tables, sidebars, illustrations, in a meaningful and attractive way. It is not enough for the book just to ''look" good, it must also read well and be easy to surf through, as they say in computer land. You can thank Mary for that.

Most editors say *"If I can understand this material, then so will the readers; if I can't, neither will they.''* We hope that is true of this book: that it is clear, easy to read, informative. And maybe even fun. At the Museum where I worked for many years, the motto was "It's fun to find out!" Let's hope when you get through with this book, you'll have found out a few things and you'll have had a really good time doing it! ✷

Lorraine Welsh

Needham, Massachusetts

TRANSITS — Celestial Passages

by Lorraine Welsh

How astrologers answer the inevitable "What's Up Doc?" by looking at the journey of the planets through the horoscope

Do transits work? You bet they do! It doesn't take a genius to figure out daily events just by using keywords to describe planet energies, and an ephemeris to plot out planet movements. It's one of the reasons astrologers are rarely surprised when a momentous event occurs — the planets have already foreshadowed what the newspapers will print tomorrow.

Take, for example, these four events from the front pages of the nation's newspapers. Look what happens when you use just some conjunctions (direct hits) and an occasional square (stress):

When tragedy struck Nicole Brown Simpson, draining her life and turning her death into a tabloid extravaganza, Neptune and Uranus (mystery, intrigue sudden, unexpected action) were opposite her natal Mars (energy violence). Transiting Mars (a knife) in the sign of Taurus (the throat) was conjunct her natal Mercury (life-giving breath, spirit). Even more ominously, transiting Pluto-Node conjunct natal Jupiter (an overwhelming, transforming life-death experience) and opposite her 8th house Sun, dealt a devastating blow to her life force. With Neptune-Uranus opposite her chart's Midheaven, or public viewpoint, notoriety for the slain victim was assured.

Less than a month earlier, Jacqueline Kennedy Onassis had passed from the scene, dying at home, her loved ones at her bedside (transiting 8th house Venus sextile natal Neptune-Midheaven). Jupiter (blessings), transiting from the 12th house of retreat and transition — the Last Stop in the chart, was square her Sun (life-essence), draining her energy but granting her swift surcease from pain. In a strange by-play, transiting Moon, the timer, was conjunct her natal Mars (vitality) in the house of public recognition, while transiting Mars (quick, decisive action) was conjunct her natal 6th house Moon, denoting her physical woman's body.

Months before, figure skater Nancy Kerrigan , considered by many to be a shoo-in for a gold-medal at the winter Olympics, had been brutally attacked and severely injured, allegedly by the husband and friends of her arch rival, Tonya Harding. For a while, Nancy's leg injuries threatened to halt her ice skating career. Even as the assailant's weapon struck, Nancy was experiencing a Mars Return, that is, the transiting Mars was conjunct her natal Mars in the sign of Capricorn, which rules the knees. Mars represents not only the violent act, itself, but also the metal instrument with which Nancy was assaulted. Jealousy and vengeance characterized the act. At the time of the assault, transiting Pluto in Scorpio was conjunct Nancy's natal Neptune (confusion). Remember her disbelief, "Why me?"

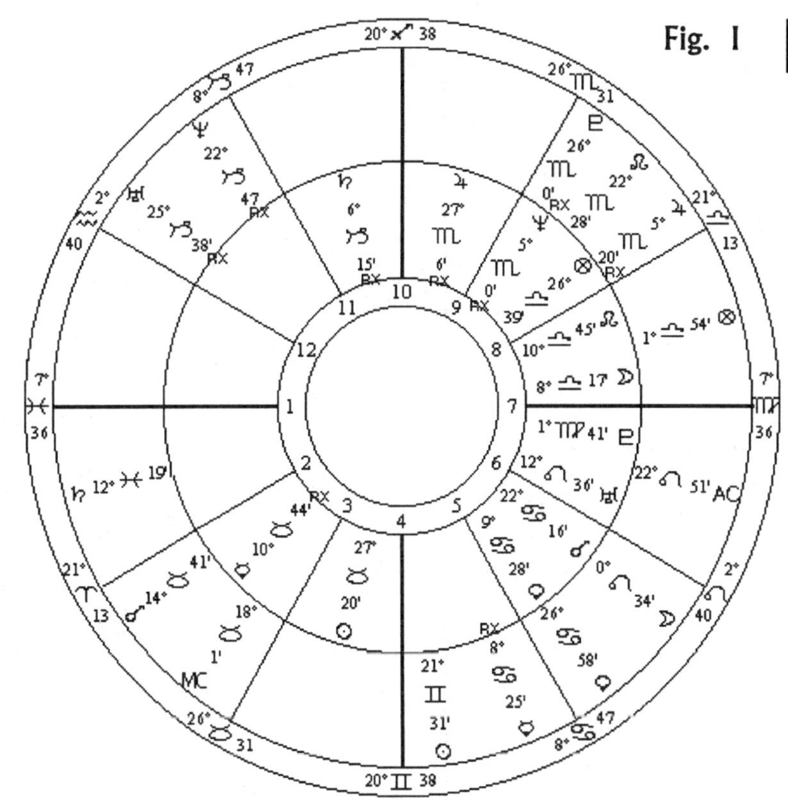

Fig. I

Inside: **Nicole Simpson**
dob 5/19/1959 2:00 AM, MET Frankfurt am Main, Germany 50 N 07, 8 E 40 Koch
Transits: **Murder**
6/12/1994 10:32 PM, EDT Brentwood CA, 33 N 55 117 W 54

Essentials of Intermediate Astrology

Finally, if we can believe the birth-time currently in favor, President William Clinton's chart is also a classic example of transits in action. The President's Sun — his true self, his ego — is in Leo. Unfortunately for him, that outgoing and generous Sun has been under assault for much of his term of office.

For starters, trouble-making Pluto, in the water sign Scorpio, has been transiting the President's 2nd house of money (Whitewater?). There, opposite transiting Mars in Taurus, it also sets up a harsh T-square to the Sun, his very essence, in the 11th house of friends (old chum Vince Foster's death, purges in the White House staff). That same Pluto transit has activated the natal Moon, planet of women, in his 8th house of sex (scandals). The 8th house also signifies other people's money (Whitewater again, but also the national budget).

Meanwhile, just as transiting Saturn (structures, forms, debts, delays and limitations) moved into his 6th house of health, the President's massive health plan, keystone of the administration, came under damaging fire. Battles with Congress and troubles abroad — famine and starvation, disease of epidemic proportions, nuclear proliferation, genocidal war — all vie for his attention. With all his Libran planets (Mars, Neptune, Venus, Jupiter), the President wants to avoid confrontation and just "make nice" with everyone, but the transiting Neptune-Uranus conjunction (confusion, delusion, unexpected eruptions) square his Jupiter from the bottom of the chart, doesn't help.

Simplistic readings? Of course. Obviously, a single transit – or even two or three – does not describe an event fully. Even in the quick case studies cited above, more than a few transits of equal significance can be found to corroborate the original delineation.

But transits are not the only telescopes through which to view a chart. Accomplished astrologers use transits, of course, but they also employ a number of other techniques: progressions, directions, planetary returns, harmonics, fixed stars, asteroids, transneptunian planets; eclipses, planetary pictures...and so on. Each technique adds substance and color to the chart reading.

Fig. II

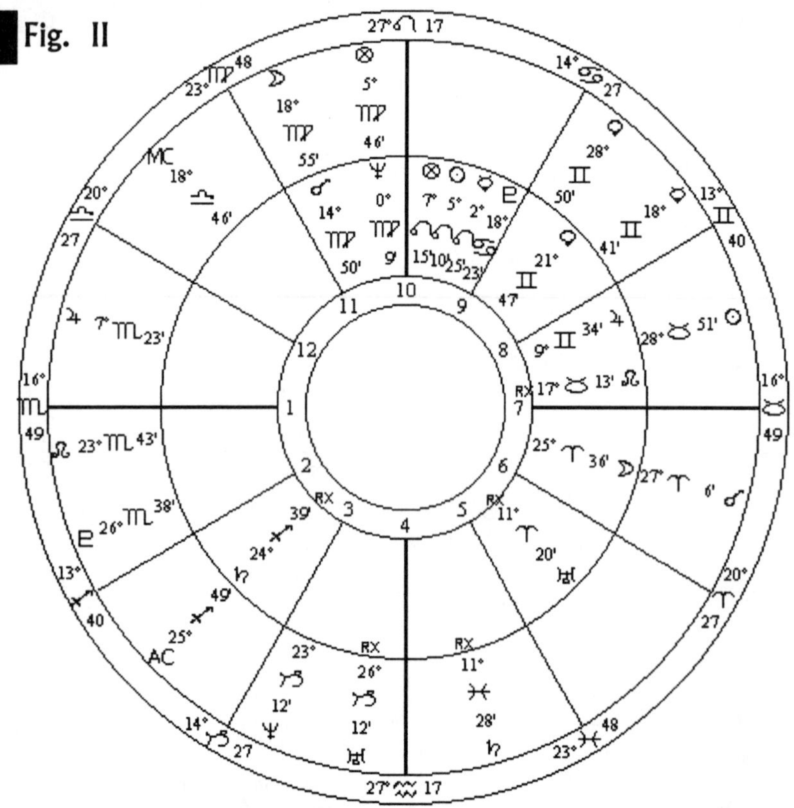

Inside: **Jacqueline Kennedy Onasis**
dob 7/28/1929 2:30 PM EDT, Southhampton NY 40N43 72W23
Transits: **Death** 5/19/1994 10:15 PM EDT, New York, NY 40N45 72W23

But the truth of the matter is, whatever other techniques astrologers may use, THEY ALL USE TRANSITS. Transits are, perhaps, the one unifying thread of astrology today. Whenever anyone asks *"What's going on up there?"*, the answer is found in transits. If a client says *"Something's happening in my life,"* check out the daily transits. And when an astrologer looks at a calendar and notes, *"Christmas looks like a difficult period this year,"* it's transits, transits, transits.

Just exactly what is a transit? Simply speaking, a transit is the movement of a planet on its journey through the solar system. When we refer to the position of a transiting planet, we're talking about where it is NOW — at this instant in its journey.

From the Latin *transire*: to cross over, the word transit actually means "passing over, or through." The dictionary defines "transit" as a passage of one heavenly body across the disc of another.

Thus it is not enough merely to know the present location of a planet: We need also to know about the planet's journey. To do that, we must understand Cycles – not only where the planet is now but where it has been, where it is going, and what it meets up with along the way.

The Planetary Lineup

Let's just review, for a moment, the model of our solar system. Our own bright star, the Sun, is at the center of the whirling mass of planets and stars. Forever circling around that Sun (all right! "forever" is a relative word, but let it suffice for now!) ... forever circling around that Sun are the nine planets that comprise our solar system.

Planet nearest to the Sun is Mercury, then Venus then our home planet, Earth, with its Moon twirling around it and marking off the days of our lives.

Looking outward from Earth toward space, there's the red planet Mars, then giant Jupiter, the many-ringed Saturn, Uranus with its unusual rotation, foggy Neptune, and finally small, dark Pluto.

(Technically, as this is written, the two outermost planets in order are Pluto first, and *then* Neptune. Due to its somewhat elliptical orbit, Pluto is presently circling the Sun from within the orbit of Neptune. It will continue to do so until 1999, when Pluto once again becomes our outermost planet. Most of us, however, continue to think of the planetary order with Pluto at the tail end of the list. All astrological references respect that traditional sequence.)

The planets revolve around the Sun at varying speeds. Because they are intrinsically tied to the Sun, those closest to the Sun move fast. Astronomically, Mercury circles the Sun in 88 days; it takes Venus about 245 days to do the same. Earth, of course, takes one full year, 365 1/4 days.

This is how the astronomers would call it. Astrologers, on the other hand, see things from our point of view on Earth. To us, it takes Mercury and Venus almost a year to circle the HOROSCOPE because these planets travel with the Sun and that's how long it takes the Sun to visit all 12 zodiacal signs. Mercury is never more than about 28° from the Sun (one zodiacal sign on either side of the Sun), Venus never more than 48° away (one or two signs on either side of the Sun).

That's the hard part. From here on out, astronomers and astrologers agree on planet periods. As one moves farther away from the Sun, the circles or orbiting paths grow bigger, and the planets take longer to travel the distances. On the average, Mars takes two years, Jupiter 12, and Saturn 29 1/2 years.

Uranus goes the distance in just under 84 years. It takes Neptune twice as long – almost 168 years , or 14 years in a sign – to circle the Sun. While most of us can wish for good health and the *joie de vivre* to see it through a Uranus return (and three Saturn returns), Even the best of us — including those who eat yogurt every day and live quietly in the Russian steppes – can

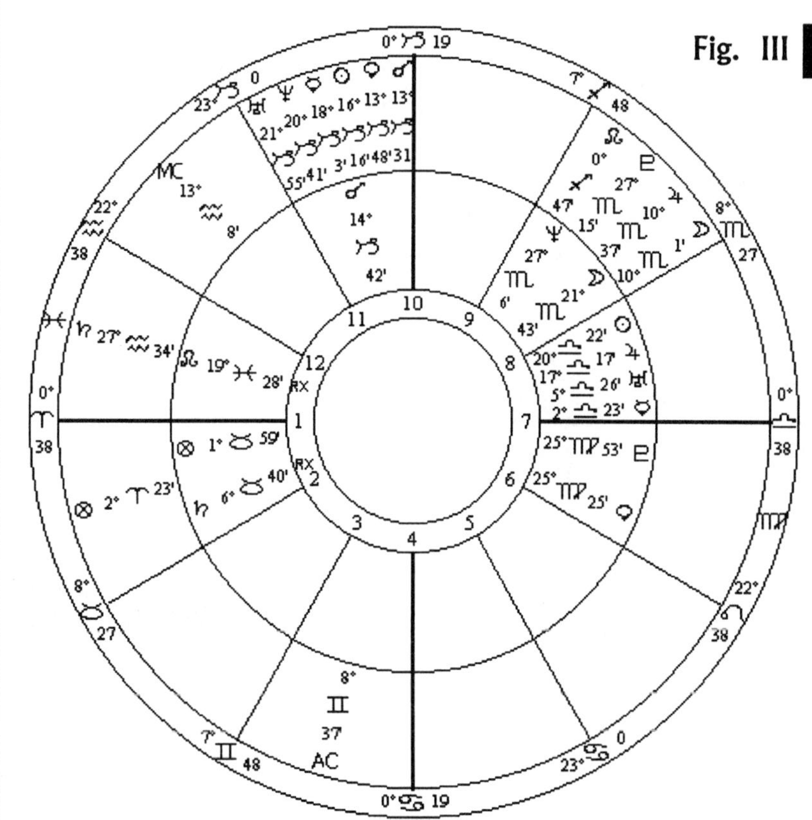

Fig. III

Inside: **Nancy Kerrigan**
dob 10/13/1969, 5:17 PM EDT Woburn MA, 42N28 71W09
Transits: **Assault** 1/06/1994 , 2:30PM EST, Detroit MI 43N20, 83W03

only hope to see Neptune pass through seven houses of our chart. Eight houses would be really pushing it!

Pluto, the smallest and most distant planet, takes 245 years just to make one revolution. No one (let's not talk Methuselah!) has ever lived long enough to see that planet traverse the zodiac. No one has ever recorded, from one person's viewpoint, the effect of, say, Pluto in Sagittarius, where it took up residence in 1995, and Pluto only a sign away, in Capricorn, where it was when our nation was born.

In the year 2008, some of you now reading this material will experience the return of Pluto to the sign of the Goat. Because there is nothing in your immediate life experience to help you understand the commingling of those energies, you lucky next-century folks will have to go back through the pages of history to surmise what might occur.

Even then it won't be easy to figure out. In 1776, Pluto was part of a grand trine involving Neptune and Uranus. In 2008, Pluto will be trine Saturn, semi-square Uranus, and septile (51½°) Neptune. Very different energies, indeed.

Frequent Visitors: The Moon and Inner Planets

Also considered in transit study is the movement of our own satellite, the Moon. Revolving around our home planet, the Moon takes 29½ days to travel from one New Moon phase to the next New Moon, and almost the same time (27½ days) to pass through one zodiacal sign after another until it visits all 12. That takes about 2½ days for each sign. During that lunar passage, we mark off the First Quarter, Full Moon, and Last Quarter phases of the Moon and their special meanings in our chart, noting also the Moon sign.

In the natal chart, the Moon can be interpreted on many levels. It represents one's emotions, moods, and innate reactions to events. It signifies the mother and important women in the chart. It has some relationship to money and other temporal needs. In combination with the Sun, it can give a pithy but perceptive view of the chart native.

Fig. IV

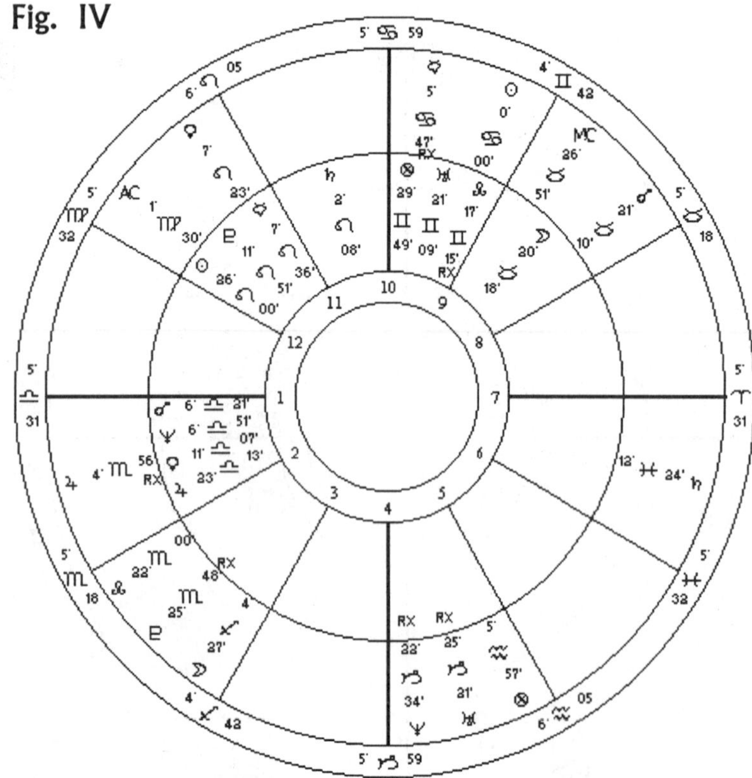

Inside: **William Jefferson Clinton** (*ne* Blythe)
dob 8/19/1946, 8:51 AM CST, Hope AK 33N40 93W35.
Transit: **Summer Solstice** 6/21/1994, 10:48 AM EDT, Washington DC, 38N53 77W01

In transit, however, the Moon acts more as a timer, setting off events signified by the planets it contacts and describing one's actual reactions to those events. A natal Moon in Scorpio may make you a person with deeply intense emotions and many secret places of the heart. A transiting Moon in Scorpio may push some of those emotions to the front, briefly turning you — and everyone else —into someone with a sharp tongue who lashes out at anyone and everything. (Note the word "may"; these are probabilities for the sake of demonstration, not actualities.)

Astrologers synthesize the Moon phase, sign, house position, and aspect it makes to another celestial body in order to paint a picture of a particular moment in time. Keeping a diary of the Moon's daily travels and noting not only what happens as it passes from sign to sign but also how you react to each new move is perhaps the quickest and best way to understand transits and learn the distinction between the planet's natal influence and its transiting influence.

Recording planet energies works better with some planets than with others.. It works well with the Moon because the Moon moves so rapidly and makes such frequent contacts, but also because the Moon describes the often high drama of emotional responses.

On the other hand, Mercury in transit tells you very little. It is, however, The Messenger of the Zodiac, come to tell you something, and you should listen to its call, especially around the time of its stations (more later) when its message is especially meaningful.

What Mercury in transit does do is to describe the prevalent mental attitude concerning an upcoming event, but not much about the actions it concerns. Mercury may suggest travel, an increase in communication, more talk than action. It is sudden inspirations, a life-spirit, the air, or breath. In weather study, it is the wind. Perhaps because it is such a fast-moving planet, "mercurial" in nature, its effects are not very long lasting, and it rarely has any serious significance in transit charts.

For that matter, neither does Venus. Another swift-mover, tied in closely with the Sun and Mercury, Venus is almost too predictable. As the activating planet in a transit chart, it casts a pleasant glow over an event, momentarily granting peace and lovely visions. Transiting Venus conjunct natal Mars in the 5th house might give a very pleasant day. Maybe a party is in the offing or a brief romantic encounter. The Venus energy is subtle, leaving you with a feeling of being loved and appreciated. Alas, the transiting energy is all too fleeting and soon the glow is gone.

Before continuing this run-down of planetary energies in transit, let's pause for a moment to discuss several other important pieces of the transit puzzle: orbs of influence, aspects, houses, retrograde and direct stations and the "act*or* or act*ee*" factor.

Orbs: Close Encounters

First orbs. Orbs are the distances allowed between planets when noting the effectiveness of an aspect. If

The solar System – Fig. V

The Solar System

Mars is at 10° of Taurus and Jupiter is at 8° of Leo, they are 88° apart, or just two degrees away from a perfect square (90°). Since most astrologers would allow an orb of five or six degrees to exist between two planets in square relationship, Mars and Jupiter in this example are said to be well within orb.

At least this would be so in a natal delineation. In transits, the rules are tighter, stricter. We are talking here about a moving or changing relationship.

While two planets in a natal chart are forever locked in their initial embrace, transiting planets move into position, make contact, and then move on in their relentless journey around the horoscope.

Because transits represent such "fleeting" contacts, astrologers tend to use very tight orbs. Some suggest only one degree difference should be permitted. Others, slightly more liberal, recommend two degrees in an applying aspect (that is, approaching) and one degree separating, or moving away from the contact. Sometimes, if an astrologer feels an "overshadowing" effect of a planet, like Saturn, the orb of influence is increased to three or maybe even four degrees.

(An aspect is the name for the relationship between two planets: the way one planet "looks" at another as, say, a good friend or a not-so-good friend. When planets are 60 or 120° apart, they are said to be in "easy" aspect.

When they are 90 or 180° from one another, they are in "hard" aspect. Conjunctions, or "in-your-face" aspects, are sometimes good, sometimes not so. Other aspects fall either in one camp or the other. See Fig. VII)

An exception to the rule of tight orbs is taken by the well-known astrologer-author, Betty Lundsted. In her book on *Transits: The Time of Your Life,* Lundsted recommends using as much as 10° for an orb of influence. She is talking here about the influence of a planet, whose approaching transit can often be felt as much as a year in advance and of the astrologer's role in alerting the client to the upcoming event. She agrees, however, that for predictive work only a tight orb should be considered.

Fig. VI

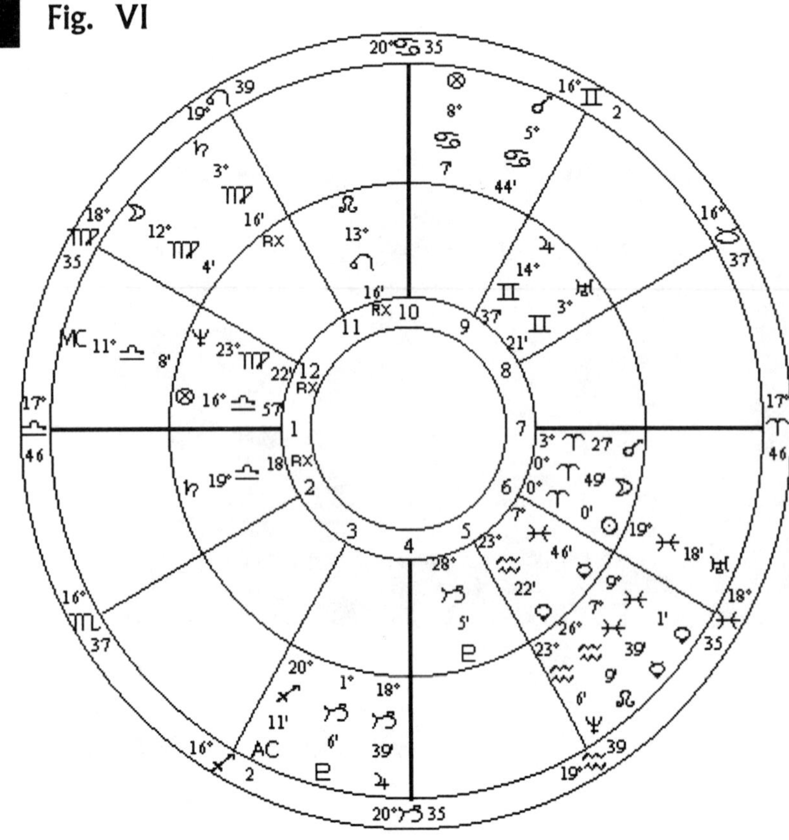

Double chart for Aries Ingresses, 1776 and 2008

Aspects: What To Look Out For

Again — because she is talking about "stress management" — Lundsted notes that she doesn't work with the trines (120°) and sextiles (60°) because "we don't usually need help in handling them."

True enough. While these so-called "easy" aspects can deliver some information, most of us are really concerned only about the difficult days ahead and the roadblocks we must surmount. For that reason, the most effective aspects in transit work are often the "hard" aspects, in particular the conjunction (0°), opposition (180°) and square (90°).

(However, there are occasions when we are on the lookout for just those "easy" aspects. In electional work, for example, when we are trying to find a suitable time to start an

endeavor, we try hard to avoid the squares and oppositions that might cause problems, and look instead for the sextiles and trines to indicate success.

No one wants to get married, start a business, buy a house, or even take a chance on the lottery when the aspects all point to tough going. It's at times like these that we want the trines and sextiles to kick in.)

Also fruitful in transit work are the semi-square (45°), the sesquiquadrate (135°), and the quincunx (150°). Sometimes, a transiting planet completes a particularly meaningful pattern, such as a grand trine, a T-square or grand cross, or a yod . These often carry very special messages and highlight particularly meaningful times in our lives.

Houses: Where the Planets Live

Planets are not among the zodiac's homeless; they live somewhere in the chart. Though they are clothed with their signs (like Uranus in Capricorn) and hang-out with one another (Uranus conjunct Neptune), they reside in that portion of the horoscope we call "Houses." In transit work, where the planet is living is almost as important as all the other information:

If Uranus and Neptune are living in your 3rd house where they affect your communications, your learning processes, your siblings, or your neighbors, for example, they will act very differently from Uranus-Neptune living in the 8th house of joint finances and wills and mortgages and death and occult matters.

The transiting planets move from house to house, visiting first this planet-cousin then another. Some houses are compatible and welcome the visitors with open arms. Some houses are already heavily tenanted, and the tenants may be in harsh aspect to other neighbors.

The whole dynamic of transiting planet to natal planet in a certain house in aspect to another planet in another house can be tense and dramatic. Along comes the astrologer like a social worker trying to make sense of it all and hoping everyone will learn to live in peace and harmony. Some task we have set out for ourselves!

Fig. VII Table of Most Commonly Used Aspects

name	*# degrees separating planets*	*influence*
CONJUNCTION	0 degrees	generally constructive
semi-sextile	30 degrees	mixed, inharmonious energies
semi-square	45 degrees	sometimes malefic
septile	51½ degrees	benefic, spiritual
SEXTILE	60 degrees	beneficial, easy, the bridge
quintile	72 degrees	mildly benefic
biquintile	144 degrees	mixed, mildly benefic
SQUARE	90 degrees	unfavorable, stressful, motivational
TRINE	120 degrees	most beneficial
sesquiquadrate	135 degrees	sometimes malefic
quincunx	150 degrees	mixed, inharmonious energies, adjustments, health
OPPOSITION	180 degrees	good–bad, needs balance, malefic, friction, me-you

* *Aspects in capital letters are the so-called Ptolemaic aspects, mentioned in Ptolemy's work, the Tetrabiblos, and are the aspects most in use by all astrologers today. Some astrologers use all of the aspects above beyond the basic five; some astrologers use only a few. There are even other aspects — the decile, nonile, bi-quintile, etc., but these are not in common use.*

Retrogrades and Stations: The Stop-and-Go Factor

So far we have been talking about the planets moving ahead in their eternal journey, but occasionally even they seem to stand still, turn back, and go over the same ground again. This retrograde motion is only "apparent," that is, it only seems that way to us on Earth because we, too, are on a moving planet racing to catch up with the fast-movers, passing some by and continuing on our way.

To explain retrogradation, the example usually used is that of two trains traveling at different speeds but on adjacent tracks. As the one on A track catches up with the one on B track, both trains seem to be standing still, taking stock of each other. For a few brief minutes, passengers can actually wave to one another or — if the windows were open — exchange notes or handshakes. Then A's speed appears to accelerate and B seems almost to be moving backwards.

In reality, both are still moving forward. Soon the slower moving B is left behind while speedy A moves on to its next encounter with another train, this one perhaps on C. track, where the same thing happens.

With planets, the apparent "stand-still" occasions are called "stations." When a planet is forging ahead, pauses, and (apparently) moves backward, it is said to be making a retrograde station. It continues to move backward until, once again, it pauses, and this time moves forward. Now it is making a "direct station." Both these stations have particular significance in transit delineation. It's as if the planet were shouting, *"Hey! Look at me!* I'm trying to tell you something!" What that something is, is either an exhortation to review past events: *"You need to go over this again"* or an urging to assimilate what you have learned and apply it in the future: *"Got it? Now move on!"*

Being alert to these stations gives the astrologer an edge in assessing future events. Saturn, especially, because it ticks off important periods of the life every seven or so years, makes one sit up and take notice when it retrogrades back and forth over another planet. These planetary stations are often referred to as great "learn-

Fig. VIII Average Planetary Periods and Retrograde Stations

Planet	(symbol)	Solar orbital period	time in a sign	retrograde station	length of Rx
Sun	☉	system center	(*1 year)	never	does not apply
Moon	☽	27½ days	2 ½ days	never	does not apply
Mercury	☿	88 days	(*1 month)	3 X yr	approx 20 days
Venus	♀	225 days	(*1 month)	every 18 mos	42 days
Eartht	⊕	365 ½ days	1 month	never	does not apply
Mars	♂	2 years	2 mos.	every 24-26 mos.	60-80 days
Jupiter	♃	12 years	1 year	every 9 mos.	4 mos.
Saturn	♄	29 ½ years	2 ½ yrs.	every 8 mos.	4-5 mos.
Uranus	♅	84 years	7 yrs.	every 7 mos.	5 mos.
Neptune	♆	168 years	14 yrs.	every 7 mos.	5 mos.
Pluto	♇	245 years	avg. 21 yrs**	every 7 months**	5 mos.

** From the Earth-centered (geocentric) viewpoint, the Sun moves through the zodiac one sign at a time per month. Mercury and Venus are closely tied in to this apparent cycle, therefore, to astrologers they also seem to move through the horoscope about one sign per month. In reality, the planets are circling the Sun in the times noted in the Periods column above.*

*** Pluto has a very erratic orbit, speeding up as it traverses some signs and slowing down in others. It spends the shortest time — 12 to 14 years — in Virgo, Libra, Scorpio, Sagittarius, and Capricorn; the longest, 31 years, in Taurus and 30 years each in Aries and Gemini. It goes through Leo and Aquarius in 19 years, and through Cancer and Pisces in 25. A person born in 1900, when Pluto was in Gemini, was 67-68 years old before that natal Pluto was squared by transiting Pluto in Virgo. That person's grandchild, born in 1970 will experience the square (from Virgo to Sagittarius) at about age 30 or 31. Abraham Lincoln, born in 1809 when Pluto was at 14 Pisces, died at age 56 with Pluto at 12 Taurus, approaching a sextile. Had he lived, he would have been over 100 years old at the square!*

ing experiences": Saturn isn't called The Great Teacher for nothing!

But perhaps the most difficult retrograde experiences occur with the planet Pluto. By its very nature, Pluto brings out dark, hidden secrets, forces us to face uncharted and undesired territory in the psyche, and often leaves us feeling wearied and worn down — and, yes, even a little bloodied.

While Saturn's effect is more surface-like and handleable, Pluto demands a great deal of us. When the planet hits a sensitive spot in your chart by transit, then retrogrades back over that spot, then turns direct and moves forward, hitting it once again — you know it! And you feel it. And you are never the same again. That's why Pluto is The Great Transformer. (But Not To Worry! Transformation is often desirable and many times marks the beginning of a new and fortuitous phase.)

Act*or* or Act*ee?* Who Does What to Whom?

One of the more difficult tasks an astrologer has is deciding which planet exerts the dominant energy, the planet in the natal chart or the transiting planet. Certainly the energies of both planets must be synthesized, but in general it is the transiting planet that causes the natal planet to react.

Suppose you are a stay-at-home kind of person, used to watching the same tv programs from the same chair while eating the same-old dinner. Along comes a visiting friend full of pep and excitement who teases and cajoles you into going out for a fun evening of dinner and dancing. You finally agree, but you don't go to the wild new club in town but rather to the friendly family restaurant down the street, with soft music and a small dance floor. Your friend has forced you to act a little differently than usual, but still in character. You both actually have a good time.

You've just experienced
transiting Jupiter to your Saturn.

Now the tables are turned. You visit your fun-loving friend and decline an invitation to go out. Instead, you stay home, order in, sit and listen to records, and talk about the good old college days long ago. You maybe eat too much and drink too much and stay up much too late, but at least you saved a little money and wear and tear on the car. Once again, you both enjoyed yourselves, albeit in a restrained atmosphere. This time, you played transiting Saturn to your friend's Jupiter.

In each of these cases, both you and your friend remained in character. How you expressed yourselves was determined by outside pressures, such as time, place, and other people. In transit work, the planets do not "cause" you to act differently or work against the promise of your chart. You are who you are but you are shaped by the changing events and moods that are

Fig. IX Earliest, Latest Saturn Returns

Born at Saturn Station turning Direct *(earliest return possible)*

first return	28 years 5 months
second return	58 years 3 months
third return	87 years 5 months

Born when Saturn is conjunct Sun *(average return)*

first return	29 years 1 month
second return	58 years 4 months
third return	88 years

Born at Saturn Station turning Retrograde *(latest possible return)*

first return	29 years 9 months
second return	58 years 10 months to 59 years 1 month
third return	88 years 8 months

As noted in the Retrogrades and Stations Table above, the periods of planet returns listed are average. In reality, a Return can occur earlier or later than these averages.

The table above shows that Saturn Returns can occur as early as 28 years 5 months and as late as 29 years nine months.

The difference depends on whether you were born before, during, or after a Saturn retrograde station. Thus two friends born a year apart experienced their return almost at the same time; a friend born in-between had already had hers! (Thanks to Frances McEvoy for this data.)

chronicled by planetary visitations — transits — to your natal chart or birth imprint.

When the transiting planet affects a personal planet like Venus or the Moon, you tend to feel the effects on an inner emotional level. You experience changes to yourself, or to the people or places dear to you. When the outer planets like Uranus or Pluto are being transited, the effect is more external, often manifested by changing events in your life over which you have little control.

For example, consider transiting Mars in a square relationship with your natal Mars. At that time, you may be impatient, quarrelsome, or angry. You may find yourself speaking sharply and lashing out at everyone. You tend to act impulsively. You may drive too fast, or trip over your own feet in your haste to get somewhere. Your actions will be unbridled. Mars is also a planet of energy, and you may work too hard or take on too much responsibility, thus draining your physical stamina. Solution? Take a deep breath, slow down, put one foot in front of the other, and think before acting.

On the other hand, when that same Mars is square your natal Pluto, you may find yourself in stressful situations, exerting your energy against what seem to be overwhelming, manipulative forces. There may be power struggles at work. You are edgy, nervous, perhaps with deep-seated anger and impending sense of gloom. Control becomes an issue as you strive to keep your place in the cat-bird seat where you are in charge of yourself and your immediate surroundings. Not so easy. Fortunately, Mars transits are relatively swift and you can pass through this ordeal in a seemingly short while, but it takes courage to keep your chin up.

Noteworthy Transits: Return of the Native

While all transits are meaningful, some have longer lasting effects than others, and some — in particular planet "returns"— are especially so. A "return" chart is drawn for that moment in time when the planet in question returns to the exact same degree and minute it held at the moment of your birth. Controversy exists as to whether you use the place of birth or your current residence for the location of the new chart. Some astrologers even go so far as to travel, even for a day, to a location that will support a more favorable chart. You'd be wise to check out all options and choose the one that seems best for you. In other words, "You pays your money and you takes your choice."

In an average lifetime, all the planets from Sun out to Uranus might be expected to return at least once (as noted earlier, a Neptune Return is an outside chance a Pluto Return is an impossibility). Therefore, return charts can be drawn for each of these planets, but the ones most commonly in use are lunar, solar, and Saturn returns. These provide useful information for an astrologer looking ahead to plot a course of action for the days and months to come.

Figure X

Generational Differences Three Outer Planets

	Uranus	*Neptune*	*Pluto*
1925	Pisces	Leo	Cancer
1950	Cancer	Libra	Leo
1975	Libra	Sagittarius	Libra
1995	Capricorn	Capricorn	Scorpio

Return charts are always used with the natal chart; you really can't have one without the other. Obviously, what is about to happen is colored by your basic responses to life's energies.

A Lunar Return marks the return of the **Moon** to its natal position. Because the Moon is both a timer and a barometer of one's personal moods, the lunar return chart gives you a picture of the events that will occur over the next few weeks, and also of your internal reactions to these events.

Every year on your birthday, the Sun returns to its place-of-birth position in your chart. Don't we always feel "full of ourselves" on our birthday? Isn't it "our" day, and don't we often make resolutions for the year ahead? We are responding to the energy of the **Sun,** our Self, Ego, the "Me" of the chart. The Solar Return is said to foreshadow the events of the coming year, and it most certainly describes the birthday period itself. Following the Sun's transit through this chart as well as through the natal chart highlights the areas of your life that will play an important role in the coming 12 months.

Without a doubt, though, the **Saturn** Return is one of the most anticipated and often feared times of your life. Tracing Saturn's journey around the horoscope leads you through all the important rites of passage that eventually shape and form the real You. How you endure (a good Saturn word!) those exhilarating and powerful changes makes your autobiography such fascinating reading!

In the 29 1/2 years (on the average) that it takes to traverse the chart, Saturn ticks off the formative stages of your life. At age seven, when the transiting planet reaches its first square to natal Saturn, the world finally sees you emerging as a person able to stand alone, ready to face the consequences of your actions. You have reached the "age of reason" and are now held accountable for all you do. Your start school and make friends on your own. Mistakes there are a-plenty. Seven years later, at the opposition, you have reached puberty. Religion tells a boy he is "a man," nature tells a girl she is "a woman," you know you're still a kid, but even you don't want to admit it. Now you have to maintain a balance between temptations from the outside and the guidelines your parents laid down. Life begins to get complicated.

At 21, school days are over and you're ready to face the world. This square of Saturn to its natal position urges you to set a course for your life. If you get a job and work hard toward success, maybe you'll weather this passage. If you chuck it all and travel to the South Seas because "I deserve it!", you may have blown a great opportunity you'll regret later on.

Saturn Watches and Makes Notes.

Somewhere between age 29 and 30, you'll experience your first Saturn Return. If you did it right, you'll find yourself settling down, maybe in a new career. You'll probably leave home if you haven't already. Maybe you'll get married, have a baby, buy a house. Now you're in for it: you have just drawn up the blueprint for the next 30 years of your life. And the Saturn Return journey begins again: another seven years another square; seven more years, the opposition; and so on. If you made all the right choices, you have nothing to worry about.

On the other hand, if you frittered away your opportunities, a Saturn Return can be difficult. You may wind up at age 30 (or 60) jobless, with no meaningful relationships and very little prospect for turning things around. Not that it can't be done: Hard work can put you back on the right track, Jack, but it won't be easy.

As a matter of fact, Saturn's passages are never easy. They all — even the good ones — require diligence . A steady hand and a stout heart, as they used to say. Accept that fact early-on and the transit is not quite a piece of cake, but not cracker crumbs either.

The "fun" part of a Saturn passage (ha, ha) is that, having weathered it once, you get to do it all over again for the next 30 years or so and then maybe even for a third time. *(See Fig. XII)* By then, it is hoped that you will have learned your lessons (the Great Teacher at Work!).

The Rest of The Gang

All of the planets in transit poke at the natal chart. The Moon does it every day. and **Venus** are quick travelers and their messages are most often positive. **Mars** can be full of energy and excitement, spurring you on to action and excitement, or it can remind you of the violent god of war for which it was named. Saturn we've already discussed in detail.

But **Jupiter**, the giant planet of expansion, called the Great Benefic and noted for the good times it brings, can also be a problem. Spending about one year in each sign — and house — of your chart, Jupiter can sometimes be just Too Much. As the giant planet strikes off sensitive spots in your natal chart, you need to be aware of the excesses that may occur, as well as the benefits.

For example, Jupiter in your first house or conjunct your Neptune may lend an aura of glamor to your persona, or let you indulge in music and the arts to your heart's content. Give in to its excesses, though, and you'll totally forget your diet, which could do damage to your health to say nothing of your wardrobe. Conjunct your Venus or fifth house, transiting Jupiter might introduce romantic encounters into an otherwise dull life – just be sure you're not blinded by the wine and roses.

Usually when Jupiter enters the sign of your Sun you can expect a lucky year. When Jupiter is in square or opposition to a planet like Pluto, there may be more sorrows or losses than you thought possible. Check back to 12 years ago when it was in the same place to see what happened then and you can get a handle on the next 12 months. Not only do the planets in orbit repeat themselves, but so, in a way, does history. Looking back is the best road to the future.

After Saturn, the next planet out from the Sun is **Uranus,** planet of the Unexpected. Things seem to happen under Uranus transits that in no way could have been anticipated. Called the Great Awakener because it really does seem to strike with a jolt when it goes into action, Uranus fulfills the astrologer's perception of it as the planet ruling the unusual, the odd-ball, the out-of-the-mainstream. Even astronomers have a problem trying to make it act like its sibling-planets: the planet was recently discovered to have a system of rings, like Saturn; it has an inside-out moon, Miranda. Uranus lies nearly flat on its side with its north pole facing Earth; and, just to be contrary, it revolves on its axis counter-clockwise!

Because of its perverse nature, Uranus is never unnoticed as it works its way around your chart. When you see Uranus approaching a planet, just make up your mind that you are probably in for a surprise or two.

What you should expect is that the transit will mark off an important cycle in your life. Because Uranus reaches its half-way point around your chart at about age 42 — just about the time you're also undergoing an opposition from Saturn — it personifies the Mid-Life Crisis, that time when nothing seems to happen quite the way you thought it would. Even when it goes its full course and completes 84 years — about 10 years more than the average life span — you aren't necessarily down for the count. Sometimes Uranus adds a new burst of energy, and Old Octogenarian You is off again and running.

As we said before, the Uranus journey is not uneventful. As it travels through your horoscope, visiting this house, touching that planet, you will more than likely experience changes, some even profound. When this planet crosses into the 4th house, for example, you may move unexpectedly to another home. If the Moon is there, you may find the changes occurring with your mother or your female friends. In the 7th house, Uranus may disrupt the order of your marriage or perhaps you'll experience an unexpected break-up with a business partner. On the other hand, the transit could just mean that you're going to meet a very unusual person who will have a great impact on your life.

Wherever Uranus travels, however, expect some sparks. Let's say the planet meets up with Jupiter, for example. Here, the changes may be fortunate and you could win a lottery, or make the front page of your local newspaper. With Mars, you should be on the alert for accidents that seem to occur out of the blue. With Mercury, Uranus can shower you with inspirational thought and almost compel you into a new line of work or play.

When transiting Uranus is in aspect to natal Saturn you get the "want-to-go, want-to-stay" urge, and that in itself can cause trouble in your neatly ordered life. Often, with Uranus, you just have a yearning to be free and independent. The point is Uranus is not always bad, but it's not always good, either. It's what you least expect, and that's what makes a Uranus transit so interesting.

Of course, all the planets in transit are interesting, none more so than **Neptune.** This is the planet of illusion and delusion, when we see and hear what we want to see and hear, but find out later 'taint so. Because things appear cloudy and unclear under a Neptune transit, you can find yourself "taken in" by a rascal or two. You tend to be dreamy-eyed and romantic. You hear violin melodies and your feet want to tap-tap into a never-never land. Alas, when you wake up, all has dissolved.

Want an example? In recent years, the world has been living under a conjunction of transiting Uranus and Neptune in Capricorn. The sudden break-up (Uranus) of government structures (Capricorn), personified by the literal breaking up of the Berlin Wall, was bathed in an idealism and euphoria (Neptune) that left the world unprepared for the stark reality of what such a dissolution would entail.

Or how about Cuba, where tough emigration laws (Capricorn) were suddenly relaxed (Uranus) causing a mass exodus of ecstatic (Neptune) islanders eager to escape (Uranus) to a promised land (Neptune), by boat (Neptune), only to find their dreams shattered (Uranus-Neptune) as they were either turned back or their admission to America delayed (Capricorn).

By the way, some people hate Neptune transits because they never seem to know what's going on around them, so strong is the Neptunian fog they live under. Others look forward to Neptune aspecting a planet or visiting a house, because they revel in the dreaminess and peacefulness it seems to bring for them, when all worries and cares are washed away. It helps to know that Neptune stays only about 14 years in one sign. By looking ahead, we can tell when its effects will begin in a certain area, and when to expect the fog to lift. More later on how to look ahead, but first, let's finish the planets with a discussion of Pluto.

Pluto, densest of all the planets, smaller than most, and farthest out in our solar system (see earlier discussion), is also slowest in its journey around the Sun. It takes 245 years to orbit the Sun, moving anywhere from seconds to no more than one or two minutes a day through the horoscope. (Refer to note at end of Figure IX.) Obviously, then, the effect of this planet lasts for a long, long time. You will feel its approach long before it makes a close aspect. Some say it has an effect from the second it enters a new sign: Thus all Sagittarians (and by reflex action, other mutable signs) were already sensing Pluto's "charms" even while the planet was still in the last throes of Scorpio.

Pluto is like the long-ago river that carved out the Grand Canyon. The river moved along on its path, relentlessly wearing down and eroding everything in its way. In the end it created a magnificent vista, but think of each granule of sand which had to scurry out of the water's way. So also with Pluto. The planet often signifies the masses, and thus has political overtones reflecting the way a People act or react. The American Revolution was a Uranian event; the Social Revolution and attendant Civil Rights Reform are Plutonian events. These things will happen, no matter how many years will pass, no matter how many prisoners are taken.

In an individual's chart, Pluto signifies power and control issues, and when it moves in transit it conveys a transforming process, a grapple with deep or hidden emotions, a delving into the psychology of an event. Where it strikes in your chart is where you will undergo a profound and transforming experience, even a "little death."

Former President Richard Nixon had Pluto in his 10th house of career and public projection. Often, when this planet in transit crossed an angle or aspected a planet in his chart, he literally fell from prominence, re-invented himself, and rose again to supreme recognition. Finally, as Pluto opposed his Saturn and trined his Neptune, he died, reviled by some, deeply respected by others.

This is not to say that death will actually occur during a Pluto transit, only that this is a planet not to be trifled with. When Pluto in transit touched one woman's natal Sun, she met the man she later married and lived with happily for nearly 40 years. When Pluto transited the North Node in the 4th house of another woman's chart, she was able to put to rest - satisfactorily - some old family matters that had been decades in need of solving. Pluto to the Moon may bring on excessive emotionality; with Venus, there may be an obsessive romance; with Mercury, you may embark on a new course of study or research.

The three outer planets, Uranus, Neptune, and Pluto, are "generational" planets. Because they move so slowly, each planet stays in one sign for long periods of time — Uranus seven years on average; Neptune, 14; Pluto, 21 (actually anywhere from 12 to 31, depending on its sign. Refer to *Fig. VII.*). Almost everyone you went to school with shares your Uranus, Neptune, and Pluto signs. Even though these planets traverse 12 different houses in your friends' charts and meet up with different planets along the way, at least these Big Three define certain basic beliefs and opportunities common to your generation. Not understanding these energies — particularly Pluto's — is the basis for the disruptive Generation Gap between parents and their children.

Think of it. Let's say your grandparents have Uranus in Pisces, Neptune in Leo, and Pluto in Cancer (1925); and let's say your parents sport Uranus in Cancer, Neptune in Libra, and Pluto in Leo (1950). You, yourself (1975), have Uranus in Libra, Neptune in Sagittarius, and Pluto in Libra. (See *Fig. X*) Now, compare your feelings on love and marriage, home and family, national pride and world view. Finally, consider the

1995 transits of Uranus and Neptune in Capricorn and Pluto in Scorpio and Sagittarius, affecting each one's chart differently. Makes for some interesting conversations around the holiday dinner tables, doesn't it?

(In transit work as in all astrological work there are other sensitive areas in the chart to be considered. In addition to the planets and chart angles discussed here, many astrologers also use the lunar nodes, Part of Fortune, East Point or Equatorial Ascendant, and vertex.

Others go even further, using all the planetary nodes, many more Arabian Parts, the West Point, Antivertex, house cusps, and eclipses to say nothing of asteroids, comets, pre-natal and post-natal eclipses, transneptunian or hypothetical planets ... and so on. In time, you will no doubt find your own particular favorites beyond the 10 basic bodies [eight planets and two lights].)

Reading the Signposts

There are many techniques astrologers use in their predictive work, such as secondary or tertiary progressions or solar arc directions. The quickest guidepost to future events, however, is the use of transits, as already discussed. To look ahead to track the moving planets, you need to use an ephemeris or listing of planet positions for each and every day of the year. A quick glance at a page in your ephemeris book will show you what degree and sign each planet is visiting, and when the planet turns retrograde or goes direct.

Figure XI shows the chart of former President Richard M. Nixon. *Figure XII* is a page from *The American Ephemeris for the 20th Century* by Neil F. Michelsen, showing the months of July and August 1974. On August 9, in an unprecedented action, Nixon resigned as President of the United States. Without a doubt, the events leading up to this date must have been among the most stressful and traumatic of the President's life.

Fig. XI

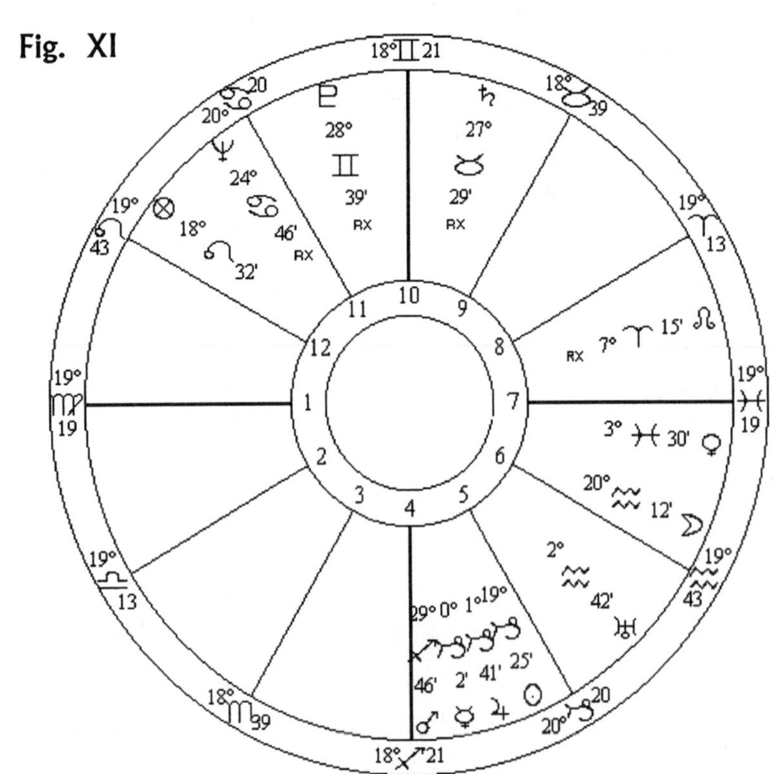

Richard Nixon *dob* 1/09/1913 9:44 PM PST 33N53 117W49 Koch

Look at the ephemeris page for July 1974 shown in *Fig. XII.* Notice that Uranus (of the earth-shaking and unexpected occurrence) seen here in the third from the last column, started off the month still retrograde but turning direct the next day. The Astro Data box on the lower left of the page tells us that the direct station occurred on the 2nd of July at 21 minutes after midnight GMT. In the columns, the *R* (retrograde) has changed to a *D* (direct). This direct station gave added emphasis to the actions of the planet, which until now had been tearing away at the President's innards.

Now Uranus starts to move, creeping slowly up to join in an opposition with the transiting Moon, both to square Nixon's 11th house Neptune. A sudden and unexpected shattering of his delusional hopes and

***Figure XII** — Ephemeris page, courtesy ACS, San Diego CA*

JULY 1974 LONGITUDE

Day	Sid.Time	☉	0 hr ☽	Noon ☽	True ☊	☿	♀	♂	♃	♄	♅	♆	♇
1 M	18 34 40	8♋47 51	29♏18 22	5♐29 50	19♐24.6	8♋32.7	5♊55.4	13♌29.1	17♓47.7	8♋23.5	23♎39.6	7♐26.2	4♎ 8.3
2 Tu	18 38 37	9 45 3	11♐38 30	17 44 38	19R 25.5	7R 57.0	7 6.5	14 6.1	17 48.9	8 31.3	23D 39.5	7R 24.9	4 8.9
3 W	18 42 33	10 42 14	23 48 33	29 50 31	19 25.6	7 22.3	8 17.6	14 43.1	17 49.9	8 39.2	23 39.6	7 23.6	4 9.5
4 Th	18 46 30	11 39 25	5♑50 46	11♑49 34	19 24.7	6 49.3	9 28.8	15 20.2	17 50.7	8 47.0	23 39.6	7 22.3	4 10.1
5 F	18 50 26	12 36 36	17 47 9	23 43 45	19 22.7	6 18.4	10 40.0	15 57.3	17 51.3	8 54.8	23 39.8	7 21.0	4 10.7
6 Sa	18 54 23	13 33 47	29 39 38	5♒35 3	19 19.6	5 50.3	11 51.3	16 34.4	17 51.7	9 2.6	23 39.9	7 19.8	4 11.4
7 Su	18 58 19	14 30 58	11♒30 15	17 25 33	19 15.7	5 25.5	13 2.6	17 11.5	17R 52.0	9 10.4	23 40.2	7 18.6	4 12.1
8 M	19 2 16	15 28 9	23 21 14	29 17 38	19 11.3	5 4.3	14 14.0	17 48.6	17 52.0	9 18.1	23 40.5	7 17.4	4 12.9
9 Tu	19 6 12	16 25 20	5♓15 8	11♓14 6	19 7.0	4 47.3	15 25.4	18 25.8	17 51.8	9 25.9	23 40.8	7 16.2	4 13.7
10 W	19 10 9	17 22 32	17 14 58	23 18 10	19 3.3	4 34.6	16 36.9	19 2.9	17 51.5	9 33.7	23 41.2	7 15.1	4 14.5
11 Th	19 14 6	18 19 44	29 24 10	5♈33 27	19 0.6	4 26.7	17 48.4	19 40.1	17 50.9	9 41.4	23 41.6	7 13.9	4 15.3
12 F	19 18 2	19 16 57	11♈46 33	18 3 56	18D 59.1	4D 23.8	18 60.0	20 17.3	17 50.2	9 49.2	23 42.1	7 12.8	4 16.2
13 Sa	19 21 59	20 14 10	24 26 8	0♉53 37	18 58.9	4 25.9	20 11.6	20 54.5	17 49.3	9 56.9	23 42.7	7 11.7	4 17.1
14 Su	19 25 55	21 11 23	7♉26 50	14 6 12	18 59.8	4 33.4	21 23.3	21 31.8	17 48.1	10 4.6	23 43.3	7 10.7	4 18.1
15 M	19 29 52	22 8 38	20 52 0	27 44 29	19 1.2	4 46.2	22 35.0	22 9.1	17 46.8	10 12.4	23 43.9	7 9.6	4 19.0
16 Tu	19 33 48	23 5 53	4♊43 45	11♊49 45	19 2.6	5 4.5	23 46.7	22 46.4	17 45.3	10 20.1	23 44.6	7 8.6	4 20.0
17 W	19 37 45	24 3 8	19 2 17	26 20 57	19R 3.2	5 28.3	24 58.6	23 23.7	17 43.5	10 27.7	23 45.4	7 7.6	4 21.1
18 Th	19 41 42	25 0 24	3♋45 10	11♋14 10	19 2.4	5 57.5	26 10.4	24 1.0	17 41.6	10 35.4	23 46.2	7 6.6	4 22.1
19 F	19 45 38	25 57 41	18 46 58	26 22 28	19 0.0	6 32.2	27 22.3	24 38.4	17 39.5	10 43.1	23 47.1	7 5.7	4 23.2
20 Sa	19 49 35	26 54 58	3♌59 26	11♌36 33	18 56.0	7 12.4	28 34.3	25 15.8	17 37.2	10 50.7	23 48.0	7 4.8	4 24.3
21 Su	19 53 31	27 52 16	19 12 30	26 46 2	18 50.7	7 58.0	29 46.3	25 53.2	17 34.7	10 58.3	23 49.0	7 3.9	4 25.5
22 M	19 57 28	28 49 33	4♍15 56	11♍41 12	18 45.0	8 48.9	0♋58.3	26 30.6	17 32.1	11 5.9	23 50.0	7 3.0	4 26.7
23 Tu	20 1 24	29 46 52	19 0 58	26 14 35	18 39.6	9 45.1	2 10.4	27 8.0	17 29.2	11 13.4	23 51.0	7 2.2	4 27.9
24 W	20 5 21	0♌44 10	3♎21 35	10♎21 44	18 35.4	10 46.6	3 22.6	27 45.5	17 26.1	11 21.0	23 52.2	7 1.4	4 29.1
25 Th	20 9 17	1 41 29	17 14 57	24 1 20	18 32.7	11 53.2	4 34.7	28 23.0	17 22.9	11 28.5	23 53.3	7 0.6	4 30.4
26 F	20 13 14	2 38 48	0♏41 7	7♏14 38	18D 31.7	13 4.8	5 46.9	29 0.5	17 19.5	11 36.0	23 54.6	6 59.9	4 31.7
27 Sa	20 17 11	3 36 8	13 42 18	20 4 37	18 32.1	14 21.3	6 59.2	29 38.0	17 15.9	11 43.4	23 55.8	6 59.1	4 33.0
28 Su	20 21 7	4 33 28	26 22 4	2♐35 12	18 33.3	15 42.7	8 11.5	0♍15.5	17 12.1	11 50.9	23 57.1	6 58.4	4 34.3
29 M	20 25 4	5 30 48	8♐44 33	14 50 37	18R 34.5	17 8.7	9 23.8	0 53.1	17 8.1	11 58.3	23 58.5	6 57.8	4 35.7
30 Tu	20 29 0	6 28 9	20 53 56	26 54 56	18 34.9	18 39.3	10 36.2	1 30.7	17 4.0	12 5.6	23 59.9	6 57.1	4 37.1
31 W	20 32 57	7 25 31	2♑54 5	8♑51 47	18 33.7	20 14.1	11 48.7	2 8.3	16 59.7	12 13.0	24 1.4	6 56.5	4 38.5

AUGUST 1974 LONGITUDE

Day	Sid.Time	☉	0 hr ☽	Noon ☽	True ☊	☿	♀	♂	♃	♄	♅	♆	♇
1 Th	20 36 53	8♌22 53	14♑48 24	20♑44 15	18♐30.5	21♋53.0	13♋ 1.1	2♍45.9	16♓55.2	12♋20.3	24♎ 2.9	6♐56.0	4♎40.0
2 F	20 40 50	9 20 16	26 39 39	2♒34 52	18R 25.0	23 35.8	14 13.7	3 23.6	16R 50.6	12 27.6	24 4.5	6R 55.4	4 41.5
3 Sa	20 44 46	10 17 40	8♒30 8	14 25 40	18 17.4	25 22.1	15 26.2	4 1.2	16 45.8	12 34.8	24 6.1	6 54.9	4 43.0
4 Su	20 48 43	11 15 5	20 21 41	26 18 23	18 8.2	27 11.7	16 38.8	4 38.9	16 40.8	12 42.0	24 7.8	6 54.4	4 44.5
5 M	20 52 40	12 12 31	2♓15 58	8♓14 38	17 58.1	29 4.2	17 51.5	5 16.6	16 35.7	12 49.2	24 9.5	6 53.9	4 46.0
6 Tu	20 56 36	13 9 57	14 14 37	20 16 9	17 48.0	0♌59.3	19 4.2	5 54.4	16 30.4	12 56.3	24 11.2	6 53.5	4 47.6
7 W	21 0 33	14 7 25	26 19 31	2♈24 59	17 38.9	2 56.6	20 17.0	6 32.1	16 25.0	13 3.4	24 13.0	6 53.1	4 49.2
8 Th	21 4 29	15 4 54	8♈32 53	14 43 35	17 31.5	4 55.8	21 29.8	7 9.9	16 19.4	13 10.5	24 14.9	6 52.7	4 50.8
9 F	21 8 26	16 2 24	20 57 28	27 14 56	17 26.2	6 56.5	22 42.6	7 47.7	16 13.7	13 17.5	24 16.8	6 52.4	4 52.5
10 Sa	21 12 22	16 59 56	3♉36 26	10♉ 2 25	17 23.3	8 58.3	23 55.5	8 25.5	16 7.8	13 24.5	24 18.7	6 52.1	4 54.2
11 Su	21 16 19	17 57 29	16 33 20	23 9 37	17D 22.4	11 0.8	25 8.4	9 3.4	16 1.8	13 31.4	24 20.7	6 51.8	4 55.9
12 M	21 20 15	18 55 4	29 51 39	6♊39 47	17 22.7	13 3.9	26 21.4	9 41.3	15 55.7	13 38.3	24 22.8	6 51.6	4 57.6
13 Tu	21 24 12	19 52 40	13♊34 18	20 35 20	17R 23.3	15 7.1	27 34.5	10 19.2	15 49.4	13 45.1	24 24.8	6 51.4	4 59.3
14 W	21 28 9	20 50 17	27 42 53	4♋56 50	17 22.9	17 10.2	28 47.6	10 57.1	15 43.0	13 51.9	24 27.0	6 51.2	5 1.1
15 Th	21 32 5	21 47 56	12♋16 48	19 42 16	17 20.8	19 12.9	0♌ 0.7	11 35.1	15 36.4	13 58.7	24 29.1	6 51.0	5 2.9
16 F	21 36 2	22 45 37	27 12 28	4♌46 25	17 16.1	21 15.2	1 13.9	12 13.1	15 29.8	14 5.4	24 31.3	6 50.9	5 4.7
17 Sa	21 39 58	23 43 19	12♌23 0	20 0 54	17 9.0	23 16.7	2 27.1	12 51.1	15 23.0	14 12.1	24 33.6	6 50.8	5 6.5
18 Su	21 43 55	24 41 2	27 38 45	5♍15 9	17 0.0	25 17.3	3 40.3	13 29.2	15 16.1	14 18.7	24 35.9	6 50.8	5 8.4
19 M	21 47 51	25 38 46	12♍48 45	20 18 15	16 50.1	27 17.0	4 53.6	14 7.2	15 9.1	14 25.2	24 38.2	6D 50.8	5 10.2
20 Tu	21 51 48	26 36 32	27 42 36	5♎ 0 51	16 40.4	29 15.5	6 7.0	14 45.3	15 2.0	14 31.7	24 40.6	6 50.8	5 12.1
21 W	21 55 44	27 34 19	12♎12 21	19 16 37	16 32.2	1♍13.0	7 20.3	15 23.5	14 54.9	14 38.2	24 43.0	6 50.8	5 14.0
22 Th	21 59 41	28 32 7	26 13 27	3♏ 2 48	16 26.2	3 9.1	8 33.8	16 1.6	14 47.6	14 44.6	24 45.5	6 50.9	5 16.0
23 F	22 3 37	29 29 56	9♏44 49	16 19 50	16 22.6	5 4.1	9 47.2	16 39.8	14 40.2	14 50.9	24 48.0	6 51.0	5 17.9
24 Sa	22 7 34	0♍27 46	22 48 15	29 10 36	16D 21.1	6 57.7	11 0.7	17 18.0	14 32.8	14 57.2	24 50.5	6 51.1	5 19.9
25 Su	22 11 31	1 25 38	5♐27 27	11♐39 26	16R 20.9	8 50.0	12 14.2	17 56.2	14 25.3	15 3.4	24 53.1	6 51.3	5 21.9
26 M	22 15 27	2 23 31	17 47 11	23 51 20	16 21.1	10 41.0	13 27.8	18 34.5	14 17.7	15 9.6	24 55.7	6 51.5	5 23.9
27 Tu	22 19 24	3 21 25	29 52 32	5♑51 23	16 20.4	12 30.7	14 41.4	19 12.8	14 10.1	15 15.7	24 58.3	6 51.8	5 25.9
28 W	22 23 20	4 19 20	11♑48 27	17 44 17	16 17.9	14 19.1	15 55.1	19 51.1	14 2.4	15 21.7	25 1.0	6 52.1	5 27.9
29 Th	22 27 17	5 17 17	23 39 21	29 34 8	16 12.9	16 6.1	17 8.7	20 29.4	13 54.7	15 27.7	25 3.8	6 52.4	5 30.0
30 F	22 31 13	6 15 15	5♒28 59	11♒24 18	16 5.1	17 51.8	18 22.5	21 7.8	13 46.9	15 33.6	25 6.5	6 52.7	5 32.0
31 Sa	22 35 10	7 13 14	17 20 20	23 17 22	15 54.7	19 36.3	19 36.2	21 46.1	13 39.1	15 39.4	25 9.3	6 53.1	5 34.1

Astro Data	Planet Ingress	Last Aspect	☽ Ingress	Last Aspect	☽ Ingress	☽ Phases & Eclipses	Astro Data
Dy Hr Mn	Dy Hr Mn	Dy Hr Mn	Dy Hr Mn	Dy Hr Mn	Dy Hr Mn	Dy Hr Mn	1 JULY 1974
♅ D 2 0:16	♀ ♋ 21 4:34	30 1:55 ♃ △	♐ 1 1:20	1 18:45 ♅ □	♒ 2 6:46	4 12:40 ○ 12♑10	Julian Day # 27210
♃ R 7 16:13	☉ ♌ 23 5:30	2 23:42 ♅ ✶	♑ 3 12:19	4 7:38 ♅ △	♓ 4 19:26	12 15:28 ☽ 19♈54	Delta T 45.0 sec
☽0N 10 1:11	♂ ♍ 27 14:04	5 11:52 ♅ □	♒ 6 0:41	6 10:41 ♀ △	♈ 7 7:15	19 12:06 ● 26♋27	SVP 05♓36'40"
☿ D 12 1:56		8 0:39 ♅ △	♓ 8 13:25	9 6:22 ♅ ☍	♉ 9 17:13	26 3:51 ☽ 2♏48	Obliquity 23°26'31"
☽0S 22 22:16	☿ ♌ 5 11:42	10 1:13 ♃ ☌	♈ 11 1:10	11 17:07 ♀ ✶	♊ 12 0:15		⚷ Chiron 24♈10.3
	♀ ♌ 14 23:47	12 22:39 ♅ ☍	♉ 13 10:21	13 18:31 ♅ △	♋ 14 3:49	3 3:57 ○ 10♒27	☽ Mean ☊ 18♐20.4
☽0N 6 7:49	☿ ♍ 20 9:04	15 2:25 ☉ ✶	♊ 15 15:54	15 19:42 ♅ □	♌ 16 4:26	11 2:46 ☽ 18♉04	
☽0S 19 8:44	☉ ♍ 23 12:29	17 10:37 ♀ ☌	♋ 17 17:56	17 19:44 ☿ ☌	♍ 18 3:42	17 19:02 ● 24♌29	1 AUGUST 1974
♆ D 19 3:38		19 12:06 ☉ ☌	♌ 19 17:43	19 3:42 ♃ ☍	♎ 20 3:45	24 15:38 ☽ 1♐05	Julian Day # 27241
♃△♄ 22 5:19		21 11:03 ♂ ☌	♍ 21 17:10	22 4:21 ☉ ✶	♏ 22 6:37		Delta T 45.1 sec
		22 21:29 ♃ ☍	♎ 23 18:19	23 13:16 ♂ ✶	♐ 24 13:34		SVP 05♓36'35"
		25 20:49 ♂ ✶	♏ 25 22:45	26 14:11 ♅ ✶	♑ 27 0:15		Obliquity 23°26'31"
		27 6:39 ♃ △	♐ 28 7:00	29 2:52 ♅ □	♒ 29 12:53		⚷ Chiron 24♈29.7R
		30 6:11 ♅ ✶	♑ 30 18:11				☽ Mean ☊ 16♐41.9

dreams. The south node (a so-called karmic, Saturn-like energy) approaches his Midheaven, or status-career position.

As the days wore on, repeated Midheaven and vertex transits set off a natal yod involving Mars-Mercury-Jupiter quincunx to the Saturn and Neptune sextile, with Pluto at the midpoint. To put it mildly, the President was in deep doo-doo.

Meanwhile, Pluto, inching its way through his first house, had been stripping away the public persona he had cultivated for so many years and was revealing the true face of the President. Never before was the need to re-invent himself more evident. Pluto's steady erosion would change Mr. Nixon forever. Uranus, conjunct his natal 2nd house south node, would cause him to re-think his value system and start building anew.

Natally, Mr. Nixon's chart is a gold mine for further study. Astrologers couldn't have made up a better case history! Progressions and directions, (plus some of the added points and parts mentioned above) give even more data — enough to fill a notebook. But it is transits alone that act like an indelible pen, tracing the course of history, underlining the days of importance, and recording the events without emotion. Just look at an ephemeris page and you will see planetary actions as a series of waves, constant, relentless, nonjudgmental. Without a doubt, an understanding of transits is your best bet toward understanding Life.

Watch Your Language!

A final word on the language used in this article. When two planets move into close proximity to one another, they "conjoin" each other. The word "conjunct" is an adjective, describing a condition (joined together), and is not a verb or action word; so a planet can't conjunct another, it conjoins it, or is in conjunction with it. Most of us know that, but we use the word "conjunct" anyway because it sounds good to American ears. Unlike Latin, American English is a growing and ever-expanding language, adding new words and adapting constantly to changing mores. Perhaps the lexicographers will come to recognize this special usage and change the dictionaries accordingly.

Astrologers also tend to ascribe human characteristics to the inanimate planets.

Saturn doesn't "cause" restrictions or delays
Mars doesn't "cause" anger
Venus doesn't "cause" love

and so on. Once again, this is an example of an astrologer's shorthand, or short-cut speech. What the planets do is mark off the synchronicity of occurring events. The Winter Solstice doesn't "cause" snow and bitter cold in the northern hemisphere, but they sure enough happen around the same time! From now on, when you talk astrology, please be sure you know the difference between cause and effect, or else every science- or reality-oriented person you meet will laugh at you. And we've had enough of that. ✹

Footnotes

(1) **Nicole Brown Simpson,** May 19, 1959, 2:00 AM MET, Frankfurt-am-Main, Germany 50N07, 8E40. *Source:* birth certificate, *via* Marion March. **Date of death:** June 12, 1994, 10:32 PM PDT, Brentwood, CA, 33 N 55 117 W 54. *Source:* news reports. Time is speculative, based on testimony of witnesses following discovery of her body and that of her friend Ronald Goldman.

(2) **Jacqueline Kennedy Onassis**, July 28, 1929, 2:30 PM EDT, Southampton, New York 40N53, 72W23. *Source:* Frances McEvoy from mutual friend and Kennedy confidant. **Date of death:** May 19, 1994, 10:15 PM EDT, New York City, 40N45, 73W57. *Source:* news reports..

(3) **Nancy Kerrigan**, Oct. 13, 1969. 5:17 PM EDT, Woburn, MA 42N28, 71W09. *Source*: McEvoy, from birth certificate. **Assault:** Jan. 6, 1994, 2:30 PM EST, Detroit Michigan, 42N20, 83W03. *Source:* news sources.

(4) **William Jefferson Clinton** (ne Blythe), Aug. 19, 1946, 8:51 AM, CST, Hope, Arkansas 33N40, 93W35. *Source:* His mother. **Summer Solstice:** June 21, 1994. 10:48 AM EDT, Washington, DC. 38N53, 77W01. *Source*: NCGR 1994 Mundane Data.

(5) "Transits signify periods of growth. If we wish to use the transit period for our growing, we need to begin when the seeds of the transit are planted. ... Many students attempt to interpret a transit when it is basically over, for they begin to work with it when the crops is being harvested. ...For that reason, when charting up-

coming transits, I use a ten-degree applying orb. In that way, the energy can be transformed with knowledge and understanding." — *Planets, the Time of Your Life*, by Betty Lundsted. Copyright 1980, Samuel Weiser, Inc., New York NY.

(6) Planetary patterns of special significance include the **t-cross**— two planets opposite one another and each square to a third

grand cross — two oppositions with each of the four planets involved square to two others

grand trine — three planets each within orb of 120° of two others, and all three forming an equilateral triangle

yod — two planets sextile to one another, each of which is quincunx one other planet. Some astrologers say that the slowest planet must be the one at the apex, and also that only the major planets, Sun and Moon may be used.

(7) Mercury, with its core of iron, may be a contender. As to why Pluto seems such a nonconformer, there are still many questions about the planet's origin. Most astronomers conclude that Pluto is a former moon of the planet Neptune and is similar to Neptune's moon, Triton. Pluto's own moon, Charon, named for the boatman who ferried the dead across the River Styx, is about one-third the planet's size. (Many thanks to Noreen Grice of Boston's Charles Hayden Planetarium for verifying the astronomical facts in this article.)

(8) **Richard Milhous Nixon**, Jan. 9, 1913, 9:44 p.m. PST, Yorba Linda CA, 33N53, 117W49.

Figures

(All charts in this article are tropical, geocentric, and erected in the Koch house system.)

I. Double Chart: Nicole Simpson, murder

II. Double Chart: Jackie Onassis, death

III. Double Chart: Nancy Kerrigan, assault

IV. Double chart: President Clinton, July 4, 1994

V. Line drawing of solar system, showing planets in orbit

VI. Double Chart: Aries Ingresses, 1776 and 2008

VII. Table of Most Commonly Used Aspects

VIII. Table of Average Planetary Periods and Retrograde Stations

IX. Table of Earliest, Latest Saturn Returns

X. Table of Generational Differences— Three Outer Planets

XI. Richard M. Nixon chart

XII. Ephemeris page showing August 9, 1974, date of Nixon's resignation

References

PLANETS IN TRANSIT, Life Cycles for Living. Robert Hand, 1976. Whitford Press, Atglen, PA 19310.

TRANSITS, The Time of Your Life. Betty Lundsted, Copyright 1980, Samuel Weiser, Inc., York, Maine.

MODERN TRANSITS, Lois M. Rodden. Copyright 1978, American Federation of Astrologers, Inc., Tempe, Arizona 85282.

ASTROLOGICAL CYCLES and the Life Crisis Periods. John Townley. Copyright 1977, Samuel Weiser, Inc. Out of print..

INTEGRATED TRANSITS. Vol. VII: The Principles and Practice of Astrology. Noel Tyl. Copyright 1974. Llewellyn Publications, Saint Paul, MN 55165.

THE AMERICAN EPHEMERIS FOR THE 20TH CENTURY, 1900 to 2000 at Midnight. Neil F. Michelsen. Copyright 1980. Astro Computing Services, San Diego CA 92116

TABLES OF PLANETARY PHENOMENA. Neil F. Michelsen. Copyright 1990. ACS Publications, Inc. San Diego.

The Eight Lunar Phases: A Cycle of Transformation

by Maria Kay Simms

The only constant in life is change. Nothing is static.

From the tiniest cell to the most complex organism, the cycle continues – life, growth, deterioration, death, and life again. In planetary symbolism we associate the Moon with change, in reflection of her constantly changing faces in the waxing and waning of her cycle. Four of the Moon's faces are well known, and many calendars mark those lunar phases: New Moon, First Quarter, Full Moon and Last Quarter. Not as familiar are the four cross-quarter phases, as described by the great astrologer-philosopher Dane Rudhyar in his 1967 book *The Lunation Cycle.* These four are: Crescent, Gibbous, Disseminating and Balsamic. All together, then, we have a cycle of eight - a cycle of transformation that we can see reflected in our lives.

We have a basic natal "type" according to the lunar phase in our birth chart and we go through a lifetime of phases as defined by secondary progressions. To some extent we might also relate our day-to-day activities to the monthly transiting lunar phases, although lunar transits go by so quickly that most people pay little attention to anything but New Moon and Full Moon. If, however, you were to carefully examine any cycle of experience, whether it encompass a few minutes, an hour, a month, a year or a lifetime, you could define the eight specific phases of transformation from birth though death to rebirth.

The closest Moon phase that occurs before your birthday is your natal Moon phase, and its mythology and symbolism should be meaningful to you in terms of the life purpose suggested by your Sun. The brief delineations given here are, of course, generalized, and will be colored by the sign of your Sun and modified by other factors in your chart.

One of the most popular forms of the lunar cycle used by astrologers is based on the secondary progressed cycle. Secondary Progression, in general, is the symbolic form of astrological timing based upon the formula of one day equals one year of life. The progressed lunar phase is the aspect of Progressed Moon to Progressed Sun. Your progressed lunar phase should give you insight into major transformative cycles within your lifetime. A complete progressed Moon cycle, from New Moon to New Moon again, takes approximately 29 years, with each phase lasting about 3-1/2 years.

The meaning of each lunar phase also corresponds very well to the eight Pagan seasonal holidays. Although these holidays are derived from a cycle of Sun and Earth, rather than the Moon, their mythologies are similar in basic meaning. In essence, a cycle of eight is a cycle of eight. The sequence works no matter

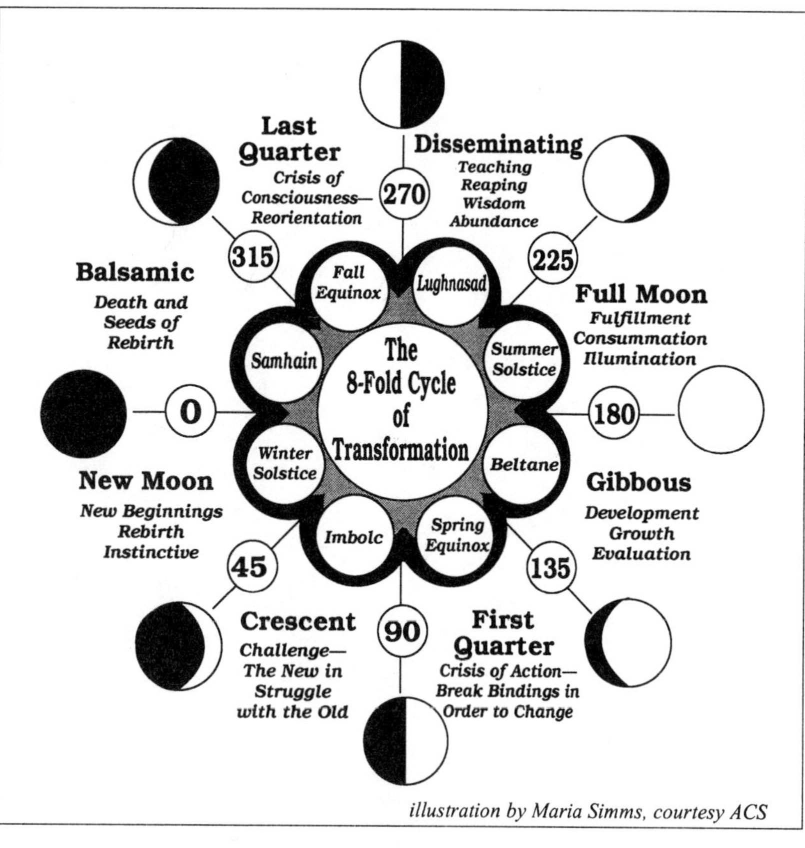

illustration by Maria Simms, courtesy ACS

which two planets' phase relationship to each other are being considered. In briefly delineating each phase, I will include references to the seasonal cycle in order to contribute to your understanding of how each phase works. Later, you might also investigate phase relationships between other planets, for the phase they are "in" should contribute nuances of understanding as to how a waxing aspect works in contrast to how the same aspect in waning phase works.

Before reading the interpretation of each phase, it would be well to know your own natal and progressed phase, and perhaps those of several friends, so that you can more personally relate to the text. This is not difficult to do.

Finding Your Lunar Phase

With Math: For those who work best with numbers, you can determine your phase by simply finding the difference between your natal Sun position and your natal Moon position. This "difference" must be the portion of the circle that places the Moon and Sun closest together.

The phase is then determined by whether Moon position is waxing or waning in relation to the Sun. Moon is waxing from conjunction to opposition, and waning from opposition back to conjunction again.

For example, look at the illustration of the Lunar Cycle at the beginning of this article. New Moon is the conjunction of Sun and Moon. New Moon is "zero," the beginning. When Moon moves 45° ahead of the Sun (a semi-square), it enters Crescent phase. At Balsamic phase, the Moon has moved 315 ° away from the Sun. This is the same as 45° away - still a semi-square - but now the Moon is "behind" the Sun, trying to catch up. At Crescent phase, Moon is in a waxing semi-square to Sun; at Balsamic phases, Moon is in a waning semi-square.

Here is an example in numbers:

• My Sun is 26° Scorpio. Within the 360° of the zodiac circle, that is 236°.

• My Moon is 6° Cancer. Within the 360° of the zodiac circle, that is 96°.

$$236° - 96° = 140°$$

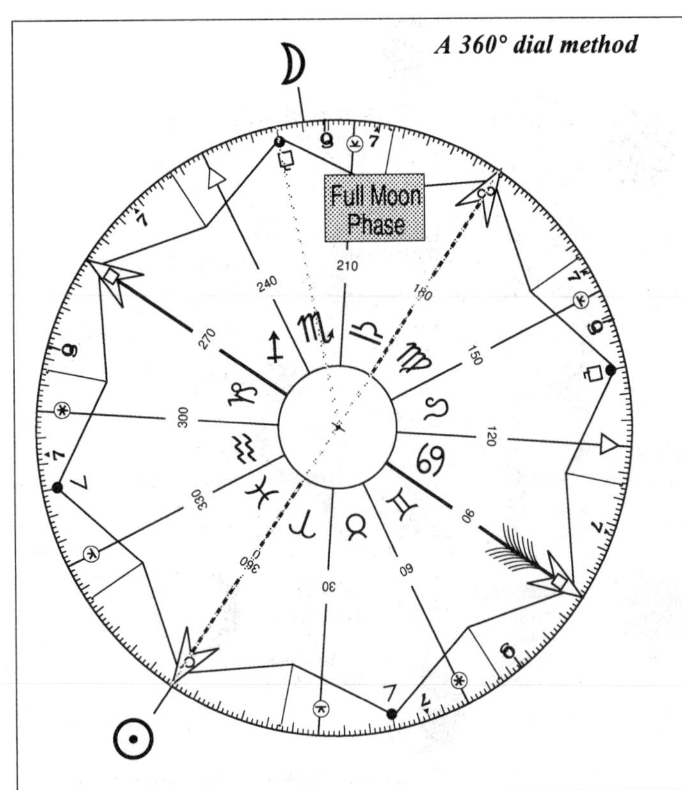

illustration by Maria Simms, courtesy ACS

140° is more than a sesquiquadrate or sesquare (135°) and less than an opposition (180°), BUT remember, the 26° Scorpio Sun is "zero." Moon in Cancer has moved PAST the opposition to Sun (26° Taurus), and is now WANING in its relationship to the Sun. It is approaching the waning sesquare, but is not yet there. Therefore, the phase relationship of Moon to Sun is still within the Full Moon sector.

You can find the progressed lunar phase by simply doing the same procedure using Progressed Sun and Progressed Moon.

With pictures: For those of you who deal more easily with visual pictures rather than numbers, you can easily find phases relationships with a 360° rotating dial, or any rotating aspectarian that shows the 45° aspect series: conjunction, semi-square, square, opposition, sesquare.

Anchor the dial on a piece of plain paper, and holding it in place, mark on your paper the positions of Sun and Moon (or Progressed Sun and Progressed Moon) in their correct sign and degree. Now, rotate the dial so that "zero" (the conjunction) is on your Sun. Note where your Moon is, on or past the degree that marks the beginning of a phase, but before the beginning of the next phase. That sector is your correct lunar phase.

With easy look-ups: There are two other ways you can find your lunar phases. *Tables of Planetary Phenomena,* by Neil F. Michelsen, contains a table of lunar phases from 1900 through 2020. You can simply look up your date.

Easiest of all is the calculation option from Astro Communications Services called *Lifetime Lunar Phases.* This is a one page report that lists your natal lunar phases plus the entry dates for each progressed phase through three complete lunar cycles, which encompasses an entire normal life span of about 86 years. A number of computer programs also contain this option.

Interpreting the Lunar Phases

New Moon: This is the dark of the Moon. Conjunct the Sun, she is, of course, not visible in the night sky. In the cycle of the seasons, Yule or Winter Solstice represents the rebirth of the Sun (the light). Here, during the longest night of the year, the Goddess gives birth to the Sun Child and hope for new light is reborn in joy and celebration. This particular mythology has been carried out in multiple religious traditions, including Christianity, in the choice of Winter Solstice as the birth of the Son, Jesus. Lucina, the Sun Goddess, who rekindles the Sun and brings new light, is known today as Santa Lucia, who wears a wreath of candles on her head.

At this time, the light is born, but is not yet clearly visible. We expect it, but its manifestation is not clear. The newborn baby does not yet show a distinctly clear individuality. The baby operates on instinct, full of potential, full of hope — but what will he or she become?

The **New Moon-born** individual projects the self on the world with a sense of creative new beginning brought forth largely through instinct or sheer impulse.

Here is one who operates best when meeting the challenge of the moment dynamically, often dramatically, who moves forward with the urge to get things going but may not yet have the process well thought through.

When you are at **Progressed New Moon** some new creative energy is released that marks the beginning of a major new cycle of your life. But it is not yet firmly established, and it is not yet certain just how it will develop. Often an event (or events) will occur at this time that "marks" the new cycle - but you may not even be aware of its importance until you look back on it later. This is a time of gradual awakening to new goals. It is not yet a definite break with the past, but it is a time when old familiar patterns seem to lack vitality and you instinctively feel a sense of creative new beginnings.

New Moon in any month is a good time to initiate something new, or to plot a new plan. The "new" phase of any cycle of experience or thought is when the first impulse occurs.

Crescent: In the monthly lunar cycle this is the time when the first silvery crescent of light appears in the night sky - the newborn light begins to manifest . In the yearly seasonal holidays, this is known as Imbolc or Candlemas (February 2, traditionally, but in terms of actual cross-quarter 45° aspect from Winter Solstice, more like February 4). The newborn Sun God is seen as a small child nursing at the breast of the Mother Goddess. New beginnings are nurtured, seeds stir beneath the earth, and a few little sprouts may appear through the snow.

The weather is unpredictable - one day it may snow, and the next it is sunny and warm. The days are visibly longer, the light can be actually seen to have "returned." Spring is obviously coming, and it is time to think of spring cleaning, as winter and its death cycle are swept away. The energy is directed toward empowering new beginnings.

If you are **born at Crescent Moon**, you feel a strong impulse toward action, but you seem forever to be involved in intense challenges. In one way or another you are trying to break with traditions of the past (sweep away the winter). You may be involved in attempting to change from one social or economic class to another, or perhaps in attempting to break away from family expectations, or to improve your status in the world. In some way or another you represent the new in perpetual struggle against the old.

At the time of your **Progressed Crescent Moon** the new beginnings that were released at Progressed New Moon begin to crystallize and take form. You "see the light." Your new beginning now takes on some manifested form, however incomplete. You are challenged to carry forward, but in order to do so, you may have to break from something in the past. Old habits may pull you back. Or nay-sayers may weaken your resolve. You may make excuses, yourself, why you are not getting done what you really want to do. You may spurt ahead, then stop, yet the will to proceed nags at you.

When the first Crescent appears in the monthly sky, you should be seeing some visible manifestation of your plans made at New Moon. Now your challenge is to proceed and not make excuses. This is true of the Crescent phase of any cycle of experience or thought.

First Quarter: Half of the Moon is now visible at night, in the monthly cycle - a balance between dark and light. In the yearly seasonal cycle this phase corresponds to Spring Equinox, or Eostar, when days and nights are of equal length. This is a point of equilibrium, just before light "springs" forth. The chains of winter are broken, and light will reign as the days grow longer. Rituals of this holiday may involve the breaking of bindings to empower self-change. The God and Goddess are children at play, and holiday festivals affirm the child within, and celebrate the new growth (birth) now appearing visibly on Earth with brightly colored eggs.

This phase of the lunar cycle has been called the crisis of action. You who are **First Quarter born** may feel that your life is one crisis after another. The challenge is action. It is decision time. No waffling back and forth on what action to take for you! You are attracted to action, noise, and movement because you sense in yourself a constant urge to get going - to progress - even if the end goal you are moving toward is still just a little bit hazy. You feel that you have to clear away old forms or structures that you perceive as obstacles, so that you can create new ones. You are strong willed and are likely to develop skills in management.

Progressed First Quarter brings a crisis of action in the new direction that you are establishing in your life. The stages of plotting and then struggling with whether or not to go forward are over. This is the time to make it happen - to be aggressive in pursuing your goals. If there is anything from your past that is holding you back, this is the time to resolve that issue and clear it away once and for all.

When the Moon in the sky is "half and half" and waxing, it is decision time, action time. Get off your duff on that new beginning and make something happen. This is the time in any cycle of experience or thought that you make a firm decision or make a decisive action.

Gibbous: The Moon in the sky is increasing in light, but not yet full. The seasonal correspondence is to Beltane or May Eve, the time of sacred marriage which honors the life-giving fertility of the blooming earth. The Maiden Goddess and the young Sun King have now come of age, bursting with self-discovery and racing hormones. Seasonal celebrations involve the race of courtship, weaving the web of life around a Maypole, and leaping the Beltane fires for luck and for future fulfillment of wishes.

You who are **Gibbous-born** give much attention to self-discovery. You are developing your capacity for personal growth in your desire to make your life something of value. You constantly evaluate - constantly ask "why" - where you are going, how you are growing, what you are doing that has significance.

Nothing is taken for granted. It is important to you to make things clear, to discover better ways of doing things. You could become caught up in working for a cause. You are very conscious of improving your skills.

At the **Progressed Gibbous Moon** you are challenged to perfect the methods of your new direction in life. You could call this the period of apprenticeship. Your new direction is established but not yet fulfilled. This is a stage of development in which you must analyze and evaluate your growth and reorganize or improve your techniques so that you can grow beyond technique and reach out for true fulfillment.

When the Moon is almost, but not quite full, it is time to work on that project, evaluate how it is going, and persist in its development. This is the time in any cycle of thought or experience when you've almost "got it," but not quite – soon, just around the corner. Gotta keep going!

Full Moon: The Moon now shines opposite in the zodiac from the Sun, reflecting his light in all her fullness. In correspondence with the seasonal cycle, it is now Midsummer, or Summer Solstice. At this, the longest day, light triumphs, yet at the same time begins its gradual decline into the dark. From here on, the waning cycle begins. This is the symbolic sacrifice of the Sun King, who embraces the Queen of Summer in the consummation of love that also portends death. In his maturity, he now recognizes that the consequences of his love for the Goddess will mean a fatherly responsibility to his people. His energy goes into the womb of the Mother, to become the harvest grain, which must eventually die in order to feed new life. His carefree days are over. He is fulfilled, but now he must assume the responsibilities of that fulfillment. It is a season of celebration, consummation and abundance, and yet at the same time, it is a recognition of the other side, the ending that will eventually come, but is not yet quite real.

As the Full Moon stands at polar opposite to the Sun, so will the **Full Moon- born** be strongly involved in issues of relationship. Long before the mature realization fully sets in that the only sense of true completion in life is within self, you may go through considerable crises in your relationships with others. Perhaps more than with other phase-types, it is through relationships that you will achieve objectivity and clarity about your own purpose in life, just as the seasonal God comes to recognize his sense of purpose through his love of the Goddess. It is the discovery of purpose that is paramount. Fulfillment - even abundance - is not enough. You must find illumination, a worthwhile reason for your life, and ultimately it must be achieved through a sense of balance within yourself that is not dependent upon the approval of, or lived vicariously through, another person.

Progressed Full Moon is a fulfillment or climax of the new direction that began about 14-15 years ago at your Progressed New Moon. It's a high period. The new structures you've been building work! Now what? As at Summer Solstice, the light triumphs — but does that also mean that now there's only one way to go - into decline? Is further growth possible? A bit scary, isn't it? It is important at this time to pause for illumination, to consider the meaning or purpose for what you are doing. You need also to integrate any opposing issues from within or without. If there is no illumination, your vitality and enthusiasm for what you are doing is likely to wane and the structures begin to crumble as your direction loses clarity. But if what you have built is truly meaningful, you have much to give back to the world in the coming phase.

At the time of Full Moon, or at the "full phase" of any cycle of experience or thought, you should see the fruits of your progress in whatever you started at New Moon (or first tangible idea), provided you have persisted through the challenges of the previous phases. In "making the most of it" you may need to seek inner balance.

Disseminating: The round Moon is now a bit flat on one side, but still bright in the sky. This phase corresponds to the seasonal festival called Lughnasad or Lammas (traditionally August 2, actually the Leo cross-quarter, more likely August 7). Here the God becomes the first fruits of the harvest, the early grains. The survival of his people is nearly assured. The full harvest is nearly ready, but not complete, still vulnerable to weather and change. It is a time of further maturing, and energy is directed toward prosperity, growth in wisdom and the reaping of plenty.

Illumination is reached at Full Moon, and at Disseminating Moon it is spread. You, who are **Disseminating-born,** like to convey ideas that are meaningful to you. You are a natural communicator, a born teacher. If a particular cause has become important to you, you could be quite a crusader. The main purpose for your life - what you live for - is to share your wisdom, your beliefs, your interests.

During the period of your **Progressed Disseminating Moon** it is time to give back to the world from what you have received. Share the fruits of your achievements, of your Full Moon culmination, and more importantly, the wisdom of your illumination. This is the time to teach others what you have learned.

During this first waning period of the monthly Moon, or in the Disseminating phases of any cycle of thought or experience, it is time to share with others what you have done, are continuing to do, and what you have learned from it.

Last Quarter: Once again the Moon is half light and half dark. At the corresponding seasonal phase of Autumn Equinox, the days and nights are equal. At this point of equilibrium, however, it is the light that will give way to increased darkness. This is the time of full Harvest Festival, and as such it is a time of joy and thanksgiving. At the same time, it is a time of leave-taking and perhaps sorrow, for we know that life will soon decline, and the Earth will take on the barren cloak of winter. Seasonal rituals may depict the symbolic death of the God, or his eventual passage into the invisible world. He is now the Dark Lord, and the Mother Goddess gives way to her mature aspect as the Crone. Still, the festival emphasis is on the message of rebirth that is seen in the potential of the seeds of the harvest that will be saved for planting.

Last Quarter is the time of crisis in consciousness and you who are **born during Last Quarter** phase know deep inside yourself that somehow you do not "fit in" with the accepted way that prevails around you. You are likely to seem different on the surface (to others) than what you really perceive yourself to be inside. New ideas germinate within you, but you may not let them show. You could even seem inflexible to others, for you will, on the surface, stick to established structures and patterns because you are not yet ready to "come out" with your inner reorientation. There will be times, perhaps when your progressions reflect that you are ready, when a "new you" comes suddenly to the surface, surprising others who did not realize the changes that were going on inside you.

During your **Progressed Last Quarter** period, you will experience some crisis in consciousness that will lead you away from the dominant activities of your current progressed lunar cycle and will begin to prepare you for a new direction at the next Progressed New Moon. You may begin to resist previous ways of doing things because it seems that somehow they no longer serve you. What was to be accomplished since the last New Moon has been done. Deep inside you something new is germinating, even though on the surface you may not show this to others.

When the Moon is "half and half" and waning, it is a time when introspection is appropriate. At the Last Quarter phase of any cycle of experience or thought, you may still be carrying on with that which was begun at New Moon, but you are beginning to wonder what may lie beyond. Why is this no longer as satisfying to me as it once was? What else is there? You begin to seek answers within.

Balsamic Only a sliver of light now remains in the night sky - the waning crescent Moon. The Balsamic Moon corresponds to the seasonal festival of Samhain or Hallows, a holiday that is more popularly know as Halloween. This is said to be the time when the veil between visible and invisible worlds grows thin, when souls who are leaving the physical plane pass out, and souls who are reincarnating pass in. Darkness is increasing. The Goddess reigns as Crone, the elder Wise Woman (who is the secular model for the Halloween witch). The God, as Dark Lord presides over the invisible world. Here he will assist the passing of the souls, and here, quietly beneath the earth, unseen within the womb of the resting Mother, he is the seed of his own rebirth.

As **Balsamic-born,** you could be one who seems somehow out-of-sync with the majority, one about whom it could be said "listens to the beat of a different drummer." You may have a sense of the prophet about you. You are certain that you have a special destiny but you are not very clear on just what it is or where you are going - but you are ready to flow with it.

Many experience the **Progressed Balsamic Moon** period as a true "dark-of-the-Moon," but it should not be looked upon as a fallow period when nothing is accomplished. You will probably try several new starts in your attempt to reach out for your new cycle, "your new sense of destiny." Some of these attempts will fall by the wayside, but others - or one - will prove to be the successful conception (seed form) of the new cycle, which you will begin to realize at progressed New Moon. Do not mourn for what has ended - it has served its purpose. Know that every ending is the seed of a new beginning. The wheel keeps turning.

When that final little waning sliver of the Moon appears in the sky, it is an appropriate time to let go of that which is finished. It is a good time to end a bad habit, bury an old grudge, bring a project to closure. The Balsamic phase of any cycle of thought or experience, is the time when you may think about future potentials without demanding that they happen now. You may come to the realization that something is finished, and let it go.

The beginning illustration and much of the interpretive text for this article is exerpted from *The Eight-Fold Cycle of Transformation* by Maria Kay Simms, which is appears in Neil F. Michelsen's *Tables of Planetary Phenomena,* ACS Publications, 1990. It is used by permission of the publisher.

APPENDIX

Perhaps the most popular method of calculating solar arcs, and, in my opinion the easiest, is to subtract the position of the Sun on the directed date (July 26) from the position of the Sun on the birthday.

Some Planetary Concepts

by J. Lee Lehman, Ph.D.

> "Nothing was ever discovered by logic. All things are discovered by intuition, as the lives of the great mathematicians and scientists prove again and again. Logic plods after intuition,and verifies discoveries in its own pedestrian way."*

The field (if we may use the 20th century concept from physics) in which all astrology plays out is the zodiac, along with the latitude that allows the placement of any point within our system. A field is like a playing field in sports: it is the surface upon which everything occurs. It is the space.

Through our definitions of the astrological signs (tropical or sidereal) we state that the field is not all of the same quality. The play will vary. First base is different from second base, and both are different from the outfield.

The planets are our Celestial players. They each have different jobs. The function of the Sun is different from the Moon, as the pitcher's job is different from the third baseman's. Once we have learned the functions of the various planets, and the qualities associated with the signs, we want to put the system together. We are interested primarily in the team after all, whether the team in our sense is an individual, a country, a question, and event, or even literally, a baseball team.

To understand the entity as a whole, we also need the third great component of astrology: the *houses*. They are analogous to the innings in baseball: they begin with the ascendant (or the First Inning), and proceed through the various phases of life. A baseball game proceeds from the First until the 9th Inning. If there's a tie, more innings proceed. With our cycles in astrology, if the entity "lives" long enough, various cycles may repeat.

I assume that the reader is basically familiar with the meanings of the planets. The purpose of this chapter is to present some information about how to interpret the planets given their zodiacal placement through the use of a series of related rulership concepts: dispositors, dispositorship, and mutual reception. A related concept is also discussed: decanates.

Since most of this material involves Rulerships, it is best to begin with a discussion of this concept.

In the history of astrology there were five Essential Dignities. In the last two centuries, three of them have often been ignored, but here we shall present them in their entirety.

Essential Dignity and Debility are both based on the zodiacal placement of a planet or position. The Essential Dignities and Debilities are given in Tables One through Four. Point values are assigned to each Dignity or Debility; their use will be considered presently.

Table One is the most familiar. However, the reader who learned astrology with many modern sources will notice that Uranus, Neptune and Pluto are not represented in this Table. There are good historical reasons for this: I discussed them in detail in *Essential Digni-*

Table 1

Sign	Domicile (+5)	Exhaltation (+4)	Detriment (-5)	Fall (-4)
♈	♂	☉	♀	♄
♉	♀	☽	♂	-
♊	☿	☊	♃	☋
♋	☽	♃	♄	♂
♌	☉	-	♄	-
♍	☿	☿	♃	♀
♎	♀	♄	♂	☉
♏	♂	-	♀	☽
♐	♃	☋	☿	☊
♑	♄	♂	☽	♃
♒	♄	-	☉	-
♓	♃	♀	☿	☿

Essential Dignities and Debilities: Whole Sign Types. *Point Values Given per Lilly*

**Colin Wilson. 1984. Religion and the Rebel.. Salem House: Salem, NH. Pages 102-103.*

ties, Chapters One and Four. In brief, the "modern" Rulerships were assigned after the true meaning of "Rulership" was lost. In the modern sense, "Rulership" is associated with analogy or likeness: Aries is believed to be "like" Mars. In the true traditional sense, "Rulership" meant "strength."

There is one major difference between the traditional Exaltations and the Rulerships: there are no duplicate Exaltations, and thus, not all signs are associated with planetary Exaltations. Thus, the signs Leo, Scorpio and Aquarius are not used in the Exaltation system. It was this fact that tempted some astrologers to play fill-in-the-blanks. This is a completely different operation than eliminating one planetary rulership and substituting another. Thus, while the two operations have often been performed in one breath, they cannot be justified together.

Table 2

Sign	Ptolemy: Day	Ptolemy: Night	Ptolemy: Mixed	Lilly: Day	Lilly: Night
♈ ♌ ♐	☉	♃	♂	☉	♃
♉ ♍ ♑	♀	☽	♄	♀	☽
♊ ♎ ♒	♄	☿	♃	♄	☿
♋ ♏ ♓	♀	☽	♂	♂	♂

Triplicities as given by Ptolemy and William Lilly. *Point value is +3 for chosen type.*

Planets in Domicile (Sign)or Rulership are strong. They are captains of their own fate, so to speak. They set their own agenda. Planets in Exaltation are more in the position of honored guests. Things are done for them, on their behalf. These things are supposed to be for their benefit, but exalted planets do not control their own agenda.

Table Two shows the Triplicity rulers. There are actually several variants of this table, but the two given are the most significant. Johannes Schoener attributed his Triplicity table to Ptolemy, but Schoener reversed the positions of the Moon and Mars in the Water columns from that given by Ptolemy. Claude Dariot, Lilly's immediate predecessor, gave water using Schoener's transposition (thus, the error was transmitted), and then in his own turn Dariot inverted Mars and Saturn as the mixed ruler of Earth and Fire respectively. Thus, by Lilly's time, the three ruler Triplicity system had been significantly corrupted from Ptolemy.

Lilly's simplification is justifiable based on a reading of Ptolemy, however. In Ptolemy's discussion of the Trigons or Triangles, short shrift was given to the mixed ruler of the three Trigons other than Water and Mars was mentioned as the primary Water ruler. Thus, Lilly's two ruler system could be understood to represent the spirit, if not the letter, of Ptolemy. Ptolemy's use of the third or mixed ruler - other than in the case of Water - was principally in describing the effects on the weather. *Planets in Triplicity are generally considered lucky.*

The *Terms* are probably the most difficult of the Essential Dignities to understand, because the origin of the Terms seems the most arcane. The simple fact is that we may never know what they are, but only that they were derived empirically. The question is, empirically from what? Was it a case of the Babylonian astrologers sitting down in their teams of observers and tabulating when particular kinds of questions were asked, and what degrees the planets occupied then? Or were the Terms a translation of something else, as Tester thought that they were derived from heliacal rising times? *We don't know.*

What we *do* know is the Ptolemy listed two term tables, those that we now call the Ptolemaic (Lilly called this set Chaldean) and the Egyptian. The two tables were variously adopted by astrologers, although there did seem to be an eventual Catholic–Protestant split, with the Catholic contingent under the "leadership" of Placidus favoring the Egyptian Terms, and the Protestant group including Lilly favoring the Ptolemaic ones.

The basis for assigning Terms seemingly was to reward those planets with greater numbers of Essential Dignities (Sign, Exaltation and Triplicity) in a Sign by making that planet the first term ruler, and to assign benefics more degrees than malefics. The planet which is

Table 3

Ptolemaic (Chaldean) and Egyptian terms. *Point value is +2 for chosen type.*

Ptolemaic

♈	0♃6	6♀14	14☿21	21♂26	26♄30
♉	0♀8	8☿15	15♃22	22♄26	26♂30*
♊	0☿7	7♃14	14♀21	21♄25*	25♂30*
♋	0♂6	6♃13*	13☿20	20♀27*	27♄30
♌	0♄6*	6☿13	13♀19*	19♃25*	25♂30
♍	0☿7	7♀13	13♃18	18♄24*	24♂30*
♎	0♄6	6♀11*	11♃19	19☿24*	24♂30
♏	0♂6	6♃14*	14♀21*	21☿27*	27♄30
♐	0♃8	8♀14	14☿19	19♄25	25♂30
♑	0♀6*	6☿12*	12♃19*	19♂25*	25♄30*
♒	0♄6*	6☿12*	12♀20*	20♃25*	25♂30*
♓	0♀8	8♃14	14☿20	20♂26	26♄30

Egyptian

♈	0♃6	6♀12	12☿20	20♂25	25♄30
♉	0♀8	8☿14	14♃22	22♄27	27♂30
♊	0☿6	6♃12	12♀17	17♂24*	24♄30*
♋	0♂7	7♀13*	13☿19	19♃26*	26♄30
♌	0♃6*	6♀11*	11♄18*	18☿24*	24♂30
♍	0☿7	7♀17	17♃21	21♂27	28♄30*
♎	0♄6	6☿14*	14♃21	21♀28*	28♂30
♏	0♂7	7♀11*	11☿19*	19♃24*	24♄30
♐	0♃12	12♀17	17☿21	21♄26	26♂30
♑	0☿7*	7♃14*	14♑22*	22♄26*	26♂30*
♒	0☿7*	7♀13*	13♃20*	20♂25*	25♄30*
♓	0♀12	12♃16	16☿19	19♂28	28♄30

the ruler by Sign, Exaltation, or Triplicity tends to get the first term position most frequently. This falls off dramatically after the first position. As one may note from the tables, Mars or Saturn get the final position. This no doubt is the origin of the rule-of-thumb assigning the final degrees of any Sign as having malefic qualities.

Planets in their own *Terms* denote the participation of the native or planet in the business of that planet, but not from a position of power, wealth, or fortune. The issue of that planet is important, but the outcome is uncertain.

The final Essential Dignity is the *Face*. We have already seen that the Triplicity rulers and term rulers were derived from the higher ranking Essential Dignities: the Triplicity from the Sign and Exaltation, the term from the Sign, Exaltation and Triplicity. On the one hand, the derivation of the Faces is extremely clear, but the rationale behind it in light of the reasoning of the other Essential Dignities is opaque.

The division of the 360 circle into units of 10 was known as an ancient system. These 10 sections in fact represented asterisms, components of constellations, and were time markers on the way to being able to measure planetary positions to degrees, and finally, minutes. The order of the Faces is simple: begin with zero Aries. The first 10 of Aries is assigned to Mars, the ruler of Aries. From there, each Face ruler in sequence is the so-called Chaldean order: Mars–> Sun –> Venus–> Mercury –> Moon –> Saturn –> Jupiter–> Mars, and so on through the signs. Reading down any column in the Faces gives the order of the planetary ruler of the days of the week: the Sun for Sunday, the Moon for Monday, etc.

We shall have more to say about the Faces when we compare them to the Decanates later in this chapter. For now, the Face represents worry or concern about the planet in question: it is somewhat tenuous that the Face should even be considered dignified.

Perhaps the pithiest distinction between the five Essential Dignities was given by Sibly:

"The effects produced by the planets under these situations, are as follow:

If the planet, which is principal significator, be posited in his own house, in any scheme or calculation whatever, it indicates prosperity and success to the person signified, to the business in hand, or to whatever else may be the subject of inquiry.

If a planet be in his Exaltation, it denotes a person of majestic carriage, and lofty disposition, high–minded, austere, and proud.

If a planet be in his Triplicity, the person will be prosperous and fortunate in acquiring the goods of this life no matter whether well or ill descended, or born rich or poor, his condition and circumstances will notwithstanding be promising and good.

Table 4 Key words associated with the five essential dignities.

Ruler	*Exaltation*	*Triplicity*	*Term*	*Face*
power	persuasion	lucky	competency	fear
owner	guest	self–made	clone	climber
success	recognition	fortunate	adequate	danger
prosperity	comfort	well–off	settled	anxiety
strength	pride	harmony	facsimile	denial
productive	majestic	favorable	mimics	concern
authority	grace	auspicious	acceptance	loathing

If a planet be in his Terms, it betokens a person to participate rather in the nature and quality of the planet, than in the wealth, power and dignity, indicated thereby. If a planet be in his phases, and no otherwise fortified, though significator, it declares the person or thing signified to be in great distress, danger, or anxiety.

And thus, in all cases, judgement is to be given good or bad, according to the strength, ability, or imperfection, of the significator."

5/18/1868 12:00 LMT, St. Petersburg, Russia
59N55 30E15 Regiomontanus

Czar Nicolas II

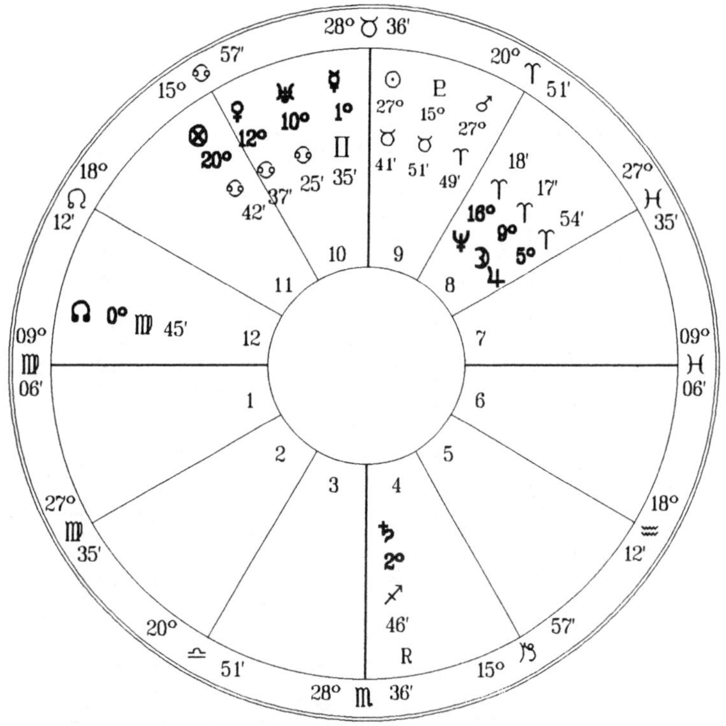

Almutens of Houses
1. ☿
2. ☿
3. ♄
4. ♂
5. ♂♄
6. ♄
7. ♃
8. ♃
9. ☉
10. ♀
11. ☽
12. ☉

Table of Essential Dignities

Points	Ruler	Exalt.	Trip.	Terms	Face	Detr.	Fall	Score	Solar	Quality of Degree
☉	♀	☽ m	♀	♂	♄	♂	--	+ 4	Occ.	Masc., Light
☽	♂	☉ m	☉	♀	♂	♀	♄	+ 4	Ori.	Masc., Dark
☿	☿ +	☊ m	♄	☿ +	♃	♃	--	+11	Occ. Beams	Fem., Light, Deep
♀	☽	♃	♂	♃	☿	♄	♂	– 5p	Occ.	Masc., Dark, Lame
♂	♂ +	☉	☉	♄	♀	♀	♄	+ 5	Ori.	Masc., Light
♃	♂	☉	☉	♃ +	♂	♀	♄	+ 2	Ori.	Masc., Light, Deep
♄	♃	☋	☉	♃	☿	☿	--	– 5p	Occ.	Fem., Light
♅	☽	♃	♂	♃	☿	♄	♂	--	Occ.	Fem., Light, Lame
♆	♂	☉	☉	☿	☉	♀	♄	--	Ori.	Fem., Light
♇	♀	☽	♀	♃	☽	♂	--	--	Ori. Beams	Fem., Void
☊	☿	☿ m	♀	☿	☉	♃	♀	--	Ori.	Fem., Dark
☋	♃	♀	♂	♀	♄	☿	☿	--	Ori.	Masc., Dark
As	☿	☿	♀	♀	☉	♃	♀	--	--	Masc., Void
Mc	♀	☽	♀	♂	♄	♂	--	--	--	Masc., Dark
⊗	☽	♃	♂	♀	☽	♄	♂		Occ.	Masc., Light

In astrological method prior to Lilly (and Lilly also did it, although he tended not to discuss it), there were two methods of obtaining the ruler of a planet, house cusp, or other placement, such as the Part of Fortune. The simple method, which is the method that survived to the 20th century, was to simply assign the Sign or Domicile ruler of the zodiacal position in question. The more complex method - which was clearly favored from the Medieval period through 1600 - was to calculate the Almuten or Dominator/Dominatrix of the zodiacal position. In order to calculate the Almuten, the exact degree of the cusp or position is needed, plus whether the entity is given by a day or night chart. For example, one may calculate the Almuten for an ascendant of 15:0 7: 30 in a night chart as follows:

• *Sign* (Domicile) ruler:	♀	5 points
• *Exaltation* ruler:	♄	4 points
• *Triplicity* ruler (night):	☿	3 points
• *Term* ruler (Ptolemaic):	♃	2 points
• *Face* ruler:	♄	1 point

Both Venus and Saturn get five points total, so they are Co-almutens of the degree. To simplify this process, I have prepared two tables, labelled Five and Six. They give the Almuten for each degree of the zodiac, given day or night.

The Dispositor

The Dispositor is the planet which rules the Sign in which the planet of interest is placed. In more extreme cases, the Dispositor could be taken as the Almuten of the degree in which the planet resides. To follow an analogy, the Dispositor is to a planet, as the ruler or Almuten is to a house cusp. (Great! Now what did she just say?!) Let's examine the use of dispositors by studying a couple of charts.

Table 5–Almutens by Day

	♈	♉	♊	♋	♌	♍	♎	♏	♐	♑	♒	♓
0	☉	♀	☿	☽♂	☉	☿	♄	♂	♃	♄♀	♄	♀
1	☉	♀	☿	☽♂	☉	☿	♄	♂	♃	♄♀	♄	♀
2	☉	♀	☿	☽♂	☉	☿	♄	♂	♃	♄♀	♄	♀
3	☉	♀	☿	☽♂	☉	☿	♄	♂	♃	♄♀	♄	♀
4	☉	♀	☿	☽♂	☉	☿	♄	♂	♃	♄♀	♄	♀
5	☉	♀	☿	☽♂	☉	☿	♄	♂	♃	♄♀	♄	♀
6	☉	♀	☿	♃	☉	☿	♀♄	♂	♃	♄	♄	♀
7	☉	♀	☿	♃	☉	☿	♀♄	♂	♃	♄	♄	♀
8	☉	♀	☿	♃	☉	☿	♀♄	♂	♃	♄	♄	♃
9	☉	♀	☿	♃	☉	☿	♀♄	♂	♃	♄	♄	♃
10	☉	♀	☿	♃	☉	☿	♄	♂	♃	♂♄	♄	♃
11	☉	♀	☿	♃	☉	☿	♄	♂	♃	♂♄	♄	♃
12	☉	♀	☿	♃	☉	☿	♄	♂	♃	♂♄	♄	♃
13	☉	♀	☿	☽	☉	☿	♄	♂	♃	♂♄	♄	♃
14	☉	♀	☿	☽	☉	☿	♄	♂	♃	♂♄	♄	♃
15	☉	♀	☿	☽	☉	☿	♄	♂	♃	♂♄	♄	♃
16	☉	♀	☿	☽	☉	☿	♄	♂	♃	♂♄	♄	♃
17	☉	♀	☿	☽	☉	☿	♄	♂	♃	♂♄	♄	♃
18	☉	♀	☿	☽	☉	☿	♄	♂	♃	♂♄	♄	♃
19	☉	♀	☿	☽	☉	☿	♄	♂	♃	♂	♄	♃
20	☉	♀	☿	☽	☉	☿	♄	♂	♃	♂	♄	♂
21	☉♂	♀	☿♄	☽	☉	☿	♄	♂	♃	♂	♄	♂
22	☉♂	♀	☿♄	☽	☉	☿	♄	♂	♃	♂	♄	♂
23	☉♂	♀	☿♄	☽	☉	☿	♄	♂	♃	♂	♄	♂
24	☉♂	♀	☿♄	☽	☉	☿	♄	♂	♃	♂	♄	♂
25	☉♂	♀	☿	☽	☉	☿	♄	♂	♃	♄	♄	♂
26	☉	♀	☿	☽	☉	☿	♄	♂	♃	♄	♄	♃
27	☉	♀	☿	☽	☉	☿	♄	♂	♃	♄	♄	♃
28	☉	♀	☿	☽	☉	☿	♄	♂	♃	♄	♄	♃
29	☉	♀	☿	☽	☉	☿	♄	♂	♃	♄	♄	♃

Almutens by Night —Table 6

	♈	♉	♊	♋	♌	♍	♎	♏	♐	♑	♒	♓
0	♂	♀☽	☿	☽♂	☉	☿	♄	♂	♃	♄	♄	♀
1	♂	♀☽	☿	☽♂	☉	☿	♄	♂	♃	♄	♄	♀
2	♂	♀☽	☿	☽♂	☉	☿	♄	♂	♃	♄	♄	♀
3	♂	♀☽	☿	☽♂	☉	☿	♄	♂	♃	♄	♄	♀
4	♂	♀☽	☿	☽♂	☉	☿	♄	♂	♃	♄	♄	♀
5	♂	♀☽	☿	☽♂	☉	☿	♄	♂	♃	♄	♄	♀
6	♂	♀☽	☿	♃	☉	☿	♀	♂	♃	♄	♃	♀
7	♂	♀☽	☿	♃	☉	☿	♀	♂	♃	♄	♄	♀
8	♂	☽	☿	♃	☉	☿	♀	♂	♃	♄	♄	♃
9	♂	☽	☿	♃	☉	☿	♀	♂	♃	♄	♄	♃
10	♂☉	☽	☿	♃	☉	☿	♀	♂	♃	♂♄	♄	♃
11	♂☉	☽	☿	♃	☉	☿	♀♄	♂	♃	♂♄	♄	♃
12	♂☉	☽	☿	♃	☉	☿	♀♄	♂	♃	♂♄	♄	♃
13	♂☉	☽	☿	☽	☉	☿	♀♄	♂	♃	♂♄	♄	♃
14	♂☉	☽	☿	☽	☉	☿	♀♄	♂	♃	♂♄	♄	♃
15	♂☉	☽	☿	☽	☉	☿	♀♄	♂	♃	♂♄	♄	♃
16	♂☉	☽	☿	☽	☉	☿	♀♄	♂	♃	♂♄	♄	♃
17	♂☉	☽	☿	☽	☉	☿	♀♄	♂	♃	♂♄	♄	♃
18	♂☉	☽	☿	☽	☉	☿	♀♄	♂	♃	♂♄	♄	♃
19	♂☉	☽	☿	☽	♃	☿	♀☿♄	♂	♃	♂	♄	♃
20	♂	☽	☿	☽	☉♃	☿	☿♀	♂	♃	♂	♄	♂
21	♂	☽	☿	☽	☉♃	☿	☿♀	♂	♃	♂	♄	♂
22	♂	☽	☿	☽	☉♃	☿	☿♀	♂	♃	♂	♄	♂
23	♂	☽	☿	☽	☉♃	☿	☿♀	♂	♃	♂	♄	♂
24	♂	☽	☿	☽	☉♃	☿	♀	♂	♃	♂	♄	♂
25	♂	☽	☿	☽	☉	☿	♀	♂	♃	♄	♄	♂
26	♂	☽	☿	☽	☉	☿	♀	♂	♃	♄	♄	♃
27	♂	☽	☿	☽	☉	☿	♀	♂	♃	♄	♄	♃
28	♂	☽	☿	☽	☉	☿	♀	♂	♃	♄	♄	♃
29	♂	☽	☿	☽	☉	☿	♀	♂	♃	♄	♄	♃

Nicholas II was the last Russian Czar. He and his family were assassinated during the Communist takeover. Nicholas' ascendant, Virgo, was ruled by Mercury, which is conjunct the Midheaven, one of the ancient signatures of royalty. His Mercury was in Gemini, its own sign. Nicholas had two planets in their own sign: Mercury and Mars. This basically means that he was able to pretty much think and act as he chose.

The kicker is this. None of the biographical materials around suggest that Nicholas was one of the bright intellectual lights of his day, and he was downright lousy as a soldier, his martial job. So what gives?

Dignity is not the same as talent. All the Dignity guaranteed was that he was able to exercise his mind and do what he wanted. He did. Look what happened!

Because he was Czar, he was able to do what he wanted. A peon with the same dignities would probably have to have more talent, because otherwise, how could he or she possibly be able to have that level of independence?

Every planet in Nicholas' chart except Mercury is ultimately disposed by Mars. Let's diagram the dispositor relationships.

☉ ♇→ ♀→ ☽ → ♂
(♅) (♃ ♆)
☿ disposes itself.

Nicholas is therefore said to have two Final Dispositors. The final dispositor(s) in a chart is/are any planets which ultimately dispose themselves. This arrangement implies that Nicholas put practically all his eggs into the military basket: all his eggs but his mind. (A terrible thing to loose, a mind!)

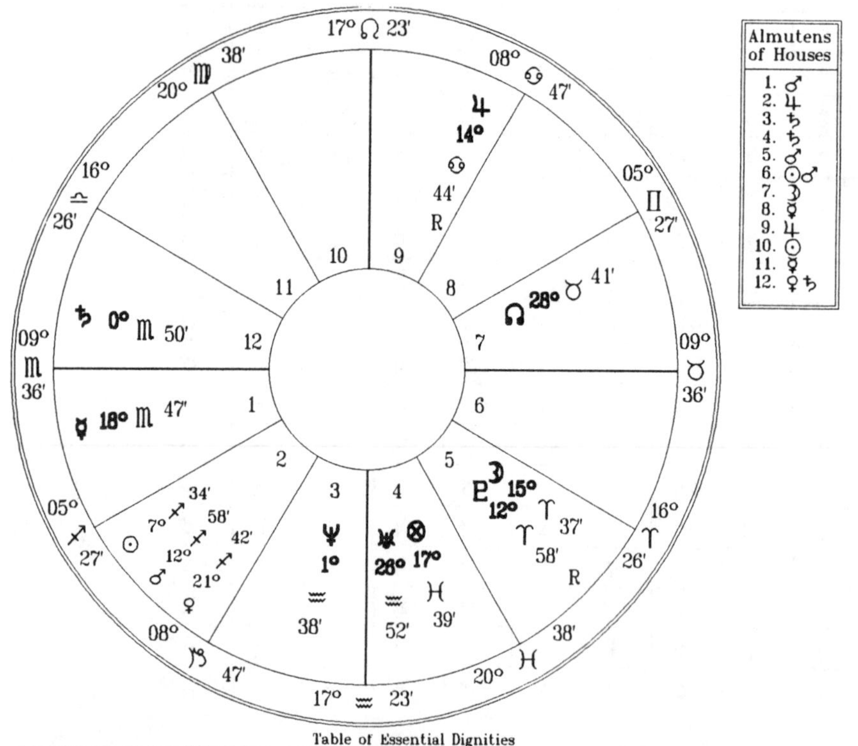

Table of Essential Dignities

Points	Ruler	Exalt.	Trip.	Terms	Face	Detr.	Fall	Score	Solar	Quality of Degree
☉	♃	☋	♃	♃	☿ m	☿	--	+ 1	Occ.	Masc., Light, Lame
☽	♂	☉	♃	☿	☉	♀	♄	- 5p	Ori.	Fem., Dark, Deep
☿	♂	--	♂	♀	☉ m	♀	☽	+ 1	Ori.	Fem., Light, Lame
♀	♃	☋	♃	♄	♄	☿	--	- 5p	Occ. Beams	Fem., Smokey
♂	♃	☋	♃ m	♀	☽	☿	--	+ 3	Occ. Comb.	Fem., Light, Fort.
♃	☽	♃ +	♂ m	☿	☿	♄	♂	+ 7	Occ.	Masc., Void, Lame, Fort.
♄	♂	--	♂	♂	♂	♀	☽	- 5p	Ori.	Masc., Dark
♅	♄	--	☿	♂	☽	☉	--	--	Occ.	Masc., Light
♆	♄	--	☿	♄	♀	☉	--	--	Occ.	Masc., Smokey
♇	♂	☉	♃	♀	☉	♀	♄	--	Ori.	Masc., Dark
☊	♀	☽	☽	♂	♄	♂	--	--	Ori.	Masc., Dark
☋	♂	--	♂	♄	♀	♀	☽	--	Ori. Beams	Masc., Void
As	♂	--	♂	♃	♂	♀	☽	--	--	Fem., Void, Deep
Mc	☉	--	♃	♀	♃	♄	--	--	--	Fem., Smokey, Lame
⊗	♃	♀	♂	☿	♃	☿	☿		Ori.	Fem., Dark

Contrast this with Mark Twain. Twain's chart ruler, Mars, was disposed by Jupiter, which was disposed by the Moon, which was disposed by Mars. Here we have three planets in a ring and no final dispositor. Mars gives Twain's self image, the macho man. Jupiter ruling the second and Almuten of the 9th shows money coming from publishing. Twain was a journalist as well as a book author.

The Moon, as in Nicholas' chart, shows his wife, but also his children, since it is posited in the 5th House. Both Twain's wife and daughter had serious illnesses. Thus, we see a linkage of themes of the houses that this ring of planets rules (both by Sign and Almuten): the 1st, 2nd, 6th, 7th, and 9th! Jupiter was Twain's most dignified planet. In his case, it does show talent, because how else given his social background could that Jupiter come to prominence!

Mutual Reception

Let us begin by defining mutual reception, and for that we turn to John Gadbury, page 43:

> *"Reception is performed by House, Exaltation, Triplicity and Term: and it is a sign of a propitious Nativity, where all the Planets are mutually received of each other. This may be, first by House (ed. note: read "House" as "Sign") as Saturn in Taurus, and Venus in Capricorn: and of all Receptions this is the best. Secondly, it may be by Exaltation as Venus in Capricorn, and Mars in Pisces: and this is a good Reception also. Thirdly, it may be by Triplicity as suppose the Nativity to be by day, and Venus in Aries, and Sun in Taurus: and this is good, though not so excellent as the other. Fourthly, Reception may be by Term, thus Mars in 16 of Gemini, and Venus in 24 of Aries: here Mars and Venus are in Reception by Term. This is the meanest of Receptions yet is better then none at all:* ***Half a loaf is better than no bread.*** *In Nativities, respect the Planets that are in Reception, and the Houses they are Lords of and if you finde the Lord of the ascendant in Reception with the Lord of the Fourth, say, The Native and his Father shall agree well: the stronger the Reception is, the more durable shall their agreement be."*

So what does "strength" of reception mean? There are two answers. On the one hand, as Gadbury mentions, reception can be by any Dignity. A reception by Sign (Domicile) is stronger than by term. Secondly, there is the issue of how strong the planets in reception are apart from their reception.

One other thought. In Gadbury's day, two planets would be considered to be in mutual reception if they shared any Dignity between them. Thus, Mars in Libra was considered to be in mutual reception with Saturn in Scorpio. Saturn is in Mars' sign, while Mars, in addition to being in Detriment, is in Saturn's Exaltation.

Morinus was the first to use the term mutual reception only if the reception was of the same type, e.g., both in each other's Exaltation. He denied the usage of "mu-

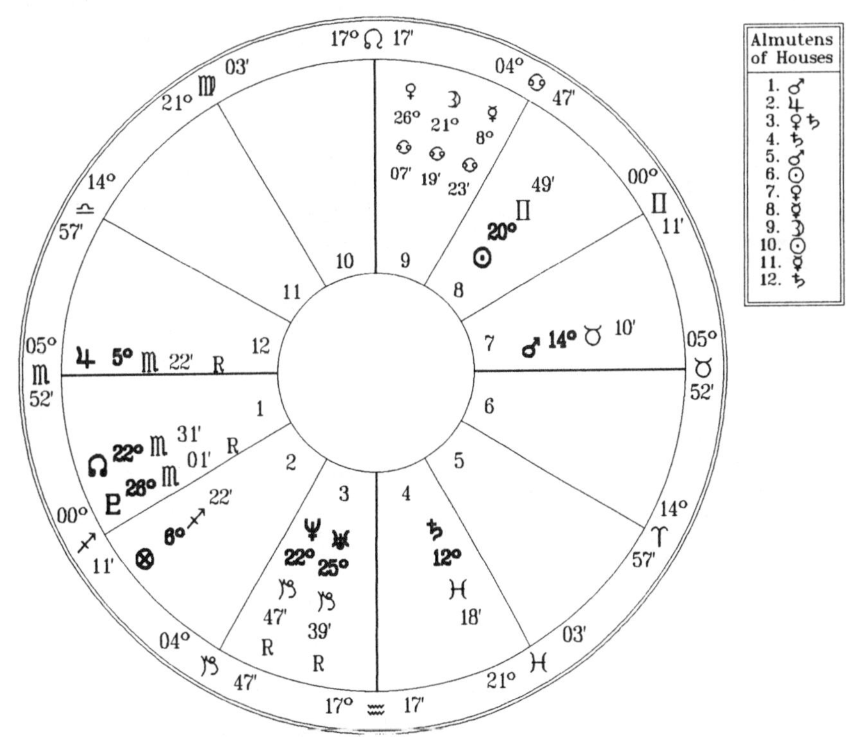

Table of Essential Dignities

Points	Ruler	Exalt.	Trip.	Terms	Face	Detr.	Fall	Score	Solar	Quality of Degree
☉	☿	☊	♄	♀	☉ +	♃	--	+ 1	Occ.	Fem., Light
☽	☽ +	♃	♂	♀	☽ +	♄	♂	+ 6	Occ.	Masc., Light
☿	☽	♃	♂	♃	♀	♄	♂	− 5p	Occ.	Masc., Light, Lame
♀	☽	♃	♂ m	♀ +	☽	♄	♂	+ 5	Occ.	Fem., Light
♂	♀	☽	♀ m	☿	☽	♂ −	--	− 2	Ori.	Fem., Light, Fort.
♃	♂	--	♂	♂	♂	♀	☽	− 5p	Ori.	Fem., Light
♄	♃	♀	♂	♃	♃	☿	☿	− 5p	Occ.	Fem., Dark, Fort.
♅	♄	♂	♀	♄	☉	☽	♃	--	Occ.	Masc., Dark, Lame
♆	♄	♂	♀	♂	☉	☽	♃	--	Occ.	Masc., Void
♇	♂	--	♂	☿	♀	♀	☽	--	Ori.	Masc., Void, Deep
☊	♂	--	♂	☿	♀	♀	☽	--	Ori.	Fem., Smokey, Deep
☋	♀	☽	♀	♄	♄	♂	--	--	Ori.	Fem., Light
As	♂	--	♂	♂	♂	♀	☽	--	--	Fem., Light
Mc	☉	--	☉	♀	♃	♄	--	--	--	Fem., Smokey, Lame
⊗	♃	☋	☉	♃	☿	☿	--		Ori.	Masc., Light, Deep, Lame

tual reception" if the reception was of a different type for each planet. Thus, Morinus was the source of our modern idea about this.)

Mutual reception is easy to grasp as a concept, but more difficult to understand in practice. Gadbury implies that a mutual reception is a good thing. But how good?

I began to search the classical literature in order to find a really satisfying discussion of the meaning of reception, as contrasted with its application. The spark for the meaning came from al-Biruni (1029), page 312 (Point 507): *"Reception. When an inferior planet arrives in one of the dignities proper to a superior one, and makes known to it the relation thus established, there is an exchange of compliments such as 'your servant' or 'neighbour'. If further the superior planet happens to be in a situation proper to the inferior one, mutual reception takes place, and this is fortified, the richer the situation is in dignities, especially when the aspects indicate no enmity nor malevolence. When reception does not take place the result is negative."*

The clue to this passage came from understanding the context of al-Biruni's culture: the Medieval period. Dismissing the cultural norms of sexism *et al,* pretend you are the Medieval lord of the manor. (After all, astrology is written for nobles. They can pay!) So you have this land and this castle. You must defend it from other lords, who covet it. How do you do this? You rely on your allies: your vassals, your immediate relatives, and your wife's relatives. The question is, how good are your allies? They may or may not show up when they say they will. They may not be numerous enough to dispel the enemy. Or, one of your allies may be strong enough so that once he helps you dispatch your enemy, he then dispatches you and takes over!

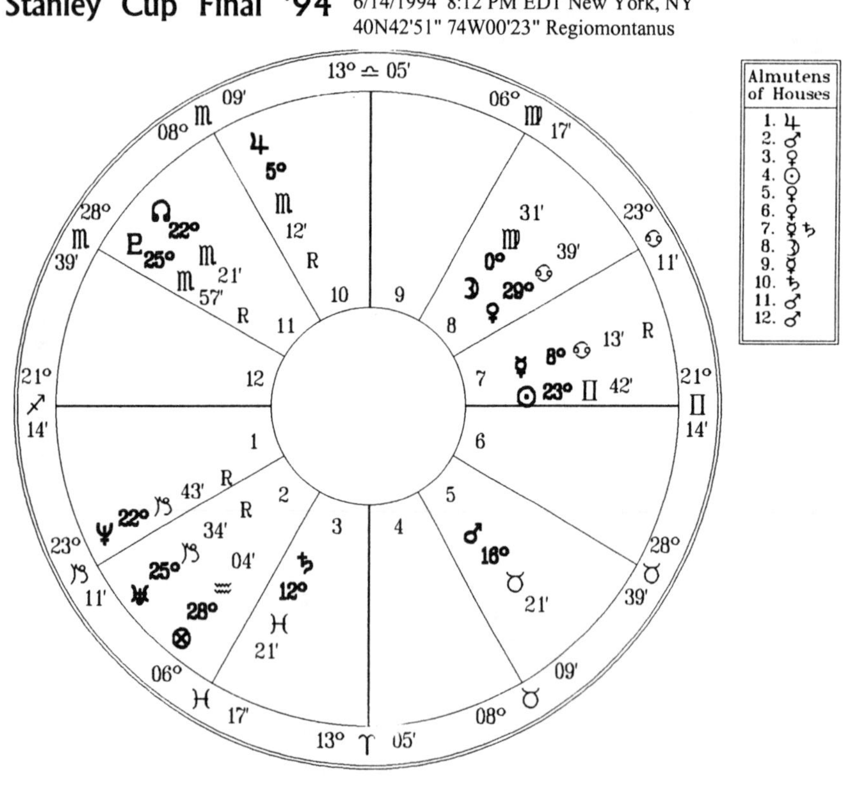

Table of Essential Dignities

Points	Ruler	Exalt.	Trip.	Terms	Face	Detr.	Fall	Score	Solar	Quality of Degree
☉	☿	☊	♄	♄	☉ +	♃	--	+ 1	Occ.	Masc., Dark
☽	☿ m	☿	♀	☿	☉	♃	♀	+ 5	Occ.	Fem., Dark
☿	☽ m	♃	♂	♃	♀	♄	♂	+ 5	Occ. Beams	Masc., Light, Lame
♀	☽	♃	♂ m	♄	☽	♄	♂	+ 3	Occ.	Masc., Void, Deep
♂	♀	☽	♀ m	♃ m	☽	♂ -	--	+ 0	Ori.	Fem., Void
♃	♂	--	♂	♂ m	♂	♀	☽	+ 2	Ori.	Fem., Light
♄	♃	♀	♂	♃	♃	☿	☿	- 5p	Occ.	Fem., Dark, Fort.
♅	♄	♂	♀	♄	☉	☽	♃	--	Occ.	Masc., Dark, Lame
♆	♄	♂	♀	♂	☉	☽	♃	--	Occ.	Masc., Void
♇	♂	--	♂	☿	♀	♀	☽	--	Ori.	Masc., Void
☊	♂	--	♂	☿	♀	♀	☽	--	Ori.	Fem., Smokey, Deep
☋	♀	☽	♀	♄	♄	♂	--	--	Ori.	Fem., Light
As	♃	☋	☉	♄	♄	☿	--	--	--	Fem., Smokey
Mc	♀	♄	♄	♃	♄	♂	☉	--	--	Fem., Light
⊗	♄	--	♄	♂	☽	☉	--		Occ.	Fem., Light, Deep

A planet in mutual reception is your ally. How good an ally is dependent on how well dignified the other planet is apart from the mutual reception. Let me illustrate this point with a couple of sports examples: games from the 1994 Stanley Cup Hockey finals between the New York Rangers and the Vancouver Canucks. These charts are drawn for the time of the opening face-off. In both cases, the home team in given by the 1st House the visiting team by the 7th. (Many modern astrologers automatically give the home team the 1st House. I don't, but in these two cases, my system lines up the same way.)

In the Vancouver game, Mars (Vancouver) is in Detriment and in the 7th House. This is bad for Vancouver. Venus has Dignity by term, which is so-so for New York. Mars and Venus are in mutual reception. Now how good an ally is your enemy anyway? This doesn't help!

The tip-off is the Jupiter rising. In sports charts I have observed that planets passing over the angles (two approaching, one separating) are extremely powerful, and will generally result in a change in the tenor of the game. Jupiter rising strongly favors Vancouver (even though peregrine), as does the Part of Fortune in the 2nd House. This is further confirmed given that it was a Jupiter (planetary) hour. (In game charts, the 2nd House is the 1st House team's friends, the 8th House is the same for the 7th House team.) Jupiter tips the game to Vancouver. Vancouver wins 4-1 and ties the series 3-3.

Three days later, the seventh and final game was played in New York. Fortuna is still in the 2nd House. (The location of Fortuna by house is a function of the phase of the lunar cycle.) Jupiter ruling the 1st House and New York now has reception by term: better than nothing, as Gadbury said. Jupiter has one of the best placements from New York's standpoint: in the 10th House. Mercury rules Vancouver, and is in mutual reception with the Moon, but not otherwise dignified. Mercury is in a good house position, being in the 7th House. It is good for the 7th House ruler to be in the 7th, or for the 1st House ruler to be in the 1st. All other factors being equal, Fortuna in the 2nd House tips the balance to New York.

But what of Vancouver's mercurial reception with the Moon? What kind of an ally is the Moon in Virgo? As I was thinking about what kind of ally, it occurred to me: Vancouver was using a new technical wrinkle as far as conditioning was concerned: barometric pressure chambers which are supposed to speed recuperation from athletic exertion. The chamber treatments appeared to work, but it was not enough to turn the tide. New York wins 3-2.

Let's also examine this concept in two nativities. Czar Nicholas II had a mutual reception between his Sun and Moon by Exaltation. Symbolically (and especially in so-called traditional society), the Sun and the Moon represent the Male and Female, and thus, locally the husband and wife. Nicholas and Alexandra

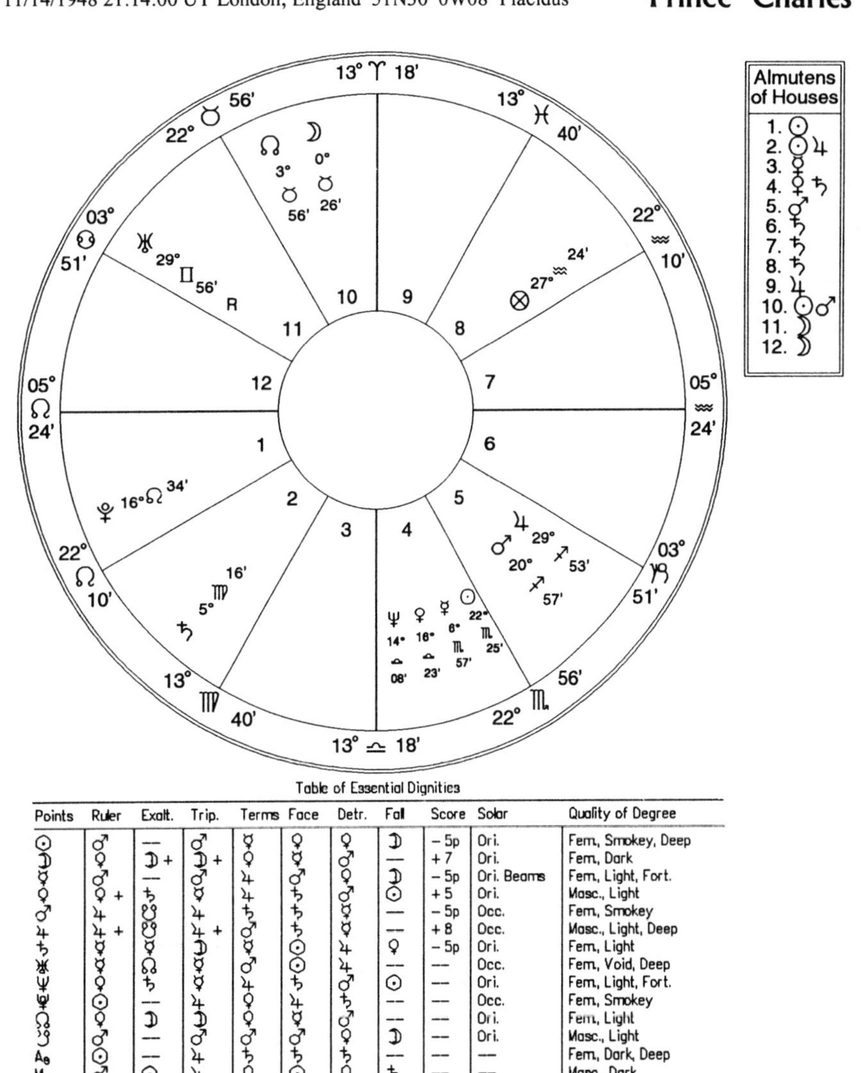

Table of Essential Dignities

Points	Ruler	Exalt.	Trip.	Terms	Face	Detr.	Fall	Score	Solar	Quality of Degree
☉	♂	—	♂	☿	♀	♀	☽	– 5p	Ori.	Fem., Smokey, Deep
☽	♀	☽ +	☽ +	♀	☿	♂	—	+ 7	Ori.	Fem., Dark
☿	♂	—	♂	♃	♂	♀	☽	– 5p	Ori. Beams	Fem., Light, Fort.
♀	♀ +	♄	☿	♃	♄	♂	☉	+ 5	Ori.	Masc., Light
♂	♃	☋	♃	♄	♄	☿	—	– 5p	Occ.	Fem., Smokey
♃	♃ +	☋	♃ +	♂	♄	☿	—	+ 8	Occ.	Masc., Light, Deep
♄	☿	☿	☽	☿	☉	♃	♀	– 5p	Ori.	Fem., Light
♅	☿	☊	☿	♂	☉	♃	—	—	Occ.	Fem., Void, Deep
♆	♀	♄	☿	♃	♄	♂	☉	—	Ori.	Fem., Light, Fort.
♇	☉	—	♃	♀	♃	♄	—	—	Occ.	Fem., Smokey
☊	♀	☽	☽	♀	☿	♂	—	—	Ori.	Fem., Light
☋	♂	—	♂	♂	♂	♀	☽	—	Ori.	Masc., Light
As	☉	—	♃	♄	♄	♄	—	—	—	Fem., Dark, Deep
Mc	♂	☉	♃	♀	☉	♀	♄	—	—	Masc., Dark
⊗	♄	♂	☽	♃	♂	☽	♃		Occ.	Fem., Smokey, Fort.

were very close: all their personal journals and writings show this. She was his closest confidant and advisor. However, Nicholas' Moon was in Aries, with no Dignity other than the mutual reception. The Moon was also applying to a conjunction to Neptune. Alexandra was under the influence of Neptune, no doubt personified by Rasputen. The Moon was also applying to a tight square to Uranus. What kind of aid could she give him? Erratic and idealistic. Not much help.

Consider Mark Twain. Mars was in his 2nd House of money and a mutual reception by triplicity with Jupiter, ruler of his 2nd House. Jupiter is exalted in Cancer. Mars ruled Twain's ascendant. The alliance of Mars and Jupiter is that he published to make money (ruler of the 2nd in the 9th) on martial subjects: male bonding and coming of age, chivalrous pursuits, "manly" arts, etc. However, in this case, Jupiter has Dignity apart from the mutual reception. Thus, it becomes a strong ally to Mars.

Table 7

Face and Decanate positions for Prince Charles.

	Face	*Decanate*
☉	♀	♋
☽	☿	♉
☿	♂	♏
♀	♄	♒
♂	♄	♌
♃	♄	♌
♄	☉	♍
♅	☉	♒
♆	♄	♒
♇	♃	♐
Asc	♄	♌
MC	☉	♌
⊗	☽	♎

Before we end our discussion of mutual reception, let me also touch upon what reception is not. The idea was proposed by Ivy Goldstein-Jacobson that planets in reception swap places, so that the Moon in Capricorn and Saturn in Cancer is like Saturn in Capricorn and the Moon in Cancer. This is not true. Goldstein-Jacobson appears to have acquired this idea by an honest misinterpretation of a translation of Ptolemy. On page 189 of the Robbins translation, Ptolemy appears to refer to reception as "exchange of signs." This translation is not accurate. The word Robbins translated as "exchange" was *enalloiosis*, alteration. The problem arose because this word is very close to *enallasso,* which has been translated by scholars as "exchange Domicile" (*c.f.* Liddell and Scott). Further examination of this root shows the use of the word "exchange" was not truly descriptive: the sense is more that of being altered as an adjective modifies a noun. Other words that come from this root are "interchange," "alternate", and "cross one another." The sense of this passage is that dispositions and receptions modify the workings of the ruling planet. In fact, the sentence in question does not appear to refer to reception at all, but rather to what happens when planets are in signs other than those in which they have Dignity.

Decanates

As mentioned above, the *decanates* are a way of breaking the zodiac up into 10 segments. The Western decanates, also called the Faces, survived as a kind of Essential Dignity, discussed above. The Oriental or Eastern decanates, usually simply called decanates, are used in modern Western astrology as a descriptive tool, not a Dignity. As such, they have splintered into several variations.

Faces are expressed as *planetary* rulers while the Decanates are expressed as sign rulers. This difference allows the reader to understand which system was the basis for any variants encountered. Thus, L. Edward Johndro's system was planetary, and hence Western in origin. This is hardly surprising, since his whole thesis was to redefine a new system of sign rulership. On the other hand, there is a new system that I have been unable to trace historically which simply counts sequentially through the signs: so the three decanates of Aries are Aries, Taurus, and Gemini. This is clearly derivative of the Oriental system.

The first question that arises is whether these two systems are in fact measuring the same, or different things? The Eastern System evolved in a system of astrology that uses the sidereal zodiac, not the tropical one. Thus, we would be justified in asking whether the Decanates really have any relevance outside of the full sidereal system.

While the Faces or Decanates are mostly ignored in modern method, this was not true through the Renaissance. Ramesey gave a listing of each Face individually and its qualities. Lilly in his eclipse book considered Solar and Lunar Eclipses in each Face position. Wing used the Faces in weather forecasting, a practice which extended at least back to the Middle Ages.

The classical descriptions of planets in their Faces is not especially complementary. Ramesey called a planet in its own Face *"at the last gasp"*; others used words like *"fear."*

When I began working with the Faces, I wasn't sure exactly what to expect. The Faces, however, supply some intriguing leads about those areas where the individual has fears or problems. Most people don't like fear, and would rather cloak fear with hatred than deal with fear directly. Consider three examples: Theodore Bundy, David Berkowitz (Son of Sam), and Sigmund Freud. The connection between the three is their spectacular dysfunction about one-half the human population, namely, women. Berkowitz stalked and murdered women in New York before he was caught and convicted Bundy killed a number all around the U.S.A. before he was electrocuted. Freud developed the theory of penis-envy, and through his followers, thousands of women have been jammed into a passive mold that Freud would have loved to impose on the women in his life! All three share Venus, the fertility or nubile side of the Goddess or female archetype, in its own Face.

Freud and Bundy also have the Moon as Face ruler of itself, a further evidence for discomfort for women. Berkowitz has the most extreme distribution in Essential Dignities of the three, having all the triplicity rulers except for Venus as Saturn, and a very high incidence of Saturn as the Dignity ruler. Freud also had as high Saturn Dignity rulership. Saturn is the Old Testament God, the dispenser of an eye-for-an–eye, for whom justice is retribution. There are no extenuating circumstances in Saturn's judgment.

In the cases of Bundy and Berkowitz, the fear represented by the Face dignities turned to violence. In Freud's case, it turned to theory. At any rate, Freud's ability to recognize that one emotion may transpose into another was clearly not based solely on observation of others!

Let us compare Faces and Decanates through a more benign example, Prince Charles. His Faces and Decanates are given in Table Six.

With Charles' Leo Rising, the Sun shows a lot about how Charles will be seen. Charles' Sun is in Scorpio, which is not a great start as far as public acclaim: he is a private man thrust into a very public position. He has a reputation for courage and for seriousness. His Sun is peregrine, which suggests that he wanders (peregrinates), not always coming to the point. The Sun's Face is Venus. Charles has the bad luck to have a wife more popular than he is. The women in his life - the Moon and Venus - both possess strong Dignity, while the male components - Sun and Mars primarily - are both peregrine. The biggest Dignity of all is the Moon, his Mother!

The planet which most dominates the Face column is Saturn. His own Saturn is peregrine. So he sits and waits in the wings. This cannot be entirely pleasant.

The Decanate column is dominated by Leo and Aquarius. Again, we see the same themes: kingship as represented by Leo service to/through the collective as represented by Aquarius.

Thus, we see that the major use of dignities and their derivatives is to gauge the strength of the planets concerned. The stronger the dignities of a planet, the easier it is for that planet to accomplish what it "wants." Precisely what those desires may be are determined by the sign placement of the planet, its house placement, and its aspects. A planet in Debility is strong, just as a planet in Dignity is. The difference is that the planet in Debility will tend to turn the normal functioning of that planet upside down to get what it wants.

Essentials of Intermediate Astrology

Dignity does not imply genius or talent, except possibly in the sense of street smarts, those qualities which help to accomplish a goal, but aren't that useful at setting the goal in the first place. Dignity implies power. It is up to the individual to choose the Light or the Dark Side of the Force. ✸

References

al-Biruni, Abu'l-Rayhan Muhammed ibn Ahmad. 1029. *The Book of Instruction in the Elements of Astrology,* translated by R. Ramsay Wright, Luzac & Co.: London, 1934.

Gadbury, John. 1658. *Genethlialogia, or The Doctrine of Nativities Together with The Doctrine of Horarie Questions.* Printed by J[ohn] C[oniers] for William Larner. In production: Regulus Publishing Co., Ltd.: London.

Johndro, L. Edward. 1934. A New Conception of Sign Rulership. American Federation of Astrologers: Washington, DC.

Lehman, J. Lee. 1989. *Essential Dignities.* Whitford Press: West Chester, PA.

Lilly, William. 1652. *An Easie and Familiar Method whereby to Judge the Effects depending on Eclipses, Either of the Sun or Moon.* Company of Stationers: London.

Ptolemy, Claudius. 1940. *Tetrabiblos.* Translated by F. E. Robbins. Harvard University Press: Cambridge, MA.

Ptolemy, Claudius. 1994. *Tetrabiblos. Book I.* Translated by Robert Schmidt. Project Hindsight, Golden Hind Press: Berkeley Springs, WV.

Ramesey, William. 1653. *Astrologia Restaurata or Astrology Restored: Being an Introduction to the General and Chief part of the Language of the Stars.* Robert White: London.

Schoener, Johannes. 1994. *Opusculum Astrologicum.* Translated by Robert Hand. Project Hindsight, Golden Hind Press: Berkeley Springs, WV.

Sibly, Ebinezer. 1817. *A New and Complete Illustration of the Celestial Science of Astrology or the Art of Foretelling Future Events and Contingencies by the Aspects, Positions and Influences of the Heavenly Bodies.* The Proprietor, at No. 17, Ave-Maria Lane, St. Pauls, London. (Posthumous edition)

Tester, Jim. 1987. *A History of Western Astrology.* Boydell Press: Woodbridge, Suffolk.

Sources for Data used:

Prince Charles: Data provided by Judith Gee, *c.f.* Rodden, Lois M. 1980. *The American Book of Charts.* Astro Computing Services: San Diego, CA.

Mark Twain: Marc Edmund Jones. Sabian Symbols. Cited in J. M Harrison. 1980. *Fowler's Compendium of Nativities.* Fowler: Romford. Original source not known.

Nicholas II: Palace records assumed. Cited in Fowler's.

Hockey game start times taken down by JLL from live broadcast.

PROGRESSIONS

Joyce Levine

The major principle of secondary progressions is that each day after birth corresponds to a year of life.

The movement of the planets show how we grow, unfold, and change in ways predetermined by the symbolic movement of the planets. When planets change signs, houses, or turn from Retrograde to Direct or Direct to Retrograde by progression, one's needs change and new ways of viewing the world are added to the natal perspective. The progressed chart does not negate characteristics of the birth chart, but adds another dimension to it.

Progressions can be seen as a predictive indicators of events or as internal psychological changes. The state of our psyche determines our attitudes and what we pay attention to. This in turn affects the course of action we take, which determines outer events.

When a progressed planet moves into an element that is missing in the natal chart, psychological changes occur. One discovers a new domain of life and begins to build in characteristics of that element. When planets progres into earth, a person suddenly recognizes the importance of money and earthly possessions and starts to make common sense decisions. When planets progress into air, one can attain a level of logic and detachment theretofore impossible. When planets progress into fire, one has more spirit and becomes more spontaneous, enthusiastic, and forward thinking. When planets progress into water, emotions become easier to express. Obviously an analysis of the birth chart is necessary to know precisely how these characteristics will manifest and what they will change.

As planets change signs, particularly when they move into a sign without any planets, the characteristics of that sign also get added on to the natal characteristics. For instance, a person born with the Sun at 0° Aries has his progressed Sun enter Taurus at age 30. Relatives and friends marvel at how he has "settled down" and begun to complete things. The Aries energy is still there, but a dimension of Taurus has been added to it.

Since inner planets (Sun, Moon, Mercury, Venus, and Mars) reflect one's personal self, their change of signs has a more personal effect than when the outer planets (Jupiter, Saturn, Uranus, Neptune, and Pluto) change signs. Since the outer planets move slowly, unless they are in very late degrees of a sign, they will in all likelihood remain in the same sign throughout one's life.

The Moon, the fastest moving celestial body, changes signs every two to two and one-half years, depending on its rate of movement. As the progressed Moon changes signs, emotional and psychological needs change. People who normally dress conservatively may find themselves more flamboyant when the Moon

Oct 12, 1942 9:56 PM EWT 41N02 73W46 **Chart 1, Susan**

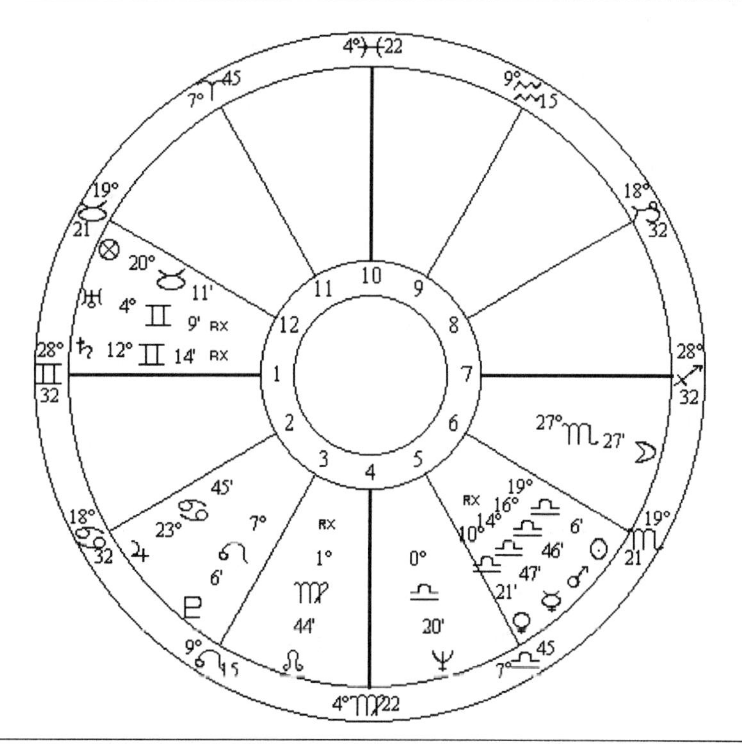

progresses into Leo and more conservative again two and a half years later when it enters Virgo. The way in which emotions get expressed also changes. Those born with the Moon in Gemini who normally intellectualize their feelings become better able to express emotions when the Moon progresses into Cancer. *(The only time I ever had any luck at growing plants was the few years my progressed Moon spent in Taurus.)*

The progressed Moon returns to its natal position around the same time as the Saturn return. Saturn's return signifies "growing up" on an external level—dealing with what might be called life's responsibilities. The Moon's return signifies coming of age emotionally. As the progressed Moon passes through each sign and house, the departments of life to which they correspond assume greater prominence. When any planet progresses into a new sign or house, that sign and house becomes integral to the expression of that planet.

The Moon entering the first house heightens an emotional response to the immediate environment. Any planet progressing into the first house affects the face one presents to the outer world as well as one's outlook on life. When the ascendant progresses into a different sign, the way in which a person projects himself changes. The change combines the sign characteristics of the natal ascendant with the sign characteristics of the progressed ascendant. For instance, a person with Cancer rising acts reserved in new situations, but once that ascendant progresses into Leo, he becomes friendlier and more outgoing and asserts himself sooner than he did earlier in life. However, the natural reserve of the Cancer Rising still exists.

Planets progressing into the second house heighten the concern for money, possessions, and security. Planets moving into the third house emphasize communication, whether that be writing, speaking, or talking with one's neighbors. They also heightens one's interest in education or short distance travels. Planets progressing into the fourth house place an emphasis on home and family concerns or real estate investments. Planets moving into the fifth house accentuate self expression, creativity, love affairs, and children. The sixth house has to do with work, one's day-to-day routine, and health. It also relates to the service that one gives and receives.

Planets progressing into the seventh house affect how one relates in one-to-one relationships, whether that relationship be marriage, business, or close friendship. Since the seventh house frequently gets projected, planets progressing here may describe the type of person that comes into one's life at the time the progression takes place.

Planets moving into the eighth house affect what one derives from relationships, whether that be sex, joint finances, or inheritances. The eighth house also has to do with death and occult interests. Planets entering the ninth house influence one's philosophy, religion, or world view as well as the interest in travel and higher education.

Planets moving into the 10th house

Chart 2 — Susan progressed, age 20

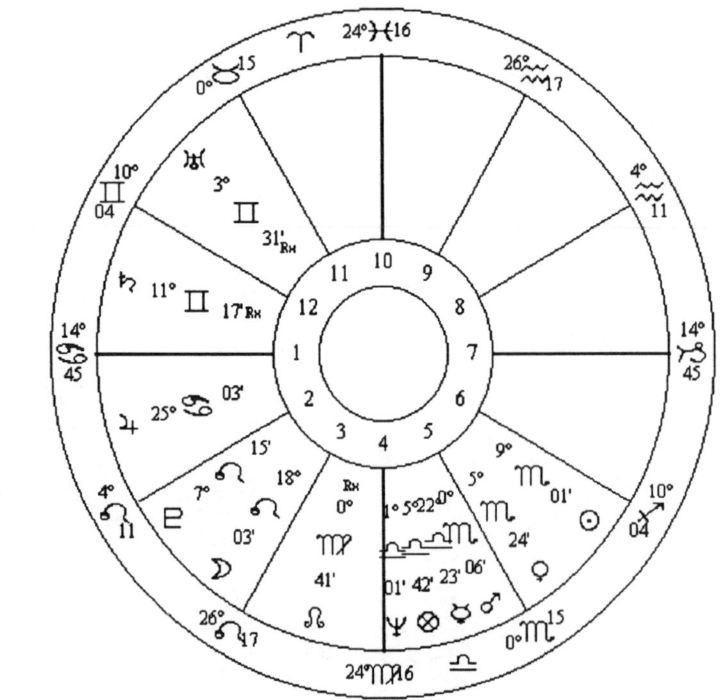

affect both one's public standing and career and also one's family life. When the midheaven changes signs by progression, one's career direction or primary career motivation changes along the lines of the progressed sign. For instance, a competitive person with an Aries midheaven becomes more concerned with material success when the midheaven progresses into Taurus. A person with a Taurus midheaven wants more intellectual stimulation and variety in a career when the midheaven moves into Gemini.

Planets moving into the 11th house influence one's goals, friendships, and participation in groups and organizations. Planets moving into the 12th house, particularly personal planets, coincide with a person wanting more time alone. One's intuition may increase as well as one's sensitivity to subliminal cues.

When progressed planets change direction either Retrograde to Direct or Direct to Retrograde, changes occur in the manner in which the planetary energy gets expressed. A person with Mercury Retrograde at birth can find himself more outgoing, or better able to directly express himself, or less introverted when Mercury changes direction. The year the planet changes direction augments a turning point with regard to the departments of life the planet rules. Naturally, the natal chart must always be considered. A person with Mercury R in Gemini natally will be more communicative than one who has it Direct in Cancer.

INTERPRETATION

Some astrologers use only the progressed ascendant and midheaven and not intermediary house cusps. I use the entire progressed chart in addition to the birth chart and compare both natal houses and planets and progressed houses and planets. As planets and house cusps move forward in the Zodiac, they make aspects to the natal chart and to each other in the progressed chart. An orb of one degree applying to exact and one degree separating from exact is used for the influence of the planetary combination. For the Sun, this represents two years. For the Moon it represents two months. The Moon, however, can touch off other aspects and keep them together.

Since the progressed midheaven moves at approximately one degree a year, and the degree on the natal MC changes approximately every four minutes, any inaccuracy in the birth time greatly affects the ability to time events. Important events show in progressions and transits and solar arcs. There is always confirmation when it comes to major changes. Years may go by without any major progressed aspects occurring. The natal chart must be taken into consideration in order to interpret progressed aspects. The nature of planets involved, natal sign and house positions of the planets, as well as the progressed signs and houses all must be considered. I also use houses ruled by planets in the progressed chart. Planets difficultly aspected to each other in the natal chart bring inherent difficulties with them. When a square becomes a trine by progression, it still has square energy. Conversely when a

Marriage — Chart 2a

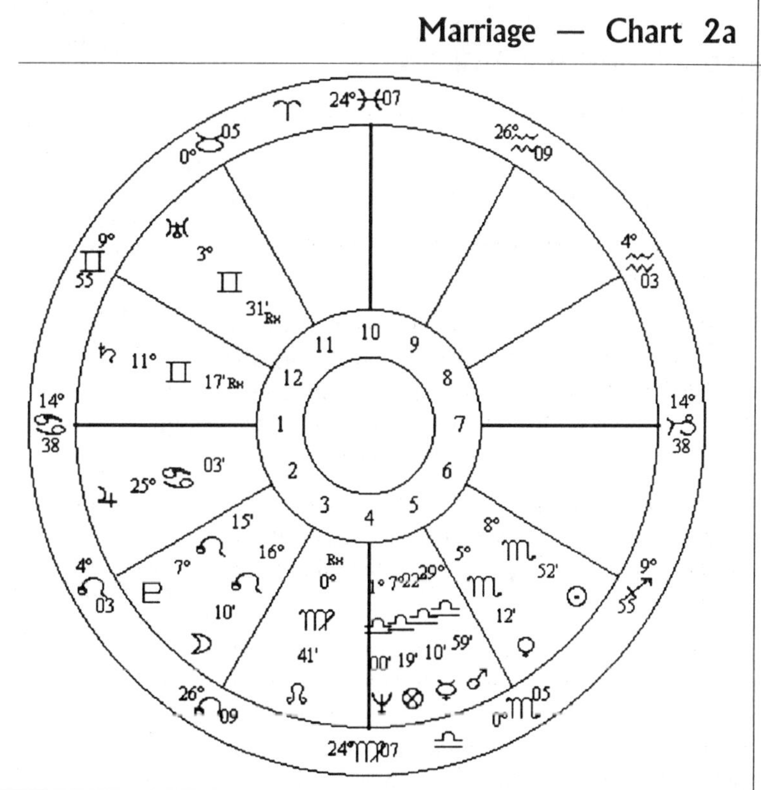

TO CALCULATE:

Secondary progressions are based on the premise that one day in the ephemeris is equal to one year of life. A progressed chart can be calculated for the first birthday by using:

1. The natal birth time (converted to Greenwich, England)
2. The birth location
3. The day *after* birth in the ephemeris.

So if someone were born on March 1, 1950 at 7 hours 12 minutes Greenwich, we would use March 2, 1950 in the ephemeris to calculate the progressed chart for the first birthday. And you would cast it for 7 hours 12 minutes on that date.

There is, however, a simpler method for calculating the progressed chart so that you can use the positions listed in the ephemeris for a given date without interpolating. Then you can easily see the progressed positions of the planets because they are the positions listed in the ephemeris. Only house cusps need to be calculated if you want an entire chart.

This method is called the ACD (or Adjusted Calculation Date) method. With this method—

a. one day in the ephemeris is equivalent to one year of life

b. one day = 24 hours (which represents one year)

c. 24 hours (one day in the ephemeris) represents 12 months by progression.

Therefore, if your were born at 0 hrs in Greenwich, the positions given in the ephemeris for your "Greenwich birthdate" would be the positions in your birthchart, and the positions for the following day would be the progressed positions for your *first* birthday.

However, since most people are not born at 0 hrs Greenwich, it must be determined what date is represented by these specific positions given in the ephemeris each day.

If you use a midnight ephemeris, the positions given in the ephemeris on the Greenwich birthdate will always represent dates *previous* to the birthdate (unless you were born at 0 hours in Greenwich in which case you would use the positions directly from the book.)

All you must remember is that by progression

1 day (or 24 hours in the ephemeris) = 1 year or 12 months of real time.

2 hours (24 ÷ 12) = 1 month and

4 minutes (120m ÷ 30 days) = 1 day of life

How to do this

1. Convert your local birth time into Greenwich Mean Time in the 24 hour system (add 12 hours to birth time for PM births). 2PM becomes 12+2, or 14:00 hours.

2. *Add* appropriate hours for AM births that are *west* of Greenwich and *subtract* appropriate hours for AM births that are *east* of Greenwich. (This time will be used in step 4.)

Example:

a. If you were born at 2:12 AM EST (Eastern Standard Time), your Greenwich Birth Time would be 7 hrs 12m (2hr 12m elapsed time from midnight + 5hr time zone increment).

b. If you were born at 2:12 minutes PM EST your Greenwhich Birth Time would be 19 hrs 12 m (12hr to noon + 5hr time zone + 2hr 12m after noon).

3. Convert your Greenwich birthdate into numerical notation, *i.e.,*

January = (month) 1
February = (month) 2, *etc.*

If you were born on March 1, 1950, you would record this as: 3–01–1950.

4. Using the 24hr Greenwich birth time *(see step 2, example a.)* divide the highest even number by 2.

Example: 7 hrs = 6 ÷ 2 = 3 (with 1 remaining.) This result will be the number of months– 3– to be subtracted from the Greenwich birthdate.

5. Take the minutes of the Greenwich birth time and divide by 4. If you have a left-over hour *(see step 4)* add 60 minutes before dividing. The result is the number of days to be subtracted from the Greenwich birthdate.

Example: Converted birth-time (with added time-zone increment) is 7hrs 12m. After dividing the highest even number of hours by 2, we have 1 hour remaining and the additional 12 minutes.

$$60m + 12m = 72 \div 4 = 18$$

In our example, the highest number of even hours of the Greenwich time is 6. When we divide by 2 the answer is 3 and this is the number of *months* we subtract from the Greenwich birthdate. The one hour that is left over is converted to 60 minutes and added to the 12 minutes of Greenwich birthtime. This becomes 72 minutes which we divide by 4. The result is 18 which is the number of *days* we subtract from the Greenwich birth date.

3–01–1950

–3–18

If you cannot subtract the days you *borrow* one month from the months column and add to the days column. You borrow the month previous to the month given and add the number of days for that month. In our example we are borrowing the month of February, so we add 28 days to the day column.

2 –29–1950

– 3 –18

11

If you cannot subtract the months, borrow 1 year and add 12 months to the months column.

14–29–1949

–3–18

11–11–1949

This means that the positions in the emphemeris for March 1, 1950 represents November 11, 1949. Then the positions given for March 2, 1950 represent November 11, 1950, the positions given for March 3, 1950 represent November 11, 1951, *etc.*

Checklist:

1. Convert local birth-time to 24hr Greenwich time.
2. Divide hours by 2. Convert remainder, if any, to 60 minutes. (Subtract result as *months* from birthdate.)
3. Add birth minutes to remainder (if any) and divide by 4. (Subtract result as *days* from birthdate.)
4 .Convert birth date to numerical notation.
5. Subtract days from days and months from months. Make adjustments based on actual days in the month if numbers won't directly subtract. Example: Sept. will "carry-over" 30 days and February 28.
6. The resulting ACD (adjusted calculation date) planetary positions equal those for that date. The next day will represent the same date the following year.

trine becomes a square, the natal trine contributes a positive effect to the planetary relationship.

While a progressed planet may make only one aspect at a time to the natal chart, all natal aspects to that planet must be considered in the interpretation. I also use transits to progressed planets and progressed house cusps. I often find that major events occur when outer planets are transiting both the natal house cusp and the progressed house cusp at once.

EXAMPLE: Susan

Susan was born on October 12, 1942 at 9:56 PM. EWT, 41N02 73W46. (See Chart 1) As you can see, Susan has five planets in Libra. This makes relationships of the utmost importance to her.

Susan married Tom on August 16, 1962. At the time progressed Jupiter was at 25 Cancer trine her progressed midheaven. Under any type of Jupiter aspect, a person feels optimistic. The world seems full of opportunities.

Chart 3 — Susan progressed age 32

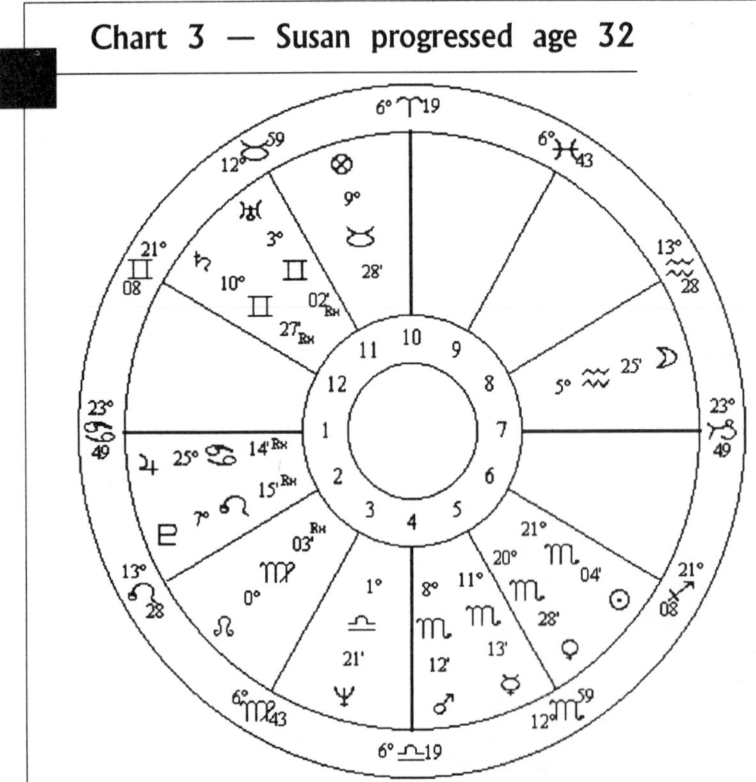

The sign Sagittarius is on Susan's seventh house cusp. Jupiter rules Sagittarius so it affects the seventh house of marriage and partnerships. Any aspects from Jupiter affect primary relationships. The midheaven represents one's standing in the world, and getting married changes one's standing (particularly in 1962). Jupiter's trine reflected this change.

Progressed Venus at 5 Scorpio was separating from a trine to the natal midheaven at the same time. Venus has to do with love, marriage, and partnerships. It rules the sign Libra. Since Susan has five planets in Libra natally, aspects to Venus play a prominent role in her life.

Natally Jupiter squares Susan's Sun and Mars and takes in Venus and Mercury because of the stellium in Libra. These aspects signal that marriage problems will eventually show up no matter how happy Susan and Tom may be at the onset of the marriage. Potential Jupiter problems have to do with excess.

Susan has Gemini Rising. Progressed Mercury, which rules Gemini, was applying to a square to natal Jupiter, ruler of the seventh house. This first–seventh house activity reinforces the I–Thou of marriage and partnerships. It also reinforces the likelihood that over-optimism surrounded the marriage.

The progressed ascendant about 15 Cancer was at the midpoint of Linda's natal Mercury–Mars conjunction in Libra. Squares have to do with activity. The progressed Node conjoined the natal Node in October, 1962. Nodes also have to do with connections.

Transiting Saturn was in Aquarius at the same time, making trine aspects to Susan's Libra planets. Saturn's influence shows that this was a long-term relationship. Susan married Tom, her high school sweetheart. Transiting Jupiter was around Susan's natal midheaven in Pisces and transiting Uranus was close to her North Node in Virgo.

Chart 3: Progressed Age 32

In Susan's natal chart, Jupiter, which rules the seventh house, squares her Sun and Mars. Since the Sun and Mars are part of a stellium in Libra, Jupiter also negatively aspects Mercury and Venus. Jupiter falls in Susan's second house of money. In January, 1974 Susan separated from Tom. She'd had enough of his expansiveness. Tom irresponsibly spent more money than he earned despite having a wife and two children and a need for security. With Jupiter afflicted in Susan's second house, undoubtedly she didn't handle money any better than he did.

At the time of the separation in January, 1974, Jupiter had come to conjoin Susan's progressed ascendant at 24–25° Cancer. The progressed Moon was conjunct the progressed descendant at 24° Capricorn. Susan felt good about separating from Tom. She was optimistic (Jupiter) that she could find a job that would support herself and the children.

Progressed Mars at 7° Scorpio was separating from the square to natal and progressed Pluto at 7° Leo and forming a quincunx to the progressed midheaven at 7 Aries. Mars symbolizes males in one's life. It also has to do with conflict. Progressed Mars' square to Pluto in the natal second house reinforces problems surrounding finances. Mars quincunx to the midheaven can be seen to symbolize Susan's change in status as well as the necessity for her to seek employment. Interestingly enough, the progressed midheaven was trine Pluto in the natal second house. This symbolized an end (or at least a perceived end) to financial difficulties at the time of the separation, and Susan's ability to get a job in order to support herself and her two children. Tom never contributed much support after the separation.

By January, 1974, Susan had had four years of Uranus transits. She was restless and willing to take risks and no longer willing to put up with what she couldn't live with. This represented a major change as Libras are more likely to keep the peace and preserve relationships whenever possible.

Transiting Pluto was conjunct the progressed IC at the same time. The fourth house represents home or family life. Pluto frequently brings an ending or loss to whatever it touches.

Transiting Saturn was also around her natal ascendant at that time. The ascendant–descendant axis reflects relationships. Saturn cycles can be times of separation, particularly if a separation is what is needed for one to take responsibility for a situation.

PROGRESSED: 1976/1977 Charts 4 and 5

On September 19, 1976 Susan started living with Jim, who became her second husband on July 9, 1977. I use the ninth house as the second husband (the seventh house = the first husband; the ninth house is the third from the seventh or symbolically the husband's brother). Aquarius is on the cusp of the ninth house. Saturn co-rules Aquarius.

Susan meets Jim 9/19/'76 — Chart 4

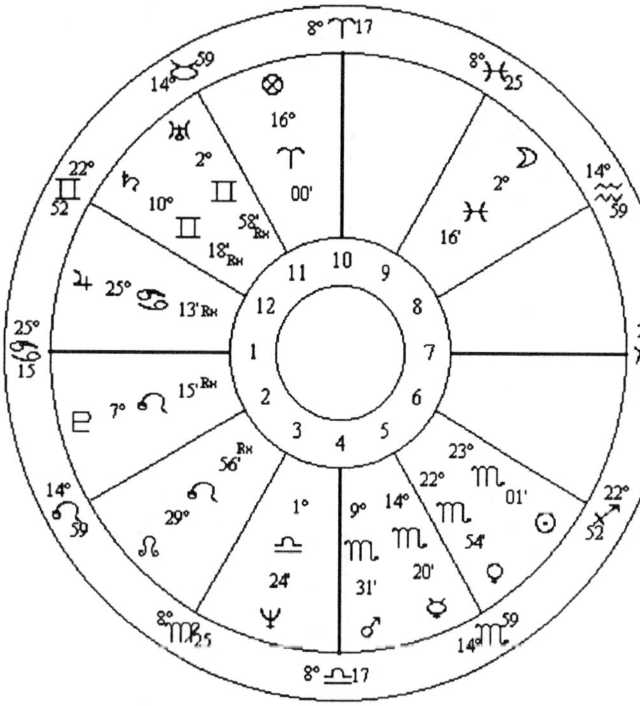

From July, 1976 through 1977 progressed Saturn was moving to form a sextile to Susan's progressed midheaven and a trine to her progressed IC. Once again, the midheaven represents one's standing in the outer world and the IC represents one's inner self as well as the home and family. Progressed Saturn semisquared to the progressed ascendant with a sessiquadrate to the descendant. The ascendant–descendant axis symbolizes marriage or one-to-one relationships.

In 1977, the progressed IC was moving to 10° Libra to conjoin natal Venus. The fourth house represents home and family life. Venus represents love and marriage.

In July, 1977 (the month of the marriage), progressed Venus conjoined the progressed Sun in Scorpio. This shows a time of much love, happiness, togetherness, and passion. The Sun represents masculine archetype, also men in a woman's life. Venus represents the feminine archetype as well as relationships.

Symbolically, the conjoining of the Sun and Venus represent the coming together of the masculine and feminine within oneself. This is mirrored in the outer world by coming together with a mate.

During this time progressed Venus was forming a trine to natal Jupiter. Progressed Sun was forming a trine to natal Jupiter. Venus signifies love and relationships. The Sun represents men in a woman's chart. Jupiter rules Sagittarius, which is on the seventh house cusp of marriage. The Sun and Venus coming together in a trine to Jupiter show a wonderfully happy and loving time in Susan's life. There is an ease of expressing love and affection (Venus) in a strongly passionate way (Scorpio).

The Venus–Sun conjunction occurred in Susan's sixth house. Shortly after the marriage, Susan and Jim opened a business together, which they both worked in daily. Progressed Mars in Scorpio formed a quincunx to progressed Saturn in September, 1977. Mars rules the progressed midheaven. The business was not successful. Progressed Jupiter in the natal second house formed a semi-square to progressed Saturn, also in September of 1977, indicating more business problems.

Chart 5: Susan marries Jim, 7/09/77

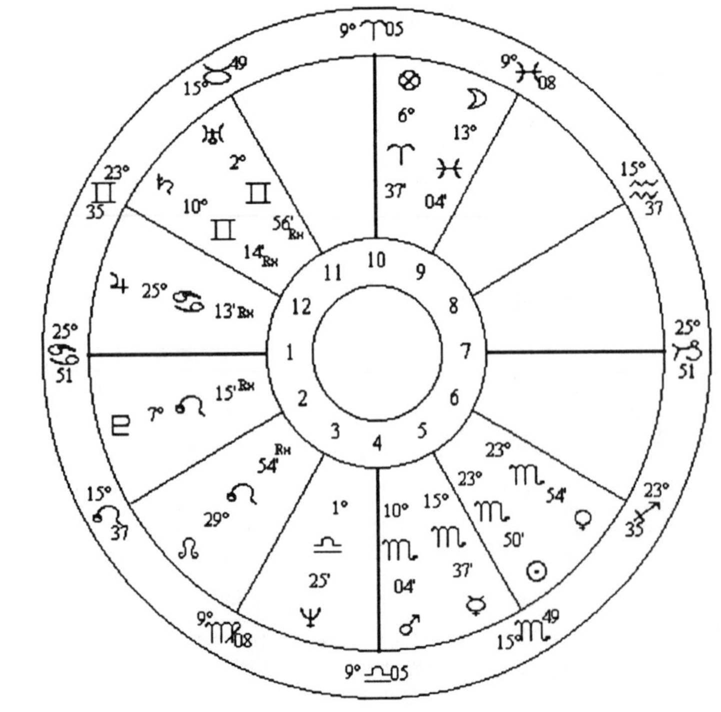

Transiting Pluto was around the progressed IC for many years. When the IC progressed to natal Venus, Susan got involved with Jim. Transiting Pluto conjunct Venus can signify the end of a relationship, or it can signify the beginning of a new romance that has great intensity. This mirrors the progressed Sun conjunct progressed Venus in Scorpio.

Transiting Neptune in Sagittarius was forming a sextile to natal Venus and Mercury during 1976 and 1977. This sextile brings forth an opportunity if one takes advantage of it. The Venus, Mercury, Neptune combination brought forth the opportunity for romance. Transiting Jupiter in Gemini also formed trines to Susan's Libra fifth house planets, expanding this romantic opportunity. Transiting Saturn in Leo formed a sextile to the Libra planets. Saturn adds a stabilizing element.

Lastly, transiting Uranus formed a trine to the natal midheaven in 1976. Since Uranus rules the ninth house of the second marriage, this aspect heightened the likelihood of a change of marital status. ✹

STUDY QUESTIONS

1. Calculate Susan's Adjusted Calculation Date (ACD).

2. Calculate Susan's chart for her ACD in 1994.

3. List the position of the progressed Moon for each month from the ACD in 1994 to the ACD in 1995

4. List the aspects formed between the progressed Moon and Susan's natal planets between the ACD in 1994 and the ACD in 1995.

5. During which months did these aspects become exact?

6. In 1998 Susan's midheaven will be moving into Taurus. What type of changes would you expect in Susan's career direction?

ANSWERS

1. Susan was born on October 12, 1942 at 9:56 PM EWT. First add 12 hours for a PM birth and her birth time becomes 21:56. You then add 4 hours (because it was war time) to obtain the Greenwich birth time, so her Greenwich birth time was 25:56. This means that it was already October 13 in Greenwich, England when she was born. Therefore, we use October 13 instead of October 12. We also subtract 24 hours from the birthtime because we are into the next day. So her birth date and time for determine her Adjusted Calculation Date is October 13, 1942 at 1:56 hours GMT.

We convert the date into numbers:

10 13 1942

We then take the highest number of even hours and divide by 2 to determine the *month* to be subtracted from the birth date.

However, since in this example there are no even hours, we convert the 1 hour into 60 minutes, add it to the minutes of birth (56) and get 116 minutes.

We then divide by 4 to get the number of *days* to be subtracted from the birth date. The result of 116, divided by 4, is 29; which is placed in the *days* column.

10 13 1942
- 0 29

You cannot subtract 29 from 13 so you borrow the preceding month from the birth month which was September and add 30 days to the days of the birth date.

9 43 1942
-0 29 1942

---

9 14 1942

So the ACD is September 14 and the Greenwich birth date of October 13, 1942 represents September 14, 1942.

2. Susan's progressed charts for the ACD in 1994.

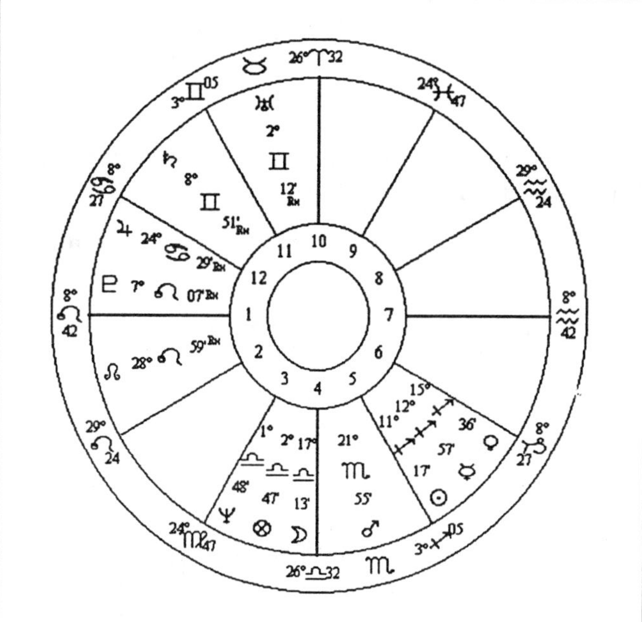

3. The progressed Moon was at 16 Libra 10 on September 14, 1994 and at 0 Scorpio 00 on September 14, 1995.

In that progressed year the progressed Moon moved 13 degrees and 50 minutes. When you subtract 12 degree it becomes 1 degree and 50 minutes or 110 minutes. When you divide 110 by 12 you get 9 and 2 left over. This means that you add 1 degree and 9 minutes to the earlier progressed Moon 10 times and 1 degree and 10 minutes twice.

September 14, 1994 16 Libra 10
October 14, 1994 17 Libra 20
November 14, 1994 18 Libra 30
December 14, 1994 19 Libra 39
January 14, 1995 20 Libra 48
February 14, 1995 21 Libra 57
March 14, 1995 23 Libra 06
April 14, 1995 24 Libra
May 14, 1995 25 Libra 24
June 14, 1995 26 Libra 33
July 14, 1995 27 Libra 42
August 14, 1995 28 Libra 51
September 14, 1995 0 Scorpio 00

4. —
Progressed Moon conjunct natal Mars
Progressed Moon conjunct natal Sun
Progressed Moon square natal Jupiter
Progressed Moon trine natal ascendant

5. —

Progressed Moon conjoined natal Mars in the month that began on September 14, 1994

Progressed Moon conjoined natal Sun in the month that began on November 14, 1994.

Progressed Moon squared natal Jupiter in the month that began on March 14, 1995.

Progressed Moon trined natal ascendant in the month that began on July 14, 1995

6. With the progressed MC moving into Taurus, money and security take on more importance in the career direction. Since Susan has no planets in earth in her birth chart and no planet have yet progressed into earth, this represents a major change for her.

THE MINOR ASPECTS
AND THEIR SPECIAL USES

by Ken Negus

John Addey's pioneering work in harmonics has clearly challenged much earlier thinking on the foundations of astrology.[1]

This is especially true of the theory of aspects. There is a compelling simplicity about the principle that all aspects are based on the division of the circle by a whole number, and its corollaries that the smaller this number, the stronger the aspect and the wider its effective orb. The favoring of those aspects derived from the smaller whole numbers, as "major" aspects, in traditional astrology bears considerable testimony to these assumptions.

In fact, the principles of harmonics have apparently always been present in astrology to a degree, although not consciously and consistently applied as now. Particularly the doctrine of the five Ptolemaic aspects as being the major aspects, as suggested above, strongly suggests that the smaller the number by which we divide the circle, the stronger the resulting aspect and the wider its orb, for these aspects are formed from relatively small numbers. Thus the conjunction is derived from the division by one, the opposition by two, the trine by three, the square by four, and the sextile by six. There appears to be an inconsistency here in the absence of five. (This will be discussed later.) But at least one through four (or conjunction through square) illustrate the above principles without qualification.

The rationale as to why the major aspects are considered such is clearly stated by Addey: "because, being primary divisions of the circle, they contain the most sub-harmonics and because they are the most likely places in the circle for these sub-harmonics to coincide and reinforce each other."[2]

STRENGTH AND ORB

Assuming that this reasoning is valid, some new possibilities immediately present themselves. The first one is that probably we should apply the principle of aspect-strength and orb-width more consistently than in the past. This would mean that if the conjunction is stronger than the opposition, the opposition stronger than the trine, the trine than the square, etc., then we should not leave out the fifth harmonic aspects (quintile and biquintile) in the series described above, if we use the sextile as a major aspect. Furthermore, we should give the quintile and biquintile somewhat less weight and narrower orb than the square (fourth harmonic), but somewhat more weight and wider orb than the sextile (sixth harmonic). This suggestion will come as no surprise to those modern astrologers who now routinely ascribe major status to the quintile and biquintile alongside the Ptolemaic aspects. There could be some unwillingness, however, to allow it a greater orb than the sextile.

Pursuing this line of reasoning further, it would be logical to place the seventh-harmonic series between the sextile and the eighth-harmonic aspects (that is, between the septile, biseptile and triseptile;[3] and the semisquare and sesquiquadrate, resp.). This would make the former stronger and wider in orb than the latter. This proposal may bring forth a howl of protest from the users of the 90° dial (of which I am one), who generally do not discriminate much between the strength and orbs of the eighth harmonic aspects and those of the conjunction, opposition and square.

But probably the most disagreeable proposal of all coming from this line of thought would be to ascribe very little strength and orb to the quincunx and semisextile, for these are mere 12th-harmonic aspects, several steps ahead in the line that we have been following, therefore much "weaker." The experience of most astrologers probably would contradict this, especially in the case of the quincunx.

The criterion of greatness or smallness of an aspect's harmonic number for determining its strength and orb seems valid up to a point, but other factors appear to modify them in many individual cases. There are at least two such factors. The first is that the higher-order the harmonic, the more specialized its application becomes. And the second: that aspect strength and orb are complicated by the fact that, in many cases, aspects of various harmonics are close to each other and partially overlap (how much depending on the orb

Essentials of Intermediate Astrology

Table 1 HARMONICS AND ASPECTS

Harmonic	*Aspect*	*Orb*	*Planetary*	*Assoc.Key Words*	*# Degrees*
1	Conjunction	7°	Sun	Unity	0°
2	Opposition	6°	Moon	Diversity, Separation	180°
3	Trine	5°	Jupiter	Unity + Diversity	120°
4	Square	5°	Saturn	Manifestation, Limitation	90°
5	Qtl,Bql	3°	Mercury, Sun	Creation,	72°, 144°
6	Sextile	3°	Venus	Harmony,Beauty,Pleasure	60°
7	Sep,Bsp,Tsp	2°	Uranus/Neptune	Esotericism	51°,103°,154°*(approx.)*
8	Ssq,Ses	2°	Mars/Saturn	Intense Energy,Power	45°,135°
9	Non,Bin,Qno	1°	Neptune/Pluto	Physical & Spiritual Extremes	40°, 80°,160°
10	Decile,Tredecile	1°	Merc./Sun/Moon	See #5 & 2	36°, 108°
11	Undecile	1°	Nep/Plu/Ur	Irrationality	32° 43' 38",etc.
12	Ssx, Qnx	1°,2°	Uranus, Neptune	Adjustment	30°,150°
16	Semioctile	1/2°	Mars/Saturn	See # 8	22° 30', *etc.*

Quintile - 72°

Biquintile - 144°

Septile - 51° 25' 43"

Biseptile - 102° 51' 25"

Triseptile - 154° 17' 08"

Semisquare (also "Octile") - 45°

Sesquiquadrate - 135°

Nonile (Also "Novile") - 40°

Binonile - 80°

Quadrinonile - 160°

Undecile - 32° 43' 38" (the remaining 11th-harmonic aspects have no names)

Semisextile - 30°

Quincunx - 150°

Semioctile - 22° 30"

(the remaining 16th-harmonic aspects have no names; they are: 67° 30', 112° 30' & 157° 30')

Aspects are also harmonics: A 90° square is a division of 360° by four, a "Fourth Harmonic". Similarly a trine is a division by three, a sextile by six, a nonile/novile by nine.

There are harmonic families: a square is half an opposition, a semisquare is half a square, a semioctile half a semisquare.

Some aspects are divisions of 360° by prime numbers (numbers that can only be divided by themselves and 1)— 2, 3, 5, 7, 11, 13.

we allow). The prime example of the latter is the quincunx (150°), which is flanked by the biquintile (144°) on the one side, and the triseptile (154°) on the other.

Further complications appear in Robert Hand's aspect model, which shows minor peaks and troughs to the side of some major aspects — for example, the trine, peaking at 120°, drops off in strength (or "amplitude") to a minor trough at about 124° (though still in effect); then it rises to a minor peak at 127°.

This concept is very convincingly argued, and should probably be considered in the "fine tuning" of any interpretation of a major aspect. In this article, however, I shall ignore these minor "bumps" on the aspect curves for the sake of concentrating on the major peaks.[4]

From this point on, we are assuming that an aspect should be assessed by three criteria: the strength of its harmonic number (the lowest being the strongest); the quality of the harmonic in question; and the extent of its overlap with aspects of other harmonics.

A fourth criterion must also sometimes be considered: to what extent the harmonic is divisible by lesser numbers, and what these lesser numbers are. The harmonic of the square (four), for example, is formed by the factors of two two's, therefore has the double the "hard" quality of the two.

The sextile (sixth harmonic) on the other hand combines two and three in its factors; therefore it has some of the soft quality of the three, added to its "twoness." The whole two-series of aspects (two, four, six, eight, etc.) has a hard quality; the three-series (three, six, nine, twelve, etc.) is soft. Obviously many of the higher harmonics are mixtures of the two, and it is often difficult to say which of the two qualities predominates.

Finally, the matter of prime numbers should be mentioned here. The prime numbers are those that are not evenly divisible by any other number except one. The first several in the series are 1, 2, 3, 5, 7, 11, 13, 17, etc. Moving upward in the series of harmonic numbers, it appears that with each step up to a prime number, a new symbolism enters into the system. This should become apparent later when we discuss them individually, especially five and seven.

CHARACTERISTICS OF THE MAJOR ASPECTS

In order to understand the qualities of the minor aspects, it is necessary to deal briefly with those of the major ones.

The qualities of harmonics one, two and three are so broad that it is difficult to ascribe precise key words to them, beyond such abstractions as unity, polarity and harmony, resp. With four, however, we do have a special quality — a Saturnian one that stands out most impressively when using the 90° dial (a fourth-harmonic device), and may be summed up with the key-words "manifestation and limitation." Ninety-degree dial indications are, in other words, generally overt, concrete, physical. They are not merely latent or potential, as are many other astrological indications. Nor are they essentially psychological or spiritual. If or when they are, then usually they are also externalized in some manner.

We begin our discussions on "minor" aspects here with the fifth harmonic, since it is not a Ptolemaic aspect, *i. e.,* not traditionally a major aspect. Attention is called first to *Table I,* which summarizes the whole system within which the individual aspects should be viewed. The details of it are my own, and are not intended to be rigidly followed. Every astrologer should eventually decide on his/her orbs, planetary association, and key words.

THE FIFTH HARMONIC

It is arguable whether traditional astrology was in error not to ascribe major status to the quintile (72 °) and the biquintile (144 °). Only Kepler, among the prominent astrologers of our Western tradition, called attention to it in the 17th century. He remained, however, a single voice that was largely unheeded by astrologers until the 20th century. Addey's work on the fifth harmonic, beginning in the Sixties, produced a major discovery of what is now called the "family pentagram," making the harmonic extremely important.[5] Also follow-up research on the fifth-harmonic chart bears further testimony to how useful in general practice the fifth harmonic can be.[6]

The special meanings of this harmonic are now clearly formulated: they pertain to the fifth house, Leo and the Sun, particularly those subsumed by the key-phrase, "creative self-expression"[7]. This harmonic also has a mercurial quality, particularly pertaining to the mental and communicative capabilities that are unique to human beings. Manifestations of fifth harmonic aspects range primarily from the procreation of children to the creation of works of art. In other words, any way in which we "give birth," putting a discrete entity from within ourselves out into the external world is indicated by the fifth harmonic aspects. Further information in this area can be derived from the fifth-harmonic horoscope.[8]

The quintile and biquintile are not, of course, so easily seen on the horoscope as are the Ptolemaic aspects, which are found simply by scanning it for the same numbers of degrees in the signs. This slight inconvenience may have been one reason why traditionally the quintile and biquintile were more or less ignored. Actually, finding them is easy with a little practice: for the quintile, one simply looks for a sextile plus 12°; and for the biquintile, it is a quincunx minus 6°. Or their arcs can be marked on a 360° dial and measured directly. The easiest method of all, of course, is to assign the job to a computer.

MARTIN LUTHER KING AND FIFTH-HARMONIC ASPECTS

An excellent example of fifth harmonic aspects is found in the birth chart of Martin Luther King. As an orator, he was a creative and performing artist, thus combining both sides of fifth harmonic symbolism — the solar and the mercurial. As would be expected, in the 360° chart we already see some general prominence of these qualities without looking for fifth-harmonic aspects. The Sun conjuncting the MC and ruling the fifth house would indicate a person who would project himself creatively in a profession. The Sun-ruled fifth house contains Neptune, indicating his role as a spiritual leader and imaginative idealist ("I have a dream"), conveyed through his verbal artistry. His Mercury in the 10th house also indicates his role as a public speaker. This planet is disciplined by a semisquare to Saturn, and stimulated by a square to the ascendant.

When we then examine the fifth-harmonic aspects involving the above-mentioned points, we find more specific details of his communicative creativity. Most powerful of all is the biquintile (144°) between the Sun and Neptune. (This shows up as a "conjunction" on the fifth-harmonic chart — see *Chart 1.*) Here we have a mathematically more precise linkage between Sun and Neptune than in house rulership. Not only does the Sun, the most creative of the celestial bodies, rule the creative fifth house, containing spiritual and imaginative Neptune; but it also is closely connected with it by an aspect that conveys traits of creativity and communicativeness. Likewise connected by this same creative aspect are Mars and the MC — whereby his aggressive energies (Mars) are channeled into his calling as orator (Mercury in the 10th; Mars in Gemini), reformer (Mercury in Aquarius) and leader (MC in Capricorn).

Then we can go on to the higher octave of the fifth harmonic — to the 10th harmonic, representing the same qualities as the fifth, with some lunar flavor as well — and encounter even tighter connections involving the Sun and Neptune, along with additional insights. King's ascendant is in Taurus, the practical, goal-oriented, persistent sign — qualities that served him well in his ministry and political actions. This ascendant, his personality, is closely linked with both the Sun and Neptune by tredecile (108°) or three-10ths of the circle). This configuration of the three points amounts to what might be called a "10th-harmonic yod," with the ascendant symmetrically aspecting Sun and Neptune on both sides.

Thus the ascendant, in addition to forming these aspects, is also at the direct midpoint of Sun and Neptune — a very powerful combination indeed. Looking at King's fifth harmonic chart, we see this combination in the ascendant's "opposition" to the "conjunction" of Sun and Neptune. The "opposition" in a fifth harmonic chart represents an aspect based on 1/10th of the whole circle (either 36° or 108°). Finally, the fifth harmonic chart shows an "opposition" of Mercury and the Moon. This represents a decile, or 36° aspect. Granted, this decile is somewhat wide, and yet is symbolically significant as representing King's creatively (10th harmonic) communicating (Mercury) with the public and with feeling (Moon).

THE SIXTH HARMONIC

The sixth harmonic, represented traditionally by the sextile, has its place as a major aspect, and therefore is not of primary concern here. Its main quality is softness and easiness, with a Venusian touch added.

Jan. 15, 1929 12 AM CST 33N44.56 84W23.17 **Martin Luther King: Chart 1**

Natal Chart rectified

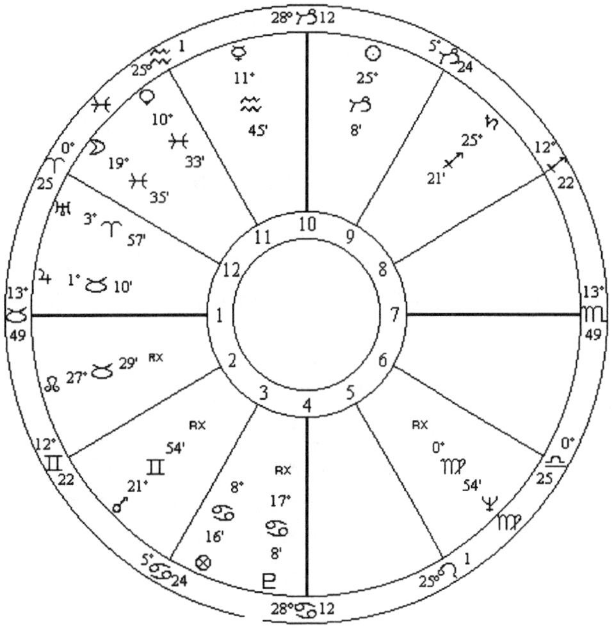

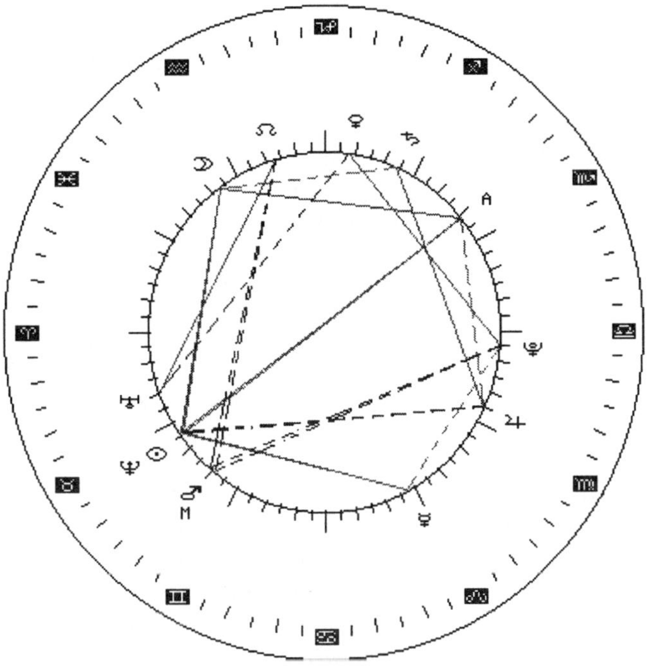

Planets converted to Fifth Harmonic —

☉	5	♉	40:20
☽	7	♒	55:55
☿	28	♋	46:35
♀	22	♐	45:45
♂	19	♉	29:15
♃	5	♍	52:00
♄	6	♐	45:35
♅	19	♈	46:10
♆	4	♉	28:40
♇	25	♍	41:45
☊	17	♑	25:15
A	9	♏	02:50
M	21	♉	01:40
V	9	♑	56:05

THE SEVENTH HARMONIC

The seventh harmonic at present holds the most promise of new and important development among the lower-order harmonics, now that the fifth has received due attention. Addey accomplished some important work with seventh-harmonic wave-analysis on the Sun positions in the charts of clergymen.[9]. Otherwise only brief and somewhat speculative descriptions of the seventh harmonic aspects have appeared to date in the major books. These aspects are the septile, biseptile and triseptile.[10]

There appears to be general agreement that the qualities of these aspects combine symbolism of Uranus (primarily) and Neptune (secondarily). Thus Addey's choice of clergymen for his seventh-harmonic study seems appropriate, at least for the Neptunian portion of the symbolism.

With these things in mind, we can hypothesize that this harmonic would be meaningfully represented in the charts of persons who live by a higher-order reality (Neptune), and in so doing are non-conforming, original or creative (Uranus). Mystics and poets, as perceived by Robert Hand, would comprise two major sub-categories thereof.[11] I have chosen the all-embracing category for this harmonic as being esotericism. An esoteric person is one who operates according to knowledge that is not widely known and understood, yet has universal meaning.

ASTROLOGERS AND THE SEVENTH HARMONIC

Upon arriving at this hypothesis, it followed that the seventh harmonic in the charts of astrologers should be examined for possible verification, since they, too, fit the above description, and also since birth information of a considerable number of them is available. Some years ago, I assembled the charts of 56 active astrologers, most professionals, and found that a great majority of astrologers had four to seven septiles, biseptiles and triseptiles in their birth charts, which usually brought together important factors thereof, such as personal points and other points appropriate for the symbolism.

Chart 2

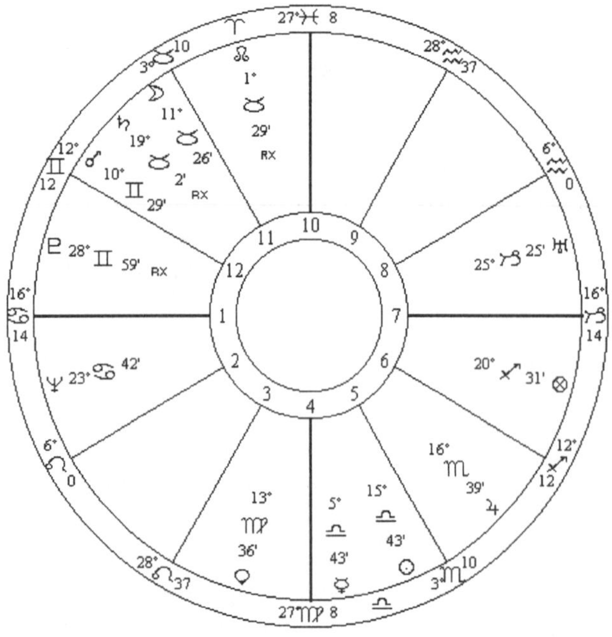

Charles Oct. 9, 1911 10:39 PM EST 39N54 75W07

Esotericism is a broad concept. Aside from the fact that it is potential in all of us, there is a considerable variety of "esoterics" in a special sense, *i. e.,* persons who command a body of knowledge that is highly specialized, yet universally applicable. In addition to mystics, poets and astrologers, we would, according to the definition, have to include many musicians, other categories of artists, and probably also those who have mastered various branches of high technology, such as computer programming.

Finding a control group that completely excludes all these categories seems impossible, especially if one considered potential talent. We have no choice but to proceed from chart to chart, modifying and expanding our findings as we go along. Usually something true eventually forms in the mind, if not on statistical graphs. The appropriateness of the symbolism, at least, becomes apparent.

CHARLES JAYNE AND SEVENTH-HARMONIC ASPECTS

There is a single, highly impressive combination in Charles Jayne's horoscope (*See Chart 2*) [12] that should probably count very heavily in any weighting system that we might devise for minor aspects: an exact (to the minute) triseptile between the Sun and Moon! In addition, there is a Mercury-Moon's Node triseptile, only mere 4' from perfect, and applying; plus a Mars-Jupiter triseptile, a Venus-Neptune septile, and a Uranus-Pluto triseptile — these last three having somewhat wider orbs. The total is six, or one above average. The seventh-harmonic strength here is not only in the closeness of aspects, but also in the heavy and exact involvement of the personal points (Sun and Moon). The aesthetic factor (Venus-Neptune) was always a major one for him. (He knew the English Romantic poets remarkably well.)

Furthermore the particular planets in the configurations are especially appropriate for astrology, and the kind of astrologer that he was. Mercury-Moon is a thinking-feeling combination. Mars-Jupiter indicates his vigorous pursuit of knowledge of all things esoteric and occult. And the Uranus-Pluto combination indicated his energetic role as pioneer and discoverer.

THE NINTH HARMONIC

The ninth is the harmonic of extremes. Being a higher power of three (the Jupiter number), multiplied by itself, does not make it particularly happy. In fact, it is found in the charts of persons whose lives vacillate between agony and ecstasy, with little to temper the extremes. The aspects with which we are dealing are: 40°, 80° and 160° (The missing member of the series, 120°),or the more powerful trine, subsumes the ninth harmonic.)

A good example of a famous person whose life was filled with extremes is Isadora Duncan. She lived at the end of the 19th and beginning of the 20th century, and is known as the creator of the modern interpretive dancing. She was enormously successful in her art, but suffered great defeats as well, primarily when she was rejected by her American audiences in the early Twenties because of her alleged Communist sympathies. Her personal life was tumultuous and, for her time, scandalously unconventional. She did not marry the fathers of her two children. Two major tragedies overshadowed her life and our memory of her. In Paris, in 1913, her two children and their nurse died when the car in which they were sitting rolled into the Seine, and they drowned. Her own death was bizarre: While riding in an open car, her scarf became entangled in the rear wheel, and she was thrown to the ground and strangled to death. She remains remembered as a superb dancer and teacher, without whom the modern interpretive dance would not be the same, but her life had the ups and downs of a roller coaster.

As always, the major aspects in her chart have much to say. Her aggressive self-assertion through rhythmic and beautiful motions is seen in the Aries ascendant conjunct both Moon and Venus, and close to their midpoint. Her imaginative artistic expression is

Chart 3

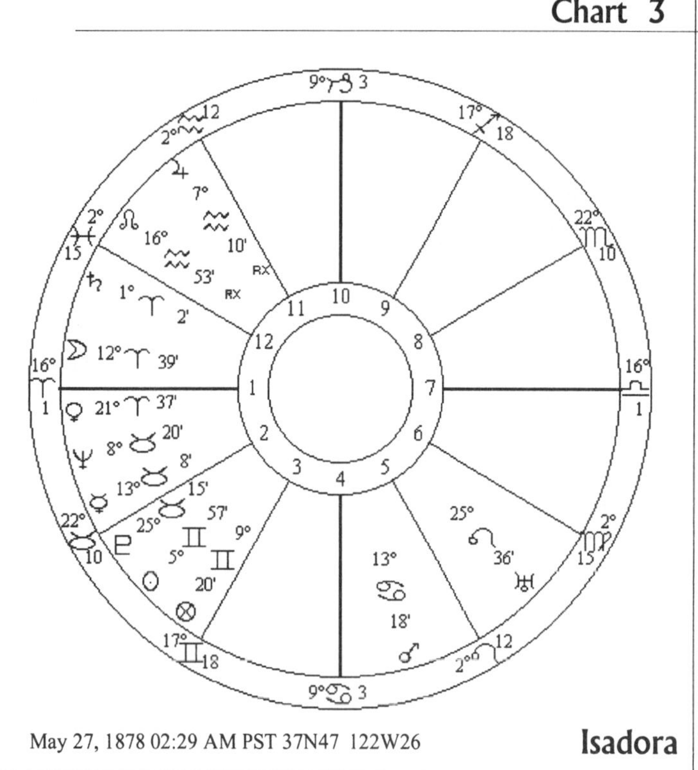

May 27, 1878 02:29 AM PST 37N47 122W26 **Isadora**

indicated by Neptune in the first house, trining the midheaven, (her career). Her flouting of convention is seen in the Uranus sesquiquadrate the midheaven, opposite Part of Fortune, and its extreme nature in the square to Pluto. Her tragic confrontations with death appear in the Pluto sesquiquadrate MC, semisquare the Equatorial Ascendant, and square the Part of Fortune and Uranus.

The extreme nature of the major events in her life, however, is still not satisfactorily covered. For these we look for the 40°, 80° and 160° aspects. Perhaps the easiest one to see is the aspect between the Sun and Uranus. If Uranus were 10° later in the zodiac, there would be a square. The separation, however, is 10° less than that, 80°, or a binonile. Thus the sesquiquadrate from Uranus to MC — meaning simply a potential unconventional tendency — is supported by the binonile to the Sun, meaning a deep, all-pervasive, and extreme unconventionality. Thus she was easily capable, in the conservative atmosphere of the early 20th century, of not marrying the fathers of her children, as well as of dancing in near-nudity before many of her audiences.

As for the wrenching loss of her children, as well as for her own death in a motor vehicle (Uranus), there is the aforementioned Uranus in the fifth house of children which squares Pluto. Also, the Uranus-Pluto square forms a "hard yod" with the MC, making the event a public as well as a private matter. Pluto, however, like the Uranus, has an important ninth-harmonic aspect: it is 40°, a nonile, away from the ascendant. Thus extreme events involving death are manifested in two events of an extreme nature.

Sometimes spirituality is attributed to the ninth harmonic, but this is of a very sublime order — therefore "extreme," as would be consistent with the above. It may be that strong ninth-harmonic people who have turned to some extreme form of spirituality may escape some of the agony that is otherwise present.

GRAY AREAS OF ORBS

Sharp cut-offs of orbs are probably inappropriate, if (as I assume) aspects are effective according to a bell-shaped curve. It would be impossible to say precisely where at the edges of the curve effectiveness begins and ends. We must assume, in other words, a gray area on the margins of orbs. To begin the series: for the conjunction, 2° on the edges (chosen somewhat arbitrarily) seem appropriate, thus assigning an area of uncertainty between 7° and 9° on each side. Thus the definite orb of this aspect plus its uncertain margin can be expressed as "7 + 2". *The whole list would then be as follows:*

Aspect	Orb
Conjunction	7 + 2
Opposition	6 + 2
Trine	6 + 1
Square	5 + 1
Quintile, Biquintile	4 + 1
Sextile	3 + 1
Seven-series	2 + 1
Semisquare, sesquiquadrate	1 1/2 + 1/2
Nine-series	3/4 + 1/4
Ten-, eleven- and twelve-series	3/8 + 1/8
Sixteen series	1/2 + 1/8

BELL-SHAPED ASPECT CURVES

Here a short digression is necessary. It seems inappropriate to use a sharp cut-off with orbs, in view of the all-pervasive wave-forms throughout astrology, and the arbitrariness involved in determining cut-offs. In other words, we would expect orbs of major aspects (in their purest form)[13] to be represented graphically as sine waves, in this manner: The orb could then be indicated with vertical lines. See inset on following page: "Gray areas of Orbs".

Thus there is a gray area on the edges of the orb in which the aspect may be in effect, although probably weaker and more intermittent than when nearer the center. Therefore I suggest that we describe any orb fully as "X" # of degrees to each side of perfect, with an additional one degree, or fraction thereof, of 'gray area'." One should probably treat all other aspects similarly.

ASPECTS AND ORBS: AN EXPERIMENTAL SYSTEM

Some guidelines can now be derived for the relative strength of aspects, and the widths of their orbs. It should be apparent that the minor aspects described above have considerable strength for the applications given. General consensus and practice no doubt would indicate, however, that, say, the fifth, seventh and ninth-harmonic aspects definitely are weaker and have narrower orbs than the conjunction on the one end, but are far stronger and operate with a much wider orb than a semi-sextile on the other side of the series. It would thus be logical to ascribe relative strength and width of orb in descending order, starting with the lowest-order harmonic — one – represented by the conjunction.

Where to begin– *i. e.*, what orb to ascribe to the conjunction at the start of the series – is a difficult question indeed. A middle-ground between the extremes, represented by traditional astrology on the one hand, with orbs up to 17° in some cases, and by modern astrology on the other, which often allows no more than five (in natal interpretation; far less for transits, *etc.*) I suggest, then, nine degrees for the orb of the conjunction. This figure places the effectiveness of the conjunction within the limits indicated by Hand's study.[14] It also is convenient for deciding on the remaining orbs, as in *Table 1*. The values in this table should be regarded as tentative — to be tested and eventually adjusted according to the individual astrologer's own experience.

QUINCUNX: BETWEEN BIQUINTILE AND TRISEPTILE

These figures have implications that would alter a few generally accepted concepts. By far the most important among these is the quincunx, to which are attributed qualities of peculiarity, unpredictability, incongruity, and the like. Among these, "incongruity," is probably the keyword that covers most of its meaning. Within the above system, there emerge some very good reasons as to why the 150° arc has heretofore been the maverick among aspects. There is much more to this arc than a simple aspect derived from a multiple of a whole number divided into 360°, because it overlaps with two relatively strong aspects to each side: the biquintile (144°) and the triseptile (154° 17'). Overlap between such diverse aspects of such an order of strength and orb does not occur anywhere else within the first 12 harmonics. Thus the area around 150° requires special consideration.

The above scheme of orbs would allow the quincunx itself to be valid only between 149° and 151°. If, then, a quincunx were on the lower side (149° to 150°), it would have a touch of the biquintile (creativity); and on the upper side (150 to 151 °), some of the triseptile quality (esotericism). If exact, it seems altogether possible that it would combine a slight amount of the other two aspects, but would primarily manifest its own quality.

PERCY BYSSHE SHELLEY

A highly instructive case study, illustrating in detail the aspect area around 150°, is to be found in the

Chart 4

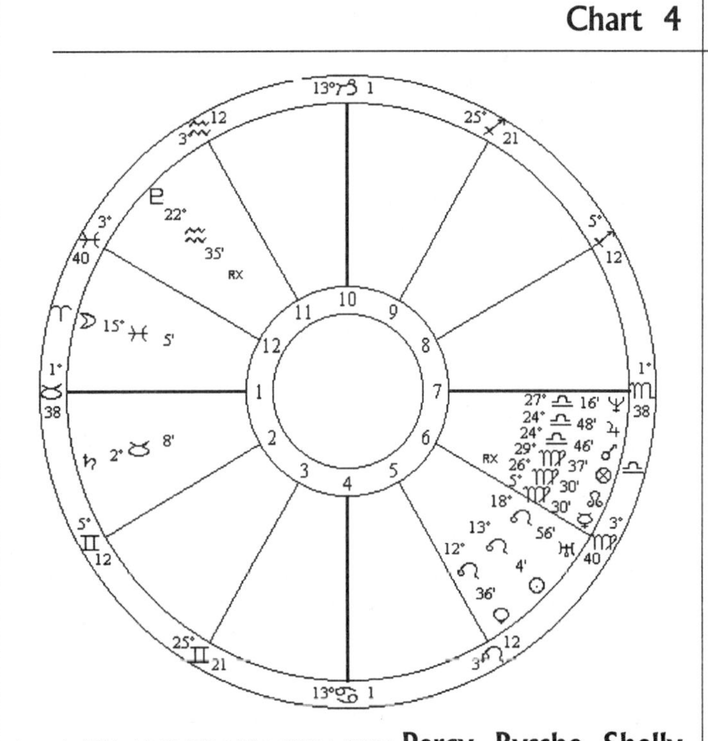

Aug. 4, 1792 10:00 PM LMT 51N04 0W21 **Percy Bysshe Shelly**

horoscope (*Chart 4*) of Percy Bysshe Shelley[14]. He has an intricate yod configuration, the positions of which are as follows:

Venus - 12 Le 36

Sun - 13 Le 04

Uranus - 18 Le 56

MC - 13 Cp 01

Moon - 15 Pi 05

Planetarily the significance of the combination hardly needs to be argued. Together these five bodies speak volumes about the poet's character — creative, dramatic, free-spirited, revolutionary, non-conforming. If my hypotheses are correct, an analysis of the finer points of the individual aspects would add the following:

Venus, the first of the three bodies forming the base of the yod, forms a slightly long quincunx to the MC, thus combining his love-life, aesthetic sensibilities and enjoyment of pleasure with his public image in an "incongruous,"or socially unaccepted way (quincunx), but also with a noticeable element of seventh-harmonic "esotericism" (his great originality as poet, but also his atheism and his unusual love-life). Among English poets, he was the epitome of the rebellious artist-intellectual, creating one scandal after another with his life-style as well as some of his writings. Here the Venus factor was certainly a major one.

The Sun-MC quincunx, on the other hand, is exact within three minutes of arc, thus would be treated exclusively as an indication of his "incongruous" public image – *i.e.,* the exercise of his will and ego would grate unconventionally and with disapproval on his identity as a famous poet.

The Sun-Venus conjunction is a few degrees short of a quincunx with the Moon, therefore out of orb for this aspect. It is, however, well within orb of a biquintile, as specified above. This is a magnificent configuration for a poet, combining creatively his aesthetic sensibility and ego-expression with the lunar principle: *i. e.,* a sense of rhythm, a strong feminine influence, and a major influence of the general public on his life as poet.

Uranus is out of orb for the yod configuration, but is indirectly connected with it by the conjunction with the Sun and Venus, thus giving added weight to "Uranian" qualities already present by virtue of the quincunx and triseptile aspects. (Note how the symbolism of these two aspects overlaps considerably with that of Uranus.) In addition, however, Uranus forms a creative biquintile (within five minutes of arc) with the MC — thus powerfully denoting Shelley's strong progressive, free-thinking, even revolutionary tendencies that were successfully brought before the world at large, although much to his loss and suffering.

Finally, the other side of the 150° area comes up again with the Moon closely triseptile Uranus — short of perfect by only 24 minutes of arc. This would add another public dimension, but this time with the "esoteric" quality described above. His unconventional relations with women would also again be indicated here. We have here reached a point where the multiplicity of repeated messages yields diminishing returns. The "esoteric," the creative, and the socially rebellious and unaccepted sides of his character have been adequately delineated with the three aspects in the 150° area.

This essay has been an attempt to provide a rationale for minor aspects within the whole system of aspects and orbs in modern astrology. Those who have been bewildered by the wide variety of strengths, meanings, and orbs, will, it is hoped, find here at least a theoretical basis for their own systems that will put the hypotheses of current harmonic research to use and to the test .

It is strongly suggested that the beginner start with only a few of the lower-numbered harmonics (especially the fifth, seventh, ninth, and 12th), proceed to multiples of these, and then up the scale to higher ones, including prime numbers such as the 11nth, 13th, 17th, *etc.* In applying the first few harmonics to the charts with which you are familiar, a limited but useful way to test them is to choose a single obvious harmonic for a given individual: *e.g.,* for an artist the fifth harmonic; for a clergyman the seventh; for a person whose life is a roller coaster, the ninth.

One should keep especially alert for harmonics in a given chart that are close to exact and interconnect several points, forming a "harmonic syndrome." Such a configuration will have as much to say as many a major aspect. We have seen this particularly in the case of Martin Luther King and the fifth and 10th harmonic.

Many of the details of the system presented here can be varied without altering its principles. In so doing, an effective way to proceed is suggested simply and clearly by Goethe in his novel, Wilhelm Meister: "Think and do; then do and think." And so on....✷

NOTES

(1) See John Addey, *Harmonics in Astrology: An Introductory Textbook to the New Understanding of an Old Science* and *Harmonic Anthology*, both published by Cambridge Circle, Ltd., Green Bay WI, in 1976.

(2) Addey, *Harmonics in Astrology*, p. 70.

(3) Septile: 51° 25' 43';
biseptile: 102° 51" 26';
triseptile: 154° 17' 09".

(4) See Robert Hand, *Essays on Astrology* (Rockport MA.: Para Research, Inc., 1982), p. 25 f.

(5) See Addey, *Harmonics in Astrology*, Ch. 12, especially p. 103 f.; also Harmonic Anthology, Ch. 10.

(6) See Joan Negus, "Fifth Harmonic Charts," *The Journal of the Astrological Society of Princeton NJ Inc.*, 2 (1981), pp. 12-19.

(7) See Addey, *Harmonics in Astrology*, p. 110 f.

(8) To calculate any harmonic horoscope, one simply multiplies the absolute longitude (*i. e.*, # of degrees from 0° Aries) of each position in the horoscope by the number of the harmonic; if the result is over 360°, then subtract as many multiples of 360° as is necessary to bring the result down to a figure between 0° and 360° This result is the new position for the harmonic chart.

(9) Addey, *Harmonics in Astrology*, p. 62 ff.; also *Harmonic Anthology*, p. 76 ff.

(10) See, for example, Robert Hand, *Horoscope Symbols* (Rockport MA: Para Research, 1981), p. 133 f.

(11) For the details of this study, see my article, "Aspects, Orbs and the Seventh Harmonic," *The Journal of the Astrological Society of Princeton NJ*, Issue #4 (1984), pp. 6-7.

(12) Information from Charles Jayne himself. It is: Oct. 9, 1911; 10:39 PM. EST; Jenkintown PA.

(13) I recognize that the true representation of an aspect curve would probably be quite bumpy, but, as stated above, I am ignoring this influence of the minor harmonics for the sake of simplicity in focussing on the major ones. See Hand, *Essays on Astrology*, p. 28 (the diagram).

(14) Shelley's chart (with "A" quality data!) is given in Lois Rodden's *The American Book of Charts* (San Diego: Astro Computing Services, 1980). The birth information: Aug. 4, 1792; 10:00 PM. LMT; Horsham, England.

SELF-TEST QUESTIONS

1. Explain the harmonic theory of aspects.

2. On the basis of harmonic theory, what is the principal factor for determining the width of orbs?

3. What are prime numbers and how do they figure in the system of aspects?

4. Briefly give the characteristics of the fifth, seventh and ninth harmonics.

5. How is the delineation of the quincunx, a 12th-harmonic aspect, complicated by other harmonics?

6. If you decided to use only one harmonic-series of "minor" aspects for a given individual, which would you choose for a:
   a. a guru?
   b. a mother of 10 children?
   c. one who frequently experiences either agony or ecstasy in his/her life, with few moderating experiences in between? Explain the reason(s) for your choice.

7. Give the aspects of:
   a. the fifth harmonic
   b. the seventh harmonic
   c. the ninth harmonic
   d. the 12th harmonic
   e. the 16th harmonic

8. Explain why the trine (120°) and the sesquiquadrate (135°) are not used as ninth and sixteenth harmonic aspects, resp., even though 120 is divisible by 40 (9th harmonic), and 135 is divisible by 22 1/2 (16th harmonic).

ANSWERS

1. Aspects are formed by the division of the circle (360°) by a whole number.

2. The higher the harmonic number, the narrower the orb.

3. Prime numbers are not evenly divisible by any number other than one. A prime number has a distinctly different symbolic quality from any others preceding it in the upward scale.

4. The *fifth* harmonic indicates creation and procreation – intellectual or artistic creativity, or the parenting and nurturing of children.

The *seventh* harmonic is that of the mystic, the esoteric, the eccentrically different qualities in a person who nonetheless has roles important to humankind as a whole.

The *ninth* harmonic is that of extremes of highs and lows in life. It can be extremely spiritual.

5. The quincunx (150°) has two relatively low-order harmonics in its vicinity: the biquintile (144°) and the triseptile (154° 17' 09"). This is an important matter when a given quincunx is inexact on the one side or the other, since it takes on qualities of the biquintile when below 150°, and of the triseptile when above.

6. a. 7th;
   b: 5th;
   c: 9th.

Essentials of Intermediate Astrology

7. a. Quintile: 72°,
   biquintile : 144°
   b. Septile: 51° 25' 43";
   biseptile: 102° 51' 26";
   triseptile: 154° 17' 09".
   c. Novile: 40°,
   binovile: 80°,
   quadrinovile: 160°
   d. Semisextile: 30°,
   quincunx: 150°
   e. Semioctile: 22 ½°, *the remainder unnamed:*
   67 ½ °, 112 ½°, 157 ½°

8. The trine (120°), although divisible by the ninth-harmonic number 40, is of the stronger, lower-numbered harmonic of three, therefore it subsumes the nine. The sesquiquadrate is divisible by 22 ½° (16th harmonic), but it is also divisible by the stronger, lower-number harmonic of eight (45°), therefore the 16th harmonic is likewise subsumed in this case.

THE DERIVED HOUSES

by Alphee Lavoie

The horoscope has 12 houses and each house has an assigned rulership over various things as well as people.

To gain a certain amount of fluency in astrology it is very important to have a good working knowledge of these different house rulerships. Once you understand the standard definitions ascribed to each house on the physical, mental, emotional and spiritual levels then you can begin to expand on these meanings by using what's known as derived houses to unveil new meanings of each house through your own delineations.

What is the derivative house system?

The first thing we learn when we study astrology is the basic meaning for each house, such as, the 2nd house rules money, the 3rd house rules your brothers and sisters, the 4th rules your home, the 5th your children and so on. The derivative house system utilizes the basic meaning of each of the houses and then applies them in relationship to each of the other houses. So the derived house system offers more depth to analyzing a horoscope. For example, on a basic level, standard house rulerships assigns children to the 5th house and money to the 2nd. By using the derived house system to find the house that rules the money of the child we follow the simple rule that tells us since the 2nd house is money we now count 2 houses from the 5th (starting WITH the 5th and counting it as #1), arriving at the 6th house. So according to the derivative house system the child's money is ruled by the 6th house. This approach can be applied to any house. The 2nd house from any house of the horoscope will tell the money or worth of that house. For instance, if we want to know the money of a business, we count two houses from the 10th (business) and arrive at the 11th house to see the finances of a company.

Counting the derived houses

Here's an example. We'll find the house that rules your sister's home. The house that rules a sister is the 3rd. The home is ruled in the natural horoscope by the 4th house. I find that it is easier to count the derived houses with a horoscope in front of you.

First, find the cusp of the 3rd house. Put your finger on it and count the 3rd house cusp as #1. Then count four houses counter-clockwise from the 3rd house cusp. The house ruling your sister's home is the 6th house.

Let's try a more complex example. Find the house ruling your sister's son's money. The sister is ruled by the 3rd house, a son is ruled by the 5th house and money by the 2nd house. Did you get it right? Place your finger on the 3rd house cusp and start counting 5 houses counter-clockwise from that cusp. You should have arrived at the 7th house cusp. Now count 2 more houses counter-clockwise starting with the 7th house cusp and this should bring you to the 8th house cusp. So, your sister's son's money is ruled by the 8th house.

Calculating the derived house mathematically

If you want to calculate the derived houses mathematically, the formula is (house + house + house) - (one

Derived Houses — Figure 1

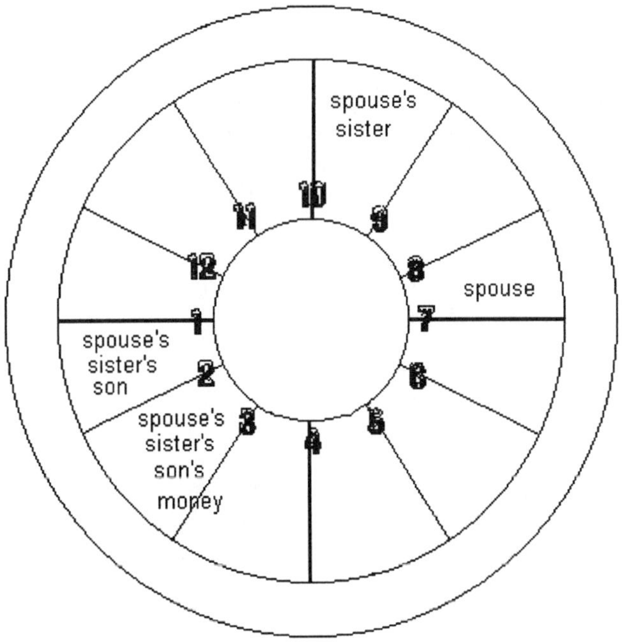

less than the number of houses added). You add the value of all the houses involved and to that total you would subtract the sum of the houses involved minus one. So if you had three houses in question you would subtract two from your total.

Here's how the formula applies to the two examples we just did. In the first example of my sister's home my sister is ruled by the 3rd house and the home is ruled by the 4th house. Mathematically you would add 3 + 4 = 7 then you would subtract 1 because you have 2 houses in question. The answer is the 6th house. Let's look at the 2nd example my sister's son's money. The sister is the 3rd house, son the 5th house and money the 2nd house. So we add 3 + 5 + 2 = 10. Now subtract (2) = 8. Remember the rule: Subtract the sum of the houses involved minus one. Since there are three houses involved we minus one (3 - 1 = 2) and now subtract 2 from the original sum of 10. 10 - 2 = 8. The nephew's money is the ruled by the 8th house. Ah! As you can see the nephew has to be ruled by the 7th house. Remember in our 2nd example we counted five houses from the 3rd house (sister) and we ended with the 7th house.

Here's another example. See how you would find my spouse's sister's son's money. We know that my spouse is ruled by the 7th house. To arrive at the proper house you would add 7+3+5+2=17-(3) = 14. Here's an interesting twist because we don't have a 14th house in the horoscope. In this instance and others like it simply subtract 12 (for the 12 houses of the whole circle of the horoscope) and you end up with two or the 2nd house. Isn't this fun! With a little practice this will open up a brand new way of delineating a chart.

A deeper understanding of the houses. A Psychological Approach

THE FIRST HOUSE — The 1st house tells you what kind of outside support you need to feel accepted and okay about yourself. It reveals how you accept the "I am" concept within yourself. In life, the 1st house is how you depend upon your own strength within. Remember, it is the house of beginnings. The placement of inner planets, Sun through Mars, in the 1st house makes the native more focused on personal energy, questioning how okay you are. When any of the outer planets are situated here it makes the native less focused on himself and more on the big picture of the world at large in questioning the issue of "okayness."

Any planets in the 1st house tells how you will enter into any situation. It represents how important it is for you to be a part of the moment. Planets like the Sun, Mars, Uranus or Pluto will give you a strong personality. The Moon and Neptune make the a person much more sensitive about themselves and in many situations a little more reserved. If the Moon or Neptune make any aspect to the Sun, Mars, Uranus or Pluto this sensitivity could manifest in a defensive way. When we first learn astrology we're taught piece-meal... little bits at a time. It is necessary in order to grow to a point where we can eventually synthesize the total picture and can see that this science really makes sense and works for all of us.

THE SECOND HOUSE —The 2nd house makes you question how much of the material goodies you need in order to feel that life really loves and appreciates you. It is through this house that you learn to put confidence in your earning ability even when your material rewards are not immediately forthcoming. It is the areas of life in which you learn to trust that you will always get what you've earned. It is here that we all understand that we reap what we sow and nothing is for free. The 2nd house is the house of the future. If you look for immediate gratification you will fall short, feel cheated and become jealous and envious of others who appear to be doing better than you. That is the weakness of the this house. This attitude promotes unhealthy feelings which inevitably create a loss of all the love and confidence that you had for yourself. As a child your parents or society rewarded you by giving you something —cookies and milk, a gift. This reinforcement boosted your confidence so that you can say, *" I must be worth it."*

The 2nd house is a succeedent house. Each of the four succeedent houses in the horoscope (2th, 5th, 8th, 11th) ties you to the physical world. And from each one we learn different lessons on how much is enough before we feel love and appreciation. These houses are very important because they make us think that we must be doing something right because we get the cookies and milk as the reward! As we mature we seek the 2nd house rewards of money to buy and own all types of possessions. The 5th house seeks somebody to stroke him, the 8th house seeks a sharing of other's material

Here are some basic keywords and concepts to briefly describe the essential nature of each of the 12 houses. Later in this chapter we'll explore each house in greater depth in relationship to the derived houses.

House 1 — I, the awareness of self, the physical body in health and appearance, personality, the image that the native of the horoscope is trying to display though clothes, hair styles, individual style and personal posturing.

House 2 — Money, material possessions, movable possessions, one's attitude toward his possessions, one's own price tag of self worth, marketable skills and traits and how much of a return one will get, confidence and determination, values, banks, earning power or income, sound investments like bonds or money certificates, the future.

House 3— Brothers and sisters, all types of communications, the way one thinks, speaks or approaches study matter, short trips, signing important papers, neighbors, drawing conclusions and making decisions, advertising, one's beliefs in his knowledge and intelligence.

House 4 — One of the parents, family, endings and beginnings, non-moveable possessions like home and land, security, the security or insecurity molded in the early upbringing, the tie to the "nest", family heritage.

House 5— Love affairs (boyfriend - girlfriend), love making, children, a birth, conception, pregnancy, gambling, betting or speculation like the stock market, self-expression, creativity, hobbies, amusements and entertainment, the games you or someone else likes to play.

House 6— Work, employees, servants, service to others, tenants, government agencies like the armed forces, law enforcers, firemen etc., health and sickness, the way that one takes care of the body, rest, work, food, and hygiene, small animals or pets, self improvement, daily habits.

House 7— Marriage and divorce, really close relationships such as a close friend, spouse, partnership, any type of unions, contracts or a business deal, lawsuits, agreements, arbitration, contests, any type of close relationship with an adviser such as a doctor or lawyer, open enemies.

House 8 — Death, taxes, surgery, wills, bank loans, other people's money such as that of the spouse, business partners, or dealings with other people's money through debts you owe, money coming from others like social security, alimony, inheritance, bankruptcy.

House 9— Religion, the church, the law, court house, long distance travel, foreign countries or connections, philosophy, higher knowledge or education, advice from others, the way you are influenced by others or listen to them, writing for publishing, preaching, teaching or wanting to say something or be heard, conscious dreams or fantasies, what one constantly prays for, one's personal commandments, belief system, spiritual understandings.

House 10— One of the parents, career, achievements, honors or reputation, any person who has some power over the native, like God or the boss, government officials, executive ability, promotions, public appearances, business. Heights attempting to be attained in this life.

House 11—Remote friends or acquaintances, clubs and memberships, one's goals, wages and pay raise from the career or profession, adoptions, social circle, hopes and wishes, how the native receives from others.

House 12 — Secret enemies, hospitals, confinements, imprisonments, secrets, self undoing, fears that hold the native back, life sacrifices, anything the native is hiding from others and Self, escapism through dependencies, such as, drugs, alcohol or denial, losses and sorrows, unconscious dreams, clandestine associates, delusions, meditation.

These descriptions of the houses reflect the native's views (the person for whom the horoscope is drawn) toward these energies, or what he is constantly setting up in life because he feels these are the things that he has to accept or challenge. On a spiritual level, these are the energies of life that one has chosen to experience for personal growth. This is why nothing happens in our individual lives unless it is clearly seen in the birth chart. The stage is always set, and when a transit, progression or direction makes an aspect to a natal planet, the curtain goes up. The growth comes from these experiences.

supports while the 11th house looks for the pay raise, socializing and respect of others in the social world.

THE THIRD HOUSE —The 3rd house tells how the native processes his mental energies to think, reason and communicate. Do I feel confident in my ideas? Is it OK to express them? Are people listening to what I have to say? Do I prefer to be silent, saying nothing at all, because I feel dumb? These are the typical concerns of the house. When the planet Saturn is in this house the native may stutter because he fears saying the wrong thing or being laughed at. Or he may speak very slowly analyzing each word with prolonged deliberation and tedious caution. Through the house energies you learn about verbalizing your ideas, mental beliefs, decision making, communications and conversation. In astrology everything starts at the ascendant. When you are really sure of yourself (1st house) you should be more aware of how much material attachment you need to feel secure and accepted (2nd house) which, in turn, stimulates confidence to communicate outside of yourself (3rd house) allowing others to know exactly who you are and what you want. This is the house of brainstorming, plotting and outlining.

Figure 2 -Derived Houses

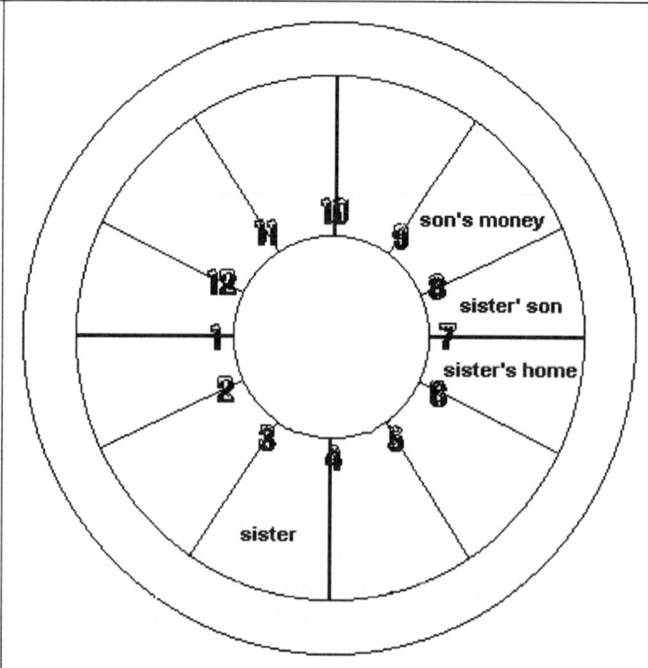

THE FOURTH HOUSE—The 4th house shows needs and dependencies of the family. It represents the programming instilled by one of your parents as your grew up as well as the emotional attachment or needs that the native hangs on to. It is everything that you have experienced in the past that affected your state of emotional security or insecurity.

The 4th house rules where you have been and its opposite house, the 10th, rules where you are going. The success of every goal and dream that you launch depends on the foundation that was built in your 4th house. The excess baggage that you continue to drag with you originates in the 4th house and only serves to slow down your growth and success.

To reach the goals of your 10th house potential it is necessary to release the unproductive past programming that stems from the 4th house. If a bird never leaves the nest it will one day realize that the comfort, caretaking nurturing of the nest has vanished and it is stuck there forever.

THE FIFTH HOUSE —The 5th house shows the talents and creations that you can market in order to feel a sense of recognition and appreciation. These talents could be channeled into games or sports that you play primarily for the attention and the glory. This creativity could be personified as a charismatic personality that makes you a terrific sales person. All of the 5th house creativity is to test your marketing skills of learning how to give of yourself. Giving is the lesson of this house. If you are good at giving of yourself you will always have lots of people loving, accepting and admiring you. This mean you have to learn to give freely with no attachments.... without demanding anything back.

THE SIXTH HOUSE—The 6th house teaches us to work, be responsible and set priorities.

How much should I go out of my way to help people? Am I spending so much time helping others that I have no time to take care of myself? Do I eat right and do all the right thing to care of my health? This is the department of the horoscope where we have to do some serious 'house cleaning' to put things in their proper places in our lives. This helps us to achieve a healthy balance of work, rest and play. All work and no play may bring about mental and physical breakdowns. By organizing our priorities, we see our daily routine more clearly which always brings about self improvement.

THE 7TH HOUSE—The 7th house speaks of how much you want to connect with anything or anyone outside of yourself. This connection is often what you feel is missing within yourself, and what others to reflect back to you. By connecting with other relationships you may gain strength by feeling more complete because it offers those qualities that you feel will restore your own balance. This rebalancing can be strongly felt even when the partner is totally your opposite. At times the energy of this house will demand that you totally surrender yourself at the cost of letting go of your own ego. This is the house of war and peace with others or within yourself.

THE 8TH HOUSE— The 8th house rules how we share ourselves or possessions with others. Through the energies of this house we learn to divide the pie in half. We learn about fairness...what's mine and what belongs to others. When we honestly feel that something is ours, then we need to be willing to die for it or for the principle it represents. Remember, the 8th house is the house of death and rebirth. If we are not willing to die for something then we should let it go without harboring feelings of feeling cheated. If we reflect to the polarity of the 2nd house where we show off our possessions on an external level then it is through the 8th house that we have to live with our own inner judgment and guilts according to how we have played the game of life. Remember, the value we print on our price tag reflects the value we acquire from the 2nd house while the 8th house demands that we live with our conscience as to whether or not that price tag is genuine or fake.

THE 9TH HOUSE—Materializing dreams through our system of faith and beliefs is the purpose of the 9th house of the horoscope. This task can be accomplished by learning to listen to the proper channel. These channels could be a good higher education, a person who knows the law, a spiritual teacher or person who truly knows whatever it is he/she is talking about. The best channel by far, however, through some form of meditation, to tune in to the Inner Self, our Guardian Angel or the God spark within. This house is often said to pertain to foreign connections and nothing is more foreign than the spiritual plane! No house in the horoscope is more content with dreams becoming reality or manifesting dreams. The difference between the 9th and the 12th houses is that in the 9th house you are in control of your dreams and vision. That's not a choice that you have in the 12th house. The 9th house ruler is the archetype of the centaurs, the man head with the horse's behind. Too many of us listen to the wrong end and wonder why everything in our life stinks .

THE 10TH HOUSE—The house shows us the ability to climb to some social status in the world. This energy inspires us to find our place on the planet. It's your life's calling representing what you want to have power over in the world. In today's society it does rule career but it rules more than just that. What about the person who does not have a career but stays at home and is the home maker? He or she has a 10th house, too. So the house poses the question to you, "If there were no such thing as a career what would you want the world to remember you by?" It could be summed up as the wording you'd like to see engraved on your tombstone. This is the place where the world measures your potential. It's the house of Capricorn and relates to status and power. Here you have to be a good mountain goat. You need to eye your goal at the top of the mountain and then climb up and never look back. Looking back will make you see all of your 4th house limitations and all the things that when wrong in the past. Looking back can implant the fear of heights into you which paralyzes you to stand in the same spot on the mountain, preventing your ever reaching the top.

THE 11TH HOUSE —The 11th house shows the ability to receive and be open to new situations. It is the house of socializing and when you socialize you meet all kinds of different people. Here you learn how close you want to be to others. Every friendship and acquaintance is different. You may have a different level of closeness with each one depending on how much you have to share and how much you are willing to open up. It is through the 11th house that you learn to deal with all kinds of people without feeling that you have to be totally committed. If a relationship or friendship compels you to be totally committed then it becomes a 7th house energy. Some people join clubs because the members of that club can do something to help their career or status. So rubbing shoulders with the proper people can make you feel important. But like the 2nd house, if your status price tag is overrated and not genuine you may not meet with the total success that this house can give you.

Remember, this house is the 2nd from the 10th which is the profit and money merited from your career.

THE 12TH HOUSE—The 12th house is the closet where you store all of your own inner fears and denial from others... and even from yourself. It is where you are escaping from confronting certain issues within yourself either by looking at it through rose colored glasses or by total denial accomplished through alcohol, drugs, sickness and even copping out with a nervous breakdown. At times some of your actions may be so unlike you that you may think that "the devil made you do it." The 12th house energy can be utilized positively by doing charity work and helping those who are in need. A lot of astrologers feel that this is the house of karma, a term loosely defined as owing something to the universe. Maybe this is why we hold the idea of inflicting pain on ourselves as penance and punishment and self sacrifice as such a noble ideal. When we are working from the 12th house our labors serve the highest purpose when they are performed to help mankind and for God's recognition and not as an expression of our own self pity.

The 12th house Shadows.

The 12th house from any house shows the things that a person does not want to face or accept about him or herself. This house is named as the house of self undoing and the house of escapism. As humans, we only try to escape things that we feel present great problems beyond our capacity to resolve. So we hide them in the subconscious of our minds believing that they actually disappeared. But we can only put so much trash in a closet and after awhile it starts spilling over.

12th house issues always come back to haunt you when you least expect it or when everything else is working against you. That's when the closet door opens up and everything falls out on top of your head! The issues never really go away because it affects decisions in the house that follows it. The 12th house from any house will carry the "shadow" issues that will influence the following house. The 12th from the first is the 12th house itself. The following house is the first. So your personality and identity are molded by your 12th house shadows.

The 1st house is the 12th from your 2nd house so your self worth will be greatly shaded by your belief in how you identify yourself. With a well energized 4th house you have a good understanding of your emotional needs and will know how to nurture others. Any problems within your early upbringing that caused you to bottle up your feelings could affect a self undoing attitude in your love relationships or with your children (the 4th house is the 12th house of the 5th house) . Remember, this is the house of marketing yourself.

If you are still hiding inside of yourself (your inner home the 4th house) no one will really see your talents and potentials. In one of his comedy routines, Bill Cosby used to say that his mother always told him *"When you grow up I hope that you have children just like you."* And he did! All the fears that you have learned

Bill Clinton Aug 19, 1946 8:51 AM CST
33N40 93W35

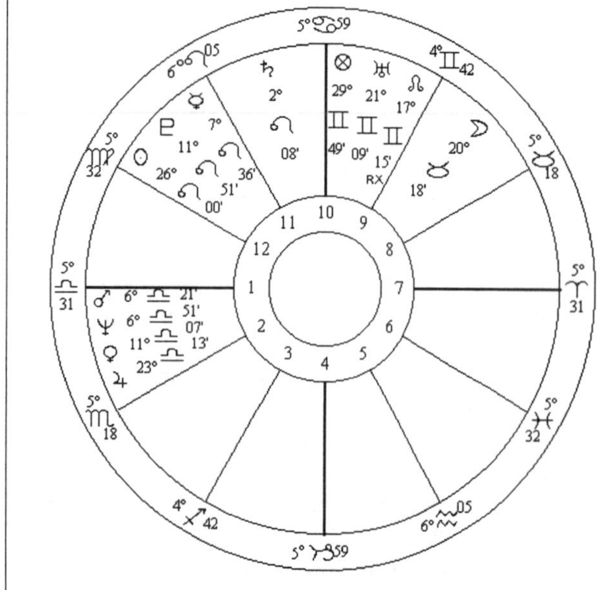

from your parents and the knowledge of how to bring up children, the 4th house, will be played out through your 5th house, the house of children. One of the most important examples on how your confusion of the 12th can effect the following house is seen as we look at the 9th which is the 12th house from the 10th.

The 10th house is the house of career or your aim in life. The 9th house is the house of blind faith to makes any dream come true. It is also the house of optimism and hopeful planning. Here your need to believe that these dreams will come true without a shadow of a doubt and that you will reach your full 10th house potential. Any doubt, fear or confusion in your the 9th house could stop you from accomplishing those dreams. The 9th house could be the way you viewed one of your parent's self undoing. It rules your philosophy of life, the rules and standards that you want to live by so if one of you parents did not agree with the philosophy your might have seen that as a limitation in them. Now let's put the derivative house system to work to understand the horoscope from a different perspective and a deeper level. For our illustration we will use the chart of President Bill Clinton.

Let's first see how the President views the communications between himself and his wife, Hillary. Hillary is ruled by the 7th house in the President's chart and communication is ruled by the 3rd house. His perception of how his wife communicates with him would then be the 3rd from the 7th or the 9th house. His 7th house shows us the way he views people with whom he has a close association and the 9th house also shows his view of the dialogues with these people.

Observe the sign on the 9th house cusp, any planets in the 9th house and the planet ruling the 9th house. You want to analyze all of the aspects to these points. The President has Gemini on the cusp which is ruled by Mercury and conjunct the planets Saturn and Pluto, sextiling his Ascendant and three out of the four planets in his 1st house. This shows a tremendous amount of energy in his communications with close associates. Uranus indicates an erratic, tense, irritable quality. He can be a good listener if the topic interests him or shut it off if there is no interest. The 9th house ruler, Mercury, conjuncting Saturn and Pluto shows careful, direct speech and a desire to control the conversation. The Pluto-Mercury could make him a little outspoken when he gets irritated and annoyed (Uranus). All the sextiles from the 1st house to Mercury brings his strong personality into his conversations.

The derived house system shows that the 9th house rules more that just communications with close associations. Being the 3rd from the 7th, the 9th house also rules the partner's advice or ideals and shows his views towards his spouse's brothers and sisters. It is also the 7th from the 3rd house, which could indicate partners of the President's siblings. Now you can see why we give the ownership of the in-laws to the 9th house. It is the 6th from the 4th - the commitment to his family and the 4th from the 6th - his parent's aunts and uncles' home or place of residence . This also rules his servants or co-worker's home. It is the 5th from the 5th house or his child's lover, children's talents and hobbies. The 9th house is the 12th from the 10th house so it's Clinton's own career secrets and undoing. It is the 11th the from the 11th house or his club or friend's goals, or his friend's friends and the 10th from the 12th house indicating his life position seen though his inner fears and limitations.

As you can see, a horoscope can be viewed in ways that go far beyond the normal house delineations. We can even go one step further. We can say that the 9th house rules his friend's son's or daughter's spouse. The 11th rules his friend, his friend's child (son or daughter) brings you to the 3rd house and the 9th house rules his friend's child's spouse. If we calculate it the formula looks like this: (11+5+7) = 23 -(2) = 21 -12 (a whole house circle) =9, the 9th house

Understanding how to work with derived houses and turning the chart is essential to accurate chart readings in horary astrology. In working with natal chart delineation or predictive work we need to use a lot more discrimination for this to be useful in helping your client. Experience is the only solution here.

But it is possible that any one or more of these areas can be triggered if a major progression, transit or direction hits the 9th house, planets within, or its ruler. I remember years ago when I was working with my chart with all types of predictive techniques and saw enough evidence that on a certain day in the month of May I could become really sick. My ascendant and my 6th house were both terribly afflicted. On the exact day that I predicted something for myself, my ex-wife's husband had a severe stroke and was on the critical list for months. My ascendant rules my ex-wife's husband as it is the 7th from the 7th and, of course, the 6th rules his health. The 6th house also rules my ex-wife's sorrows and hospitals.

Why had this happened to him and not to me? I don't know. The affliction was in my chart. This unexpected incident really played on my mind and made me realize that if you don't take care of yourself your life can be cut short. Although the energy did not hit me directly the incident left me with a major awareness involving my ascendant and my 6th house commitment to myself. This incident drove that point home. This is why it is hard to make predictions in astrology. When the stage is set you will have to experience it and learn its valuable lessons from it. But these lessons can come from all different areas. As you can see the horoscope seems to be our connection with the universe. From my chart you could see my ex-wife dealing with her unconscious patterns. In my own horoscope, I have Libra on the 6th house cusp and three planets in Libra in the 6th. One of these is the ruler of the 7th house. Does that show that my spouse, close associates and partners have unconscious fears (the 12th from the 7th) about relationships? Or, because I have my Sun and my chart ruler in the 6th does it mean that my total commitment to my work produces unconscious fears in relationships with my spouse, partners and close associations?

Before we return to more examples let's clarify a very controversial issue as to the houses that rule the mother and father. There has been a long standing dispute about which belongs to the 4th or the 10th house. Some astrologers say the 10th rules the father and some say that the 4th rules the father. I have seen thousands of client charts and after asking them particular questions about their parents I concluded that the 10th house rules the parent that has more influence in molding the native's goals or direction. It seems to represent the parent whose approval you sorely seek. The 4th house rules the parent with whom you can share and discuss your deepest emotions. If you are looking for both of the parents and consider them as a unit, then you would use to the 4th house. In horary, the standard rule is that the 10th house is the mother and the 4th house is the father. In my many years of doing horary I've had excellent success with these rulerships. The 4th house rules the family or the parent as a team. If we are looking for the house that rules the family's money or possessions then we would look to the 5th, which is the 2nd from the 4th. This house could also be your father's money.

If we take the 10th house to rule the mother then the 12th house would be your aunts or uncles from your mother's side of the family, the 12th being the your mother's sisters or brothers (the 3rd from the 10th). The same would hold true for the 6th house as it would be your aunts and uncles from your father's side of the family. If the 10th house is the mother then the 1st house rules the mother's father or the your maternal grandfather and the 7th house rules your mother's mother or your maternal grandmother. Keeping the same frame of rulerships, the 7th house rules your paternal grandfather and the first rules your paternal grandmother on your father side of the family.

Now you could expand on your family relations. The 3rd and 9th houses rule your great aunts and uncles. The 7th is your mother's mother or your grandmother and the 3rd house from there being the 9th is your grandmother's sisters and brothers. Calculate as (10+10+3) = 23 -(2) =21-12 = 9. The 3rd house holds true for the father's side of the family.

Now, how about your cousins? We already have a head start on this from the example above. Your mother is ruled by the 10th so her brothers and sisters are in the 12th house (the 3rd from the 10th). and finally their children are ruled by the 5th from the 12th. Calculates as ((10+3+5) -2 =16 -12 = 4). Therefore the 4th rules your cousins on your mother's side of the family. Isn't this fun!

Now let's go back to President Clinton's chart and see how he communicates with his father (actually his step-father, as his father died before he was born). In this instance I will use the 10th house as the ruler of the father (the most influential parent) and the 3rd from the 10th is the 12th house. In his 10th we find Saturn and Mercury. The conjunction between these two planets describes the way he sees his father. His perception might be that his father was hard to understand and very focused in his ideas. Mercury also rules his 12th so it brings that conjunction into his communications.

with his father. This shows that their conversations were more practical and focused on business matters than on small talk.

Remember, that this application does not describe the way his father actually communicated but rather it shows how he perceived his father communicating with him or the way that he wanted to communicate with his father. The President was pushing out this energy to create this type of communication with his father. His father could have been the easiest person for others to talk to about anything at all but this chart shows that Clinton had lessons to learn in talking with his superiors.. The 10th house not only rules one of the parents but it also rules anyone who has superiority over him. The lesson that he learned from the communication with his father as a youngster either helped or hurt him in the way he communicates today with his superiors. This theory is clearly shown in a family environment where one kid has difficulty talking to the father and the other sibling has no problem at all. It's the same father but two different views. If you were to examine the charts of the two children you would easily see why.

Now, let's examine the communication with his daughter, Chelsea. His daughter is ruled by his 5th house and communication with her is the 7th house (the 3rd from the 5th). The planet Mars rules the 7th house and it is receiving a sextile from Saturn, Mercury and Pluto. This shows good, direct positive speech with Chelsea. The Mars and Venus conjunction in his 1st house brings a personal pleasure and satisfaction with their communication. The conjunction of Mars and Neptune can be viewed as bringing a deeper, spiritual understand or awareness as this planetary combination is a good subconscious transmitter. The negative side of this aspect can carry with it misunderstandings, confusion and even fibbing. A conjunction can bring out both sides of the energy. This is where you have to analyze the whole situation before coming to conclusion in reading a horoscope. Here we have four strong positive aspects to Mars and one harmful aspect. Overall, it is safe to say that he is very good in communicating with his daughter, though I am sure that the Mars-Neptune will play out its negative side at some time. Let's face it, nobody is perfect! Using this approach we would also want to look at his daughter's chart to see how she approaches the communications with her dad. Remember, the President's chart indicates how he feels he should communicate with his daughter.

Let's look at President Clinton's chart again and try to apply what we have learned. We'll look at some of his aspects and see how it applies in his life. First, let's take the important aspect of the Mars-Neptune conjunction on his ascendant in his 1st house. The planet Mars has to initiate something. It shows a physical drive along with the things for which he will fight. Neptune represents misinformation or misunderstandings; things are not quite in the plane of reality. In a negative view, Mars-Neptune can feel like driving blindfolded on the highway 90 miles an hour! On a positive side this could bring out the sensitive or psychic nature of a person which can certainly help to keep him on the right road. This indicates that some of his actions could take place without his knowing all of the facts or some of his action could cause his own self undoing. In the President's chart Mars rules his house of relationships or dealings with close associates and Neptune rules his house of commitment and daily priorities. The 6th house is the 12th from his 7th house so we may conclude that he may deal with relationships and partnerships rather blindly, without considering all the consequences and his actions will always come back to haunt him later. Skeletons from his past behaviors with others will sneak out of the closet. It is also a good indicator that he may be a poor judge of others. The motto of the 12th house is "what goes around, comes around." If he utilized this energy in a positive way the 12th house would give him strong intuition and deeper inner understanding of others. Seeing that this aspect between these two planets is a conjunction he would be manifesting this force both ways.

Example 1:

This same principle can be applied to the remainder of the houses in Clinton's chart. The 7th house could be his father's career goals in life (the 10th from his 10th and the 6th house rules his father's 9th house faith and belief system (the 9th from his 10th). Bear in mind that this does not describe the way his father utilized his dreams in his career but it does describe how the President witnesses his father utilizing his dreams in his career. He thought that his father was a bit unclear with his career desires even to point where his actions were working against his success. One thing that you have to bear in mind when working with derived houses is to keep the same theme. Notice that in this example with Clinton's father, I derived both of the houses involved from the same house, the 10th house, because the 10th house rules his father.

Example 2:

Here's an example of another way of working with derived houses but as you will see after reading the example it is too confusing and contorted as its scope is too wide. You can say that Mars rules Clinton's 7th house or his father's career and Neptune rules his wife (the 12th house). Now try to delineate the wife's fears and limitations ruled by Neptune in regard to his father's career ruled by the planet Mars. Crossing themes with derived houses (the above example) will always cause confusion and lose much of the integrity of the value of working with derived houses. By keeping the same theme clearly intact your delineation will have much more value and accuracy, as was demonstrated in example 1. If you were using horary astrology you could easily work with both examples and achieve good results. The approach we use in horary is totally different from the application of derived houses in the natal chart. For example, if we ask the question "Will my niece get along with my friend's spouse"? and leap frog around the houses we will end up having to compare the 7th house with the 5th house. This is easy and accurate to do in a horary chart, but in a natal chart the energy would be too remote from you to make enough sense out of the entire question. ✸

CHAPTER QUESTIONS

All of these questions are based on President Clinton's natal horoscope.

1) Which house will tell you how the President sees his daughter's friends?

2) Which house shows how the President identifies with his daughter's limitations in her love relationships?

3) Which house rules his brother's father in law's boss's club?

4) Would you say that the President's aspect of Sun square Moon has something to do with how his wife's upbringing has an effect on the way that she markets herself and the way she gives in a love relationship? Why or why not?

5) Look at Clinton's Mercury sextile Mars. Mars rules his brother's or sister's children (the 5th from the 3rd house) . Neptune rules his friend's partners. Will Mars and Neptune indicate how the President views his friend's partner with his nieces and nephews?

Recommended Further Reading:

Planets in Houses by Robert Pelletier

Simplified Horary Astrology by Ivy M. Goldstein-Jacobson

The Concept Dictionary by Michael Munkasey

The Rulership Book by Rex E. Bills

Cycles

by Mary Downing

Astrology has returned – ironically, as it were, to a cycic universe-view.

All planetary motion was once considered not just "cyclic" but clock-gear wheels within wheels. The heavens were revolving spheres enclosing the stationary Earth like some cosmic Russian egg. But Copernicus put Terra in her proper place, third in line circling Sol, and Kepler stretched the spheres into ellipsoids. European astrologers became more self-absorbed and explored the unique individuality of their clients while de-emphasizing the commonality of mass experience. In short we tried to show very hard that each person was unique and possessed of free will. We developed a skittishness about anything that even faintly suggested a "fated" environment. Cycles are going to happen. They *are* fated. It isn't whether we will experience them, but *how*. To paraphrase Shakespeare, the problem is not in the "stars," but in ourselves for being influenced by them.

Cycles belong to that larger world. They are our link with both our "mother-nature" and our universal siblings on the planet. We all suffer them; some at specific ages as rights of passage, some on a mundane generational level. They are nature itself, a frame in which we exist.

A diurnal cycle is Sunrise to Sunrise, and a lunation is New Moon to New Moon. We commonly consider the yearly solar cycle to begin with the vernal equinox. Each planet has a specific time and path to complete its circuit of the Sun that constitutes its orbital cycle. Any element of this orbit may be used as a beginning measurement, and there may be very specific characteristics to these markers or phases — check"down hill"in the sidebar.

Two-planet cycles are timed from their mutual conjunction. These are called *synodic cycles.* Perhaps the best known is the "mutation cycle" of Jupiter-Saturn conjunctions. We are currently experiencing a Uranus-Neptune synod that last occured in 1822. The Uranus-Neptune has been used by the French astrologer, André Barbault, to predict the rise and fall of collectivism in Europe. He predicted the fall of communism in our time as early as the 1960s.

Before we discuss specific cycles, we must establish zodiacs

Western astrologers are mostly tropical. Our longitudinal measurement for Sun, Moon and planets is calibrated from the position of the Sun at the vernal equinox. In short, the first day of spring is the first degree of Aries. The alternative system is sidereal. The tropical and sidereal zodiacs no longer correspond; indeed the tropical 0° Aries is now approximately 4° of Pisces and moving backwards at the rate of 1° every 72 years. Somewhere between now and 2400 it will move into Aquarius. The exact position of sidereal 0° Aries is obviously a matter of great concern, and hotly debated among siderealists.

What are cycles?

• ***They are measurements of time*** — the simple "stopwatch." Point A around and return to Point A again.

• ***They are points of relationship between other elements.*** Planet A conjunct planet B, both around and conjunct again.

• ***They are phases that may have profoundly different characteristics:*** Going *up* the hill is a phase of the same cycle that contains going *down* the hill. "Up-hill" is the natural dissipation of the stored "down-hill" momentum. It's a closed cyclic loop. *If you're pedaling a bike, that's another story.*

Precession is obviously itself a "cycle," the grand-daddy of them all, *circa* 26,000 years. It takes approximately 2100 years for each "age," which roughly corresponds to precession through a tropical sign. We are currently in the Piscean Age, and the "dawning" of the Age of Aquarius. The heroic Age of Aries, when the zodiacs agreed, was the zenith of ancient Greece and Rome. The birth of Christ roughly corresponds to the dawn of the Piscean Age. Coincidentally, early Christians used a "fish" symbol for identification, and faith in assorted universal economic and metaphysical worldviews has been the motivating dynamic throughout this era.

Cycles operate in layers, longest to back and shortest to front. Our natural life expectancy is way less than half a Neptune or Pluto cycle; one single Uranus cycle, plus or minus three Saturn returns; seven Jupiters; 40 Mars; and 80 each Sun, Venus, and Mercury. We may never experience Neptune or Pluto's embrace (lucky us), or we may have Neptune-Uranus parked on our personal points for years. This is a generational deficit that may be experienced by certain Sun-signs and not by others. In fact our entire conceit of what makes a Capricorn *Capricornian* may be warped in the next generation by memories of the current Uranus-Neptune effect. Is the Scorpio (with Pluto-conjunct-Sun) more an eagle and less a stinger? Pluto in Scorpio — actually inside Neptune's orbit — should be somehow "extreme" since it's at the innermost limit; its top-of-the hill.

A Cycle Primer: Solar cycles: day and year

Diurnal — Every day each degree of the zodiac rises, culminates, and sets. This is called *Rapt Motion.* The Sun and planets are figuratively "carried away" by the heavens. Transiting planets follow the solar path from eastern Sunrise-ascent to mid-day zenith, to western Sunset-descent, midnight's nadir, and return. Each planet rises and sets. The fast traveling Moon "chases" the Sunrise, rising later each night until it vanishes just before dawn with the approaching New Moon. At some point, every day, our own Jupiters and Saturns will cross the midheaven.

Annual — Each day "noon," the highest reach of the Sun, occurs four minutes later than the day before. As the Sun passes from vernal equinox to summer solstice, thence to autumnal equinox and winter solstice, it marks the major corners of the yearly Earth-Sun cycle. If we attach natal planetary positions to a yearly wheel, we will see them carried east to west throughout the year. So our natal Sun, Moon, and planets also rise, culminate, and set with the seasonal flow.

While the civil year begins with January 1, the solar year begins with 0° Aries. This is the *vernal equinox,* the date when the Earth is aligned in such a way that the noon Sun is directly over the equator. As a result, the night and day portions are of equal length — thus *Latin: equi* (equal) *nox* (night).

The Earth is tilted 23° to the plane of the ecliptic. Think of the ecliptic as a flat platter running through the center of Earth from the center of the Sun. The Earth's north pole is always tilted 23° north-west. Twice during its orbit around the Sun (our year), the Earth crosses the ecliptic plane traveling north-south. When it does, the Earth's equator and the ecliptic plane align, and we have the vernal and autumnal equinox. These are the *nodes* — intersecting points — of the "up-down" dimension of the Earth-Sun orbit.

From an "in-out" perspective , the Earth is its closest to the Sun (south — *perihelion*) at the *Tropic of Capricorn;* and its farthest (north — *aphelion*) at the *Tropic of Cancer.* From our Earth-bound viewpoint, the Sun seems to stop its poleward journey and begin a retreat towards the equator. It "stands still," Latin: *sol* (Sun) *stice* (stand-still).

This process moves backwards ever so slightly , one degree every 72 years, so that the stars rising before the Sun at the equinox have steadily shifted over millennia. Now the early degrees of the constellation Pisces preceed the Sun, and soon the constellation Aquarius will "dawn" when the Sun rises on the first day of tropical Aries. The process is called the *Precession of the equinox.* The difference between Tropical 0° Aries and sidereal (constellational) 0° Aries is commonly referred to as the *ayanamsha*, after the vedic astrological term. Unfortunately constellations are not a neat 30° in length, so the exact position of sidereal 0° Aries is fuzzy. There are several *ayanamsha* is use, and they of course must be continually updated to incorporate precession.

The Sun also exhibits a cyclic pattern of "spots" and solar-flares. These average an almost 12-year period that would suggest a Jupiter-Sun interaction.

How do we use this?

Application:

• In *Horary, Event* and *Elections,* planetary potency is partly determined by house, quadrant, and the proximity to angles. Angles are a function of the *diurnal cycle.*

• In *Mundane* practice, charts are commonly set for both the *equinox* and *solstice* to predict the quarter year following. When a mundane astrologers discuss an "ingress" chart, they are normally referring to the Sun's entry into Aries — the beginning of the yearly cycle.

• *Uranian* and *Cosmobiology* practitioners use the *0° Aries* position as a "connecting point" between an individual and the larger society. Here *Aries* represents the "shared experience" of the yearly rythm.

• Any chart, tropical or sidereal, can be *"precessed,"* and *solar returns* commonly are. Very long-lived institutions — countries, cities, ruling-families — survive common transits, but may have their charts "precessed" to conjunct a fixed star. *(Lilly predicted the plague and fire of London by precessing Mars of that city's founding-chart to the fixed-star El Nath, and wound up in court for his troubles.)*

• Gauquelin's research demonstrated that *planets rising and slightly past the MC* were particularly related to "noteworthy" occupational achievement.

• Judith Hill's redheads-research showed statistically significant numbers to have Mars (a planet connected with the color red) in the first house.

• *Diurnal charts* are used to predict periods during the year when specific configurations in a natal chart are exceptionally active by their natural diurnal revolution to angles or other powerful mundane positions.

The natal planetary longitude is retained, as is the time and place of birth. However the house cusps are recalculated for progressive dates, thereby rotating the natal planets totally throughout the houses during a year. A 4th-house Jupiter will "rise" 90 days or so later, and a 12th-house Mars finally reaches the midheaven in the same period. The theory is that when a planet is being activated by its yearly transit over an angle it is more visible to the wide world and therefore more important in day-to-day affairs.

Another *Diurnal* is the application of a natal chart to an *Event*, *Horary*, or *Election*. The natal planets are entered "outside" as transits would be to a natal chart. Where the natal planets are (by house) is important. *Example:* Your boss is announcing lay-offs 8:00 AM Tuesday, and your Saturn is rising. *Resumé anyone?*

Planetary Cycles

Simple cycles: There are several ways to calculate cycles. We will take the most obvious first:

Sun – Day:
• *a sidereal day* — The passage of one star over the meridian — is 23h 56mi (Notice the four minute deficit.)

• *a solar day* — the passage of the center of the Sun over the meridian — is 24 hours.

• *a lunar day* — the passage of the Moon's center over the meridian — 24h 50 m.

Earth: revolution around the Sun is an *Earth-year–* 365.25 days. The solar cycle is really the Earth orbit around the Sun, which itself orbits the galactic center at 27° Sagittarius. The Earth's satellite, Luna, dances in-and-out. We think of the Moon as spiraling through space around us as we whiz around the Sun, but in fact it snakes first to the inside (New Moon) then to the outside (Full Moon) as we make a mutual solar orbit.

Moon: *sidereal* revolution: 27.32 days (Earth and Moon in line with same fixed star);and *synodic* revolution: 29.53 (New Moon to New Moon)

There are several other important lunar cycles we will address later in this article.

Lunar Phases: The names given to the lunar phases are applicable to Mercury and Venus as well. You might consider the implications of the Sun, Moon, Earth interaction.

They are—

New (Dark to Crescent) 0° to 45– Moon on line *inside* between Earth and Sun traveling "back" while Earth travels "forward."

Crescent (Quarter sliver to half-lit) 45° to 90°– Moon begins its pass *behind* the Earth.

First Quarter (Half-lit to 3/4) 90° to 135°–At Quarter, Moon is *behind* the Earth and beginning to travel "forward" to the outside.

Gibbous (3/4 to Full) 135° to 180°– Moon is on the *outside*, advancing, approaching the Sun-Earth line.

Full 180° to 225°– Moon is at the Earth-Sun line, *outside and advancing.*

Disseminating (3/4 decreasing to half-lit) -225° to 270°– Moon is *ahead* of the Earth and approaching its maximum advance.

Third Quarter – (Half-lit to last sliver) 270° to

315°– Moon *crosses path of Earth's orbit*, and begins circling inward between Earth and Sun.

Balsamic- (Dark of Moon) 315° to 0°– Moon approaches Earth-Sun line on inside traveling backward.

We never see Mercury more than 28° from the Sun, and when we can observe it, it is as either the Morning or the Evening Star. For an Earth-bound observer, Mercury has a yearly cycle with the Sun, as does the other inner planet, Venus.

Venus: *sidereal* 225 days (Venus conjunct a fixed star) *synodic* 584 days (Venus conjunct Earth in line with the Sun, "Inferior conjunction")

We experience Venus as part of a Mercury-Sun-Venus triumvirate. Venus, like Mercury and the Moon, has phases. When either of the inner planets crosses the imaginary line connecting the Earth to the Sun — on the same side as the Earth — it is in *inferior conjunction.* We then see it in a "New Moon" phase.

When it is on the opposite side of the Sun, it is in *superior conjunction,* and we see it in "Full Moon" phase. Venus alternates with Mercury as morning or evening star. Another name for Venus was Lucifer — Latin for bearer of light — and it "falls" from its morning-star position as it retrogrades to conjunct the Sun; falls into the flames as it were.

Mars: *sidereal:* 687 days (Mars conjunct a fixed star) *synodic:* 780 days (Mars conjunct Earth in line with the Sun)

Note: When a planet is "conjunct the Sun" in the ephemeris, it is on the *opposite* side of the solar system from Earth. It is *conjunct Earth* (on the same side of the Sun as Earth) when it is in *opposition* to the Sun. *Planets will always be closest to Earth when they are in opposition to the Sun.*

Jupiter: *sidereal:* 11.86 years, *synodic:* 398.9 days.

Saturn: *sidereal:* 29.46 years, *synodic:* 378 days

Uranus: *sidereal* 84.0 years, *synodic:* 369.7 days

Neptune: *sidereal* 164.8 years, *synodic* 367.5 days.

Pluto: *sidereal* 248 years, *synodic* 366.7 days.

Pluto has an exceptionally eccentric orbit. It's "quarter" periods are of extraordinary variation. If we use a

Cycles on a personal level:

The Saturn "return" is an astrologer's yardstick for coming of age. Each Saturn square equals a rough seven years. *Think of the simple correlation:*

0 to 7 years: Preschool childhood. Before seven a child is not considered morally responsible for his actions.

7-14: Prepubescent childhood, learning years.

14-21: Puberty and developing sexual roles, familial independence.

21-28: Establishment of own household . First Saturn return.

The second Saturn cycle mirrors the first. In the first seven years we learn our place in the home. In the second cycle we become part of the community.

28-35: Community involvement, career development

35-42: Career and community "arrival." The worker achieves "master" status.

42-49: The mid-life crisis, a second "puberty" where self-doubt can again alienate the native from family.

49-56: Worker as teacher. Establishment of a second family or career . Preparing for the next generation.

Note: In a primitive society few people live past 35-42. Even in our technological and medically sophisticated world, this is the "muscle" limit. From here on skill and experience must compensate for diminished physical capacity.

PLANETS

Mercury: *sidereal:* 88 days, *synodic:* 116 days. (Mercury conjunct Earth in line with the Sun, "Inferior conjunction")

convenient entry into a fixed sign as a "quarter" indicator we have

1. Scorpio to Aquarius, 39 years
2. Leo to Scorpio, 47 years
3. Taurus to Leo, 87 years, and
4. Aquarius to Taurus, 75 years.

You don't normally find a Full Moon phase more than twice the length that of the New! Taurus, Gemini, and Cancer natives suffer more than double the Pluto attention of Scorpio, Sagittarius, and Capricorn.

Other personal Saturn cycles

Saturn-Sun contacts create identity crisis. The native seeks to define himself in view of his perceived goals and history in achieving them. Problems emerge, attain sharp definition, and are dealt with.

Saturn to the angles (ASC, MC) prompts us to change the circumstances of our life. It particularly gives us the opportunity – and possibly the inclination – to change jobs, place of residence and marriage partners. Grant Lewi developed a schema that might be helpful —

Saturn to ASC– *Begin a new career.* First seven years spent in learning and skills development. (Also a common – and symbolically surprising – marriage indicator. One is taking one's status, or lack of it, seriously.)

Saturn to IC – *Emergence as a journeyman,* capable of practicing career without supervision. (Analogous to "leaving the nest.")

Saturn to DSC – *Emerging into the community as a spokesman, master.* Accepting responsibility. (Not surprisingly – in this instance– connected with marriage difficulties. Independence, competence and self-reliance are stressed.)

Saturn to MC – *A pay-ofj jor accumulated expertise,* wisdom. Becoming a teacher to a new generation. (A "fall from grace" for the unready.)

Mundane Cycles

I strongly recommend you obtain and read Nicholas Devore's *Encyclopedia of Astrology.* The "Cycles" entry was submitted by the late Charles Jayne, and discusses the intriguing interlocking nature of our solar "gears."

Unfortunately there are simply too many mundane cycles, and to properly present them to a student would require considerable introduction. Let me simply mention a few, hopefully whet your appetite, and introduce the intriguing realm of nodes and perihelia.

The Jupiter-Saturn mutation cycle — 19.859 years. Often called the great chronocrators because of their generational sweep. The cycle, which is close in time to the Moon's nodal cycle, groups in threes. Each one occurs 123° in advance of its predecessor. After three it returns to where it began advancing only 8.93°. After 40 conjunctions (794.37 years) it returns to within 0.93° of its starting point! It has been connected with ecconomic cycles (the Kondratieff Wave), "social-lag," civil unrest in China between 230 BC. and AD1930, and the death in office of US Presidents.

The Saros Cycle: Originally a Chaldean cycle of 3,600 years, which is coincidental with a recurrent cycle of 21 Neptune-Uranus conjunctions that returns to -6° from its starting place. Obvously the Chaldeans were unfamiliar with invisible planets beyond the orbit of Saturn.

In the present day, a Saros cycle (or series) is a lunar cycle of 223 lunations; or 18 years, 11 1/3 days. Eclipses then reoccur in the same sequence, but at a location approximately 120° west of the previous cycle. They were used to predict eclipses, and each eclipse is counted as part of 1/19 specific series. There could be problems on what consituted a real eclipse, however. Before computers and ephemerides, this was the way it was done – and by the Chaldeans in cuneiform on clay tablets.

Metonic Cycle: A recurrent 19 year New Moon cycle (happens on the same day), Discovered in the 5th century BC by an Athenian named Meton.

OTHER FRAMES OF REFERENCE

Round and round, up and down

How do we measure a cycle? We can do it in longitude by marking a position such as the conjunction with a fixed star. That is a *sidereal* cycle. We can combine two planets and wait for the combination to reoccur. That is a *synodic* cycle. We can also measure "Up" and "Down."

Planetary Nodes and other orbital mysteries.

A "node" is the place where satellite orbital planes cross each other. The primary body is the orbital attracting mass, in our case Sol. Everything goes around in elliptical orbits. Sol, with its planetary complement is headed toward the solar apex at 1°54" of Capricorn, and the entire galaxy is moving toward the galactic center at 27° Sagittarius. The South or descending nodes and aphelions (positions furthest from the Sun) are also arrayed in that direction. We are examining the points of interaction of planets and the plane of the Earth's orbit around the Sun. The Sun also has its own reference plane in its alignment to the center of the galaxy.

As we said before, think of an oblong platter — blunt end in, with the Sun as a focus. It is on a lazy-susan orbiting the galactic center. That lazy-susan is the galactic plane. The platter, (which isn't quite level) is the Earth' s orbital plane. So when we discuss a planet's latitude and nodes, we are measuring current interactions with Earth's orbital plane. With the exception of Pluto, all the planets describe very flat orbits with very little deviation from Earth or each other. But notice, however, that Earth's orbit is the reference. These nodes are points of interaction between the Earth's and other planets' orbits in their mutual dance around Sol, just as the lunar nodes are the intersection of the Moon's circum-Earth orbit with Earth's circum-Sun orbit.

If we wanted to – we could expand this to include all planetary orbits intersecting all others (not just Earth's ecliptic). Michael Erlewine in his *Interface Nodes* did just that. We're examining Earth's plane; why not examine the Sun's plane vis-a-vis the Galactic Center? Why not, indeed?

Ecliptic planetary nodes, perihelion, aphelion and helio positions are relegated to the second-tier specialty astrological studies. It isn't because they have no effect on us – they very definitely do. Nelson used such considerations to predict the solar flares that bombard Earth with measurable radiation. He described one "Earthside effect" to me in which high tension electric feeders in Scandinavia burst into flame. Anything that can create that flamboyant a result beats "synchronicity" hands down. What we are examining here can produce palpable geophysical phenomena. One must assume there are interesting mass psychological effects as well.

We really do not know the mechanism by which planetary orbits affect events on Earth. Nicholas Devore espoused gravity; Carl Payne Toby postulated magnetic attraction; and Johndro outlined an electro-magnetic field concept. Nelson, who was a radio propagation engineer, demonstrated that solar flares were related to planetary position heliocentrically by longitude. He also opined that the planets were more potent in nodal positions. If we consider activity on the solar surface to have properties analogous to Earth tidal action, we can easily imagine that planetary nodes and aphelion-perihelion transits could *actually* – not symbolically –affect gravity, magnetic attraction and whatever electro-magnetic fields might be involved (to say nothing of solar wind, radiation, and ozone layers.) Since I'm wading in waters that will quickly be over my technical head, I'll proceed to something for which I'm better qualified.

We consistently limit ourselves to geocentric longitude with little attention to the planets' "personal" cycles. Since the orbits are elliptical, they cycle from "closest – *perihelion* to furthest – *aphelion*" They are fastest when close and slowest when afar. All of which is academic unless we have a mechanism for demonstrating some useful Earthly response.

Stock market data is a bellwether of mass activity and provides a time-line stretching from the late 1700s to the present day. It is very easy to obtain, it is eminently cyclical, and it responds to human panic and euphoria. *What more could you want?* If you get handy applying it, it even pays for itself. If you have an interest in Sunspots, weather, earthquakes or plankton counts these are also available; and any narrow-focus historical research is also an option.

What we are studying?

Celestial reference systems and nomenclature

Helio: *Perihelion, Aphelion.* In-out measurement.

All of the planets have elliptical orbits. When they are closest and fastest they are at *perihelion.* When they are furthest and slowest they are at *aphelion.*

Heliocentric longitude: Measurement around the Zodiac; where the planets are as viewed from the Sun.

From Saturn outward the position is largely the same as geocentric. The inner planets vary considerably.

Heliocentric nodes: intersect position The place where any planet's orbit intersects the plane of the ecliptic. (The ecliptic is the plane of Earth's orbit). Nodes are designated North (ascending) and South (descending). Of course up and down or north and south are arbitrary in a galactic reference. With the exception of Pluto, all of the orbits vary in tilt only a few degrees.

Latitude: up and down measurement The distance a planet is above or below the ecliptic. When a planet is at 0° latitude it is at a node. When it is at maximum north or south latitude, however, it is not at ap/perihelion.

Geocentric: *Geocentric longitude:* measurement around the Zodiac, as seen from Earth perspective. Because of unequal orbits we see other planets as having apparent retrograde periods. We also see Venus and Mercury from Earthside as having much longer "years" than their actual orbital periods.

Nodes:

a. Lunar Nodes: Where the Moon crosses the ecliptic. Since the Moon is an Earth satellite, it can only have geocentric longitude. Lunar nodes move backward in a 19 year cycle. When a New or Full Moon occurs on the ecliptic, it is an eclipse. The Earth, Moon and Sun line up so that one blocks out the view of – or the light shed on – the other.

b: *Planetary Nodes* can be expressed in either helio or geocentric longitude (by correcting for Earth's orbit). Check which version your data source uses. Try to correct the positions for the date of the event. *A simple ballpark method of converting from Helio to Geo position:* Determine when a planet is conjunct its helio node. Using a geocentric ephemeris, see what its geocentric longitude is at the time of conjunction with that helio node. This is the approximate geocentric node. The outer planets are fairly consistent in either notation.

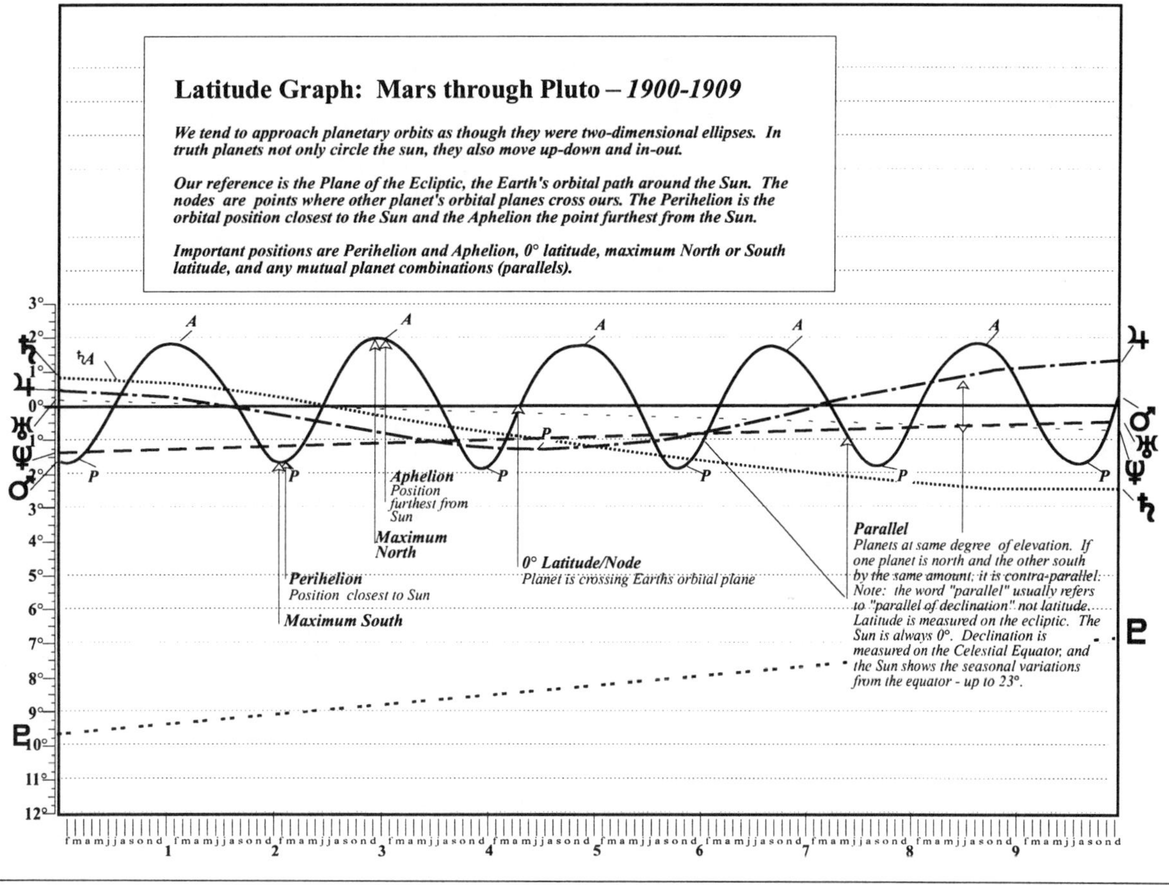

A little heresy

You may never need exact nodal or perihelion positions, at least for outer planet work. Indeed perihelia wobble and nodes creep. The only reliable data would be computer generated. If you begin your examination of any cyclic phenomenon with too tight a focus you'll impair your ability to judge if there is any global correlation. Remember you are judging interaction of ellipsoidal orbits that may have a maximum elevation of 2 or 3°'s from each other. Outer planets can ride these intersecting nodal positions for a month. Is it really logical to limit the influence of Pluto-perihelia to one day when it has an orbit of 200+ years?

A note on nodes and perihelia

They are a bit difficult to extract from astronomical reference texts. Both nodes and perihelion wobble slightly. Attached are the mean perihelion and node positions which are subject to precession of approximately 1° per century. Unfortunately the only date-corrected source is ACS *Heliocentric Ephemeris of the Twentieth Century,* and it has a computer glitch in the outer planet perihelion positions that renders – *that specific data only* – unreliable.

Sources

Zipporah Dobyns, *Node Book* (both helio and geo-corrected listings)

Michael Erlewine, *Astrophysical Directions* (nodes and perihelia, including major asteroids); *Intersect Nodes* (planet to planet, galactic plane, etc.)

Nicholas Devore, *Encyclopedia of Astrology* (planetary helio nodes)

Charles Jayne, *A New Dimension* (helio nodes)

The CCRS program lists helio and geo nodes, but converts perihelia to geo longitude -which is unfortunate. Latitude is available from most ephemerides. The frustrating thing about this is that you can get better information from *The Old Farmer's Almanac* than from astrological sources. *Raphael's* ephemerides carry a "phenomena" page.

Mean Heliocentric North Node Positions (epoch AD 2000) & Perihelion (epoch AD 1950)

planet	*Ascending node*	*mean perihelion*	*last conjution*
Mercury	18 Tau 15	16 Gem 41	*Three times a year*
Venus	16 Gem 40	10 Leo 52	*Yearly*
Earth	—	12 Can 04	Jan. 4 *yearly*, aphelion July 4
Mars	19 Tau 33	5 Pis 08	4/3/1994 (aphelion 4/25/1993
Jupiter	10 Can 29	13 Ari 31	7/10/1987
Saturn	23 Can 38	2 Can 04	1/08/1974
Uranus	13 Gem 59	19 Vir 05	5/22/1966
Neptune	11 Leo 48	14 Tau 11	7/08/1886 (aphelion 7/17/1959)
Pluto	20 Can 17	15 Sco 01	9/04/1989

Interpreting nodes, latitudes and perihelion:

Unfortunately nodal interpretive material plunges from the galactic plane into the human psyche without ever examining objective reality in passage. As an industry we have an unfortunate compulsion to exclusively examine individual emotional and socio-religious belly-buttons. Since internal satori are notoriously difficult to codify, the interpretive material on nodes abounds in tortured keywords and very abstract concepts which – valid as they might be – are guaranteed to frighten away neophytes. I would not recommend you go that route in your researches. Pick something simple and external and hammer away at it until the shell breaks and you can extract some kernel of understanding. Then see if you can repeat the process.

Example: I first began applying helio nodes in the late '60's. Neptune was transiting a Mars/Uranus midpoint on the chart of New York City when Mars ascended its helio node. There were three unrelated gas main explosions in as many days, one sending flames five stories high. Gas main explosions are fairly rare occurrences. Mars-Uranus-Neptune can certainly be a gas explosion, but three of them ?

When Mars is at its nodes or peri/aphelion, what incendiary singularities do you find in the news? What happens on the market? Will the same thing (or similar) happen at 90° or 45° aspects thereto? Is there a definable cycle that corresponds to Mars-node-perihelion? If you find yourself particularly testy, that's also worth noting; and if fellow motorists are treating your car as though it had a bullseye painted on it, I'd recommend you take note as well.

There have been several attempts to digest this material for natal charts. Zipporah Dobyns' *Node Book* and *Distance Values* are two attempts, but they relate to the geocentric positions not helio. Rinehold Ebertin also attacked distance values and developed a "kernel" diagram which never caught on, and the Ebertin Verlag offers a graphic declination ephemeris - which is also obtainable in Astrolabe's Time Graphs 2 program. Declinations were a mainstay of 19th century interpretation and still are used in more traditional practice. The operating conceit was that if planets had the same north or south declination they were *parallel,* and must be interpreted like a conjunction. If they had equal separation but one was north and the other south (contraparallel) they must be acting like an opposition. Planets are certainly more "conjunct" if they are also parallel. In fact they are "occulted"—the inner planet blocks view of the outer. It would be analogous to an eclipse. There are demonstrable economic cycles that correspond with planets at maximum north or south, and 0° declination.

Problems in using inner planet geocentric nodes:

If you use geocentric planetary nodes you can have Mercury's North and South Nodes conjunct each other, which is hardly demonstrative of orbital equilibrium. Since helio Mercury, Venus and Mars can differ wildly from geocentric position, It's a mental stretch to use their heliocentric nodes in geocentric charts. T. Patrick Davis, Edith Custer, and others in the modern helio revival use both helio and geo planetary positions with standard house cusps, which is one possible approach. However, the outer planets are fairly consistent in both frames of reference and can be interchanged, if one remembers that the helio nodes drift. Give some orb!

Charles Jayne's approach in *A New Dimension* best fits what these positions really are. He expanded on the concept of conjunctions or occultations. Unfortunately he invented a new nomenclature that confuses rather than enhances his exposition and all his examples (in that paper) are of a social nature.

Planetary nodes haven't been commonly used simply because there is no simple graphing mechanism to show them for what they really are, orbital phases. With the 12-house chart, 90° dial, and graphic ephemeris we have simple straightforward diagrams that present longitude positions. With the node-latitude-perihelion data we are introducing a three dimensional orientation that hasn't yet been visually presented in a digestible way. What *has* been assimilated, "declinations", can be shown to have real-world cyclic correspondence. Nodes are an interactive point between orbiting bodies. It is this *interactive* quality and their cyclic nature that makes them potentially very useful and with practical applications.

Astrologers experience:

Michael Munkasey remarked to me that the data-base he used of famous people in developing his midpoint weighting system was overloaded with planets on nod-

Current popular uses:

Following are snippets of natal chart usage (from Zipporah Dobyns, *The Node Book*). All reference is to geocentric positions. This book also offers a geocentric nodal ephemeris, covers lunar node interpretation, and offers many case studies. It does not cover perihelion-aphelion positions. As you can see, the descriptions are exactly what you would expect.

Mercury: "...intellectual functioning, both basic capacity and importance of study or communication to the individual."

Venus: " ...individuals involved in artistic work and in cases in which love or partnership is important. Where the north node of Venus in prominent, there may be special talent...."

Mars: "...offer predictable areas of stress, action, health concerns, self-assertion, urge to freedom, and sometimes violence, depending on context and degree of conflict."

Jupiter: "...Jupiter can also be a clue to excesses and consequent problems, and its nodes are apparently similar, bringing faith and intelligence and good judgment when favorably aspected or the reverse when negative."

Saturn: "They may mark areas of severe restriction and pressure. Or they may mark the danger of overreaching and a fall."

Uranus: " ..the unexpected, the innovative, the adventurous, the humanitarian or the crackpot revolutionary.... All professional psychics who were checked had aspects to one or both nodes of Uranus."

Neptune: "...extremes of artistic or spiritual gifts ...vs . mysterious health problems and various forms of escapism...."

Pluto: "The quality of forcefulness, sometimes carried to ruthless extremes, the association with the end of a cycle; the potential for psychic openness and interest...."

al positions, and Zip Dobyns notes that aspects to the outer planetary nodes occur with great frequency in world figures. Diana Rosenburg and Arlene Nimark have found the Uranus node prominent (and occupied) in charts of astrologers. Diana uses a 90° dial marked for nodal positions and considers them to have the purer essence of the planet than the transiting planet-in-aspect itself.

Personal interpretations:

• I consider nodal points and other orbital factors as hot-spots. Even with them and fixed stars I still have a little list of "degree areas" (operating independently of any celestial body or point) which one ignores at one's peril.

• There is a flavor to the "degree-area" that usually corresponds to the common interpretation of the (nodal) planet, but may have some other unrelated connotation — like shipwrecks, bank failures, etc..

• Regarding lunar nodes, I subscribe to the standard Cosmobiology interpretation of a connection with the public at large. I am also mindful of Barbara Watters' consideration that a planet in the degree of the lunar node (in an event chart) was often the signature of fatality. (Perhaps "closure" would be a more politic term.)

• When any planetary configuration connects with nodes, I'm sure the corresponding event will be public and not private, which is one of the reasons that I consider personal socio-religious interpretations inadequate. In the financial markets any given planetary configuration will incite a greater movement if there is temporally corresponding nodal or perihelion activity from *any* planet. *When a transit or planetary event is heavily interrelated to planetary nodes, put a mental exclamation point after it.* The difference on the stock market is extraordinary, and there must be a pandemic corresponding intensity in all human interactions.

• Latitude and declination cycles have noticeable economic correlations. I consider both maxima and 0° (nodal) positions very significant. Natally I put an added spin on anything connected with the above, much as I would conjunction with an major fixed star.

• Planets alone: I am inclined to interpret their "health" by means of phase. Jupiter at full phase is "fattest." Pluto has just completed its perihelion and started a "new" phase. It is waxing. We are experiencing new Pluto realities (AIDS?, energy sources?, economic underpinnings?). Has anyone missed the increased economic and political intensity in the last few years? A little change in the map of Europe, perhaps?

• It is one of the criteria by which I measure planetary consistency. We all know of someone who has been fired on a Jupiter transit or won the lottery with Saturn. Some people sail through a Neptune–Uranus conjunction and collapse at a Saturn square. A Jupiter transit that activates a natal Saturn Node connection may be more saturnine than jovial.

Notes:

In mundane work, I am constantly brought up short by my inability to explain a phenomena in standard geo reference frame only to find my answer evident in helio. If I insist on helio-only, I find big gaps that lunar phases, stations, and sign changes alone will fill. If I insist on an ecliptic reference mode I am chagrined to find right ascension (equator based and corresponding much more to the visual night sky positions) holds the answer. *Nothing is complete and they're all right.*

This is most evident when I am examining a time-line such as stock market prices. I have the quaint concept that if I bash my head against the phenomena long enough I'll isolate the celestial cycle that corresponds to it. Quite often I can, but occasionally only in part. There may be several cycles and more than one reference base. The problem is that astrologers have bought into an ecliptic-based geocentric system without understanding there are equally valid complementary alternatives. To assume these only work in the mundane sphere is self-deluding.

Don't be put off by the buzz words you'll find in books devoted to technical nodal material. I'm not an astronomer, nor am I a mathematician, and I haven't the time or inclination to become either. We need not be in order to understand the mechanics of what we do. Until we grok how the gears mesh we are akin to the blind man with the elephant: *"It's a snake, no its a tree, no its a...."* I use almanacs as well as ephemerides to mark lunar apogee and perigee, and the nearest passage of the planets to Earth. Think how much greater emphasis we place on a planetary configuration that accompanies an eclipse than any other New Moon. Please make the effort to understand what the reference systems you use represent. These are physical cycles and have real-world correspondences. If you live near seashore you're very much aware of the eclipse-coastal storm connection. When we experienced a "super perigee" or proxigean Moon that corresponded with the Full Moon of March 8, 1993, it spawned one of the fiercest East Coast blizzards of the century.

You'll be able to apply cycles natally with much more surety if you see clearly how (and if) they operate in weather, the stock market, the ozone layer, etc. If you can't make a cycle (node, perihelion, *anything*) work at all with any time-line data base, do you really want to apply it to human lives no matter how warm and fuzzy the interpretations may be? If you can show a real correspondence to mass activity, do you dare leave it out even if there isn't any ancient wisdom by which to interpret it?

In the case of nodes and perihelion, we have ample evidence that they correspond to physical and mass economic cycles, so we must consider incorporating them into individual charts. There are precious few directions on just how to do this however. The reading list below is "it." *Welcome to the new frontier.* ✷

Reading list:

The Node Book, Dr. Zipporah Pottenger Dobyns. TIA Publications POB Box 45558 Los Angeles CA. Ephemeris of Geo node positions.

Interface Nodes — Michael Erlewine from Matrix Software, $6.00 copying fee. Book is being reprinted.

All the inter-planetary nodes, perihelion positions, Solar Apex, galactic plane, etc. (The reference work you need if you are going to seriously study nodes.) Interpretation is based on the concept of interactions, inclinations and disinclinations.

Astrophysical Directions, Michael and Margaret Erlewine from AFA. Helio node and perihelion positions (including asteroids), star catalog.

Encyclopedia of Astrology, Nicholas Devore. Must reading for everybody. Contains several contributions by Charles Jayne that are significant.

Tables of Planetary Phenomena, Neil F. Michelsen, ACS Publications Outer planets, Earth, perihelion; aphelion; Moon Perigee/Apogee. Another "must have."

The Stars, and *The Earth in the Heavens*, L. Edward Johndro.

The Astrologer's Astronomical Handbook, Jeff Mayo.

Sun-Earth-Man, Theodore Landscheidt.

Cycles, The Mysterious Forces that Trigger Events, Edward R. Dewey.

Ephemerides

The American Heliocentric Ephemeris 1901-2000 ACS, Neil Michelsen. (Warning: the outer planet perihelion positions are wrong)

The 200 Year Ephemeris, Macoy Publish Co. Richmond VA (heliocentric longitude and latitude only, once a month. Geocentric monthly, stations, eclipses, declinations). This is a excellent reference for quick checking cyclic concepts. It also contains world-wide latitude and longitudes, information on Old Style, Hebrew and Mohammedan and Soviet calendars.

Raphael's Ephemeris: has a phenomena page (Nodes, elongations, greatest brilliancy, etc. Lists separation of conjunctions in latitude, declination.)

Applied Cosmobiology, Rienhold Ebertin (explanation of distance value interpretation.)

Software

CCRS by Marc Pottenger, available from Astrolabe, helio and geo nodes, geo perihelia (*may include helio positions by the time you read this, check.)

Andromeda Software — is a scientific astronomy and graphics "shareware company" that has some interesting programs aimed at amateur astronomers. Write PO Box 605 Amherst, NY 14226-0605 for a catalog. Programs are $5.00 and may be registered for full support if the buyer finds them useful.

Questions:

1. What is a cycle?

2. What is the difference between a sidereal and synodic cycle?

3. List the moon phases. Describe the Sun, Moon, Earth orbital positions for each phase.

4. What are nodes?

5. What two cycles interact to create the lunar nodes?

6. What two cordinate interactions define planetary nodes?

7. What is latitude?

8: What is the difference between heliocentric and geocentric coordinates?

9: What two planets determine the Mutation cycle?

10: What is the ecliptic?

Answers– *are all in this article.*

Aspects: The Parallel of Declination

by Susan Manuel

Similar to a conjunction, the parallel aspect brings together the forces of two or more planets in a horoscope.

Unlike the conjunction, astrologers rarely give the parallel of declination the attention given to conjunctions in the horoscope, but this does not mean they are of little consequence. It may be they are sometimes overlooked because they do not appear in the chart wheel and come from a different system of celestial coordinates than do the well-known series of aspects measured along the ecliptic in zodiacal longitude. It may be that parallels are given an orb so small — just one degree — that we mistakenly think they will come and go quickly, thus having little impact or meaning; or it just may be that astrologers have not studied the parallel aspect to observe its effects as closely as we should.

Definitions of Parallel and Declination in Astronomical Terms

Planets form parallel aspects when they share the same degree of declination north or south of the celestial equator. Before discussing the place of parallels in horoscope interpretation, it is necessary to understand the word declination as a coordinate used to locate the position in the sky of any planet, star, or other body. (If you have used a telescope you may have noticed that the mounting has an axis of declination which is used to locate an object and fix it in the lens.)

Just as the geographer locates a specific place on the Earth by expressing its latitude in degrees north or south of the equator, the astrologer can use exactly the

Figure 1: Latitude vs. Parallels

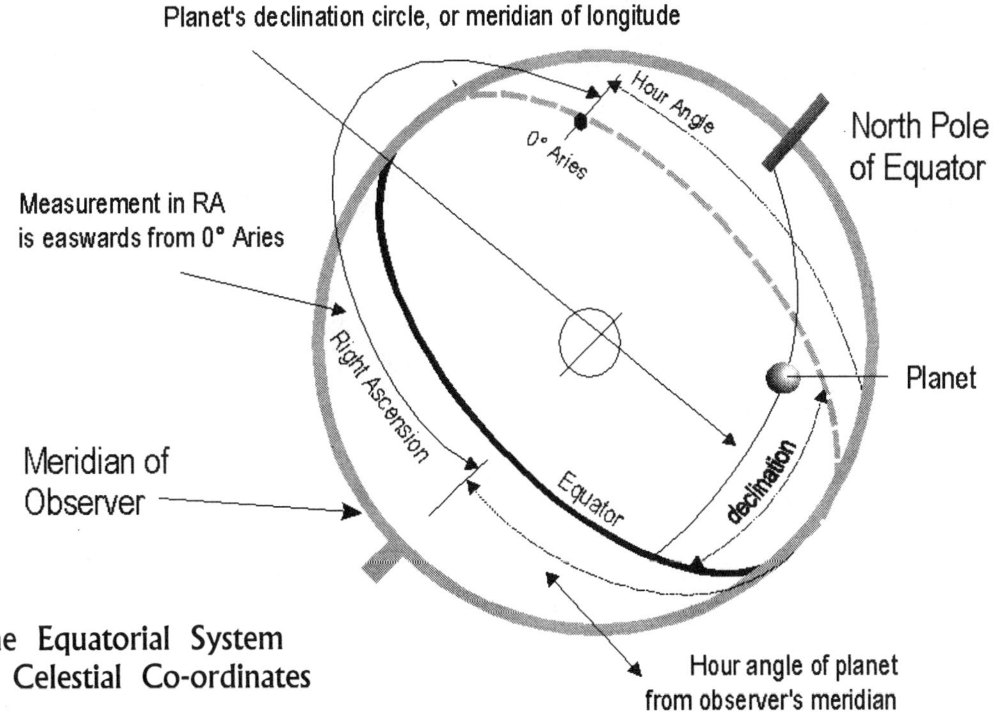

The Equatorial System of Celestial Co-ordinates

same system of coordinates to mark the position of a body in the sky. Astrologers, however, may use more than one system of coordinates to express the position of heavenly bodies.

You may know that there are three primary systems of celestial coordinates used in astrology and astronomy: the Horizontal System, the Ecliptic System, and the Equatorial System. These systems are defined and compared in the table at the end of this chapter. Parallels of declination are measured in the Equatorial System using the celestial equator as a circle of reference. In this system of coordinates, latitude is called declination, and longitude is called Right Ascension. (*Figure 1)*

Declination is a measurement in degrees north or south of the celestial equator. The celestial equator is simply the Earth's equator extended as a circle out into space so that it divides the celestial sphere into two hemispheres. The points on the celestial sphere halfway between the north and south celestial poles form the celestial equator.[1] Two planets equidistant from the celestial equator share the same parallel of declination, just as two cities on Earth share the same latitude when they are exactly the same distance north or south of the Earth's equator.

Parallels of declination are always expressed in degrees, minutes, and seconds. A planet exactly on the plane of the equator has no declination (0°). Planets north of the celestial equator are shown with a plus sign, while planets south of the equator are prefaced with a minus. The symbol for a parallel aspect is //, although sometimes a capital P is used.

When two planets share the same degree of declination, but one is north and the other south of the celestial equator, the aspect is sometimes termed a contraparallel and the symbol # is used; however, any two planets equidistant from the equator, regardless of whether they are north or south, will act together in the matter under consideration and are considered parallel. You can find the declination of the Sun, Moon, and planets listed in most ephemerides and computer printouts, and you should observe whether a planet's declination is increasing or decreasing to determine if it is applying or separating from a parallel aspect. Computer printouts will also show the declination of the ascendant, midheaven, and other points in the horoscope.

The maximum possible declination of the Sun is 23 degrees 28 minutes, which occurs at the solstices when the Sun passes the Tropics of Cancer and Capricorn. At the equinoxes, when the Sun is in the first degrees of Aries and Libra, it has no declination, since at these points the ecliptic intersects the celestial equator. However, planets at this longitude may have declination. The declination of the Moon and planets may exceed 23 degrees north or south of the celestial equator, but while the fast-moving planets may reach 27 or even 28 degrees, the outer planets rarely reach 24 degrees of declination.

Importance of the Parallel Aspect

In his classic work on financial astrology, *Stock Market Fluctuations and Cosmic Influences,* Gustave Lambert-Brahy has this to say of parallels: "These considerations concerning parallels and declinations only require a few extra glances, and the fact that they are of great interest makes the additional research required extremely worthwhile."[2]

My attention was drawn to the parallel early in my astrological career when an astrologer colleague and friend lost her son in a fatal car crash. She had not forseen the danger, nor did she see fatality in the son's horoscope as she studied it after the fact. In her shock and grief she continued to search the young man's horoscope for understanding, but the picture seemed incomplete.

Then one night her son appeared to her in a dream, standing in the road where he had been killed. *"Mom,"* the boy said to her, "*look at the declinations."* Upon awakening she did, and found there the parallel aspects which helped complete the tragic picture. I have kept this story in mind over the years as a reminder to watch the parallels.

Generally a one-degree orb is allowed for the parallel aspect. Since it is usually coincident with a conjunction, the parallel serves to give added emphasis, especially since the parallel may remain within orb after the conjunction has separated. It is also important to note that two planets need not be conjunct in order to share the same degree of declination.

In action, the parallel may seem less abrupt and its influence more subtle than the conjunction; however, the effects of a parallel aspect may last longer than those of the conjunction. While parallels involving the outer planets may remain within orb for many months, their precise interpretation at a given moment may change according to the favorable or unfavorable aspects between the faster moving bodies that form and fade during this same period of time.

Interpreting the Parallel Aspect

Specific interpretation of parallel aspects must be referred to the entire horoscope, and analysis proceeds as usual from judging the planets by sign, aspect, strength, and house placement. The student should note parallel aspects found in the natal chart as well as parallels formed by progressed, directed, and transiting planets.

The parallel aspect has its role in all branches of astrology. In horary, for example, the parallel, like the conjunction, will bring together two significators. The examples that follow come from natal astrology as well as natural and mundane events.

Long-term parallel aspects between the slowest moving planets will be activated when the Sun or any other fast-moving body reaches the same degree of declination and triggers the long-term parallel. For example, in a case from our files a woman was born with Mars, Saturn, and Uranus parallel by declination at +22 degrees. In the year when her progressed Sun reached +22 degrees of declination, her mother died. A chart for the mother's decumbiture[3] showed that the transiting Sun was in -22 degrees of declination on the day her mother was fatally stricken.

Why was it the Sun, the giver of life and vitality, that was the planet in aspect by parallel rather than one of the malefics in this woman's chart when her mother died? Here we must study the complete natal chart for an accurate and detailed understanding of the symbolism of this parallel. In this woman's natal chart we find the Sun in the 10th house, the house of one's mother. The 10th house cusp was ruled by Mars, as was her Aries Sun. The native's 8th house, where death is found, was ruled by Saturn and Uranus, so that the parallels from the progressed and transiting Sun brought together those planets signifying death and the mother. Among the many confirming aspects were solar arc Moon directed to the North Node and transiting Mercury and ascendant parallel her Node at the time she received the sad news.

Events in this woman's life included gain as well as loss during the year in which the progressed Sun was parallel her Mars, Saturn and Uranus. A completely different interpretation of these planets was necessary to explain her good fortune when she was able to afford an extended vacation and three months of travel. The Sun ruled her 2nd house while Saturn and Uranus ruled her 8th of joint finances. Saturn ruled her 7th, representing her husband. When her husband won money in a state lottery, he generously gave it to her and she was thus able to afford such an extended vacation.

Physical Correspondences Fig 2:

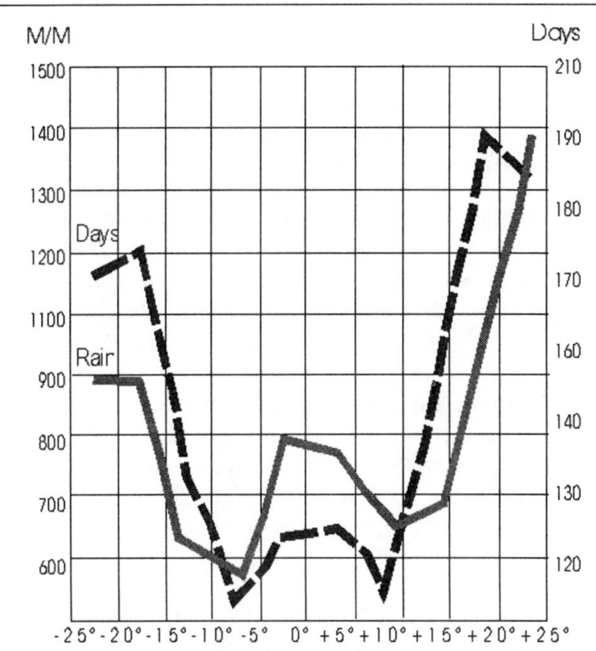

DECLINATION—
The Moon's influence on Rainfall.
Variations in the number of wet days per year and the total amount of rain as a function of the Moon's declination. *After P. Luis Rodès (Èbre Observatory).*

The Parallel in Mundane Astrology

For students interested in mundane astrology, the Declaration of Independence horoscope makes an excellent chart for study because there were five planets parallel by declination on July 4, 1776. They were the Sun at +22:48 degrees, Venus at +23:32, Mars at +23:34, Jupiter at +23:16 and Pluto at -23:40.[4] Notice that Pluto is south of the celestial equator while the other four planets are in northern declination.

A study of the most important events in American history will demonstrate that they frequently occur when progressed and transiting planets parallel these five planets in the Declaration horoscope. For instance, when the Bill of Rights became effective (December 15, 1791), the transiting Sun and Pluto formed a parallel to the Declaration chart's Pluto at -23 degrees and a contraparallel to Sun, Venus, Mars, and Jupiter. Taking Pluto as a symbol of power, this example reminds us that our founding fathers realized the need to protect and balance the rights of individuals against the power of government authority (Sun), wealth (Venus), military might (Mars), and the influence wielded by those with aristocratic tendencies and the power that high social status can bring (Jupiter).

Consider these transiting parallels to the Declaration's five planets during the Civil War: When the Emancipation Proclamation was announced on January 1, 1863, the transiting Sun, Venus (property) and Uranus (freedom) were by declination at -23:01, -23:22 and +22:58, respectively. Throughout the Civil War slow-moving Uranus, planet of rebellion, maintained a declination of approximately 23 degrees north. When the final surrender came at Appomattox on April 9, 1865, Jupiter, symbol of victory, was at -22:57, contraparallel Uranus at +23:36.

Continuing with examples of transits to the five parallel planets in the Declaration of Independence chart, we find that by the time the United States entered World War II, Pluto had moved to 23 degrees north of the celestial equator, contraparallel its natal position. On the morning Pearl Harbor was attacked, the declination of the transiting Sun was -22:38 and Pluto +23:21. Later in the war, on D-Day (June 6, 1944) at H-Hour, the Invasion of Normandy (the largest organized military expedition of World War II) began with Saturn at +22:32, the Sun at +22:38 and Pluto +23:53.[5] Victory in the Pacific came soon after the United States dropped the atomic bomb on Hiroshima (August 6, 1945), when the declination of transiting Uranus was +22:46, the Moon +23:23, and Pluto +23:29.

The Sun, Uranus, and Neptune were parallel the five planets in the Declaration chart on December 17, 1903, at the time of the Wright Brothers first successful flight.[6] Transiting Mercury and Mars were parallel these five on the day President Kennedy was assassinated. Students of mundane astrology are encouraged to continue this study of transiting parallels to the Declaration of Independence chart for a deeper understanding of the parallel aspect in mundane work.

Further insight can be gained by studying parallels in the chart of the U.S. Constitution.[7] In the Constitution horoscope the Moon is at +20:49 degrees of declination, and found in the chart's 7th house of war. On April 30, 1975, the morning on which the United States finally evacuated the last Americans from Vietnam (a scene of chaos and panic that marked the ignoble ending of America's longest war), the transiting Moon and Neptune at -20 degrees were contraparallel the Constitution Moon.[8] Students of military matters know that Neptune is the primary symbol of retreat and surrender in charts for war and battle.

Parallels to the Constitution chart's 7th-house Moon have often coincided with the outbreak of American wars. When the Civil War opened with the attack on Fort Sumter, the declination of the transiting Moon was +20:31 when shelling began at 4:30 AM. The Spanish-American War was precipitated when the USS Maine was blown up in Havana Harbor on February 15, 1898; transiting Mars, Saturn and Uranus were parallel the Constitution's Moon at the time.

Consider another example from U.S. history and parallels to the Constitution horoscope: On August 20, 1920, at the moment when the Secretary of State announced that the 19th Amendment to the Constitution (women suffrage) was ratified, transiting Venus was parallel the Constitution chart's Sun and the transiting Moon was parallel the Constitution's Venus.[9] Women were finally given the vote under parallel aspects from the only two planets astrologers define as feminine.

History is composed of great words as well as great deeds; many great and memorable speeches in U.S. history occurred at the time when Mercury in the Constitution horoscope received parallel aspects from the transiting planets. The Emancipation Proclamation went into effect when Saturn, Neptune, and Pluto were all parallel Mercury in the Constitution chart. When President Lincoln delivered the Gettysburg Address to honor and remember those who had sacrificed their lives for the Union, the Moon, Neptune and Pluto were parallel the Constitution's Mercury.[10]

Parallels to Mercury also mark times of technological advance and achievement. Transiting Jupiter and Uranus were parallel the Constitution's Mercury on that summer day in 1969 when man first walked on the Moon. Earlier in our history, Jupiter and Uranus were also parallel Constitution's Mercury on May 24, 1844 when the first message was successfully sent from Washington to Baltimore by telegrph. Combined study of progressed and transiting parallels to both the Constitution and Declaration of Independence charts is guaranteed to be rewarding.

Planets at Extreme Declination

Some studies suggest that planets in extreme declination may have an enhanced power to influence events. One research study found that there may be a significant correlation between rainfall amounts and the Moon's declination. Observations collected over a period of 20 years at the Ebro Observatory in Spain showed that there tended to be a greater amount of rain on days when the Moon was at its greatest declination from the equator, particularly when the Moon reached extreme northern declination.[11] Further observations on a worldwide scale and over long periods of time may establish the Moon's declination as a factor in rainfall amounts. *(Figure 2.)*

The natal astrologer will find that when progressed planets reach extremes of declination they coincide with years of major change in the lives of clients. For example, a man having Mars in his 5th house and ruling his midheaven started a family and began a new career during the year when progressed Mars reached an extreme of +25 degrees of declination. His first child was born under the Mars-ruled sign of Scorpio, and his new career was in the field of law enforcement. Once again, remember that a complete and accurate interpretation of the planet in an extreme degree of declination must be made by studying the planet within the context of the natal chart, in conjunction with current progressions and transiting aspects. The planet in extreme declination serves to confirm indications found by studying the complete horoscope.

Noting the years in which the secondary progressed Moon reaches extremes of declination can be telling, indicating major changes in the native's life. These are often planned changes appropriate to the native's age. For example, it may mean retirement for an older person, while in the chart of one who is middle-aged, it may indicate the time when children leave home. If you scan the Moon's declination listed in an ephemeris you will see that the Moon moves from zero degrees of declination (when it crosses the celestial equator) to its extreme degree north or south of the celestial equator approximately every seven years. Therefore, when using secondary progressions in which a day equals a year of life, the progressed Moon moves in a seven-year cycle and is thus related to the cycle of Saturn.

When the secondary progressed Moon crosses the celestial equator, changing either from north to south or south to north by declination, it can mark a period of emotional change in the life of the native. Unlike the planned changes associated with years when the Moon is at extreme declination, the native may have less control over events when the progressed Moon crosses the celestial equator. For example, in the life of a preteen or adolescent, there may be the extremes of emotion associated with the hormonal changes of puberty. Perhaps the teenager may show signs of rebellion, or may experience the emotions of young love. The progressed Moon changing directions as it crosses the celestial equator seems to relate more to internal changes or emotional states and may be associated with circumstances over which the native has little control.[12]

The declination of the secondary progressed Moon as well as progressed and directed planets can also be helpful when interpreting the chart of someone with an uncertain birth time. Years of significance can be spotted by observing both extremes of declination and years when planets cross the celestial equator.

Celestial Coordinate Systems

As mentioned in the introduction to this chapter, the parallel aspect is measured in the Equatorial System of celestial coordinates, while most of the measurements astrologers use come from the Ecliptic System. To explain the differences briefly, the apparent path of the Sun, called the ecliptic, is based on the annual revolution of the Earth around the Sun. Our zodiac of signs and familiar aspects of longitude come from this coordinate system. By contrast, the Equatorial System takes as a point of reference the diurnal rotation of the Earth around its axis. Extending the Earth's north and south poles out into space, you have the north and south celestial poles. Extending the equator, you have the celestial equator. Circles parallel to the equator are parallels of declination. (Students should note this distinction: Circles parallel to the ecliptic are measured in degrees of latitude north or south, and should not confuse planetary latitude with planetary declination.)

As a final distinction, there is a third system of coordinates used in the Horizontal System. Here the point of reference is taken from your particular location on the Earth, where the point directly overhead is the zenith, the opposite point, below the Earth, is the nadir, and at right angles to these is a plane which is called the horizon. Parallel to the horizon are the parallels of altitude.

In order to observe movements and note the positions of bodies in the sky, astrologers and astronomers must use some fundamental system of reference. As an aid to understanding the basis of the parallel aspect, compare and contrast the three systems of reference used to measure points upon the celestial sphere in the table on the facing page.[13]

It is easy for today's astrologer to find the declinations of all the planets in the ephemeris or calculate and print them out for any chart using a computer. Astrologers need to gather more information about the parallel aspect as well as planets in extreme declination. Students are encouraged to observe for themselves the action or events corresponding to these parallels and extremes of declination so that more may be learned about their influence and meaning. ✹

Questions

1. What orb is generally allowed for a parallel aspect?

2. Declination is a coordinate of which system of celestial reference?

3. The function of a parallel aspect is similar to what other aspect?

4. What sign is used to indicate declination north of the celestial equator?

5. How may planets at extremes of declination be used in horoscope interpretation?

6. How does one accurately interpret the meaning of the parallel aspect?

Notes

1. The celestial sphere is simply an imaginary background against which the observer sees the projection of planets and stars. If you picture the sphere of the Earth enlarged to embrace the visible heavens, you are imagining the celestial sphere. As with any true sphere, any circle drawn around it can be termed a circumference, but to lo-

Systems of Reference

Celestial Sphere	Equatorial System	Ecliptic System	Horizontal System
Circle of Reference	***Celestial Equator***	***Ecliptic***	***Horizon***
Poles	North celestial pole	Midheaven	Zenith
South celestial pole	Imum Coeli	Nadir	
Secondary Circles	Hour circles	Latitude circles	Vertical Circles
Parallels of Declination	Parallels of Latitude	Parallels of Altitude	
Coordinates	Declination	Celestial Latitude	Altitude
	Right Ascension	Celestial Longitude	Azimuth

cate any particular circle as a circumference implies the selection of some point of reference. In the Equatorial System, it is the celestial equator that is used as a circle of infinite radius, lying in the same plane as the Earth's equator, the two circles having the same center.

2. Gustave Lambert-Brahy, *Stock Market Fluctuations and Cosmic Influences*, ed. Norman H. Winski, trans. Phyllis Gould (Chicago: Astro-Trend Publications, 1982), p.109.

3. Decumbiture literally means "lying down," and a decumbiture chart is erected for the time when a person is taken ill, or takes to his or her bed. This chart is read to judge the possible nature and duration of the illness. It is similar to a horary chart and is used to make a prognosis in the case of accident or illness.

4. Declinations of the planets at approximately 5 PM. on July 4, 1776.

5. The Allied Invasion of Normandy began at 6:40 AM DGDT at Portsmouth, England, according to Capt. Harry C. Butcher, USNR, *My Three Years with Eisenhower* (New York: Simon and Schuster, 1946), pp. 560, 567.

6 When the times of historical events are well known to astrologers, and I am not using the Moon's declination in an example of parallel aspects, no sources will be listed in the notes.

7 The U.S. Constitution went into effect at midnight on March 4, 1789, marking the beginning of constitutional government in the United States. This chart is set for New York City, which was then the nation's capital, at 12:00:01 AM LMT.

8 The final evacuation of Americans from Vietnam began at 6:52 AM SST (-7 hours) in Saigon after South Vietnam had surrendered to the Viet Cong, according to *The New York Times*, April 30, 1975, p. 1.

9 The Secretary of State announced that the 19th Amendment was ratified in a proclamation delivered at 8 AM EST in Washington, D.C., according to *The New York Times*, August 27, 1920, p. 1.

10 History does not record the exact time at which President Lincoln began speaking at Gettysburg on November 9, 1863; however, we do know that the procession to the battlefield *"moved promptly at 10 o'clock"* in the morning, according to Bruce Catton, *Never Call Retreat* (New York: Pocket Books, Pocket Cardinal Edition, 1967), p. 271. The Moon's declination in this example is for 10 AM LMT at Gettysburg.

11 Lucien Rudaux and G. De Vaucouleurs, Larousse *Encyclopedia of Astronomy*, 2nd ed. (New York: Prometheus Press, 1962), p. 175. The data in Figure 2 is taken from a table in the *Larousse Encyclopedia,* p. 174.

13 The author wishes to thank astrologer Carol Tebbs for sharing her observations on the declination of the secondary progressed Moon.

14 A similar table appears in Nicholas deVore, *Encyclopedia of Astrology* (Totowa, New Jersey: Littlefield, Adams & Co., 1976), p. 51. Students wishing more technical information about parallels of declination and celestial coordinate systems used in astrology and astronomy are referred to deVore's Encyclopedia. Other useful references include *The Astrologer's Astronomical Handbook* by Jeff Mayo (Romford, Essex: L. N. Fowler & Co. Ltd, 1982), and *Simplified Astronomy for Astrologers* by LCDR. David Williams (Tempe, Arizona: AFA, 1969); along with NCGR study guides.

IMPORTANT POINTS IN A CHART

VERTEX AND EAST POINT

by Gary Christen

There are five great circles used by astrologers. They are: Equator, Ecliptic, Horizon, Meridian and Prime Vertical.

All important planes in astrology are created by great circles (defined as any circle that passes through the center of a sphere). Where the great circles intersect, various important points are marked off. As an example, the intersection of the Ecliptic and the Horizon in the east is called the ascendant and marks the beginning of the plane of houses. Most of these intersections have been noted by the great astrologers of ancient times through the present and we encounter them in our everyday work in astrology.

During the middle of the twentieth century, the astrologer, Charles Jayne, wondered why the intersection of the Prime Vertical and the Ecliptic in the west was never treated by the ancients. In his work, he considered these points to be very important. He called them the Vertex, the intersection of the Ecliptic and the Prime Vertical in the west and Anti-Vertex (the real name of the Anti-Vertex is the East Point) the intersection of the Ecliptic and Prime Vertical in the east. He mostly talked and wrote about the Vertex and associated it with karmic destiny. Charles was quite successful in introducing them to the other astrologers of his day.

VERTEX AND EAST POINT

The calculation of the Vertex and East Point can be accomplished in one of three methods.

1. ***For the mathematical types, one can use the following formula:***

   Vertex = arctan(cos RAMC/ [(cot latitude x sin obliquity) - (sin RAMC x cos obliquity)])

Where RAMC is the Right Ascension of the Meridian (multiply the local sidereal time by 15 to convert it from hours to degrees and you have the RAMC), latitude is the latitude of the chart, obliquity is the angle of the Ecliptic to the Equator (roughly 23° 26.5' for the latter part of the 20th century).

If the Vertex is negative, add 180°. If the value, cos RAMC is negative, add 180° to the Vertex. If both are negative, add 360° to the Vertex.

To derive the East Point (Anti-Vertex), add 180° to the newly calculated Vertex.

2. ***For the house table bound:***

   a. Calculate a chart.

   b. Take the 4th house cusp and treat it like the midheaven.

   c. Derive the co-latitude by taking the latitude of birth and subtract it from 90°.

   d. Look in the table of houses under your new 4th house cusp midheaven and find the corresponding ascendant using the co-latitude instead of the birth latitude. Interpolate both the new

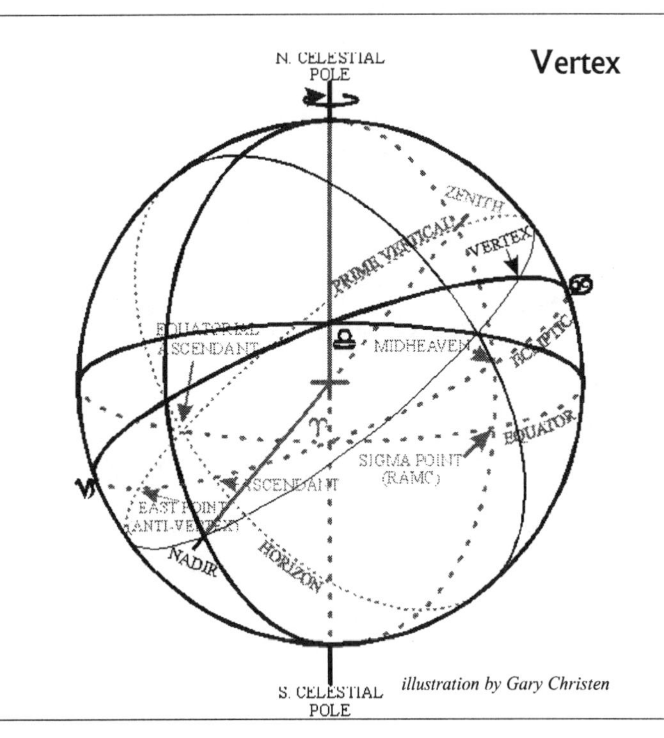

Vertex

illustration by Gary Christen

midheaven and the co-latitude for precise results.

e. Add 180° to the Vertex to find the East Point.

3. ***For the mathematically challenged:***

Use a good astrological computer program.

EQUATORIAL ASCENDANT

The Equatorial Ascendant is the intersection of three great circles, the Horizon, Equator and Prime Vertical. The Equatorial Ascendant is sometimes referred to as the East Point. This is a common mistake (and the author is as guilty as many of his peers in this regard) because the East Point is the specific name of the Anti-Vertex (see Vertex and Anti-Vertex). The Equatorial Ascendant is easy to visualize if we think of how the ascendant (the one we use all the time) is constructed. The ascendant is the intersection of the Horizon and the Ecliptic in the east. On the other hand, the Equatorial Ascendant is the intersection of the Horizon and the Equator in the east.

The Equatorial Ascendant as a mundane position (pertaining to the earth) is used in mundane astrology (forms of astrology that deal with world events, politics, social movement and change, etc.). This is because the Equatorial Ascendant is geometrically unique in the framework that astrology uses to divide the celestial sphere. In connecting the Horizon to the Equator, the Equatorial Ascendant is 90° from the Zenith (the point in the celestial sphere that is directly overhead the place that the horoscope is cast for). This makes it physically connected to the Earth and specifically to a place on the Earth.

If we consider the Equator to be the fundamental plane of the Earth and the Horizon to be the fundamental plane of a place, their intersection connects a specific place to the world at large. Events that deal with places on the earth will always have important material connected to the Equatorial Ascendant.

The Equatorial Ascendant is also used in the Meridian house system[1] as the first house cusp. The Uranian System of astrology (a form of astrology developed in Germany by Alfred Witte in the early part of this century) has very definite interpretations for the Equatorial Ascendant. They see the Equatorial Ascendant as one's own view of oneself. This contrasts with the interpretation for the ascendant which is how others view us.

The Equatorial Ascendant in a natal horoscope is a very subjective personal point. It is our inner view of our own actions, how we think we appear to others. The placement of the Equatorial Ascendant in another house system is also important. For example, if we construct equal houses from the ascendant and the Equatorial Ascendant falls into the 12th house, then we would observe the native finding favor with social groups that are outcast or hidden from the more tradition bound societies. If the Equatorial Ascendant falls into the 1st house, then the native finds himself involved with traditional social customs and morals, outgoing and open.

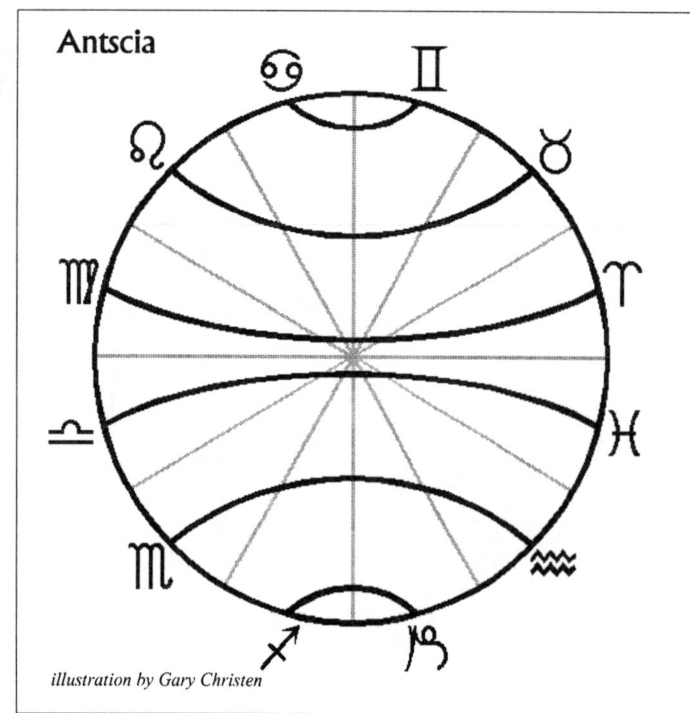

illustration by Gary Christen

Calculating the Equatorial Ascendant can be accomplished by following one these three ways:

1. ***For the Mathematical types.***

Equatorial Ascendant = arctan (tan [RAMC + 90°] x cos obliquity of the Ecliptic

Where RAMC is the Right Ascension of the Meridian (multiply the local sidereal time by 15 to convert it to degrees and you have the RAMC), obliquity of the Ecliptic is the angle of the Ecliptic to the Equator (roughly 23° 26.5' for the latter part of the 20th century)

As a quadrant check, make sure the Equatorial Ascendant is roughly 90° ahead of the RAMC.

Note that if you do not add the 90° to the RAMC in the above formula, your answer will be the midheaven. If you add 30° to the RAMC and re-run the formula, you will get the 11th house cusp of the Meridian system of houses. Add another 30° and you will get the 12th house cusp, etc. See the note below.

2. ***For the house table bound:***

Take the local sidereal time for the chart in question and add 6 hours to it. Calculate a new midheaven. The new midheaven is the Equatorial Ascendant.

3. ***For the mathematically challenged:***

Use a good computer program and most software will list (or have an option for listing) the East Point. This point is the Equatorial Ascendant. If your program doesn't include an East Point or Equatorial Ascendant, cast a chart using the Meridian house system* Find the 1st house cusp, it is the Equatorial Ascendant.

ANTISCIA

The dictionary defines the term Antiscia as meaning shadow image or reflection (as in a mirror). Astrologically, Antiscia is defined as reflections across the Cancer-Capricorn Axis (an axis is defined as a line bisecting a circle into two equal parts). These reflections connect different signs according to this rule: Cardinal signs reflect Mutable signs and Fixed signs reflect Fixed signs. *Figure 1* illustrates this and you can see that the sign Cancer is connected to or reflects Gemini, Leo is connected to or reflects Taurus, etc.

These reflections connect signs together in the way a scale or balance works. For example, when a dynamic astrological factor (a planet, angle, node, etc.), such as a transit or progression is in the degree that is an antiscia to a natal factor, the dynamic factor is expressed through the natal factor. This is one of the oldest concepts in astrology. The ancients only used whole sign notation and later specific degrees were used. So to extend our example further, let us suppose that natal Mercury is in Gemini and transiting Jupiter is in Cancer. We would say that transiting Jupiter is antiscian Mercury and that Jupiter finds its expression through Mercury.

The idea of antiscia also predates the use of parallels of declination. Until the very late renaissance, astrologers did not use declination (distance north or south of the Equator), they only used latitude (distance north or south of the Ecliptic) as their vertical coordinate for planetary positions. As you will learn, parallels (and their opposite contra-parallels) are very powerful in all forms of horoscopic analysis. When the early astrologers began to use antiscia broken down into individual degrees, the refinement of the concept of parallels of declination began to form.

Antiscia broken down into individual degrees works the same as sign antiscians as applied to specific degrees. For example, 15° Gemini reflects specifically 15° of Cancer, 14° of Gemini reflects 16° of Cancer,

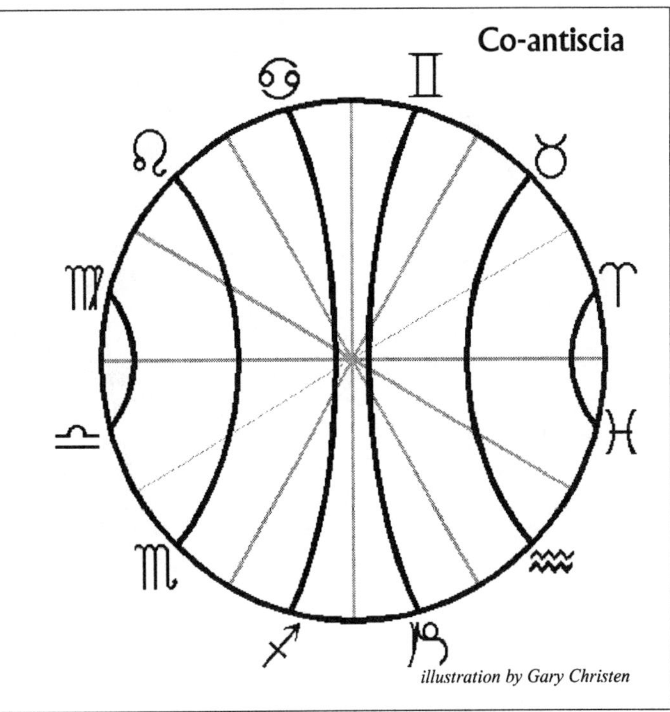

illustration by Gary Christen

13° of Gemini reflects 17° of Cancer, etc. Our rule about whole sign antiscians remains, Cardinal reflects Mutable and Fixed reflects Fixed. There are two formulas for calculating antiscia:

For factors less than 180° (from the first degree of Aries to the 30th degree of Virgo), we use the formula

Cancer plus Cancer minus factor equals antiscia or 180° - factor = antiscia.

For factors greater than 180° (from the first degree of Libra to the 30th degree of Pisces), we use the formula

Capricorn plus Capricorn minus factor equals antiscia or 540° - factor = antiscia.

For example:

Mars at 17° 22' of Aries,
antiscia is 180° 0' - 17° 22's = 12° 38 'Virgo.

ascendant at 25° 50' of Scorpio
antiscia is 540 ° 0' - 235° 50' = 4° 10' Aquarius.

You will note that the factors have been expressed in 360° notation in order to complete this formula and reconverted back to sign notation to express the answer.

In our example, a factor progressing to 12° 38' of Virgo reflects natal Mars and stands in its antiscia degree, or a factor from another natal chart occupies 4° 10' Aquarius and is antiscia to the natal ascendant. These factors are said to express through the natal positions via reflection.

Parallels of Declination can be loosely expressed in the same way as antiscians. If we use the transiting Sun as an example of this phenomenon, we will get precise results because the Sun's path is, by definition, the Ecliptic and has no latitude (all other planets can have latitude either north or south).

If the Sun's position is 17° 19' Leo, its declination is 15° 39' North. The antiscia of the Sun is (180 - 137° 19') 12° 41' Taurus. The declination of the Sun at 12° 41' Taurus is 15° 39' North. 15° 39' North is the declination for both the position of the Sun and its antiscian. This expression will hold true for the Sun in any position on the Ecliptic, however, it is not as precise for the rest of the planets because of their latitude off of the Ecliptic. It will generally be within a one degree orb of equal declination, so it is very useful for quickly finding parallels in a horoscope.

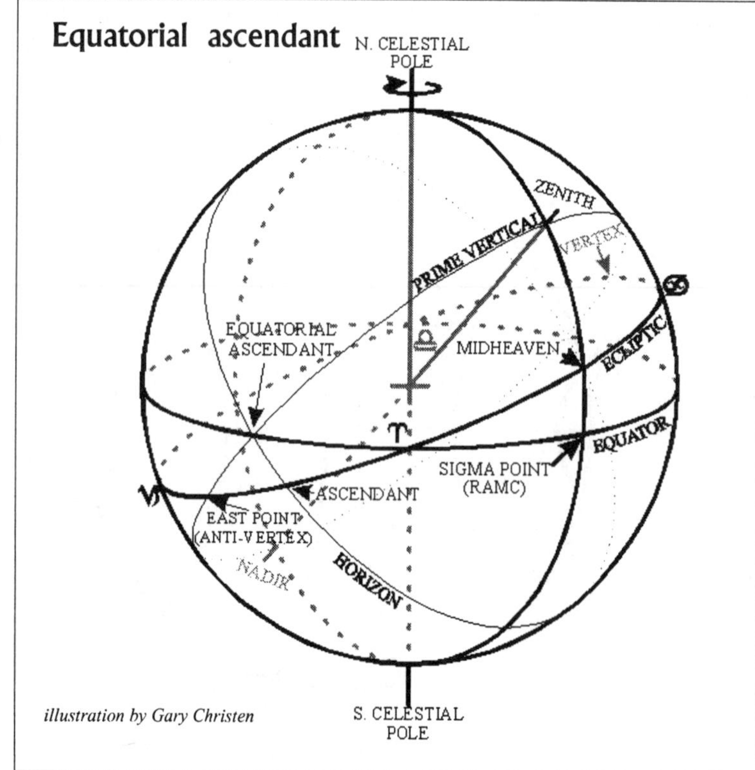

illustration by Gary Christen

If we rotate the entire system so that the main axis is Aries-Libra instead of Cancer-Capricorn, the reflections off of this new axis are called Contra-Antiscians (see *figure 2*). Contra-antiscians are almost as powerful as antiscians and show contra-parallels in declination. The formulas to determine contra-antiscians are:

For factors between the first degree of Capricorn to the 30th degree of Gemini, we use the formula

Aries plus Aries minus factor equals contra-antiscian (where Aries equals 360°, not zero)

or 720° - factor = contra-antiscian.

For factors between the first degree

of Cancer to the thirtieth degree of Sagittarius, we use the formula

Libra plus Libra minus factor equals contra-antiscian

or 360° - factor = contra-antiscian.

In our example of the Sun at 17° 19' with an antiscian at 12° 41' Taurus and a declination of 15° 39' North, the contra-antiscian is 12° 41' of Scorpio with a declination of 15° 39' South.

In this century, most work in antiscia and contra-antiscia has been in the Uranian System of astrology, a collection of astrological ideas originating with the German astrologer Alfred Witte (1878-1941) that has been refined into a unique and powerful school of astrological thought. Within the confines of Uranian astrology, the antiscian and contra-antiscian take on even greater importance than is given in classical astrology in two ways. One is the Uranian meaning of the Cardinal Axis (0° Aries, Cancer, Libra and Capricorn), the other is that the archetype antiscia formula is the prototype for all forms of Planetary Pictures (symmetrical groupings around a common axis).

Uranian astrologers consider the cardinal axis to signify the world at large and things connected to the cardinal axis are connected to the direct workings of the world in general. This has profound implications for mundane astrology and determining prominence in the horoscope. Planetary pictures are the backbone of the Uranian System, since most delineation (in this view of astrology) is derived from them. When two astrological factors are in antiscia or contra-antiscia to each other, then they are also in a very powerful planetary picture that connects the action of the factors involved into the world arena of events.

Antiscia (and contra-antiscia) are very powerful positions in horoscopic astrology and should never be overlooked. ✷

Notes

* The Meridian House System is created by making equal houses on the Equator, using the right ascension of the Meridian as the 10th house cusp and transforming the resultant positions onto the Ecliptic. The right ascension of the Meridian (abbreviated as RAMC) is a point where the meridian crosses the Equator {also called the Sigma Point}. Where it crosses the Ecliptic is the midheaven or 10th house cusp in most house systems.

LOCATION CHARTING

LOCAL AND INTERNATIONAL PLANETARY LINES

by Steve Cozzi and Michael Munkasey

Astrology is a science and an art which encompasses both space and time, but geographical space in astrology has not been fully explored...

This chapter will introduce you to some basic ideas and proven techniques of locational astrology. With these ideas you can determine how astrological influences work for any geographical location on Earth.

What does the astrology of location mean? It can mean any number of things depending on your frame of reference. This "frame of reference" is how you are noting or observing planetary influences. Although each planet moves at its own speed and within its specified orbit, astrologers, astronomers and navigators have options on how they can measure where a particular planet is located in reference to them. These options are called "coordinate systems." Each one is based on different ideas which measure a planet's position in outer space from a specific location on Earth. Stay with me during this brief but important introduction to these systems.

Why do we have different systems of measurement in space? That answer is a bit complicated, but think about these systems briefly. Look at a nearby door or window, or some other nearby object. I see a door now, and it is about six feet away; or is it 72 inches away; or is it 1.83 meters away? See what I mean about different systems of measurement? The door hasn't moved one bit, but how I measure where it is in relation to me can take on different shades of meaning. The base of my measurement can be in feet, inches, meters, furlongs-whatever I choose.

This analogy applies to the three systems used in space. The most widely used system of measurement in space is based on the Ecliptic. This is one of the three basic coordinate systems used in locational astrology. The Equator system, and the Horizon or Local Space system are the other two. The reason why these different systems are used is because we, on Earth, have different frames of reference. We see our local horizon, and that gives us one point of reference. But the Earth has to be located in reference to the Sun, and that gives us another system. Then the planets have to be located in reference to the Sun, and thus we have a 3rd system of reference.

It is important to remember that a planet's position can be measured in any of these three systems. Each of these coordinate systems has its particular point of reference which has developed into a certain point of view. But, regardless of how you measure where the planet is in reference to you, as you stand on the Earth, the planet is still in the same place in space. It is just like that door, and what was it? Six feet? Seventy-two inches? 1.83 meters? It just depends on your frame of reference really, doesn't it?

These systems are divided by circles which serve as the basis for measurements in the systems. The circles in these various systems have names, and they all intersect. This is good, because that makes the math of transferring from one system to the other a whole lot easier. If this did not occur it would be much more difficult to calculate a natal chart or plot a planetary line somewhere on the Earth. For example, the intersection

Circles and Projections – Figure 1

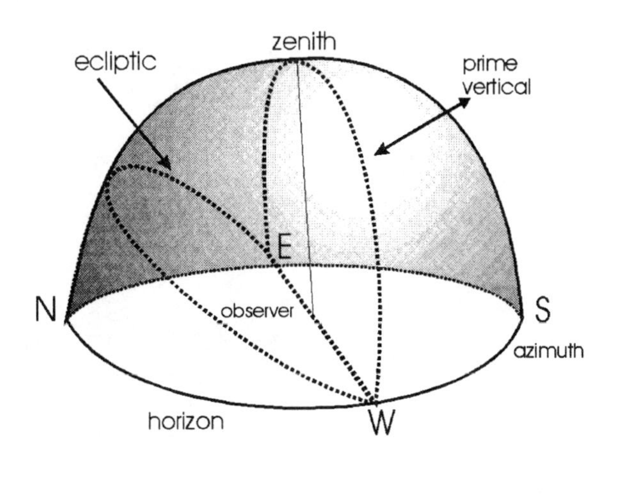

of the Ecliptic and the Horizon gives you the ascendant -descendant position.

An example is appropriate here to help you visualize how these circles interact around you. Picture yourself in the middle of a large geodesic dome, as in *Figure 1.* The circle of the floor that surrounds you is descriptive of the Horizon-Local Space system. See where the planets are positioned on the compass. Directly over your head is the main beam that connects east and west. This is the Prime Vertical-Campanus system, and the beam actually runs under you too, thus completing the circle. On an angle running along the side wall of the dome is the Ecliptic-Zodiac circle. It is also only half visible above the horizon (floor).

Charles Jayne, a pioneer researcher in this area, used to say that the Horizon-Local Space was like the merry-go-round; the Prime Vertical like the Ferris wheel; and the Ecliptic like the tilt-a-whirl. Local Space is on the surface of the Earth, Prime Vertical above and below it, and the Ecliptic is tilted in an arc across the sky.

Now you have some idea of how astrologers plot planets in various locations. Astrology is like a grand clock, with all its gears and circles turning within. Although these systems may be a bit confusing at 1st, the basic intent here is to teach you to read accurate time, not to become clock repairman.

THE SIGNIFICANCE OF THE BIRTH CHART ON LOCATION

The astrological chart wheel that you are familiar with is simply a convenient way of looking at planets at certain degrees, in signs and houses. What isn't very obvious is that the different house systems give a 12-fold division of the Earth's surface. The round wheel of the chart does in fact represent the sphere of the Earth. *See Figure 2.*

The place where we are born is important because in locational astrology it becomes our starting point. Long ago astrologers noted marked changes in behavior and events when a person moved from their birth location. Sometimes the distance was near, sometimes far, but measurable changes appeared none the less. Since the houses exist all around your worldly space, thus the planets are contained within this space too.

The birth chart is like a dial that rotates counter-clockwise when moving west, and clockwise when moving east. The rate at which your birth chart changes is about

Figure 2 – 12-fold division of Earths surface

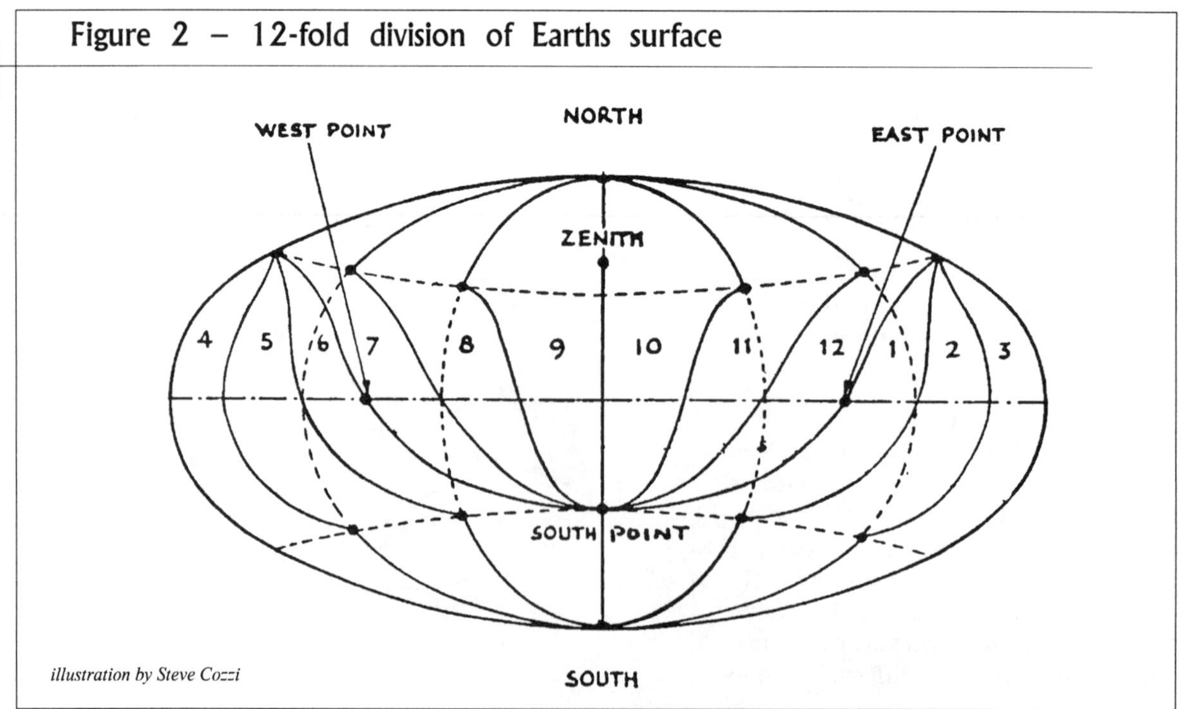

illustration by Steve Cozzi

one degree for every 50 miles of movement. (Keep in mind that I am not downgrading the natal-birth chart. Quite the contrary. Because it gives basic information, we have to return to it again and again to determine the helpful or difficult influences of each planet.) This one-degree change will be added or subtracted from the degree of the sign on the MC, or the 10th house cusp in the birth chart, if you are using a house system that is tied to the 10th house. If the movement is toward the west then one degree is subtracted for about every fifty miles of movement. If the movement is to the east of the birth location, then add one degree. If west subtract, if east add. The ascendant is obtained by obtaining the new latitude and also using the new 10th house cusp.

In your astrological studies you have probably learned that the conjunction is an intense and powerful aspect. Therefore, when a planet is on or conjunct either the 1st, 4th, 7th or 10th houses (i.e., the chart angles), we have a strong focus and display of that planet's energies in the affairs connected with one of those major angles or houses. (Other angles, or Personal Sensitive Points, which can be just as important in local space work, can also be used. These include the vertex, the equatorial ascendant, *etc.* See the article on "Astronomy" in this reference for more information on the Personal Sensitive Points.)

As you move in location, the planets will change houses, make different aspects to the four most used chart angles, and new ASC and MCs will appear. However the planets conjunct the four cardinal house cusps (1, 4, 7, 10) have been shown to demonstrate considerable influence over the affairs in a person's life. So, it is movement, east or west, on the Earth's surface that you want to determine. Just how far do you have to move to bring, say, your Sun to conjunct your ascendant?

The whole basis of locational astrology rests on the premise that "we can modify. in varying degrees. the influences in our birth chart." We certainly can't change the aspects between the planets themselves, but may have the opportunity to bring more favorable aspects to the angles, and more importantly, to place helpful planets on (conjunct) an angle. You can't really change your Mercury conjunct Mars natal aspect. But, it is possible to shift the chart so they trine the ascendant and-or sextile your 10th house cusp. If you should have a diminished 12th house Jupiter, you may wish to move that toward your ascendant.

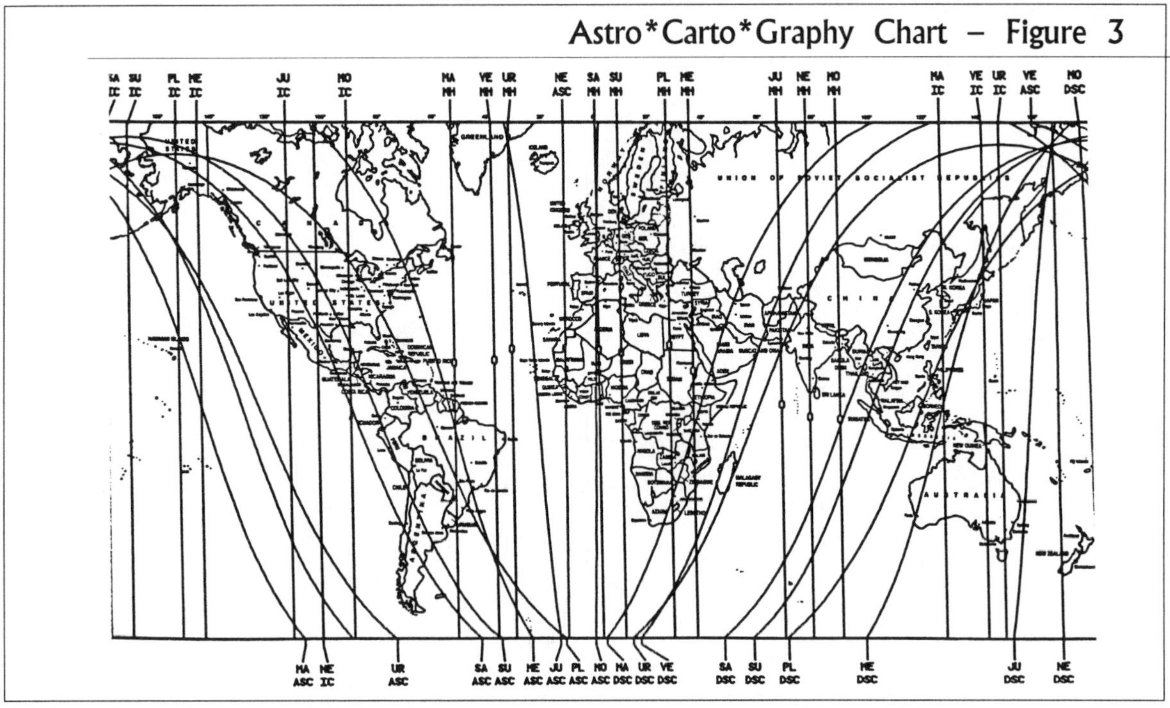

Astro*Carto*Graphy Chart – Figure 3

LOCATIONAL ASTROLOGY TO THE RESCUE

Prior to 1975 astrologers were caught in a dilemma. A client would come and ask if the north side of town would be better to live in, and will my love life improve in Miami, and should I invest in real estate in Denver, and what about the job offer in Boston. This would require at least four charts cast for each area. Now, that you can see the planetary lines over just one map, and you can save much time and energy.

Early researchers drew in each of the planetary lines, similar to that you see in *Figure #3.* Then several astrological graphing techniques, like Astro*Carto* Graphy, became available in the mid-1970s. These techniques produce computer drawn maps, and henceforth I shall refer to these types of charts or maps as Astro-Locality Maps.

HOW TO USE ASTRO-LOCALITY MAPS

When looking at an Astro-Locality Map you will see a series of lines. Each line represents a planet either conjunct or in major aspect to an angle. In the Astro-Locality map I use, the 10 planets are shown on all four angles for a total of 40 lines. The 20 curved (sometimes dashed) lines represent the planets in conjunction with either the ascendant (or 1st House) or descendant (7th house). A recommended orb of 100 miles (about 2°) is used either side of the lines. The 20 solid straight lines represent planets in conjunction with either the MC or 10th house cusp, or the IC, 4th house cusp. Unless otherwise noted the planetary symbols on top refer to the ascendant and MC, and the ones on the bottom the descendant and IC. Some of the available computer programs and services show close ups of countries, regions and even metropolitan areas. (Programs in development will offer selections for aspects and latitude crossing lines.)

Measurement in right ascension (RA) for the planets is used to compute both the MC-IC, and the ASC-DSC There will be a difference in the planetary positions in RA (*i.e.,* on the Equator) and the Ecliptic positions. This occurs only the across the ascendant-descendant angle. For most of the planets the difference is minor. However with Pluto, the difference can be 3°, and with the Moon and Venus about one degree each. To compensate for this, allow an orb of about 200 miles with Venus and the Moon, and 350 miles with Pluto, on either side of the line.

When looking at the series of lines a process of elimination begins to take place. At least half of the lines

Figure 4 – Jupiter opposes Saturn in a locality map

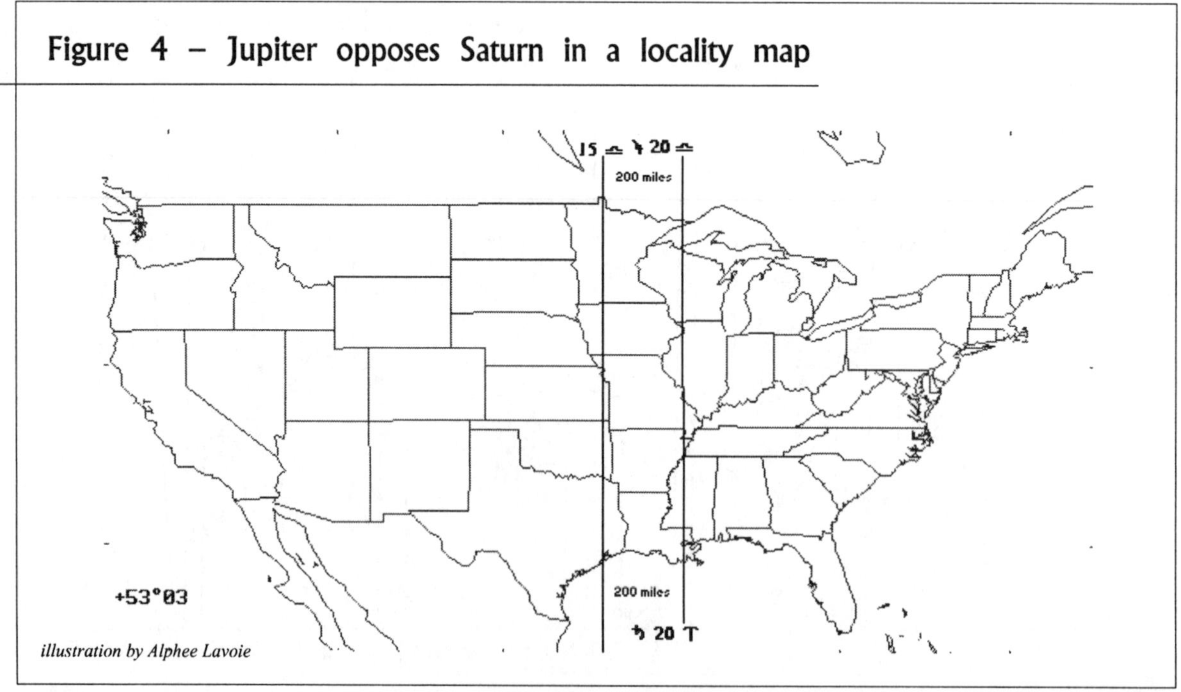

illustration by Alphee Lavoie

will be more then several hundred miles out into the oceans. This fact will limit the chances of individual ever experiencing them. There will also be lines in remote and or extremely cold places. The social and political climate of many countries will make other lines undesirable. The number you have to really look at will be usually less then 10, especially if the client is only concerned with locations in , say, North America.

Actually there are slow moving progressed and transiting planetary lines that continuously move from west to east, unless the planets are retrograde. They can come in off the ocean and offer some long-term opportunities, or they can cause problems, depending on the planet

We remain connected with the whole world because even though we may never visit the great majority of planetary lines and places, they will in a sense visit us. This is no abstraction: "people are places." People who are born, or those that have lived exclusively, in a location where we have helpful lines tend to help us. People from places where we have difficult lines tend to hinder us in some way. People are places.

When you or a client are concerned with a certain city it's advisable to do a standard chart for the new place in question. Simply use the true time of birth, with same day, month and year, but put in the relocated latitude and longitude of the city. Check with the formula of 50 miles is equal to one degree to see if you are correct.

The reason for doing this is threefold. You want to see if there are any aspects to any of the angles, within a one-and-a-half degree orb. You will also want to check to see which planets have shifted into new houses, and if the birth ascendant or MC has changed. Remember, if you are living in a place other then your birth location, the new or relocated chart will get stronger with time but it will not override the birth chart.

Charles Jayne use to call this type of astrology "Progressions in Space." His reasoning was that if you observed that a transit or progression were to come into conjunction with an angle a few years from now, you would have to wait for that time. Let's say your progressed ascendant will move down and conjunct your Jupiter in the 2nd house when you are 38 years old. You are now 36, and you would have to wait two years for this aspect to culminate. Yet in some location in the world Jupiter is already on your relocated ascendant!

Chart shows heavy Eastern Seaboard activity – Figure 5

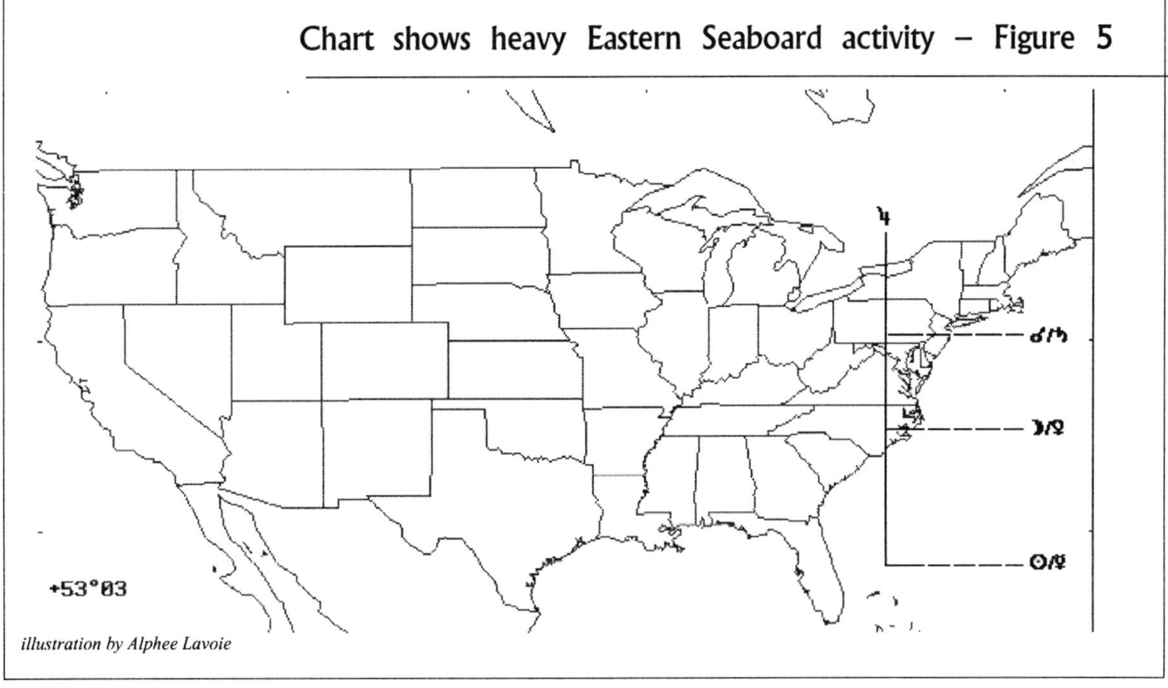

illustration by Alphee Lavoie

Locational astrology offers you greater choices, including a chance to move toward financial independence, a chance to enjoy retirement or vacation, a chance to find a comparable mate, etc. In reality there is no perfect place, only locations that offer what we think we want and more often then not, what we really need.

Many or few such alterations or modifications to the birth chart can be made, but there is a limit. It is possible to get the best out of difficult aspect providing a constructive move takes the form of good aspects.

Perhaps another example will help illustrate how we can alter our destiny for the better. Look at *Figure 4.* You will see a map and part of a chart illustrating the opposition of Jupiter and Saturn close to the 10th and 4th houses respectively. Jupiter is at 16 Libra in the 9th and 4° from the 10th house. Saturn is conjunct the 4th house cusp at 20 Aires. Let's say you moved 200 miles to the west. The degrees on the 10th house cusp would decrease by four, putting Jupiter conjunct the 10th. Saturn would now be 4° from the 4th cusp at 16 Aries. Yes, you would always have a Jupiter opposition Saturn but note that you have decreased the restricting energies of Saturn and emphasized the expansive energies of Jupiter.

HOW TO USE THE LATITUDE CROSSINGS

Looking at *Figure 3* you will see a series of straight lines that cross curved lines. What this means is that at that specific latitude a planet is on either the ASC-DSC, or 1st or 7th cusp, while another is on the 10th or 4th. Because both of the axes are activated, the energies of both planets create what could be called a personal power spot. A crossing extends out to a diameter of about 300 miles. For most people born at mid-latitudes, the majority of crossings occur in the polar regions. The interesting thing about crossings is the latitude of the crossing remains active all across the Earth, so anywhere on this latitude you would have the combined energies of these two planets.

There are two ways in which crossings are used. In the absence of major planetary lines (*i.e.,* a planet conjunct one of the angles), a crossing or a cluster of two more can demonstrate a considerable influence. Look at *Figure 5* and you will see that this individual has Jupiter on the MC-10th. This line goes through the whole of the eastern seaboard. It is obvious that this person will have some degree of luck, happiness, success, etc., there. Where would you advise this person to live: New York state, North Carolina, Florida? In other words where would his or her successes be most pronounced?

Figure 6 – A local space map

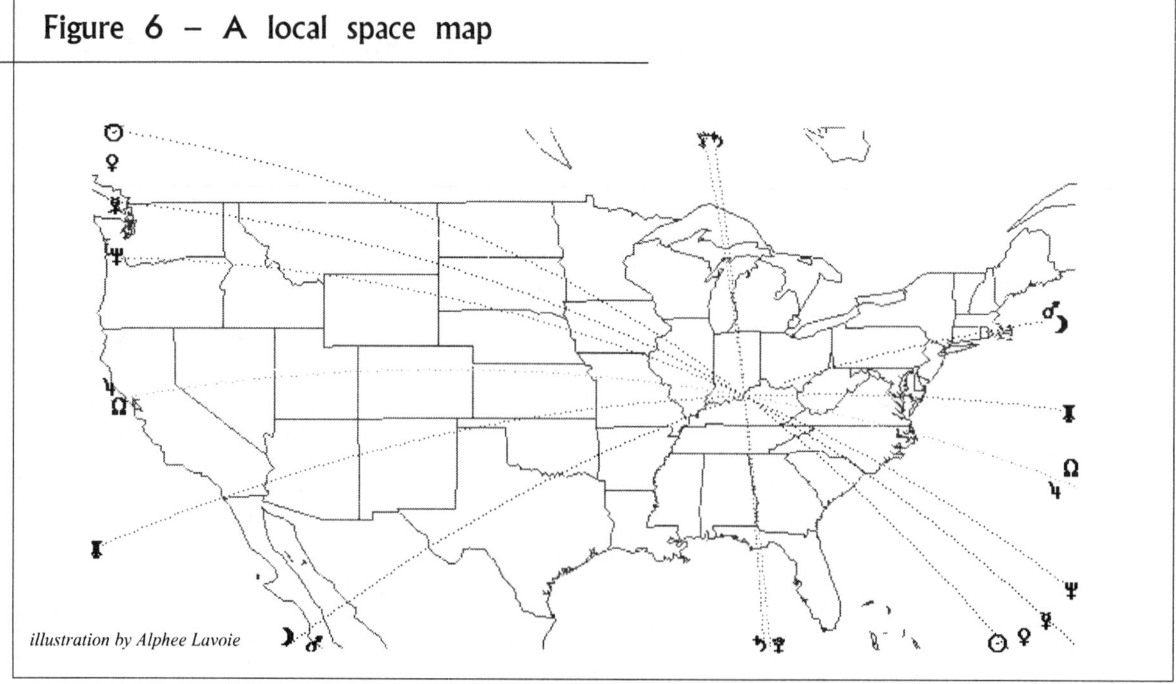

illustration by Alphee Lavoie

This is where crossings become important, because they can point to the latitude along this line that will be most favorable. The planets involved with the crossing must be harmonious or supportive of the major planet in question. In this case a Moon-Venus or Sun-Mercury crossing should prove helpful. The Mars-Saturn crossing would tend to weaken the Jupiter somewhat, but for a person whose Jupiter is very strong in the birth chart, it could bring added energy to make good things happen.

HOW TO USE THE LOCAL SPACE-HORIZON LINES

Earlier the Local Space-Horizon system was briefly mentioned. Picture yourself out in a boat, or out in a very flat field. Then point to where the sky meets the Earth or water, and turn around 360°. This is your Local Space horizon. In this system we simply take the planets off the Ecliptic-Zodiac and place then on the horizon. This gives each planet a compass bearing that can be followed on the surface of the Earth. The individual degrees are now called degrees of Azimuth.

This Local Space chart can be used for the birth location and for the person's present location. The Local Space lines from one's birth can give you a general overview, but the lines for the present location show you what's going on now. *See Figure 6.*

These lines represent planetary energy just like the ones in an Astro-Locality map. However there are some differences. When you travel on the Local Space lines they can show you possible routes of travel, and long distance connections with others via phone lines and mail routes. When a person travels on one of these Local Space planetary lines it can give them some real insight as to why the journey is being made. The basic nature of the planet in question and how it works for the person must be taken into consideration. Local Space lines do not create crossings when they intersect with themselves or lines from the four standard angles.

In *Figure 7* you see a Local Space chart wheel. Notice that there are four cardinal directions, and the degrees circumference are the 360° of azimuth. They increase going clockwise. Zero azimuth is at the north, with 90° at due east, 180° at due south and 270° at due west. Even though the planets are given an azimuth on the Earth's surface they are actually in the sky above or below the horizon. This is called their altitude. In a Prime Vertical-Campanus chart this elevation is called amplitude. The aspects formed on the horizon and in the Local Space chart do not seem to work as they do in the Zodiac-Ecliptic system.

The Matrix Computer program Local Space chart is different. It lists the degrees of azimuth starting from the east in a counter-clockwise fashion. Both charts will place those planets in the same parts of the wheel, only the numbers will differ. (Michael Erlewine and his wife Margaret did ground breaking research in Local Space in the early 1970's. The term "Local Space" was coined by them.)

IMPORTANT POINTS

A Local Space chart is always calculated for the present location, or any such location that is under consideration. After about fifty miles in any direction, the lines begin to change. The compass directions and azimuth degrees of a planet can move in two directions. If it runs northeast, it also runs southwest; if it is north it is also south; if it is AZ-30 it is also AZ-210, *etc.*

There are some rather intimate connections between Local Space charts, maps and the birth (or relocation) charts, and their graphic counter part the Astro-Locali-

A local space chart – Figure 7

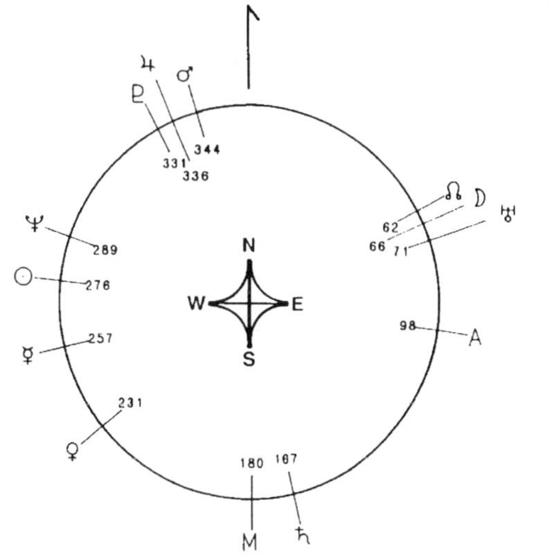

N
W
E
S
344
331
336
289
276
257
231
180
187
62
66
71
98
A
M

Fig 8 – Floor plan with overlay

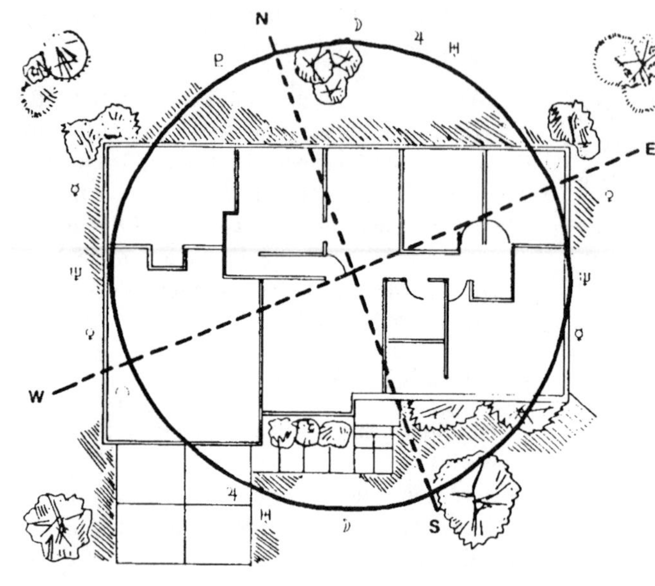

Figure 9 - City map with overlay

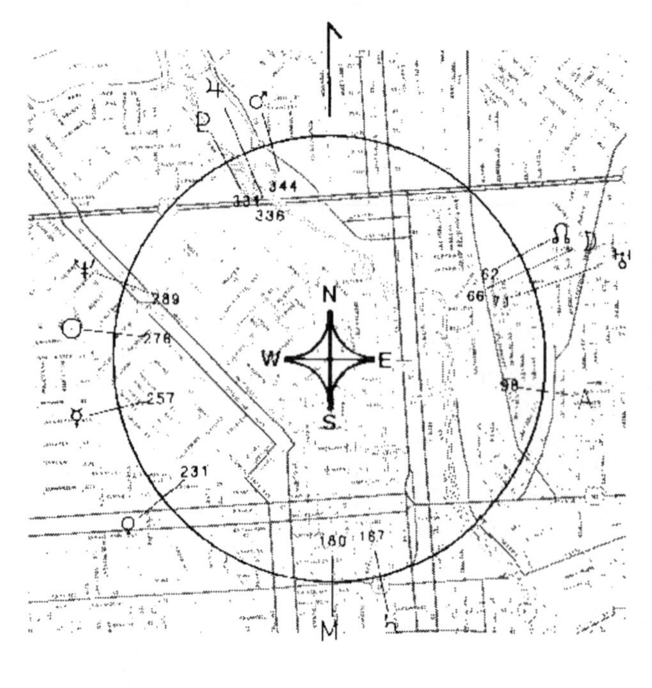

ty maps. In the northern hemisphere the MC-10th house is the same as due south, provided of course that you are in the same location that it has been calculated from. This makes the IC-4th the same as due north. Reverse this for southern hemisphere. When you look at a street map or an Astro-Locality map, north should always be at the top, and south at the bottom.

What about east and west directions? The ascendant and descendant do not lie due east or west. Looking at a standard chart only the vertex lies due west and the anti-vertex due east. (In a Local Space chart they are simply labeled as west and east). The theory here is straightforward. If we include north and south in a standard chart we need also to include east and west. Please do not try and arbitrarily mix the two *(i.e.,* azimuth and the zodiac degrees). Just keep in mind that north and south in the one is the same in the other, *i.e.,* the IC and MC The vertex and anti-vertex in one is the same as west and east in the other.

There is an affect called "bunching." This is where the planets tend to position themselves close to the east-west parts of the Local Space chart. This occurs when someone is born in the middle latitudes and moves more than 10° of latitude to the south, (reverse this for the southern hemisphere). The farther south the one goes, the greater the bunching. The problem is solved by using the Prime Vertical-Campanus chart as if it were a Local Space chart. The top lies north and west is on the left, etc.

LOCAL SPACE TECHNIQUES

We have already explained the basics of how to use the Local Space lines over certain distances. The next we look at is the Local Space chart within the community. By that I mean the city or county where a person lives. Having an accurate Local

Space chart for the location in question, you can begin to determine just how the planetary lines work within your community. (To double check your accuracy, compare the Local Space positions with those on the relocation chart or map. Remember MC = south, IC = north, vertex = west and anti-vertex = east. Planets close to either of these points should be very close to the same in both charts.)

Your first step is to take your Local Space chart to a copy store and have a transparency made of it. Next, get a detailed map of your area. If the person lives on a street that is aligned either north-south or east-west, then the center of the chart is placed over where the person lives. Next align the top of the chart with the top of the map, because both should be due north. When a person lives on a hilly or curved street there are a number of things you can do. You can look at the original blueprints, check with surveyors, or ask a boy scout to give you true north by the compass correction from magnetic north. All you really need is one direction, so if it's close to the Spring or Autumn equinox you know that the Sun always rises due east and sets due west at that time.

Earlier it was said that it may not be necessary for most people to travel long distances from their place in an attempt to improve their lives. The fact is that the majority of people (those with offices in the home are partially excluded) travel frequently on certain planetary lines. The route to work is usually the most traveled. It has been shown that we tend to invoke or gather whatever planet's line is traveled on. Its energies are symbolically and actually drawn into our life through this usage. All well and good if it is a helpful planet, but what if it is a planet that is difficult in the birth chart, or in a difficult temporary situa-

A LOCATIONAL ASTROLOGY PROCEDURAL CHECKLIST

1. Go through a process of elimination and center in on the continent, country or region that is under consideration.
2. It is important to have a working knowledge of how each planet works for the individual. Helpful, difficult, or a mix, a temporary condition or somewhat permanent.
3. Always use the true time of birth. All you are changing is the latitude and longitude. Use the 50 miles = 1 degree rule to double check.
4. Next in importance after the planetary lines (*i.e.,* planets conjunct First, Fourth, Seventh or the Tenth angles) is to see if a planet is conjunct the Vertex/West or Anti-Vertex/East. These positions are just as important as the other four angles.
5. Check to see the latitudes and what type of planetary pairs are found in the pair crossings.
6. Observe the Local Space lines from the place of birth.
7. Observe the Local Space lines from the present location.
8. Look to see where the progressed positions place the planet lines.
9. Look at the progressed crossing latitudes.
10. Observe the progressed Local Space lies from the present location.
11. Use the Local Space chart in the community, and in the home.
12. Do a standard relocation chart, and look for new aspects to all six angles. Also note when planets are placed in a new houses.

tion from transits or progressions? This is not to say that Saturn is always difficult, but wouldn't you rather travel twice a day, five or six days a week, on a Jupiter line?

Let's assume *(Figure 8)* this person travels to work on a Neptune line. The chart is centered over where the person presently lives. Let's assume that he or she has a difficult Neptune placement. This individual writes for a living, but he or she has experienced frequent melancholy moods and confused thinking when traveling to and from work. When a move was made to the northeast side of the city, the person now traveled along their Mercury line. Then it becomes possible to think in a more orderly fashion on the morning drive, and to systematically review the day on the evening drive. Some of the most important directions are those used to work, school, when visiting loved ones, a doctor, bank, supermarket, automobile repair, exercise places, etc.

In the final method the same transparency is used to uncover information about your home or office. The chart can be placed over a drawing of your home, or place of business. If the company has a floor plan, then put the center of the chart over the center of this area. This will show how the company views the individual. The chart can also be placed over the center of the your office to see how you view the company. Remember to align the chart, and then align the overlay using a cardinal direction, as in *Figure 9.*

The final use of the Local Space chart is in the home. Naturally it is placed over the center of the house. Problem planets will cause problems in that area of the home that they run through. Remember that the planetary lines go in both directions and be observant. There is no end to the discoveries that can be made.

Most people spent over 80% of their lives in the home. Yet it was not until the last decade that astrologers developed a methodology for practical use in the home or office. Things get noticed on the Sun line, there are arguments along the Mars line, things appear more beautiful along the Venus line, *etc.*

Using the Local Space chart in the home and community is a modern and western version of the Chinese geomancy called Feng Shui (wind and water). Feng Shui has a wealth of information which blends quite well with Local Space. Some of the Feng Shui practices are general, some practical, and in others certain facts remain a secret. Local Space has the advantage of using the planetary lines based on near exact birth times, something that was rare in Feng Shui practices.

There is a great amount of cross cultural information about the directions in general. Source material for this we are given in the recommend programs and reading list. ✷

QUESTIONS

1. Name the three systems used to measure a planet's position? ANSWER: Ecliptic-Zodiac; Horizon-Local Space and Prime Vertical-Campanus.

2. The astrological houses actually represent a 12-fold division of the Earth's _____? ANSWER: surface

3. At the mid-latitudes, 50 miles = how many degrees of right ascension on the MC? ANSWER: 1 degree

4. When doing a chart for a new location the only two pieces of data that change are the_________and________? ANSWER: latitude and longitude.

5. If the MC-10th is south, and the IC lies north, then the vertex lies and the anti-vertex lie where? ANSWER: west and east.

6. In locational astrology we look at how many angles? ANSWER: At least Six. The ascendant, descendant, MC, IC, vertex and anti-vertex.

7. When looking at an Astro-Locality Map the curved lines represent either the ______or _____and the straight lines the_____or_____?AN SWER: 1st or 7th cusps, and the 10th or 4th cusps.

8. Crossings are measured along ? ANSWER: latitude

9. In a Local Space chart the planets are taken out of the Ecliptic-Zodiac and placed on the ? ANSWER: compass or horizon

10. Local Space lines should always be observed from the—location? ANSWER: present

RECOMMEND BOOKS AND PROGRAMS

Planets in Locality, Steve Cozzi, Llewellyn Publishers, St. Paul, MN.

*The Astro*Carto*Graphy Book of Maps,* Jim Lewis and Ariel Guttman, 1989, Llewellyn Publishers, St. Paul, MN.

Astro-Maps High Res by Matrix Software, Big Rapids, MI

Local Space-Astro-Locality Report Writer I, with CityScope, by A.I.R. Software, West Hartford, CT

MUNDANE CHARTING

by Bill Meridian

Mundane charting is a fascinating branch of astrology about which very little material is currently in print.

A recommended reading list appears at the end of this chapter. Charles A. Jayne conducted what is likely the most extensive study of mundane astrology from the late Thirties to the Fifties. Many of the applications that follow are derived from his valuable work.

Writing in 1946, Charles Jayne defined and described mundane astrology as being the astrology of national and international developments. On one hand, he stated that mundane was more difficult than individual astrology because of the number of charts involved. On the other hand, an individual has a certain freedom that a group does not have. Therefore, in a large group there seemed to be a more narrow degree of freedom and, correspondingly, a greater amount of predictability. Before looking at the meaning of the planets, let's introduce a trio of essential concepts.

Basically, mundane tools can be divided into several broad categories: transit cycles, individual political horoscopes, and astro-geography methods.

Transit Cycles

Transits of the outer planets are one obvious indicator of longer-term world trends. Passages of planets through signs, such as Neptune through the signs, are important. Barry Lynes has pointed out that the transit of Neptune through earth signs has usually brought monetary deflation while its journey through fire signs usually heralds inflation.

In addition, aspects of the outer planets are powerful. Ptolemy said not to overlook, "any *of the hundred and nineteen conjunctions, for in them depends the knowledge of worldly operations, whether of generation or corruption."* One of the best known is the conjunction of Jupiter and Saturn which occurs every 20 years. Of these, Frederic von Norstrand said that

> *"The conjunctions of these two chronocrators were known to set the world's pace for years ahead, their least conjunctions disposing of the course of mundane affairs for twenty years thereafter."*

Commander David Williams has shown that the conjunction tends to occur at lows in the economy, and mark the beginning of a new period of expansion. The last three, in 1920, 1940, and 1980, did just that.

The aspect occurs in one element for about 240 years. It has been in earth since January 26,1842. The shift of the conjunctions into a new sign was termed a Great Mutation, and was considered of greater importance.

The value of the Jupiter-Saturn conjunction charts was proven in the 'war or peace' predictions made by one American astrologer prior to WWII. While Edward Johndro, using his locality method for the capital cities of Europe, predicted peace; and Grant Lewi, using the birth charts of world leaders concurred; Elizabeth Aldrich, utilizing a fine set of timed charts of countries and leaders plus the Jupiter-Saturn charts set for the capitals, predicted the slow beginning and the eventual spread of the war throughout Europe and the world. Specifically, her interpretation of the Jupiter-Saturn chart for London led her to predict that London would be bombed, but not invaded. Quite a prediction in view of the fact that aerial warfare was not widespread before 1939.

In recent times, the Uranus-Neptune conjunction of 1993 has generated much commentary. This aspect has coincided with mass shifts in consciousness such as the seeming change of heart in the communist bloc. The previous conjunction in 1821 coincided with the rise of communism. Previous conjunctions brought the settlement of the Americas, the Renaissance, and the Reformation.

There are, of course, other major outer planetary aspects of importance: the Uranus-Pluto conjunction, Saturn-Uranus conjunction, Saturn-*Neptune, etc.* As Jayne pointed out, very long-term cycles are created by the return of outer planet aspects to certain degree areas. These recurrence cycles of hundreds and thousands of years formed the bases of many civilizations.

To determine the local effect of these aspects, set up a chart for the major capitals of the world. The angles of such charts are very important in determining the expression of the planets in that locale.

POLITICAL HOROSCOPES
Base Horoscopes and Modifiers

The mundane astrologer erects horoscopes for the birth of a nation and its leaders. The accuracy of birth time data is a significant challenge to the mundane researcher. Often, charts set for noon or sunrise must be utilized due to the lack of a birth time. The most extensive effort to provide an accurate group of mundane horoscopes is the *Book of World Horoscopes* by Nicholas Campion.

To the 'base' charts of nations and leaders Charles Jayne would add those set for the beginning of rule, such as a coronation or oath of office, major political changes, and the outbreaks of wars. The base charts described the traits and aspirations of a society. These horoscopes might be set for the moment of a great military victory or a proclamation or the establishment of a new form of government.

Here's how the modifying charts work. Let's assume that a base chart has a Sun-Mars sextile. This would indicate that the people favored athletics and had a good martial spirit. They would take to soldiering well and would provide the material for a sound army. Now assume that a new regime comes to power or a change in the form of government takes place. This chart reveals a Sun-Mars square. This must be added to our interpretation of the base chart's sextile. The new leader or society may not handle the military well or prevailing social trends might turn anti-military as they did in the US during Vietnam. So, the base chart is 'modified' by the new horoscope.

The changing fortunes of France were Jayne's favorite example of this concept. The base charts were considered well-aspected for military success, but were modified by later French charts. Thus, the Napoleonic era ended in defeats in Russia and at Waterloo. The loss in the Franco-Prussian war followed. But the base chart was again modified by new charts. Although France took a beating in the World Wars, the country eventually emerged on the winning side. Post-war horoscopes suggested declining French power.

Significant Moments

Charles Jayne and, more recently, Nick Campion, believe that horoscopes of moments that were significant in the development of a country or a culture. Jayne found that there may be several charts for a country are important. His contemporary, Margaret Morrell, pointed out that in addition to the July 4, 1776 chart of the Declaration of Independence, one might use the horoscope for Washington's inaugural address on April 30, 1789. She felt that this was the chart for the government of the US as opposed to a horoscope that would more directly represent people. Jayne wrote that the April 19, 1775 (Battle of Concord) chart used by William Leary was a more representative chart for the citizens. He felt that the Declaration of Independence in 1776 was an important chart, but not the chart for the US.

The Meaning of the Houses

Following are the standard keywords for interpreting the mundane houses:

house	*interpretation*	*house*	*interpretation*
1	National character, self image	7	Foreign relations, partners or enemies
2	Material resources, wealth	8	Financial relations
3	Transport, communications	9	Foreign trade, religion
4	Land, community, agriculture	10	Ruling class, government, prestige
5	Pleasure, art, sport, birth rate, speculators	11	Institutions, legislature
6	Workers, the military, health	12	The hidden, hospitals, underground

America declared its desire for independence, but did not effectively achieve it until Cornwallis surrendered at Yorktown on October 19, 1781 at 10 am LMT. More recently, Julian Armistead has promoted the use of a chart set for July 2, 1776. A. H. Blackwell has demonstrated that the horoscope of the US Constitution has reflected subsequent legal changes in the country. Thus, each chart is representative of a different facet of life of the country.

The question then arises as to when an entity is born in the eyes of the mundane astrologer. This was not necessarily clear in all cases. A country revolves around a culture. It develops in stages, one of the last of which will likely be the establishment of a political form such as a republic. After studying the history of a country one might very well have many charts, each describing a different facet of life. There are few 'wrong' charts. Each has its value in describing a different aspect of the life of a political entity.

For example, if one were to analyze US-USSR relations, one might have three charts for each country and one for each country's leader and his date of inauguration. Then we might have two more dates representing treaties between the two countries that would be representative of their relationship. Once this analysis is completed one would likely come up with certain degree areas that were important. Rather then be overwhelmed by a large number of horoscopes, the astrologer could then concentrate his analysis on these areas.

Shared Degree Area

The previous discussion illustrates Jayne's statement that "Breadth is essential in mundane astrology." Once a country's history has been studied and a series of horoscopes had been collected, the connections between the charts emphasized certain degrees of the zodiac. This is a vital concept because the mundane astrologer will find that future stimulation of these degrees leads to major events. To draw an analogy, the process resembles a pinball machine. Sometimes, a single pinball sets off many lights and runs up a big score.

An example from German history will illustrate the point. Many historical German charts show strong connections to 0° Capricorn. The eclipse that coincided with Germany's victory in the Franco-Prussian War fell at 0° Capricorn on December 22, 1870. This was a very significant event because Germany defeated a much larger army. The French loss so shocked the world's military leaders that they copied the Prussian style of wargaming, planning, and rigid control. The adoption of these practices led to the chain reactions of mobilizations that ignited WWI. Pluto's transit over 0° Cancer in 1914 set matters off in Sarajevo with the Assassination of Ferdinand. Pluto was at 1° Cancer when the Lusitania's sinking brought the US into the war. The 'race to the sea' and the ensuing stalemate that led to the hopeless trench warfare began with the transit of Saturn over 0° Cancer.

By 1918, all sides were desperate to break the stalemate. The British developed the tank and unleashed it on the Germans at Cambrai on November 20, 1917. They tore a big hole in the enemy line, but were unable to exploit it. The Germans were also planning to break the British lines by training special storm or shock troops. The British assault at Cambrai gave them an additional idea: to use the captured British tanks in their counterattack. This commenced on March 21, 1918 when the Sun was at 0° Aries. After the war, all military leaders saw the value of the tank but none put the strategy and tactics together better than the Germans.

Heinz Guderian developed this new warfare in the face of stiff opposition from the infantry. Finally, he got Hitler's attention during a maneuver. The event which enabled Guderian to get the audience that he required was his senior commission which took place on June 22, 1916, with the Sun at 0° Cancer. On June 22, 1940, France surrendered to the blitz. On June 22, 1941, the Panzers attacked the USSR in the greatest blitzkreig in history. The Sun was back at 0° Cancer on both dates.

Other key events show planets in these degrees. The first known aerial bombing took place on June 24, 1849 when the Austrian army sieged the rebellious city of Venice. Austrian engineers floated balloons that had flaming material in carriages underneath that were dropped on the city. They did no damage, but we note the 3° Cancer position of the Sun. The WWI armistice and the 1918 German republic chart both have Mars near or at zero Capricorn. The following table summarizes the data. In addition, note how 10 to 14 degrees Aquarius also stands out. The fall of the Berlin Wall on November 9, 1989 occurred with Uranus at 2° Capricorn. A solar eclipse at 6° Aquarius on January 26, 1990 hit the important Aquarius degrees right after the fall. This example highlights the importance of transits over significant degree areas. Research by Jayne found that all cultures had sensitive degree areas that were created by aspects of the outer planets that fell at the time of major changes in the given culture. Any leader whose Sun fell in these degrees was bound to have a very important effect on his civilization. Transits and eclipses in these parts of the zodiac set off events of major significance.

Horoscopes of Phenomena

Here, we are not confronted with the difficulty of obtaining accurate birth times. The accurate times of eclipses, lunations, and ingresses are known in advance. The mundane astrologer then erects the horoscope for the locale in question. Again, the angles of these charts are a very important factor in their delineation.

Ingress Horoscopes

These charts are set for the time and date of the entrance of a planet into a sign. The most widely accepted convention is to erect charts for the Sun's entrance into the four cardinal signs, Aries, Cancer, Libra, and Capricorn.

This horoscope set for a given location then describes conditions in that area for the quarter. One school of thought assigns greater importance for a given year to the Aries ingress, while another emphasizes the Capricorn ingress. England's Charles Harvey stresses that these charts are most valuable when viewed as part of the larger cycles of the planets.

KEY DEGREE AREAS IN GERMAN HISTORY

event	*date*	*degree*	
EMPIRE ECLIPSE	12/22/1870	0°	Cap
HITLER BIRTH ECLIPSE	12/22/1889	1°	Cap
FERDINAND ASSASSINATED	6/28/1914	1°	Can (Pluto)
LUSITANIA SUNK	5/7/1915	1°	Can (Pluto)
1st AERIAL BOMBING	6/24/1849	3°	Can (Sun)
TREATY OF GHENT	12/24/1814	2°	Cap (Sun)
GUDERIAN RECEIVES COMMISSION	6/22/1906	0°	Can (Sun)
CAMBRAI COUNTERATTACK	3/21/1918	0°	Aries (Sun)
WW1 ARMISTICE	11/11/1918	0°	Cap (Mars)
GERMAN REPUBLIC	11/9/1918	29°	Sag (Mars)
FRANCE SURRENDERS	6/22/1940	0°	Can (Sun)
GERMAN INVASION OF THE USSR	6/22/1941	0°	Can (Sun)
FREDERICK THE GREAT	2/4/1712	14°	Aq (Sun)
GERMAN EMPIRE	1/18/1871	10°	Aq (Mc)
NAZI STATE	1/30/1933	10°	Aq (Sun)

Lunations and Eclipses

As with ingress charts, these maps are set up for the moment of a new or full moon for a given location. These horoscopes described the affairs in the locale over a very brief period and were regarded as subsidiary to the ingress charts.

Those lunations that were eclipses were given greater weight. Jayne and Edward Johndro felt that eclipses were the single most powerful influence in astrology. Jayne taught that events that occur near eclipses always take on greater importance. Events commencing in the week prior to the eclipse rarely work out as expected. The Republic of Texas signed a peace treaty with the Mexican Emperor, Santa Anna, one day before the solar eclipse of May 14, 1836. The Emperor then marched across the Rio Grande in violation of the agreement. After winning two small battles, the powerful Mexican army was routed at San Jacinto by an army of frontiersmen.

When the disgraced Santa Anna returned home, he found that his rivals had used the defeat to topple him from power. Note that the treaty worked out unexpectedly for both parties. Attempts to reconcile remaining differences resumed just prior to the solar eclipse of September 18, 1838. Those talks proved fruitless. The key lessons are that events near eclipses take on a greater importance, and that events in the week before eclipses are fated to work out unexpectedly.

Cycle Charts

These horoscopes are cast for the time when a planet moves from south to north declination. Interest in this method has been revived by Joan Quigley. Due to the lengths of the declination cycles, Mars, Jupiter, and Saturn are of the greatest value. These charts stay in effect until the next declination cycle begins.

The method stipulates that subsequent transits of, say, Mars over other planets in the chart are important. By erecting the chart for a given place, one can see the effect for that area, as with the previous horoscopes.

Astro Geography Methods

Various practitioners have attempted to project the planets in spacc onto the surface of the Earth in an attempt to find where the planetary energies would manifest.

Geodetic Equivalents

One of the earliest attempts assigned the 360 degrees of the zodiac to the 360 degrees of geographic longitude. The zero meridian running through Greenwich, England is designated to be the equivalent of zero Aries. The next 30 degrees to the east represent the sign Aries, and so on around the globe. So Paris, at 2° E 20 longitude, is assigned a midheaven of 2° Aries 20. Transiting planets at these degrees are believed to have an effect on their equivalent area on the Earth.

Eclipse Paths

The shadow of an eclipse has historically been seen as an omen. Astrologers traditionally have felt that the area and the peoples shadowed were unusually energized. Indeed, the single country most traversed by eclipse paths from the post-war years to 1960 was Vietnam. We can also see this at work in the life of the individual. The path of the eclipse nearest birth is usually significant in the life of an individual. For example, the path associated with the birth of Mao Tse Tung (Chart 1) slices China in half.

Charles Jayne made an extensive study of paths for over a decade. His method was to associate eclipses and their paths with a country's history. He demonstrated that these old paths stayed warm or energized, and could be ignited by future eclipses and transits.

One of his favorite examples was the path of the eclipse near Columbus's discovery of America. It ran from New Orleans over the eastern seaboard and across the Atlantic to England. Although Columbus was an Italian sailing for the Spanish, America's future was to be more closely linked with England.

At the end of WWII in July of 1945, a shadow connected the USA and USSR over the poles. The path was pointing to the two cold-war antagonists. It also traced out an attack route that was not accessible to armies of that age.

But the development of the missile and long-range bomber was to eventually lead the USA to construct the DEW line of radar stations to monitor attacks along this path. Curiously, the birth eclipse path of Mikhail Gorbachcv follows the same route.

Astro*Carto*Graphy

The development of ACG maps is rooted in the idea that planets at one of the four angles of the horoscope are strong. If a country or person has Jupiter on the midheaven, then that same relationship exists on a north-south band of longitude, and not only at the precise location of the birthplace. This can be best understood by considering relocation horoscopes.

If one is born in one city and moves to another, astrologers commonly set up a relocated birth chart for the new location. Thus, one could move to a place where Jupiter would have been on the midheaven if the person had been born there. By the same token, he could move to a place where Mars would have been rising in his chart. Again, Mars was rising somewhere in the world at the time of birth, just as Jupiter must have been on the midheaven somewhere. Lines can be drawn on a map to pinpoint these areas.

If one moves to a Jupiter line, he is more likely to encounter Jupiterian expansion there. On a Mars line, aggressive energies and Martian themes are emphasized. So, four lines, one for each angle, can be plotted for each planet. President Carter's Mars lines ran through the lands where warfare and conflict troubled him, like Iran and Ethiopia. Kennedy, Johnson, and Nixon all had difficult lines running through Southeast Asia.

ACG maps can be plotted for ingresses, lunations, eclipses and other phenomena. An annual publication, *The Astro*Carto*Graphy Source Book of Mundane Maps*, includes all of these valuable maps.

THE MEANING OF THE PLANETS
Focus on the Sun

Many of the following interpretations were drawn from the work of Charles Jayne. The keywords are standard mundane interpretations. With so many charts to analyze, Jayne stressed focusing on the Sun. He felt that this, and the progressed Sun, were the most vital bodies in a mundane chart. Being the life energy of any person or organization, the light's position is important. The 1992-1993 solar eclipse hits to the Suns of both President Premadasa and the republic of Sri Lanka are a fine example of the power of the Sun as an indicator of the assassination of this leader.

Key words and concepts—

–The supreme authority-the king, queen or president.

–The general nature of the country.

Special Significance of the Outer Planets

The discovery of the outer planets marked a great shift in man's consciousness. Therefore, Jayne considered the erection of horoscopes for their discovery to be important. These charts represented man's relation to these new energies. It was felt that the outer planets had a greater effect upon mundane astrology and the collective then they did upon individual charts. This occurred because individuals simply did not live long enough to experience all of the outer planets' cycles.

This influence was symbolized in the horoscopes of the discoveries of the three outermost planets. The Moon in each chart was very close to the Lunar node, indicating that the Moon was very close to the ecliptic. In other words, the Moon had little latitude. Jayne stressed the use of latitude (see his book *A New Dimension in Astrology)*. This type of aspect represented situations in which individuals had little latitude, or little free will. Because the Moon represents the people, one can interpret the discovery charts as saying that man has little latitude or freedom of action in relation to the three outermost planets.

Pluto, The Planet of Government

Pluto is the glue that holds political entities together. The Pluto effect is a binding one, in contrast to the effect of Uranus which is an 'unbinding' one. Pluto represents the power of the state that enables it to survive. Analysis of the horoscopes of 13 charts representing the 10 national states that Jayne felt were most significant during WWII revealed that the Sun was opposite Pluto in eight cases.

This combination symbolizes a strong central power and a hierarchal political structure. It represents the ability to govern a vast group of diversified people who were heterogeneous in racial, cultural, and religious make-up, and were living over a large area. It is interesting to note that there was not a single opposition of Mars, Jupiter, or Saturn to the Sun. Leaving a wide 18° orb, one would expect 1.3 oppositions in 13 instances, but there were 8. This occurs by chance only 1 in 18,000 times. So, Pluto-Sun appears to be a necessary ingredient for a lasting government.

The trio of countries that did not have the opposition did feature a trine between the pair. The three were Germany, Fascist Italy, and Japan, all Axis powers that obviously did not last. This set them apart from the US, Britain, France, China, British India, Brazil, and the USSR.

Like Neptune, Pluto was related to mass movements, but with quite a different flavor. Pluto's changes are drastic, authoritarian, severe, unwavering, and irrevocable. Its action is similar to Mars, but its scope is more vast, and the changes are more deep and slow. Pluto was opposite Mars upon discovery on January 21, 1930, which may account for its harsh nature.

Jayne saw the Russian Revolution and the Fascist takeovers in Italy and Germany as taking place under the influence of Pluto, so they differed from the Uranian American revolution. While the Russian (the USSR was formed on December 30, 1922 with Sun opposite Pluto) and Fascist entities differed in some respects, they shared the totalitarian means of control.

Jayne noted that some judgement was necessary in assessing the affect of the Sun-Pluto upon the entity. In the case of Brazil, note that the Sun is opposite Pluto in the September 7, 1822 chart of independence and in the map of the November 15, 1889 chart of the republic. Only the horoscope of the 'New State' declared by the contemporary dictator, Vargas, on November 10, 1937, had the trine. So, the 'base horoscopes' of Brazil were strengthened by the Sun-Pluto opposition, but the regime of Vargas did not suggest a long life for his particular government. The astrologer could then conclude that Vargas' regime would not last but that Brazil itself would remain intact. This was the difference in the interpretations between the hard and soft aspects.

At the war's conclusion, many astrologers looked to Pluto in an attempt to predict the onset of one-world government. No one succeeded, but Jayne did note that the prevailing Saturn-Pluto opposition of 1946 was likely to foil any such attempts in the mid-'40s.

Key words and concepts-

- Wealth located below the earth,
- Nuclear energy,
- Oppression and its backlash : terrorism, hidden secrets, secret police
- Crime
- Drastic changes.

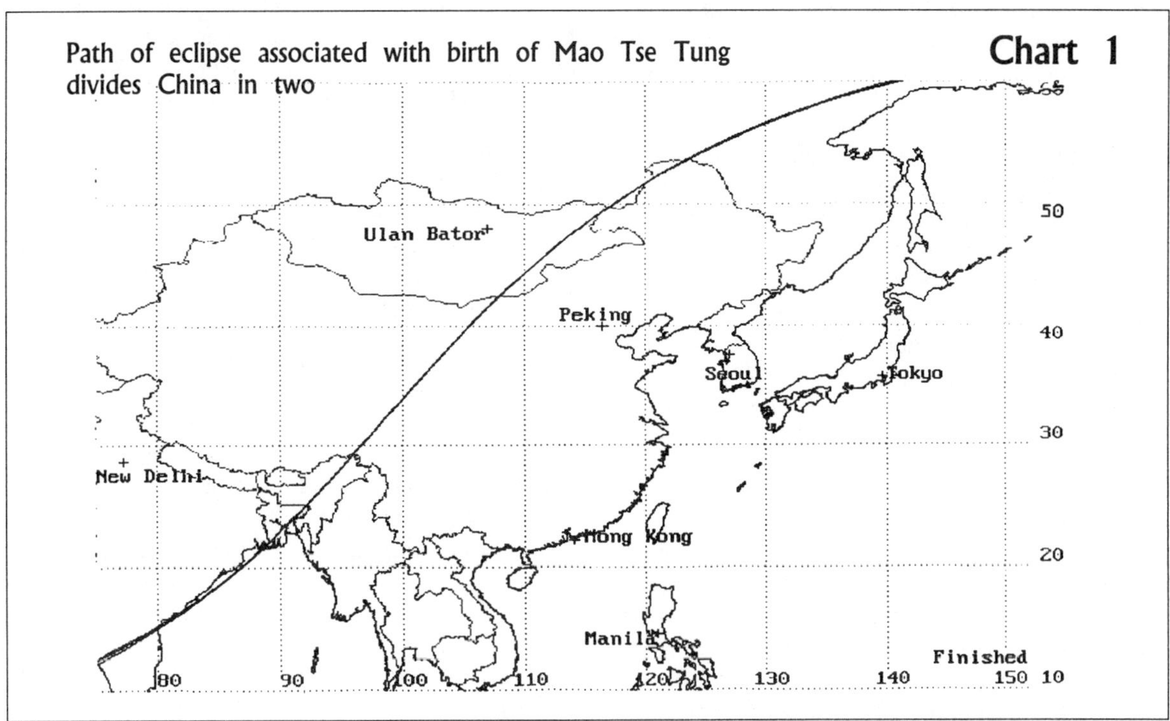

Neptune—
Planet of the Masses

This planet rules mass movements and the mass mind. Neptune has a liberal character and symbolizes social idealism and collectivism. Jayne cited it as being the single most prominent factor in the dissolution of countries or organizations. This usually occurred through a loosening of the social mores or laws of the land, and frequently was accompanied by monetary inflation. Hard Sun-Neptune angles usually represent an idealistic or even deceptive situation, usually due to the faulty appraisal or assessment of conditions. There is an inability or unwillingness to deliver on the promised reforms. The horoscope of the British rule of India, November 1, 1858, has a Sun-Neptune sesquiquadrate. This negative angle more than offset the Sun-Pluto opposition.

Neptune was first sighted, and thought to be a star, in May of 1795. From that date until discovery on September 23, 1846, the planet's effect intensified. Because it was conjunct Saturn upon discovery, its effect upon mankind was more gradual than that of Uranus. Neptune infiltrates while Uranus shatters. Utopian socialism was born and folks began mass movement by rail and steamship. Communism, spiritualism, worldwide communications, and the growth of international organizations were all Neptunian developments. Labor organizations and cooperatives, somewhat akin to socialism, also fell under its rule.

The First International was established by Marx on September 28, 1864 with Neptune opposite the Sun and Uranus square it. True to the rule that Neptunian organizations do not last, the movement was out of business by 1876. Subsequent labor organizations such as the International Labor Organization (April 28, 1919) had a Sun-Neptune square while the World Federation of Trade Unions (October 1945) had the conjunction. As one can gather from these descriptions, Neptune rules majorities while Uranus represents minorities.

After the war, Jayne interpreted Neptune as being the planet of large-scale finance. We can see this in the three Jupiter-Neptune conjunctions of 1971. Thirty days prior to the third conjunction, Nixon took the US completely off the gold standard on August 15, 1971, setting off the great inflation of the '70s. This phase ended with the Saturn-Neptune square of March 25-26, 1980 when the attempted corner of the silver market by the Hunt brothers collapsed within 24 hours of the aspect. A decade of deflation in commodities followed. Passage through fire signs has coincided with price inflation in the past while transit through earth signs has heralded price deflation.

Key words and concepts—

- Welfare state, utopia, socialism, liberal groups,
- Subversion,
- Dissolution of morality,
- Propaganda,
- Hospitals, charities,
- Minorities,
- Oil.

Uranus-The Planet of Individuality

According to Jayne, the dramatic effect of Uranus upon the Earth could be read in the discovery chart of March 13, 1789. Uranus opposed Saturn and Mars and squared the Sun. This was certainly indicative of the upsets and readjustments that to occur. Uranus was discovered only 12 days after the Articles of Confederation were ratified on March 1, 1781 in the US, so this body has a special connection with America. England, too, felt the planet's energy. The last Stuart king was ousted, and the new rulers, William and Mary, were forced to agree to terminate the divine right of kings and transfer the power to Parliament. The 1789 French Revolution led to the Rights of Man declaration.

The effect upon industry was also dramatic. Watts' construction of the steam engine in 1782 can be considered the beginning of the industrial revolution. The first research paper about uranium was read in the summer of 1786. The first atomic explosion occurred on July 16, 1945, the week before Uranus crossed the ecliptic.

Hard aspects to the Sun create entities that usually do not last long. British rule of India commenced under a quincunx, so rule there was marked by rebellion. Fascist Italy had a Sun-Uranus trine, but here is where the principle of the modifier changed the interpretation. Italy joined the Berlin-Tokyo alliance on November 7, 1937 when the Sun was opposite Uranus, drawing it into the Axis-Uranus sphere. Modern Italy (June 10, 1946) has the Sun conjunct Uranus and the North Lunar Node, symbolizing the many changes in leadership. The hard aspects, particularly the opposition, were symbolic of dictators and dictatorships. The aspect brought arrogance, self-will, and violent revolutionary changes that are upsetting and not always progressive.

The Sun-Uranus square has an interesting history. It seems to be connected to social dissent and the affirmation of human rights; the movements are in conflict with prevailing authority. When the Chinese Revolution began on October 11, 1911, the Sun squared Uranus. The November 7, 1917 Bolshevik Revolution also occurred during this aspect. Marx established the First International on September 28, 1864. The Second International began in Paris on July 14, 1889 and was reformed on May 25, 1923. Each had the square aspect, each expressed revolt, and each was too difficult to hold together.

Soft Sun-Uranus aspects represent a progressive trait. Many international and humanitarian organizations carry the sextile or trine. The Covenant of the League of Nations on June 28, 1919 occurred on a trine aspect. Other such organizations with the trine or sextile are: International Chamber of Commerce (June 30, 1920), International Association for Labor Legislation (July 28, 1900), Geneva Convention of International Red Cross (August 22, 1864), and the International Postal Union (October 10, 1874).

Uranus symbolizes the entrepreneurial freedom expressed in free enterprise and the 'right to strike.' In the post-war period, Uranus was seen as representing US labor.

Key words and concepts—
- Revolution and change,
- Technology, innovation, electricity
- Legislative assemblies
- Sudden shifts of power, dictators.

Saturn— Also a Planet of Government

Saturn-Sun aspects were second only to Pluto-Sun connections in the charts of long-lasting political entities. Squares, oppositions and trines, respectively, were most frequently present. Like Pluto, Saturn added to the glue that held entities together. Sun-Saturn trines indicated a continuity from the past and some support from the previously established order. The planet was interpreted as ruling big business after the war.

With this in mind, the 1993 Saturn-Pluto squares can be read as clashes between the Clinton administration and big business. Curiously enough, Jayne associated Saturn itself and the Jupiter-Saturn polarity with war (secondarily progressed Mars was also frequently cited as a harbinger of conflict). Here was his reasoning from the April, 1948 issue of *American Astrology:*

> *"It is our own belief that hostility, every-man-for-himself, division and what we might term 'defensive aggressiveness' are all Saturnine.... We can correlate Jupiter and Saturn with empire and peace, and with strife and division (not as wholly a negative phase as it might sound since progress is made and material matters)."*

Key words and concepts—

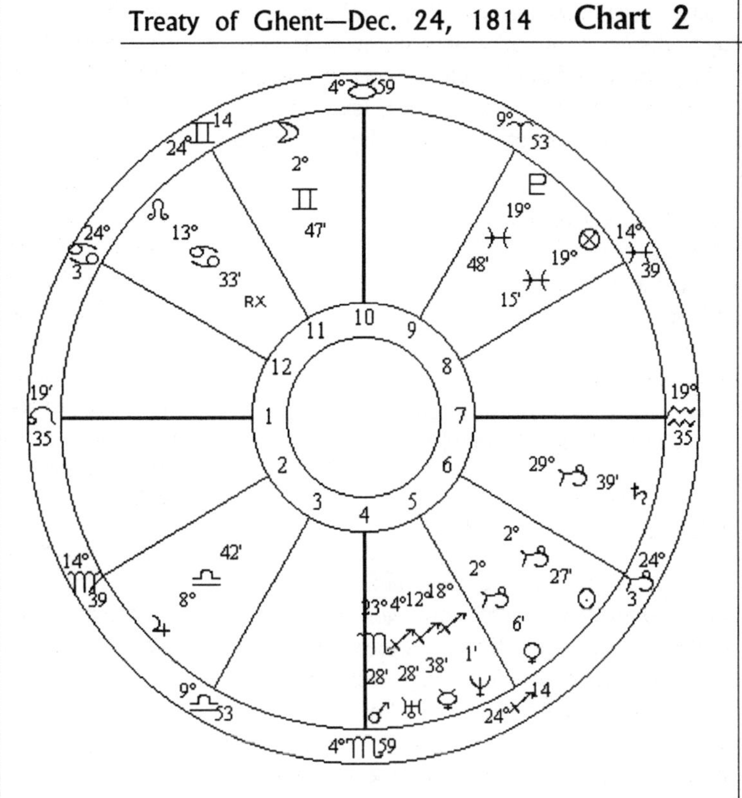

Treaty of Ghent—Dec. 24, 1814 **Chart 2**

– Practical matters
– Defensive aggression
– Land, buildings
– Senior citizens, bureaucrats and state employees
– Law and order, legal system, civil service,
– Conservative groups.

Jupiter-The Planet of Expansion

The horoscopes of Britain and the US illustrated the point. The British chart for the Glorious Revolution of January 28, 1689 had the Sun closely conjunct Jupiter. The American and French conjunctions were wider, and the countries expanded less rapidly. Mussolini's Italy (October 31, 1922) shared this aspect, but did not survive the expansion of fascism due to its otherwise weak solar axis. This was the type of Jupiterian expansion that led to war. In addition to the traditional interpretations of the Greater Benefic, Charles stressed its less materialistic side. In fact, he once related a story in which an astrologer tested his peers' ability to predict. He found that astrologers were most often incorrect where Jupiter was the most potent factor. Jayne called Jupiter the planet of the soul, and its growth as an expansion of consciousness. This manifested through religion, philosophy, and education. It was also the planet of reform and the righting of wrongs, thus the connection to law and justice. Jupiter-Sun aspects gave a somewhat progressive or liberal tone to a national chart.

Key words and concepts—
– Wealth
– Bureaucratic waste
– Judges
– Banks
– Philanthropy
– Churches, values and belief systems
– Institutes of higher learning, law.

Venus and Mars: *Significators of Peace and War*

The interpretations of the Lesser Benefic and the God of War are no surprise to any astrologer. The way in which the planets were utilized is of great interest. Johndro stressed that a well-placed Venus was necessary to establish a lasting peace. His favorite examples were the successful Treaty of Ghent and the infamous Treaty of Versailles. The Treaty of Ghent concluded the British-American War of 1812. It was signed on December 24, 1814 at Ghent sometime 'in the evening.' Johndro set the chart (Chart 2) for 8 PM. Note the Sun-Venus conjunction. The agreement did not reach London until the 26th, the day of a lunar eclipse. The striking development was the exact conjunction of Venus to the eclipse degree. Johndro wrote that this denoted "...a peace and friendship that would eclipse all others as an example of what peace and friendship can really mean between amicable and reasonable peoples." He quoted Ptolemy as saying:

> *"The planet having closest configuration with an eclipse dominates it."*

Thus, the inclusion of the eclipse chart in the analysis of this treaty reinforces the strength of Venus in the agreement. To complete the study, the treaty arrived in Washington on February 14, 1815 with Mercury and Venus conjunct. The Senate approved it on the next day with Moon sextile Mercury and Venus. Johndro concluded by noting that the progressed Mars of the eclipse chart squared the eclipse Mars in 1941-1942, indicating a crisis period and increased military activity for the US, Britain, and Canada. He also correctly projected that Neptune passing over the treaty Jupiter in 1945-1947 was beneficial, but that the US would likely give its gold hoard away in an unwise post-war largesse.

The Treaty of Versailles was signed in Paris on June 28, 1919 time unknown. Venus was conjunct Saturn and the Sun was conjunct Pluto. The solar eclipse of May 29, 1919 rules the agreement. The eclipse was conjunct Mars, and the US Senate fought over the contents of the treaty during the month of May. Sun-Pluto reflects, among other things, that the terms of the treaty were to be kept secret until the signing. But a senator leaked the terms to the press and then presented a copy to the Senate, thereby forcing its publication and setting off another row. Quite a different story than the Treaty of Ghent!

In natal charts, Johndro noted that Venus square Saturn was not the configuration for a peace negotiator. Roosevelt, Hitler, Chamberlain and American Secretary of State Hull all shared this aspect. History tells us what ensued.

Venus key words and concepts—
– Holidays, festivals, celebrations
– Art, amusements

– The ability to mediate or negotiate
– Victory, peace, the harmony that keeps societies together.

Mars key words and concepts—

– War, soldiers
– Engineers
– Epidemics, droughts, great activity, accidents such as fires and explosions
– Threat of war to dominate the population.

Mars Retrograde and Direct

Jayne utilized the stations of Venus and Mars frequently in prediction. When these bodies are retrograde, they are closer to the Earth and exert a greater influence. Aggressive actions seemed to be more successful when they began at the direct station and culminated when Mars reach maximum speed of 41 minutes of arc per day. The retrograde period slowed attacks down and were not the most auspicious time for launching new campaigns. In fact, it was not wise to be over-extended at such times. Peace efforts made during Mars retrograde frequently failed after the Red Planet went direct. In fact, these intervals were usually used by one side or both to re-arm for fresh fighting.

The Nazi-Soviet pact is one example. Germany and Russia also signed their post-WWI peace pact under a retrograde Mars. Curiously enough, Rudolf Hess parachuted into England on a retrograde Mars. Also, the US and Japan discussed peace during Mars' retrogradation, followed by the attack on Pearl Harbor. The effective force of the planet was most apparent when it traversed a band of the zodiac for the third and final time. Therefore, if direct Venus were making its third passage at the same time that Mars was retrograde, the Venusian influence would dominate and would warrant greater emphasis from the astrologer.

Many military campaigns began shortly after Mars resumed direct motion. The 1935 station heralded the Ethiopian crisis which became a war in the following fall. The Sino-Japanese conflict commenced after a station in the summer of 1937. The war in Europe followed the summer station in 1939 by a little more than a week. Pearl Harbor followed the November, 1941 directional change. The winter station of 1944 preceded the big American push in the Pacific while the early 1946 one marked the US-USSR crisis over Iran. The 1948 and 1950 events roughly coincided with the Israel crisis and the outbreak of the Korean War. No major events of similar nature seemed to occur before or after this series. To quote Charles Jayne in 1956, "*We must think of Mars as a 'trigger-force' which sets off a charge of dynamite, but only when and if other and more massive and slower planetary influences have already operated.*"

Mars' opposition to the Sun during the retrograde period marked the time of the greatest build-up of energy. The point of release seemed to occur in the approximately two month period between the direct station and the subsequent square of Mars to the Sun. Quoting again, "We suggest, therefore, that when-and just after- a planet is closest to the Sun-and farther away, too- its influence is increased."

The fact that not all direct Mars stations sparked major world events left a piece out of the puzzle. Charles felt that oppositions, conjunctions, parallels, and contraparallels to Jupiter contributed greatly to the likelihood of conflict. Another major contributing factor was the distance of Jupiter from the Sun. Its influence was magnified when it was near (perihelion) or far (aphelion). Second to these influences were contacts to Neptune. So, combinations of the direct station of Mars to the Sun, Jupiter, and lastly Neptune were most likely to generate action.

If these Martian influences were indicators of attack, then what were the planetary indications of defense? They were primarily Saturnian. Jayne wrote that Saturn in Gemini was a big negative for the Allies because it opposed the Sagittarian Suns of both King George and Stalin whilst also passing over the Gemini sector of the American independence chart.

Grant Lewi writing in *Dell Horoscope* in 1940 added this:

> *"Saturn transiting Mars is more disastrous for the attacker than for the defender. One can defend as Saturn transits his Mars, but he can hardly hope to succeed if he attacks. Thus Britain can defend better than Hitler can attack."*

The Moon and Mercury

The Moon traditionally rules the people in a mundane chart. Green also associated it with water and women and children.

Key words and concepts—

- People, popular opinion, the masses
- The prevailing mood.

Mercury represents the transportation and communication systems. Jayne found Mercury significant in the history of China. He felt that it symbolized the communication and transportation problems of this populous nation. It also reflected the many dialects.

Key words and concepts—

- Writers, speakers, teachers
- News
- All communication and transportation systems
- Trade and commerce ✹

Suggested Reading

Mundane or National Astrology by H. S. Green. Symbols and Signs, North Hollywood CA,1977.

Raphaels's Mundane Astrology by Raphael. Symbols and Signs, North Hollywood CA, 1977.

Precepts in Mundane Astrology by Frederic von Norstrand. Macoy Publishing NY, 1962.

Mundane Astrology by Baigent, Campion, and Harvey. The Aquarian Press, Wellingborough, UK, 1984.

Book of World Horoscopes by Nicholas Campion. The Aquarian Press, Wellingborough, UK, 1988.

Accurate World Horoscopes by Doris Doane. AFA, Tempe AZ, 1984.

Planets in Locality by Steve Cozzi. Llewellyn Publications, St. Paul MN,1988.

The Astrology of the Macrocosm anthology edited by Joan McEvers. Llewellyn Publications, St. Paul MN, 1990.

*Astro*Carto*Graphy Source Book of Mundane Maps* by Jim Lewis. Astro Numeric Service, Box 336, Ashland OR, 1994. Issued Annually.

REVIEW QUESTIONS:

1. An astrologer must prepare a forecast for a city and surrounding region for the next three months. Which techniques would be employed?

Answer: Lunation, ingress, and eclipse charts set for the location. Also, the relation of these charts to any relevant natal charts, such as one for the city or its leaders.

2. Arrange these horoscopes in order from most powerful to least powerful: The prime minister, the country, the Jupiter-Saturn chart set for the capital, a horoscope set for the beginning of the most recent era of the culture.

Answer: The chart for the most recent era of the culture, the country, the Jupiter-Saturn chart, the prime minister. The culture is the larger and more lasting entity. The country will likely be second in longevity. The conjunction chart lasts for 20 years. The leader may only last for a few years.

3. An astrologer is asked to assess the prospects for a country. The person makes his forecast based upon the horoscopes of the republic and the president. What does the analysis lack?

Answer: Breadth. If there are very vital degree areas from the old charts of cultural change or significant moments, they will be missed. These may make the difference between a relatively minor event and an historic one.

4. A question arises about the relations between two countries. What methods might be applied to obtain an answer?

Answer: Synastry between the national charts and their leaders. Horoscopes set for the significant moment that the two first had contact or made war or treaties. Astro*Cart*Graphy lines and eclipse paths that connect the two countries.

5. You are asked to analyze the economic prospects for an area. How would you approach this question?

Answer: Focus on Jupiter and Saturn for expansion and contraction. Look at Uranus for innovation. Jupiter and Neptune for inflation. Saturn and Neptune for deflation. These planets can be checked in: the chart of the country, the Jupiter-Saturn chart set for the capital, ingress and eclipse charts, or the Jupiter cycle chart.

6. What are the methods available to determine the prospects for war in a given region?

Answer: The planets to focus on are Mars, Jupiter, and Saturn. The stations of Mars and Venus are important. Uranus and Pluto can be revolution. The charts to check are: the national charts, the leaders' charts, important degree areas for the culture. Eclipses and their paths and the Jupiter-Saturn conjunction charts set for the capital.

SOLAR ARC DIRECTIONS

by Warren Kinsman

This article will allow readers to use solar arc directions as part of their interpretation of a horoscope.

It is not going to be philosophical or argumentative such as solar arcs *vs.* secondary progressions. I'm a firm believer that , no matter what a user decides upon in the way of house systems, progressions, solar arcs, secondary progressions or user-arcs, our guides step in to help us with our interpretations; and we all end up at about the same place, with the client being helped. This assumes, of course, a dedication on the part of the astrologer.

Before going much further, it would be useful to define the terms in this article. I used the words "secondary progression" above. *Secondary progressions,* the so-called day-for-a-year method, is the most commonly used form of forecasting in astrology. More astrologers use secondary progressions than any other form of directing a horoscope. I believe the reason for this is related to the fact that most astrology text books teach secondary progressions only. More modern books, such as those by March and McEvers, Tyl, or Hastings, cover solar arcs, but most others do not.

A progression is obtained by taking the age of the client, let's say 25, and counting ahead in the ephemeris 25 days after the day of birth. An easy example would be someone born July 1 of any year. July 2 represents the second year of this life (age 1 to 2), and July 26 represents the 25th year of this life (age 25 to 26). Then, using the placements on July 26 from the ephemeris, calculate a horoscope exactly as you did the natal horoscope, only these planets and house cusps now become the secondary progressed horoscope.

Solar arc directions are based on the same day-for-a-year system as secondaries, but here it is the position of the Sun only that holds the key. I use a method taught to me by Barbara Watters when I was studying with her more than 20 years ago. She took the motion of the Sun on the directed date in the ephemeris and from it subtracted the position of the Sun in the ephemeris on the natal date. This became the solar arc and was added to all the planets and the MC. The new ASC and intermediate house cusps were derived by looking them up in a table of houses for the latitude where the client lived on the directed birthday. (A more thorough way of calculating directions is shared in the Appendix).

The interpretation of solar arcs is basically the same as interpreting the natal horoscope, with some very notable exceptions. *First, do not read anything into the directed horoscope that is not also indicated in the natal horoscope.* We've all heard of so-called astrologers who tell clients they need to be careful of some horrible fate based on a directed chart, when the natal chart showed nothing of the kind.

Second, aspects in the natal chart are reinforced in the directed chart. A directed square, opposition, sextile, trine, or conjunction to a natal planet will activate

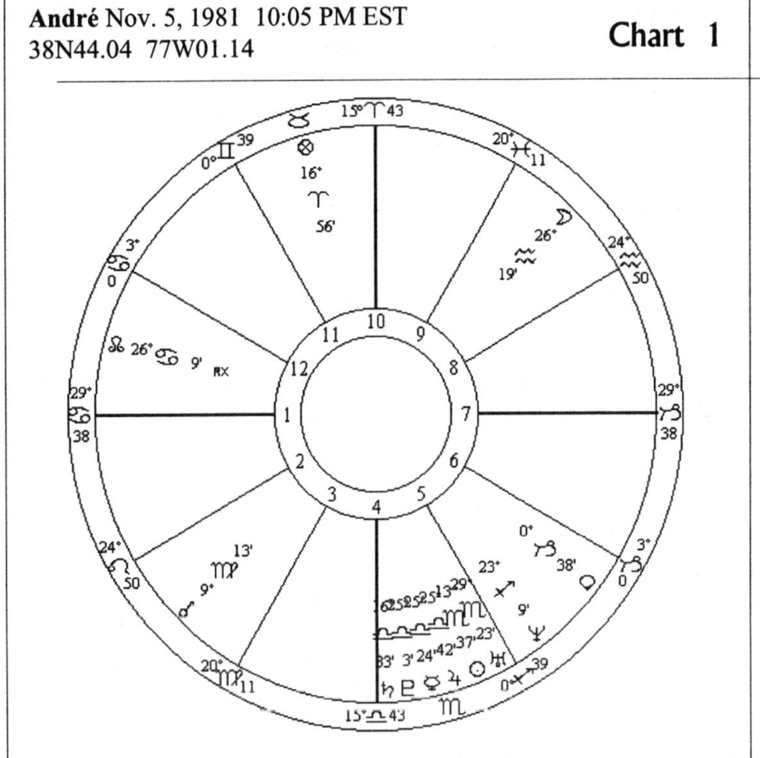

whatever natal aspects the chart is making. This means, to reinforce the point, that a directed trine to a natal planet squaring another natal planet will activate the natal square. This doesn't mean some disaster will develop, as lots of positive outcomes are initiated on squares, but it does suggest some effort will be needed to direct the energy in a positive way.

Third, solar arc directions hitting natal planets may or may not be activated based on the transits happening at that time. In my experience, it is more likely that an aspect will pass unnoticed when there are easy (trines and sextiles) aspects by arc and transits rather than hard ones (conjunctions, squares and oppositions).

Don't expect every solar arc aspect to indicate an event in a client's life; however, taken with transits, there is a good possibility that an event will manifest outwardly in the person's life.

For example: I recently consulted with a gay couple, Harry and Greg (not their real names). Harry had Venus square Saturn by solar arc. The symbolism suggests that Venus (the love nature within) would probably experience some frustration (Saturn) in finding expression, but it didn't appear that anything else was going on in his chart. Greg, however, had transiting Uranus conjunct his natal Sun, which symbolizes a desire for more freedom. At the time that the transiting Moon was making a square to his Uranus-Sun, Greg informed Harry that he wanted more space. After some discussion it turned out there was no serious problem between these two, but that Greg (Uranus-Sun) wanted to spend some time with friends he hadn't seen for a while and was feeling guilty over leaving his lover.

When Harry, who knew some astrology, discovered that these friends did not threaten the partnership, he simply told his partner to take as much space as he wanted, and the two are continuing to grow together as these aspects now wane. Had Harry been possessive and clinging, he undoubtedly would have lost his friend. Had Greg wanted a sexual liaison with others, the relationship would probably have ended as well.

If secondary progressions are the most frequent form of direction used by astrologers, why even bother with solar arcs? The example given above is one reason. Solar arcs seem to indicate events in people's lives that for the most part manifest externally. I've heard some astrologers suggest that secondary progressions make themselves known on an internal level and that solar arc directions manifest on an external level. I do believe this is generally true, but there are enough deviations from this rule to suggest applying it with caution. In the examples I'm providing, however, the external manifestations will be quite evident.

Let's take a look at a young boy's chart. We'll call him André. (Nov. 5, 1981, 10:03 PM. EST, 38N53, 77W02). Here is a child who keeps a great many things to himself with his water sign rising, five planets in the 4th house, and the Moon in the secretive 8th. Most Cancer rising individuals are devoted to home and family, or the *idea* of home and family, even when circumstances arise to make this part of life very difficult. Mercury, Jupiter, Sun in the 4th sound great, but when you add the conjunction of Pluto to the Mercury-Jupiter and then square the ascendant to these three, the picture becomes more complicated. The recipe becomes further complicated by adding the Saturn in opposition to the MC (mother). Now we have set up a potentially difficult family picture in the life of this child. With the chart ruler in the 8th house square Uranus from the 5th, we see an added dimension around women in the life of this young man.

The solar arc is calculated to April 15, 1989, when André was taken away from his mother due to her neglect of her children and her abuse of cocaine (crack). Note that Neptune by direction is exactly conjunct natal Venus, ruler of the home 4th. Neptune's less evolved manifestation is involvement with drugs. Its conjunction with Venus is telling us that there could be something unclear about the home situation. As it turned out, we have a child who worshipped his mother, covered her drug abuse from others (he had been removed once before when he was younger, but that date is unavailable), and set about taking care of his two younger brothers.

For 10 days, this 7 ½-year-old boy was left totally to his own resources. He got himself up in the mornings, washed, dressed, and went to school where he was given breakfast and lunch. These were his only meals of the day. Immediately after school he would come home and begin knocking on the doors of his neighbors to beg food for his two younger brothers then aged 3 and 4. Had it not been for this concern about his family

(Cancer rising), André might not have taken the care that he did, and his brothers could have died. After 10 days of this begging, one neighbor finally called the police, who found the parent absent; and the children were finally placed in foster care.

Notice the directed Saturn within 1°01' of natal Pluto. Some astrologers would say that orb is too great for a solar arc, which operates more within 30' or even 15'. Three factors made me think otherwise: first, André's removal from his mother was terribly confusing for him (Neptune on Venus); second, this trauma meant he would live with his next youngest brother but be separated from his youngest sibling (whom he adored); and third, he was placed in a foster home with a woman who was big on discipline and short on demonstrated love.

All this told me that André's directed Saturn was manifesting roughly one year before its exact aspect. Indeed it continued to operate, as he took almost three years to accept — albeit grudgingly — that he wasn't going home anytime soon. Furthermore, he had to adjust to a foster mother who was a hard-nosed Capricorn with a very needy Leo Moon. This woman spent a great deal of time complaining of her sacrifices for "these children" while making sure her every whim was satisfied. *(I admit to having very little objectivity toward this particular foster mother.)*

In looking at his younger brother's chart (we'll call him Leroy, May 24, 1984; 9:49 AM EDT; 38N53, 77W02), notice that his rising sign is also Cancer, and only one degree away from André's rising degree. Leroy has an 11th house Sun opposite Uranus, making him ready to march to his own drummer (much to the frustration of all his elementary school teachers). He also has Pluto in the 4th square the ascendant, and a Mars-Saturn conjunction, also in the 4th. That both of these boys would have problems in their early years around home issues is hardly surprising. Again, by directing the chart to the date they were taken into protective custody (April 15, 1989), we see directed Saturn conjunct natal Mars in the home 4th ruling the maternal 10th. Stress in the home at this time involving the mother is certainly one of the interpretations of this aspect. However, is it the only thing that could have happened to this child? Certainly not! In some charts directed Saturn to a natal 4th house Mars might mean a move, perhaps a difficult move for the child. It could mean the mother and father were at war with each other and the child was feeling trapped. It could also mean that absolutely nothing at all occurred in the life of the child. That's why I'm less inclined to try impressing clients with past events and more inclined to ask what occurred when I see aspects in the past indicating potential trauma.

If I were to read this chart when this child reaches adulthood and say something to the effect that he may have had a tough time at home when he was 4 years old, he would fill in the blanks, and be sufficiently impressed with astrology to believe that there must be something to it. Were I to predict his mother and father probably argued all the time and this led to their separation when he was four, he would, undoubtedly,

Leroy May 24, 1984 9:49 AM
38N55.04 77W01.14 **Chart 2**

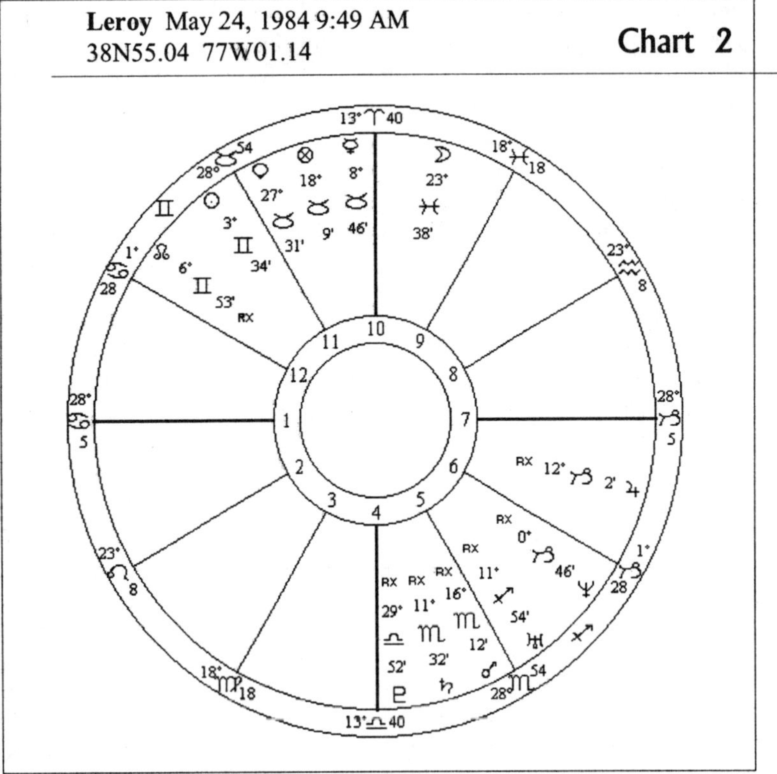

be most unimpressed, since his mother and father had been separated since he was a baby.

So what did it look like for these two boys at the end of 1994 when they were supposed to be reunited with their birth mother?

Over the spring and summer of 1994, their mother got herself a job, went out and found an apartment for herself (waiting for the city to provide housing is like trying to nail jello to a tree!), and consistently came up negative in her weekly drug tests. I had a long talk with her in August, and she appeared to really want to "get it all together" this time. The fact that she was in her Saturn return year made me additionally hopeful.

She told the social worker she wanted her children back, and the court determined her boys could begin spending weekends at her home beginning in September. However, when it came time for her to have her preliminary hearing, she failed to show up in court. In checking with her job, it was discovered she had been let go, and she stopped showing up for her drug tests.

This has been a consistent problem ever since her boys were taken from her. She would constantly promise them she'd be getting them back; and then she would constantly sabotage herself whenever she got close to making these promises a reality. André's natal Moon square Uranus is certainly an indication of sudden upsetting events and circumstances or unpredictability around the women in his life. Unfortunately, I do not have a timed chart for his mother, but we should be able to look at the boys' horoscopes to see how things look down the road.

On October 30, 1994, André had directed Saturn in the 4th square his ascendant. This brings home the natal influence of problems in the home that have a strong impact upon the personality. If you take this with transiting Pluto square his natal Moon setting off his natal Moon-Uranus square, you can see additional problems through a woman or women (*i.e.*, foster mother, or teachers). Other Uranus transits in the fall are Uranus square Pluto, square Mercury, square Jupiter.

I'm a firm believer that those who try their hand at predicting precisely how Uranus is going to manifest in a chart are the astrologers who end up with egg on their faces. This isn't to say we can't look at potential areas and possibilities, but I just don't feel comfortable getting too specific with the planet of unpredictability.

Having said this, let's provide a few more details around André's life in the fall of 1994.

All his life André has been a top-rate student. In fact he was reading when he was two years old, and these weren't "Dick and Jane" books. His grandmother would give him books to read so that by the time he was in kindergarten, his principal, who didn't believe anyone that young could read, tested him by giving him a newspaper. André not only read from several articles but, in his own words, told the principal what they meant. His grades have always been A's and B's until the year he turned 13, when the pressure from peers not to be "nerdy" took over.

In the fall of 1994, André brought home a report card with C's and D's, and he became a constant discipline problem for his teachers. His foster mother appeared unable (or less willing) to keep him in tow, as she had in the past. I had been trying for three years to get her to allow him to go into counseling, which is provided by the foster care program. She steadfastly refused, no doubt because she knows her less-than-stellar care will surface for all to see.

The organization for which I volunteer learned of her reluctance and reported her to the social worker. As a result, André began getting the counseling he had needed, and the fact that he started it before December when the court made its final decision as to whether to reunite him with his mother or place him along with his brother in long term foster care, may prevent him from internalizing all the negatives in his life.

His brother's chart was less stressed by traditional aspects in the fall. However, if we direct his solar arc Neptune, we see it makes a sesquiquadrate (sesquare) to the midpoint of the Moon/ascendant. Noel Tyl describes this as *"Self-delusion is possible; feeling 'wiped out'; loneliness; deception by a female."* In fact, this midpoint picture to his solar arc planets looked very challenging.

In December 1994, the court surprised a number of us working with André and Leroy by ordering these two brothers to be reunited with their mother. Her drug tests, which she began taking again in November, were negative; and she indicated a desire to have her children together again. A big factor was the boys' pleas to be reunited with their real mother, and the fact that what came out in the hearing about the foster mother may prevent her from ever again being assigned additional children in need of foster care. At this time, André's second brother joined André and Leroy on December 23 (his birth time is unavailable so I haven't included his chart).

In the five and a-half years I have been working with these first two brothers, I have never seen them more content. They are less stressed and more relaxed now than they were with the foster mother. When they were around her, they had to walk on eggshells, as her mercurial temperament kept things very unstable around the home. If they literally looked at her in a way she felt or perceived as questioning in any way, they were yelled at or sent to their room. If they are so happy now, why do the solar arc midpoints show such stress in 1995?

It's important not to be myopic in doing anyone's chart. Quite simply there are other things going on in these young boys lives as well as being reunited with their mother. There is the stress of relocating to a new neighborhood, a new school for Leroy, and an impending further change of residence as their mother looks for a larger apartment to house her reunited family. She's found a larger apartment in a better building, but the neighborhood that one has to walk through to get there leaves much to be desired. Newcomers to any neighborhood will be tested by other youth, so they have this rite of passage to anticipate as well.

With André's solar-arc ascendant semi-square his Mars/Saturn midpoint through January 1995, he had to struggle in his neighborhood; he struggled in his school (he's got major work to make up as a result of his poor first advisory grades); he struggled in defining his relationship with his mom. With solar-arc Uranus square his Jupiter/ascendant midpoint, he was able to pull out of his funk quite unexpectedly. (Tyl says *"fortunate adjustment to one's status saves the day".*)

Solar-arc Mars was sesquare his Uranus/MC midpoint (he challenged his teachers and found himself in arguments with them). SA Neptune was semi-square his Sun/Uranus midpoint (a possible threat to a relationship - he had a new girlfriend), and SA Saturn was semisquare his Venus/Uranus midpoint (the relationship with the girlfriend was curbed because his mother had threatened to take away his telephone privileges).

With André's move to another part of town, he was considered an out-of-boundary student at his junior high school. This school is a "magnet" school with advanced programs; and because André was rebelling against his teachers in the fall (female authority figures), he was put on notice that one more misstep would find him at a regular junior high school in his neighborhood. The junior highs in his current neighborhood and in the neighborhood to which he was moving were highly undesirable places for this gifted student to be. However, if he even looked at any of his teachers the wrong way, he would be transferred.

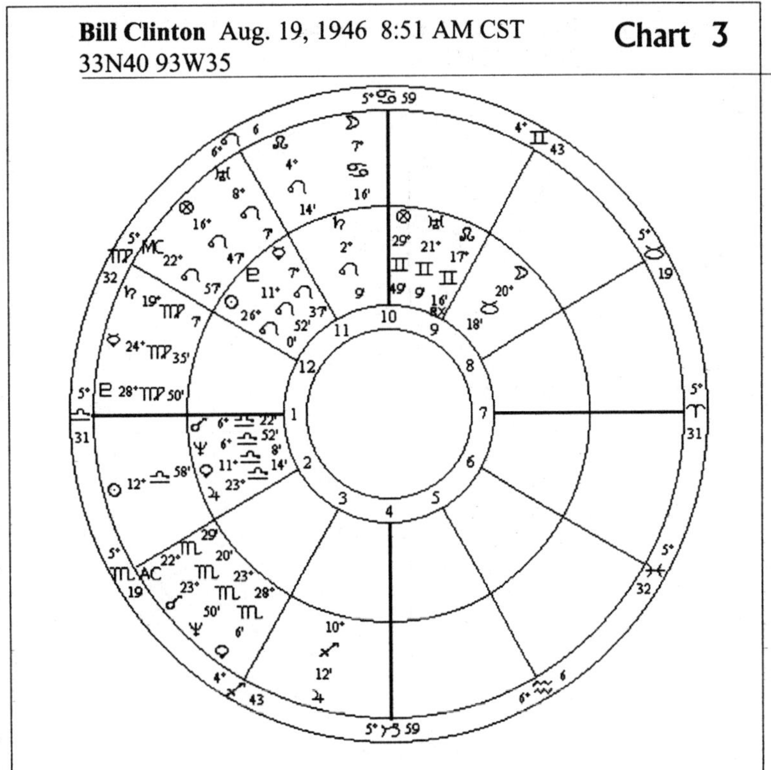

Although his current excellent principal has a reputation for taking no nonsense from children, she was sympathetic to his need for time to adjust to his new living conditions.

The Libran planets in André's chart manifest in his desire to be liked by everyone. This can sometimes be used to get him to conform. On the other hand, this approach didn't work with brother Leroy at all. This lad's natal Sun-Uranus opposition make him the natural rebel. For this reason, I was concerned about a SA Uranus square his Mars/ascendant midpoint in late January 1995.

The entire symbolism is argumentative. Leory has a temper, and under this aspect he was ripe for an explosion. I arranged for him to go to an out-of-boundary school and got him into the same program his brother is in, which will provides him with a mentor through junior high school and guarantees him a college education (provided of course that he qualifies). Should he show his hind-side and cuss out his teachers, or fight with the other students, he will be out of this school and out of this once-in-a-lifetime opportunity.

On the other hand if we can help Leroy direct this energy positively, and find constructive things for him to do around school and home, he can take advantage of his SA Pluto opposition to his Node/MC midpoint (which, according to Tyl, shows leadership and success). This aspect in late March '95 preceded a SA Sun square the Pluto/ascendant midpoint, which is also very success oriented

Although I said above that there were other things going on in the boy's lives than their readjusting to their mother, I don't mean to make light of this adjustment. I'm very concerned with how their mother is going to readjust herself after having had almost six years of freedom and separation from her children. When she last had them they were ages seven, four and three. Now they are 13, 10, and 9, and she must learn how to be a parent and cope with the difficult teenage years. She acknowledges she may be a little too permissive, because she feels a great deal of guilt at having put her two oldest through an experience with a foster mother who seemed to have wanted a check more than she wanted the children. (Let me add here that the youngest boy has had a great experience with his foster mother.)

Chart 4 **Ralph Waldo Emerson** July 4, 1776 2:21 AM EST 39N57 75W10

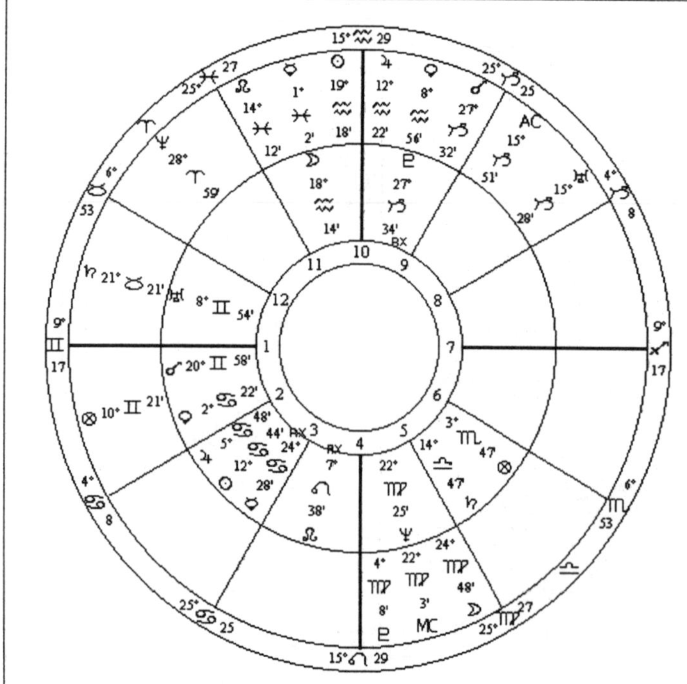

We are providing counseling to André at the moment. The counselor (male) has indicated a desire to work with Leory and do family counseling as well. We have a social worker (female) who is willing to work with the mother. We are cautiously optimistic about the resources we can provide, and I am walking on pins and needles based on my reading of the horoscope. There is no question I feel a strong emotional attachment to these children, and I wonder how objective I can be about looking at future events. I may pat myself on the back and say I've done fairly well over the past six years, but each day it's a whole new ball game.

Now let's take a look at something more mundane. Barbara Watters preferred solar-arc directions in all her work, but would use them exclusively in mundane work. She wouldn't even consider a secondary progression in doing something such as the US horoscope. With the upheaval in Congress after the November 1994 elections (when the Republicans wrested control of both houses of Congress from the Democrats after 40 years), it might be interesting to see what appears to be indicated by solar-arc directions in the Gemini rising chart for the United States. I am using this chart because it is the one most commonly used, and because July 4th is a date we consciously celebrate as the birth of our nation. (Charles Emerson chart for the USA: July 4, 1776, 2:21:05 AM EST, 39N57, 77W10.)

Right away I would think that there should be something connecting the 11 house, which is the legislature (Congress) in a mundane horoscope with Pluto as the planet of significant change or transformation. As it turns out, SA Mars, co-ruler of the intercepted 11th house (Koch Houses) made an exact conjunction with natal Pluto in the 9th on November 29, 1994. That the Congress would change under these aspects should not be a surprise. That this is a turning point from where we have been is certainly indicated.

An early analysis of the elections suggests that only 39% of those eligible to vote went to the polls. A very committed constituency, specifically the religious right, did get out to vote. One could say that Mars by SA direction in the 9th house representing religion among other things, energized this segment of the voters to get out and express their point of view. I do not mean to imply that the religious right controlled the election, but they certainly helped in the election of candidates more supportive of issues dear to their hearts.

How this will all play out in the next Congress is somewhat up in the air. If you do a chart for January 3, 1995 when the new legislature was sworn in, there is a prominent retrograde Mars. Mr. Clinton had the same aspect for his inauguration. I expect lots of anger and not a whole lot of progress over the next two years, but that's not in the solar arcs as much as it is in the mundane chart for the new Congress. The transformation of the Congress, however, was in the solar arc directions of the USA horoscope.

Finally, wouldn't it make sense to discover some kind of solar arc direction related to President Clinton's chart, that will suggest some changes regarding his own beliefs as to how he can best accomplish his goals? Solar-arc Uranus had made an exact conjunction with natal Mercury in the President's chart before the election; however, it was still within orb (30').

Since Mercury rules his 9th house of philosophical beliefs, we would expect some change in this direction. And since the American people (those who voted) have expressed a desire for change, the President, with all his Libra planets will want to be on the side of the majority. So he'll just change to accommodate the more conservative element who have made their wishes known.

SA Uranus is also about to make a conjunction with Mr. Clinton's 11th house. He will find new ways of working toward his goals, even if this goes against his old principles. (Isn't there an old saying *"The man who stands for nothing will fall for anything?"*) His friends all say the man has strong principles. That may be, but unless he demonstrates this to the public at large, his negative rating will continue to haunt his popularity.

Well there you have it on solar arcs. I feel strongly that they manifest in direct events experienced by individuals. That an external event may help a person to go within and reflect upon what is going on in his or her world should suggest that solar arc directions can be indicated for both internal and external events. But in my opinion, you will find solar arcs more frequently in events that manifest for the world to see than you will find secondary progressions. My advice to anyone is to try using solar arcs and judge for yourself.

APPENDIX

Perhaps the most popular method of calculating solar arcs, and, in my opinion the easiest, is to subtract the position of the Sun on the birthday from the position of the Sun on the directed date. See the following example: Birth date–July 1, directed date–July 26.

July 26	Sun	3 Leo 16' 26"
July 01	Sun	9 Can 25' 25"

Since we can't subtract 9 from 3, or 25 from 16, we need to do some converting. It's not that hard. We learned in elementary school that there are 60 seconds to each minute and 60' to each hour. We know also that a circle contains 360° and if we divide that by 12 equal signs we get 30° to each sign. If we add 30° to the 3° of Leo, we get 33°. Now, because we need to add 60 minutes to the 16' on July 26, we borrow one degree from the 33 Leo, making that 32; and adding 60' to the 16'. This gives us the following:

July 26	Sun	32 Leo 76':26"
July 01	Sun	09 Can 25':25"
		22° 51' :01"

By adding 22° and 51' (seconds can be rounded off) to the Sun, Moon and planets, we come up with the solar-arc directed planets. The most popular way of directing the house cusps is to add our increment to the natal MC and look up the new ascendant and remaining house cusps in a table of houses for the location in which the client is living on the directed birthday. Again some astrologers prefer to add the arc to the ascendant and all the other natal house cusps as well.

Some astrologers take the motion of the Sun on the day of the client's birth and calculate its movement, which will be roughly between 57' and 61' a day depending on the season in which you were born (slower in spring-summer and faster in autumn-winter. They multiply this figure by the age of their client and add this figure to the natal sun and planets. Using our July 1 birth date, the sun moves approximately 57' and 12" each July 1. If the client is 25, then 57' and 12 secs. are multiplied by 25:

57min	*12 sec*
x 25	*x 25*
1,425	*300*

300" /60 = *5'*
1425 ' /60 = 23° 45'

23° 50' total solar arc

We add the 5' we converted from seconds to the 45' and our final figure for our solar arc is 23° and 50'. This figure would be added to the natal Sun, Moon, and remaining planets to get the solar arc directed chart for the client's 25th birthday.

Houses can be done two ways. Either add the arc to the natal MC and go into a table of houses for the new ascendant and house cusps using the latitude for the location of the client on the 25th birthday; or add the increments to all the houses in natal horoscope. The former method appears to be the most widely used. As you can see, the difference between the average and the precise methods shown above can, over the years, add several degrees. By the time one is 60 years old, this can amount to as much as 3 degrees, making predictive work difficult if not impossible. For this reason, I prefer the first method. ✸

ASTROLOGY AND THE CELESTIAL SPHERE

THE ASTRONOMY OF THE BIRTH CHART

by Michael Munkasey

What's in a word? The very words "astronomy" and "astrology" seem so similar that many people confuse them

Both words derive from Greek roots; *astro* from the Greek means star; *nomy* comes from the Greek root *nomos*, meaning name; and *logy* from the Greek root *logos*, meaning the study of. Astronomy and astrology are quite different. Astronomy derives from an idea people had about the naming of the stars, while astrology derives from early idea concerning the study of the impact of the stars. The ending for astrology – *logos*, or *logy* in English– can be found associated with words like biology (the study of life, or *bios*); histology (the study of *histos* or tissue matter), *etc.* Today the student word, astronomy, of the parent word, astrology, has a slightly different meaning. Astronomy is said to be "scientific" while Astrology is said to be "pseudo-scientific." Astronomy is concerned with the physical properties of space and the universe. Astrology is concerned with the meanings of this universe as applied to everyday life.

Why dwell on this fine nit-picking distinction of these two basic words? Because the astrology which is practiced *in both the east and the west* is descended from the philosophy, ideas, and practices of the Greek people and culture. Astrology as it is generally known today is a shadow of the thought which was put together from ideas passed on to the Greeks by the Egyptians sometimes around or before 400 BC. The Egyptians got their ideas from the Persians, who got theirs from the Babylonians who got their ideas from the Mesopotamians, who got theirs from the Assyrians, etc. This may not be the historically precise sequence for the passage of this knowledge, but it is close enough for you to realize that astrology, the study of the stars (or the heavens) is old, old, old as an idea; and more importantly, it carries with it a heritage and a tradition of which all astrologers should be proud.

The commonalty between astronomy and astrology is "the stars, or the heavens." This encompasses the planets, the Sun, the Moon, the stars, the asteroids, the comets, etc. The telescope was invented about the year 1600. Before that people who observed the sky did so with the naked eye. There is a popular myth that astrology was "invented" by shepherds watching the movement of the bodies in the sky while they tended their animals. I think that is a far-fetched notion. I think that "the ancients" had a better idea of the mechanism of human consciousness and how it worked than we generally have today. They also had a more refined understanding of how the movements and patterns in the cosmos mirrored what happened to our inner selves. I think that part of that understanding was the inherent and almost universal awareness that our

Figure 1: Celestial Sphere

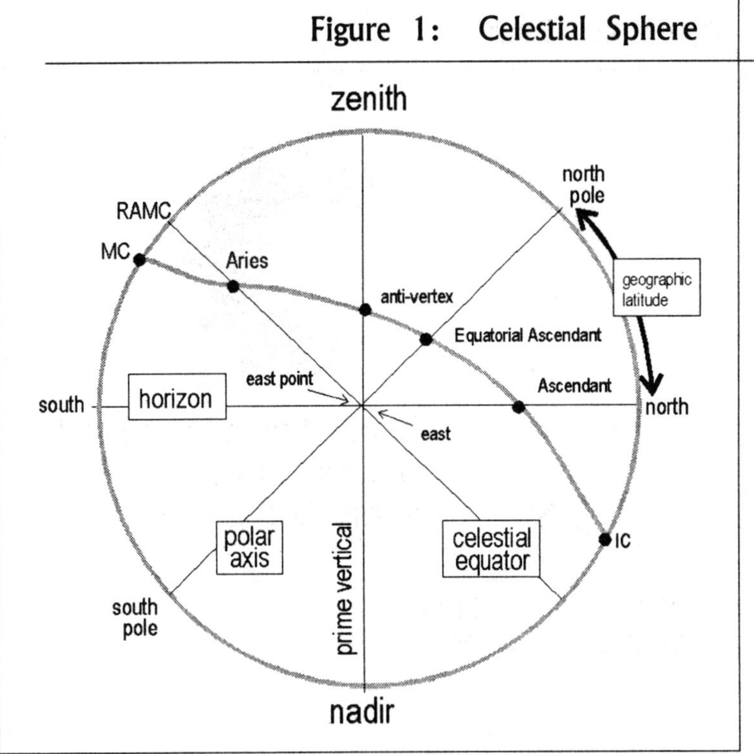

minds, our bodies, our lives, our perceptions, *etc.*, are indeed mirrors of our physical universe. They are not the universe, but somehow these people knew and realized, better than we do, that we are likened to the universe in ways which science has yet to be understand. They named this linkage and the study of its implications "astrology." Astrology to them was not some casual study, it was a subject which formed the very basis for their everyday thinking and living.

The Sky

The body of astrological knowledge which comes to us from these people tells us that there are seven distinct tools available to astrologers for the practice of their craft: planets, signs, houses, aspects (or harmonics), the Personal Sensitive Points (or the chart angles), the fixed stars, and long precessional cycles. All qualified Greek "astrologers" around the year 300 BC understood this. Their reply to this fact would probably be "so what?" Yet, today, toward the close of the 20th century, some 2300 years later, most "astrologers" could not even name or define these parts. *"Use harmonics? Use the fixed stars? Include long precessional cycles? What is this stuff?"* would probably be their reaction. *"We use 2000+ asteroids and that is enough."* Enough, maybe, for a few, but if you want to understand the heritage and knowledge of people who have practiced the astrological craft for thousands and thousands of years, you have to understand the sky, and you have to understand how to use the astrological tools – all of the tools, not just one or two of them.

It is difficult to find today, in this era of computers, a decent coherent text to explain the terminology of the sky. Surprisingly, one of the better books available to explain the various physical components of the universe is also one of the cheaper ones. It is called *Astronomy Made Simple* by Meir H. Degani, Made Simple Books, a division of Doubleday and Company, New York City.

This book covers the components and design of the universe, and discusses subjects like telescopes, the planetary bodies, the Celestial Sphere, navigation, etc. While these ideas should be attractive to students of astrology, it is the Celestial Sphere which should be studied and understood most completely. Information needed to erect a birth chart comes to astrologers through the Celestial Sphere. If you understand the divisions and parts of the Celestial Sphere then you may understand the astronomical reality behind a natal birth chart.

That is what this article is all about: the Celestial Sphere. Understanding the Celestial Sphere and its various components lies at the core of the "Astronomy for Astrologer's" section of this work.

The Celestial Sphere is a skeleton which allows you to divide the sky into parts, and then use those parts for your own purposes. It is like a road map to the heavens. It provides names for the important pieces and parts of the sky, and it provides your first look at the logic behind the complexity of planetary movement. As you read this text ,it would be helpful having a book beside you like *Astronomy Made Simple*, or *The Astrological Thesaurus, Book One, House Keywords*, by Michael Munkasey, Llewellyn Publishers, 1992.

Figure 2: Earth

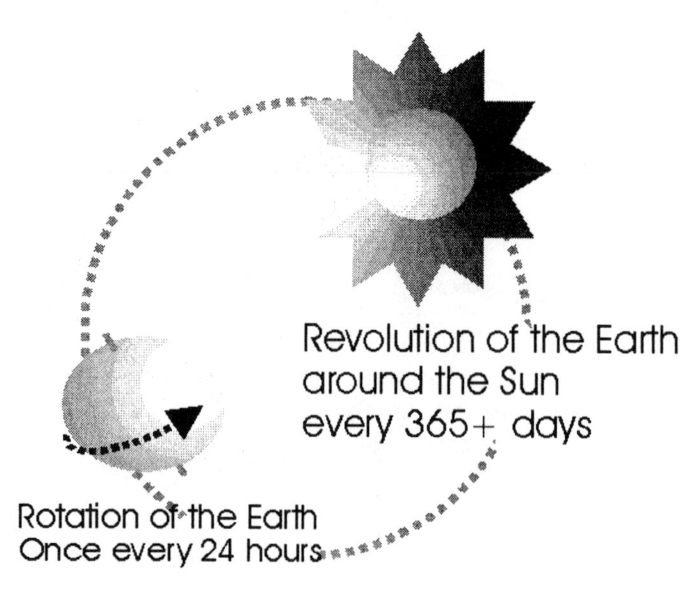

Those Three Planes

We measure the movement of the solar system in three planes, called the ecliptic plane, the equatorial plane, and the horizon plane. Each of these planes derives from a mathematical idea of how to divide and name certain parts of the space around us. This origin is actually a necessary thing. We stand on the Earth, and if we have a relatively clear day we can see where the Earth and the sky meet off in the distance. This meeting is our visible horizon, or, often, just "horizon," and it is generally about six or so miles away if the ground is flat and you are not standing on a hill or higher up in a structure. This horizon is your first orientation to the ideas of "up and down," and "around." For all practical purposes this visible horizon is the anchor for your everyday reality. It is also the place you intuitively look to differ between the concept of night and day. When the Sun is over the horizon it is day, when it is below it is night.

As you view your horizon, the Earth is spinning on its axis — pretty fast too, some 23,000 miles an hour. Besides this 24 hour daily rotational motion, the Earth is moving around the Sun even faster. It moves around the Sun at such a speed that about every 365 days (our year) it returns to about the same position *vis-a-vis* the background of stars it started from a year earlier. Thus, if we really want to measure where we are against a universal background of planets and stars we need measurement tools for anchoring these daily rotational and yearly revolutional motions. The mathematical names given to these three basic skeletons are the horizon plane, the equatorial plane and the ecliptic plane. Understanding what these planes are, how they interconnect, and the names for their various parts is the secret to understanding the astronomy behind the birth chart.

Why, you might ask, are these planes so important? The answer is that they set the framework, the foundation, for translating the physical reality of our universe into the symbolic notations of astrology. It is through their interaction and inter-connection that astrologers are able to place and then read the seven astrological tools mentioned earlier. Those astrological tools, the planets, signs, houses, PSPs, aspects, fixed stars, and precessional cycles not only derive from but also are dependent upon these planes. Therefore, we need to understand the diagram of the Celestial Sphere, *figure 1,* to place these planes into perspective.

The Celestial Sphere

Let us take the Earth and each plane in turn, in isolation, and then combine them overall into the Celestial Sphere. We will start with the Earth itself, and then proceed to the other planes. I start with the Earth because the terms used to divide and place people and cities on the Earth's surface may already be familiar to some of you, and thus an analogy from the Earth's terms to the Universe's terms may be helpful.

Figure 2 can help you associate the Earth with its terminology. The terms to pay particular attention to are equator, longitude, latitude, longitude circle, latitude circle, pole, North Pole, and South Pole. You should learn the definition of these terms. Their definitions are given in the appendix to this article.

Figure 3: Horizon Plane

A Cross Reference of Terms Used in the Co-ordinate Systems

Earth System	*Equatorial System*	*Ecliptic System*	*Horizon System*
North & South Pole	Celestial Pole	Ecliptic Pole	Zenith; Nadir
Equator	Celestial Equator	Ecliptic	Horizon
Latitude	Declination	Zodiacal Latitude	Altitude
Co-Latitude	Polar Distance	Polar Elevation	Zenith Distance
Parallels of Latitude	Diurnal Circle	Zod. Latitude Circle	Altitude Circle or Latitude Circle
Meridian	Hour Circle	Longitude Circle	Vertical Circle
Longitude	Right Ascension	Zodiacal Longitude	Azimuth Angle
Greenwich Meridian	Hour Circle of 1	Local Meridian	Prime Vertical

The Personal Sensitive Points and Their Intersections

Personal Sensitive Point Name	*Its Opposites Name*	*Intersection of the Ecliptic and...*	*General Location in the horoscope*
Ascendant	Descendant	Horizon	Left
MC	IC	Meridian	Up
Equatorial ASC	Equatorial DSC	Polar Axis	Left
Vertex	Anti-Vertex	Prime Vertical	Right
Co-Ascendant	Co-Descendant	Co-Equator	Left
Polar Ascendant	Polar Descendant	Co-Polar Axis	Right
The Aries Point	Libra Point	Equator	Zero Aries
Moon's North Node	South Node	Moon's Orbital Plane	As defined

The horizon plane has the following parts and names associated with it. The horizon plane is shown in *figure 3.* The terms you should pay attention to are azimuth, altitude, and the cardinal points of the compass, north, east, south, and west. Distances in altitude are measured in plus degrees if they are up, or minus degrees if they are down. Distances around are measured in terms like "30 degrees east of north." Surveyors and air or sea navigators used to use terms and descriptions like these in their daily work before certain satellites were launched to take over this work and make it easier to find where you are.

The equatorial plane has its owns terms too. Notably, these are celestial equator, declination, right ascension, and hour circles. See *figure 4* for a diagram of the equatorial plane. The ecliptic plane introduces a third set of terminology. I think the people who invented this used different names because then they could write books which people would have to buy, and they could become rich (ha ha, joke!). Note the terms zodiacal latitude, zodiacal longitude, meridian, and ecliptic. *Figure 5* may help you keep these terms separated in your mind.

You, the reader, are now given a homework assignment. Take some time and look over the various diagrams provided with this article. Become familiar with the different terms and how these planes inter-connect. This is a time to move beyond words and into some mental visualizations.

The Role of the Celestial Planes

Learning about these celestial planes would just be an intellectual exercise except for two important reasons. These planes define the role of space and the role of time in our lives. If we consider that "I am in a bad (or a good) space today!" or "I am running out of time!", then we are invoking the elements of both space and time in our daily lives. Space, in general is shown by the houses of the birth chart. Time, in general, is shown by the PSPs in the birth chart. Whether or not an astrologer uses houses or the PSPs (Personal Sensitive Points) does nothing to lessen their over-all importance within the practice of astrology.

Astrologers often get confused about the choice of which house system to use. They will also say that they have never heard of or will not use certain of the PSPs. Chapter 5 of *The Astrological Thesaurus, Book One, House Keywords* presents a theory and discusses some ideas on how to choose a house system. There is little material available in modern astrological literature for some of the PSPs, but that does not lessen their over-all importance.

Short astrological definitions for the PSPs have been included in the appendix to this article. The role of the celestial planes is to divide time and space so that their over-all impact can be presented through the birth chart. You should understand the framework of the celestial planes because understanding their physical role and nature will help you integrate them into their place in your psychological world. Astrologers should strive to understand their physical world to draw inferences about the astological framework they have available.

Figure 4: Equitorial Plane

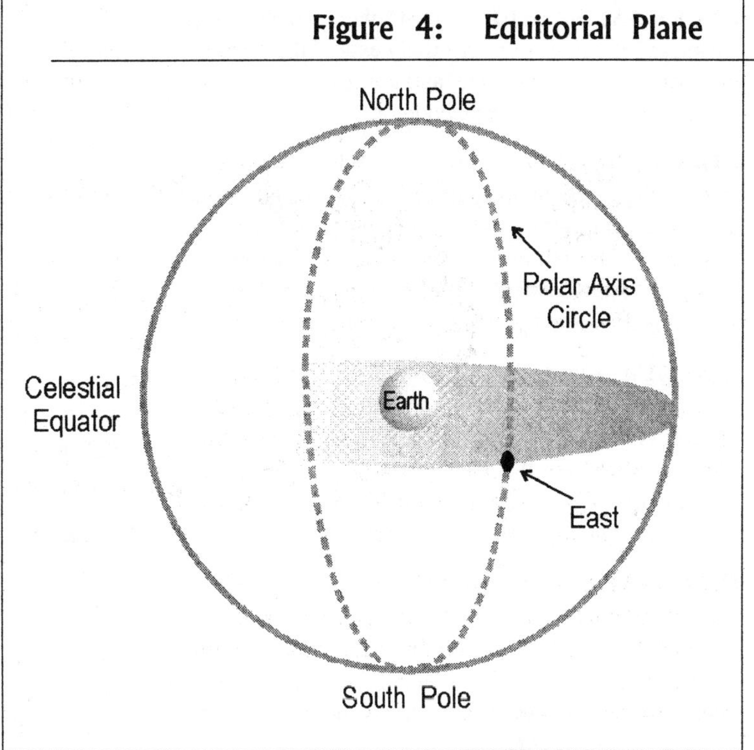

Definitions for Some Astronomical Terms

ARIES POINT — (1) The point where the equatorial plane and the ecliptic plane intersect as defined by the passage of the Sun through these points in month of March. (2) The starting point for the measurement of either right ascension or zodiacal longitude. (3) One of the PSPs (Personal Sensitive Points) used by astrologers.

ASCENDANT — One of the PSPs of astrology. It generally refers to the mechanism of the thinking and observing mind as it tries to place the circumstances of location and environment into a context for you.

BIRTH CHART — A map of the heavens, popularly miscalled a horoscope, which is used by astrologers for astrological purposes.

BODY — A planet, a star, or some similar object which exists in space and time.

CELESTIAL EQUATOR — A great circle denoted by an extension of the Earth's equator infinitely projected into space. This is the circle along which the measurement of right ascension is made.

CELESTIAL SPHERE — That sphere which would be formed if one were to infinitely extend the "sphere" of Earth outward into space, and use the an extension of the Earth's equator as its equator.

CO-ASCENDANT — One of the PSPs of astrology. It generally refers to that part of mind which allows us to obtain and interpret information which does not come or go through one of the five physical senses. This point is associated with ESP, and also with unspoken gender identification, voice inflections, etc.

CO-EQUATOR or **CO-LATITUDE** — The mirror image of the Earth's equator as located from measuring from the poles down toward the equator. It is the same distance from the poles as your latitude is from the equator. If you are at latitude 40°, then the latitude of your co-equator is 90° - 40°, or 50°.

CONSTELLATION — A division of the sky. The ancients originally defined 48 such divisions, and associated them with certain myths. More modern definitions have expanded this to about 78 such divisions, mainly by carving out the ancient divisions and adding in those portions of the southern sky not visible from places where the original constellations were defined.

CO-POLAR AXIS CIRCLE — The great circle formed when the mathematics used to derive the polar axis circle is mirrored from the Earth's poles, rather than from the Earth's equator. It is formed by the axis of the Co-Equator.

DECLINATION — A measurement in the equatorial plane of the amount of distance, up or down, a body is located off of the Celestial Equator. Measurements are generally stated as: 14 N 21. For the planets, the measurements rarely exceed about 23 ½ ° due to obliquity.

ECLIPTIC — That great circle of the celestial sphere which the Sun traces, when seen from the Earth, in its yearly travels against the backdrop of the sky.

ECLIPTIC PLANE or **SYSTEM** — The mathematical plane which contains the Solar System, with the Sun as its center, and its planets in their motions around the Sun. A sphere of space using the ecliptic as its equator.

EQUATORIAL ASCENDANT — One of the PSPs of astrology. It generally refers to that part of self or mind which evaluates the ongoing conditions of life and sets rules for coping with everyday existence. This is generally a sensitive and tender part of the human psyche, and generates ideas not easily shared with others.

EQUATORIAL PLANE — The mathematical plane whose center is represented by infinitely extending the Earth's equator into space.

EQUATORIAL SYSTEM — A sphere of space using the celestial equator as its main central circle or equator.

GREAT CIRCLE — A circle contained within the celestial sphere which has as its center the center point of the celestial sphere.

HORIZON — A great circle, for which there are four associated terms: Visible, Rational, Sensible, and Celestial. In the way that we use these terms, the Visible Horizon is our view of where the Earth and the sky meet off in the distance from where we stand on or near the Earth. The Celestial Horizon is the horizon we use mathematically as our starting point to calculate houses and sensitive points, and it is the visible horizon as if that horizon were starting at the center of the Earth (as opposed to where we are located on or near the surface of the Earth) and was extended infinitely into space.

HORIZON PLANE or **SYSTEM** — That place where the Earth and the sky meet off in the distance. The same as the celestial horizon. A sphere of space, with the Celestial Horizon serving as its equator. See also: *Horizon.*

HOROSCOPE — The ascendant of a birth chart. This term is often misused to represent the entire diagram used by astrologers. See "Birth Chart."

HOUR CIRCLE — A great circle which is perpendicular to the Celestial Equator and which passes through a particular body in space.

HOUSE — A division of space defined by using various circles of the Celestial Sphere to divide this space. This is one of the seven tools used by astrologers in their work. Houses, in general, represent the things of every day life.

HOUSE CIRCLE — A great circle which has as its poles the North and South points of the Horizon, and which is perpendicular to the Prime Vertical.

LOCAL SIDEREAL TIME — The time calculated for a horoscope when a time of event is added to the longitude correction, the time zone correction, the acceleration, the delta T correction, and the sidereal time from an ephemeris.

LONGITUDE CIRCLE — A great circle which starts at the pole of the ecliptic and travels around the Celestial Sphere perpendicular to the ecliptic. It is like a circle of longitude, but in the ecliptic system, as opposed to on a globe of the Earth.

MC, or **MIDHEAVEN** — Onc of the PSPs of astrology. It generally refers to that part of mind which maintains continuity for living from one day to the next. It also helps define that inner part of maturity which helps you grow as a person.

MERIDIAN — A great circle of the Horizon system which passes through the Zenith, the Nadir, and the North and South points of the horizon.

NADIR — The South Pole of the horizon system. Opposed to the Zenith.

OBLIQUITY — The angle in space formed between the ecliptic and the celestial equator. Presently it is about 23½° and decreasing slowly with time.

PERPENDICULAR — 90°. Circles which meet at 90° angles.

PLANET — The Sun, Moon, Mercury, Venus, Earth, Mars, Jupiter, and Saturn are the visible planets. Uranus, Neptune and Pluto are not visible to the naked eye.

POLAR ASCENDANT — One of the PSPs of astrology. It generally refers to that part of our mind which allows us to connect, in an ESP way, to many people or events, and not necessarily those in our immediate

Figure 5: Ecliptic Plane

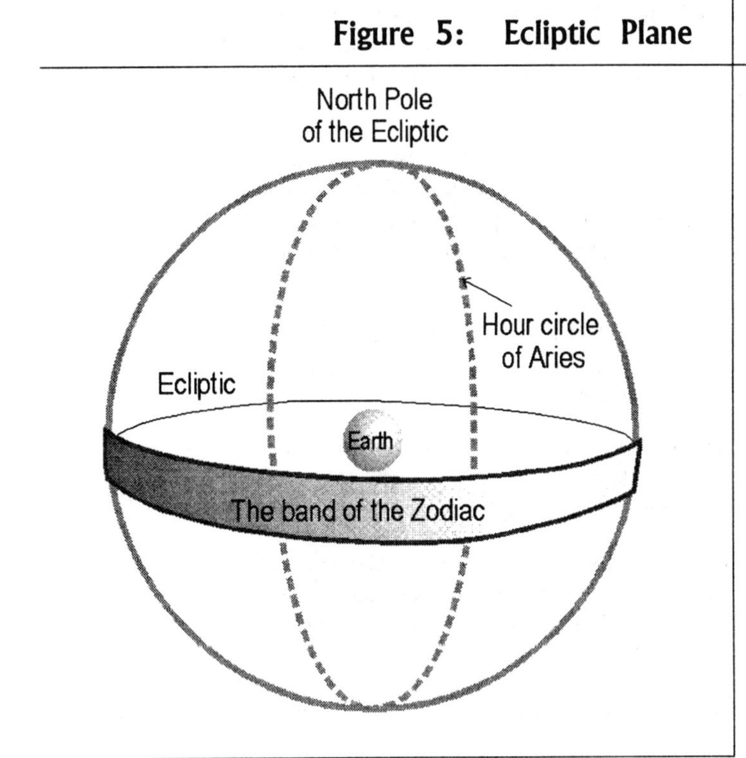

or conscious environment.

POLAR AXIS CIRCLE — A great circle which passes through the North and South Poles of the Earth and the East and West points of the horizon.

POLE — When describing three- or four-dimensional space (using time as a fourth dimension) a pole is a mathematical point that is 90° everywhere from a circle. For instance, the Earth's North or South Poles are 90° from all points on the Earth's equator.

PSPs — The Personal Sensitive Points of astrology. These always exist as a pair across the birth chart. There are eight of them, named earlier in this article and defined elsewhere in this glossary. No one is any more or less important than the others, although in most 20th century astrology only the ascendant and the MC are popularly utilized. Each PSP is formed by a real intersection in space.

PRIME VERTICAL — A great circle which passes through the Zenith, the Nadir, and the East and West points of the horizon. It is 90° from the meridian, and vice-versa.

RIGHT ASCENSION — A measurement along the celestial equator, in the equatorial plane, used for locating a body's position in space. Measurements start from 0° Aries, and are generally stated as: 14 Hrs 36 Mins.

VERTEX — One of the PSPs of astrology. It generally refers to that mechanism of mind which somehow allows us to connect with people or circumstances to effect those conditions we need to go through for personal growth.

VERTICAL CIRCLE — A great circle which is perpendicular to the horizon and passes through the Zenith and the Nadir.

ZENITH — The North Pole of the horizon system. The point in the horizon system which is over your head. Opposed to the Nadir.

ZODIAC — A small portion of the celestial sphere which is about eight degrees on either side of the ecliptic circle. It is in this space that the planets move for most of their cycles.

ZODIACAL LATITUDE — A measurement in the ecliptic plane, up or down from the ecliptic, to a designated location, usually a body. Measurements are generally stated as: 3 N 16.

ZODIACAL LONGITUDE — A measurement in the ecliptic plane, starting from Aries, to a designated location, usually a body. Measurements are generally stated as: 7 Taurus 12, or 23 Libra 56. ✹

The Celestial Sphere *Michael Munkasey, 1994*

ASTEROIDS : THE MINOR PLANETS

by Frances McEvoy

The asteroids are minor planets that revolve around the Sun, falling mostly between the orbits of Mars and Jupiter.

As early as 1598, Kepler had suggested that there might be a planet between Mars and Jupiter, based on the regular progression of planetary placements with a gap between those two planets. The empirical law of planetary distances was stated by J. D. Titius about the same time. In 1772 Johann Bode called for a search for the missing planet. In 1781 Herschel discovered the new planet, Uranus, and it confirmed Titius's law, being exactly where it should have been by progression. A society of two dozen famous astronomers then devoted their time to finding the missing planet.

On January 1, 1801, Giuseppe Piazzi of Palermo, not a member of the society, noted a small star which he had not seen before and noticed that it was moving. Ceres was retrograde at the time and thus orbiting closest to the Earth. He also noted when it stationed and began to advance forward. A year after Piazzi's discovery, Heinrich Olbers of Bremen confirmed the discovery and it was named Ceres.

Ceres was located precisely where there should have been a planet according to the Titius-Bode law of planetary distances.

Three months later Olbers discovered Pallas nearby and its distance from the Sun was the same as that of Ceres. The orbit of Pallas was inclined at 34°, greater than any of the other planets. In 1804 Juno was discovered and in 1807 Vesta. Vesta is the brightest of the group and often visible to the naked eye in spite of its small size.

The first theory presented was that the four small planets were part of a larger planet that had exploded at some point, and there was speculation that Pluto might have been the hard magnetic core which was flung into outer space to become the outcast from the solar system. In 1830 a 5th asteroid, Astraea, was found, though it has not been used as yet by many astrologers. The actress Helen Hayes had Astraea conjunct her Sun. Currently we know there are well over 10,000 asteroids in this belt between Mars and Jupiter, and over 5000 of them have been assigned names or numbers. This article treats only the Big Four: Ceres, Pallas, Juno and Vesta. Chiron is included here although it is not an inert asteroid, but rather the largest comet nucleus known. Chiron is huge by comet standards, some 25 times the diameter of a typical comet like Halley. Chiron is now known to be a refugee from the Kuiper Disk, a reservoir of comets which extends from the orbit of Neptune out toward the spherical Oort Cloud. Comets such as Chiron have been designated Centaurs. Chiron Also has a devoted following of astrologers who would never do a chart without it.

The asteroids tend to form families which share orbital characteristics. Some scientists believe each family came from a separate planet which may have collided and shattered. The gravitational pull between Jupiter and the Sun would have prevented a very large planet from existing between Mars and Jupiter. Small fragments of asteroids may account for meteorites which rain down on the Earth, causing craters.

Jan 5, 1893 8:30 PM TZ: 5E30 – 26N45 83E22 **Yogananda**

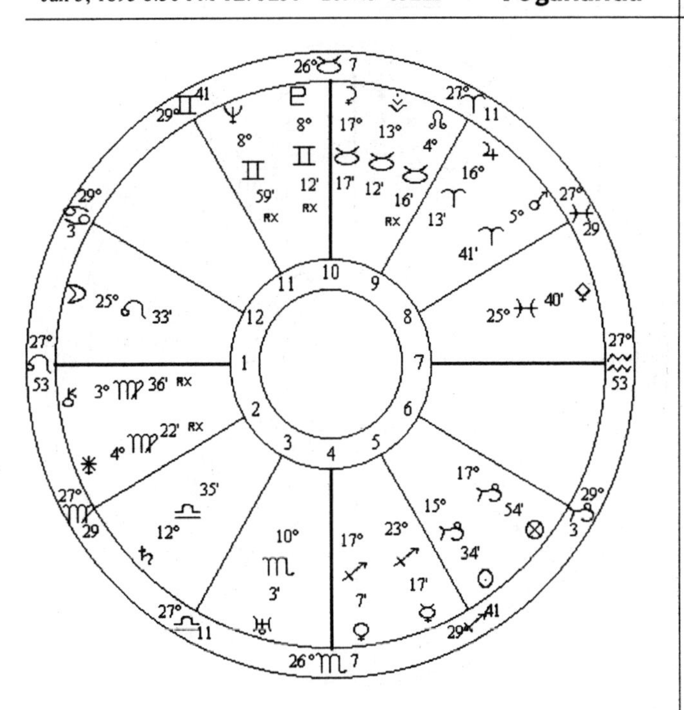

Though the basic four asteroids were discovered nearly half a century before Neptune, no ephemerides of these small planets existed until January 1973. Astrologer Eleanor Bach was responsible for this first ephemeris of the first four asteroids, and in 1976 Zip Dobyns and her son published a complete asteroid ephemeris for the 20th century. In the 20 years since those first ephemerides appeared astrologers have been using at least the first four asteroids and many now find it difficult to delineate a chart without them.

THE ASTEROID CERES

The largest and brightest of the asteroids, Ceres, has a 23-year cycle, returning at the end of that time to the same degree and sign on nearly the same day. Within that 23-year cycle it circles the zodiac five times. It completes the zodiac once every four and a half years, turning retrograde about once a year for three months and moving back 14°. When in direct motion Ceres moves about three and a half to four signs and remains direct for 12 to 13 months.

In Greek and Roman mythology, Ceres-Demeter was worshipped as the Earth Goddess of fertility and agriculture. The foundations of astrological iconography were laid during the Age of Taurus, when the sign of the bull stood at the Spring Equinox, and during this period the Great Goddess was worshipped as the natural mother of all living things. Myth has always connected the feminine with the planet itself, with the flesh, and with the processes of birth, growth and death. In Sanskrit the Earth is called *prithivi* and represents all that is solid, substantial and tangible, things felt, touched and measured.

Ceres-Demeter was the maternal archetype, providing physical, psychological and spiritual food to all living things. When her need to nurture was thwarted, she became frantic and depressed. When her beloved daughter, Persephone, was abducted by Pluto and taken to the underworld (inner Earth) she stopped planting and the Earth's fertility cycle was interrupted. All growing things withered and died while she searched for her daughter. The Eleusinian mysteries were established by the goddess herself, who promised not only agricultural fertility but the ennoblement of human life and cultural gifts which enriched Earthly experience.

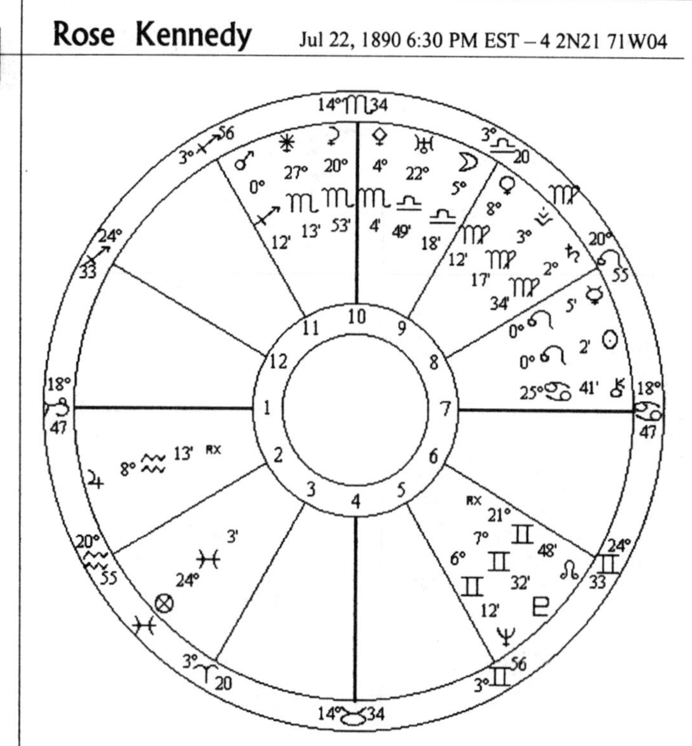

"The Goddess," declared Socrates, *"gave us the fruit of the field when she came to Eleusis, and the Eleusinian rites which gave us hope for existence as a whole."* The first grain was sown and harvested on the plain of Eleusis. Demeter-Ceres was the central figure of the fertility rites of ancient Greece. Pluto was the god of agricultural wealth and not just death and the underworld, and, therefore, he was also bound up in the fertility cult. Dionysus, the son of Persephone, also became part of the celebration of the Earth's rebirth every Spring when the Sun entered the sign Taurus.

In astrology, the asteroid Ceres is the most powerful significator of parenting, nurturing and feeding. Women with Ceres strongly placed in their charts pay special attention to their children's physical, mental and spiritual welfare. These women enjoy feeding others, serving food and drink, often grow and cook their own food, and share their harvest with others. They have an aura of the Earth Mother about them.

Queen Victoria of England was born with Ceres rising in her chart, conjunct the Sun and Moon in Gemini. Even though her Sun and Moon were in the mutable air sign not usually noted for a maternal instinct, she gave birth to nine royal children and became the royal matriarch of all Europe. Today she is the ancestress of virtually every royal family in Europe.

Rose Kennedy, mother of the nine Kennedy offspring, was born with Ceres in Scorpio on her midheaven. Three of her sons have died violent deaths in the service of their country, and her oldest daughter is retarded. Rose passed away at the age of 104 and was the matriarch of her family right up until her passing. The country can never forget her image as the grieving mother the morning that her son Robert was assassinated. Rose is the archetypal image of Ceres-Demeter. Like the goddess, Rose Kennedy was concerned not only with the physical nurturance of her children, but with their spiritual and intellectual growth as well, encouraging them to read and study.

Her daughter-in-law, Ethel, is also a strong Ceres woman. Born with Ceres rising just above her ascendant, conjunct Mars and opposite Juno and Neptune, Ethel was pregnant with her 11th child when her husband was killed. She also experienced the grief of the mother who has lost her child when her son David died of a drug overdose at age 29.

The Goddess Demeter came from a long line of mother goddesses. She was granddaughter of Gaia, the primal Earth Mother, and daughter of Rhea who was the mother of the first generation of Olympians. Both Gaia and Rhea had to protect their children from masculine abuse. All three husbands and fathers displayed a lack of paternal concern, all three goddesses suffered the loss of children, and all three persisted in having these children restored to them. With Ceres-type women, the mother-child relationship is primary. Ceres women are apt to marry men who are either jealous or lacking in paternal concern, and who leave the parenting to their wives. These men may be absent because of their careers, because of ill health, because of philandering natures, or they may be passive men who prefer to leave the job of parenting to their wives. Ceres women usually come from a long line of matriarchal women.

The largest of the asteroids was discovered January 1, 1801, the first in size, on the first day of the first month of the first year of the new century. The facts surrounding its discovery are interesting. Scientists had suspected the existence of a planet between Mars and Jupiter for centuries on the basis of the empirical law of planetary distances.

When Uranus was discovered in 1781 it was in the exact spot indicated by this law, and this increased the interest in finding a planet in the empty spot between Mars and Jupiter. During the next 20 years a group of European astronomers devoted themselves to the search, and on New Year's Day 1801, while examining a region in the sign Taurus, they observed the small planetary body, which was then making a station and about to turn direct. The new planet was smaller than they had expected, having a diameter of less than 500 miles, but was in the exact place where a planet should have been according to the planetary law.

Apr. 11, 1928 3:30 AM CST – 41N51 87W39 **Ethel Kennedy**

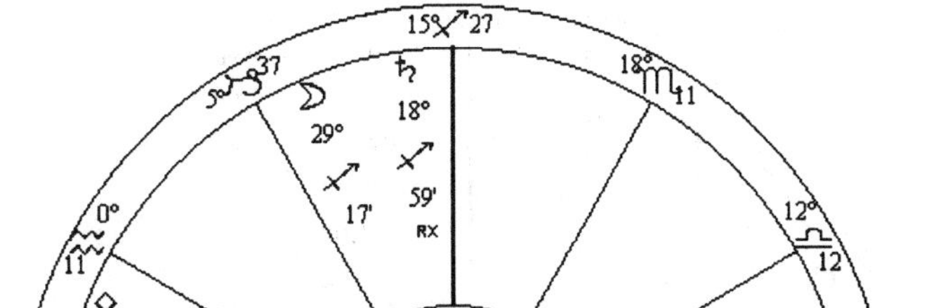

The 23 year Ceres Cycle and Dates When It Entered Zero Aries.

4-7-1901	4-8-1924	4-11-1947	4-12-1970	4-14-1993
2-12-1906	14-1929	2-16-1952	2-18-1975	2-10-1998
5-7-1910	5-8-1933	5-10-1956	5-13-1979	5-15-2002
3-13-1915	3-15-1938	3-16-1961	3-17-1984	3-19-2007
6-17-1919	6-22-1942	7-27-1965	7-3-1988	
9-13-1919 R	9-5-1942 R	8-28-1965 R	8-21-1988 R	
1-10-1920	1-13-1943	1-15-1966	1-17-1989	

Ceres is often strongly aspected in a chart where there is the loss of a parent or a child. For instance, President Clinton was born with Ceres retrograde in Aquarius opposing his natal Saturn in Leo, and his father died three months before his birth. His mother was forced to leave him for the first four years of his life in the care of his grandparents while she went to New Orleans to study nursing. His earliest memory is of her grief on saying goodbye to him when they were separated. Clinton's concern for the rights of children is also indicated by this Ceres-Saturn opposition.

A three-year-old child born with Sun-Ceres conjunct in Leo on his midheaven recently lost his father from an asthma attack. The boy's father had lost his own father when he was two years old. This child will be raised by his mother and grandmothers in a strongly matriarchal family, and undoubtedly will be aware of his grandmother's grief over the loss of her son. He is surrounded by a strong family unit that is overwhelmingly matriarchal.

Ingrid Bergman Aug 29, 1915 3:30 AM CET – 59N20 18E30

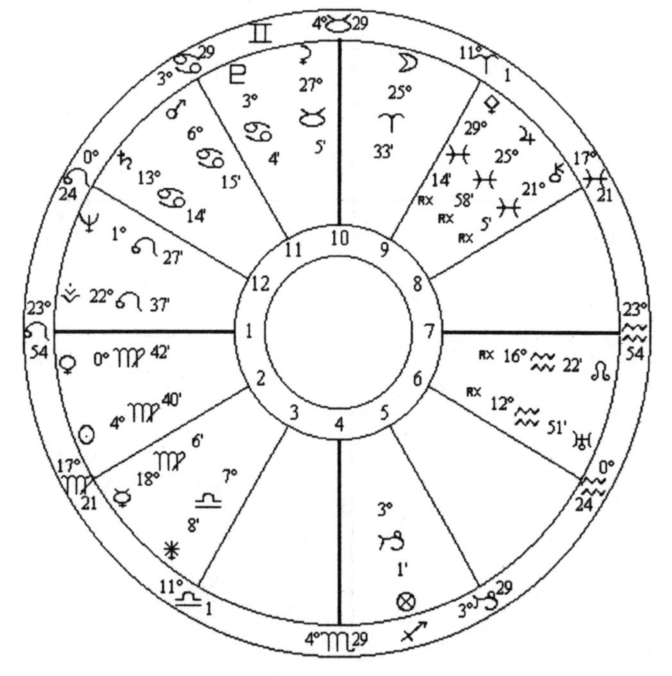

Ceres-Pluto and Ceres-Saturn aspects are found in the charts of young children who are the victims of parental abuse. David Azar, who was convicted of killing his four-month-old daughter, Geneva in 1988, was born with Ceres conjunct Saturn in Scorpio, square Pluto in Leo on his ascendant. The child had Pluto exactly conjunct her father's Ceres-Saturn conjunction, and a stationary retrograde Ceres in early Aries conjunct Mars, both opposite her father's Sun in Libra. The loss or separation of a child usually is indicated by a Ceres-Pluto or Ceres-Saturn configuration between parent and child.

Liza Minelli, daughter of Judy Garland, was born with Ceres on her midheaven, opposite Moon, Saturn and Mars in Cancer. She has grieved over her mother's tragic life and death, and has tried to live with Judy's legend all her life. This is a case of child grieving for the loss of a mother.

Gloria Vanderbilt was born during a lunar eclipse with Ceres near both her South Node and Uranus. She was still an infant when her father died and she became the pawn in a court battle between her aunt and her mother. Divorce and death have haunted her own life and she lost one of her sons when he committed suicide at a young age.

Uranus in aspect to Ceres is often found in the charts of unwed mothers, or women who give up their children for adoption. Liv Ullman has Ceres conjunct Uranus and the South Node in her 10th house, opposite Venus on her North Node. Her famous love affair with Swedish film director Ingmar Bergman resulted in the birth of their daughter Linn. Dancer Isadora Duncan, born with Ceres rising conjunct Venus and the Moon, with all trine Uranus in her 5th house, had three children by three different lovers. The children were drowned in Paris in 1913.

The actress Ingrid Bergman was born with Ceres in Taurus in her 10th house square a rising Venus in the first degree of Virgo. She was the wholesome Earth goddess of the screen, who shocked the nation when she became pregnant with the son of Roberto Rossellini, Italian film director, while married to Dr. Peter Lindstrom. Bergman left her husband and child to live in Italy with Rossellini and was not allowed to see her daughter for many years. Later she was forced to live separately from her younger children when she divorced Rossellini. Her grief over the separation from her children is recorded in her autobiography. Bergman had the asteroid Juno square Pluto and Mars and was married to two macho men who felt the children were the property of the husband. In her third marriage she grieved that she could no longer have a child because of her age. Ingrid had lost her own parents while a very young child.

Eleanor Roosevelt was born with Ceres in Virgo near her midheaven and was an orphan at a very young age. She felt that her mother-in-law usurped her maternal role with her own children. Eleanor expressed her Ceres urge to help people in need. Her son said of her that *"mother neglected her own children and mothered the whole world."*

The actress Shirley MacLaine was born with Ceres, Mars and Sun all in Taurus in the 8th house. Ceres was square Saturn in Aquarius in the 5th. She was estranged from her own daughter for many years because the child lived with her father in Japan while Shirley pursued her career. When Pluto and Saturn transited through Scorpio, opposing her natal stellium in the 8th, she played the role of the mother in the movie "Terms of Endearment" and won an Academy Award. The film was a modern dress version of the myth of Demeter and Persephone. The story dealt with the loss and death of the daughter, and ended with the mother determined to raise her grandchildren. When MacLaine won the award her daughter was with her in the audience and the two were reunited in recent years.

Ceres stations coincide with concern for the rights and welfare of children, and with fertility. Around Halloween 1989 Ceres stationed conjunct Jupiter in early Cancer and a bumper crop of babies was born the following July, breaking records in hospitals all over the country. In San Francisco they blamed it on the Earthquake which occurred about the same time, but cities

Jan 9, 1908 4AM CES – 48N52 2E20 **Simone de Beauvoir**

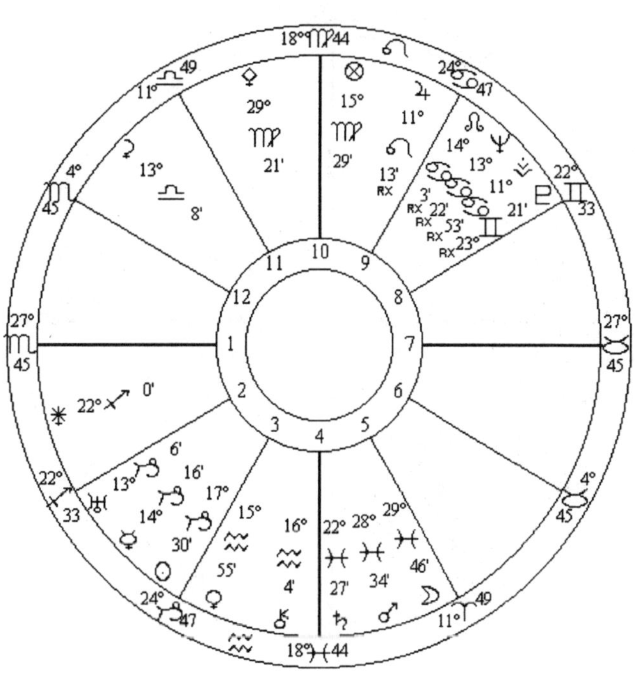

Planetary Stations of Ceres during the Final Decade of this Century

Nov 2, 1989	5 Cancer R	Feb 7, 1990	21 Gemini D	Mar 2, 1991	3 Scorpio R
Jun 5, 1991	20 Libra D	Jun 4, 1992	10 Aquarius R	Sep 16, 1992	26 Capri D
Sep 2, 1993	6 Taurus R	Dec 12, 1993	22 Aries D	Dec 20, 1994	20 Leo R
Mar 22, 1995	6 Leo D	Apr 11, 1996	15 Sag R	July 19, 1996	2 Sag D
July 9, 1997	13 Pisces R	Oct 21, 1997	19 Aquarius D	Oct 11, 1998	13 Gemini R
Jan 17, 1999	29 Taurus D	Feb 6, 2000	8 Libra R	May 8, 2000	25 Virgo D

in other parts of the country reported the same phenomenon. In late 1992 and early 1993 when Ceres was in Aquarius and conjunct Saturn, attention was focused on the legal rights of children, and legislation was introduced to protect their rights against neglectful or abusive parents. A young boy was allowed to "divorce his mother" and choose his foster parents as his legal guardians.

Ceres circles the zodiac about every four to five years. When it turns retrograde it can make three passes over half of one sign. After 23 years it repeats its cycle, stationing on the same degree and sign within a day or two of the same date. In 1996 Ceres retrogrades in Sagittarius between April 11 and July 19, and spends most of that year in that sign. Entering Sagittarius January 23, 1996, remains in that sign until November 14, 1996 when it enters Capricorn.

PALLAS ATHENA: THE WARRIOR GODDESS

The second largest of the asteroids, Pallas, was discovered in March 1802 in the sign Virgo, one week after a lunar eclipse in that sign. The new asteroid was almost the same distance from the Sun as Ceres, which had been discovered the year before in 1801, and the two have the same 23-year orbit. Pallas, however, has the greater eccentricity and its orbit is inclined at more than 34° to the ecliptic.

Gertrude Stein Feb. 3, 1874 8AM LMT – 40N28 80W01

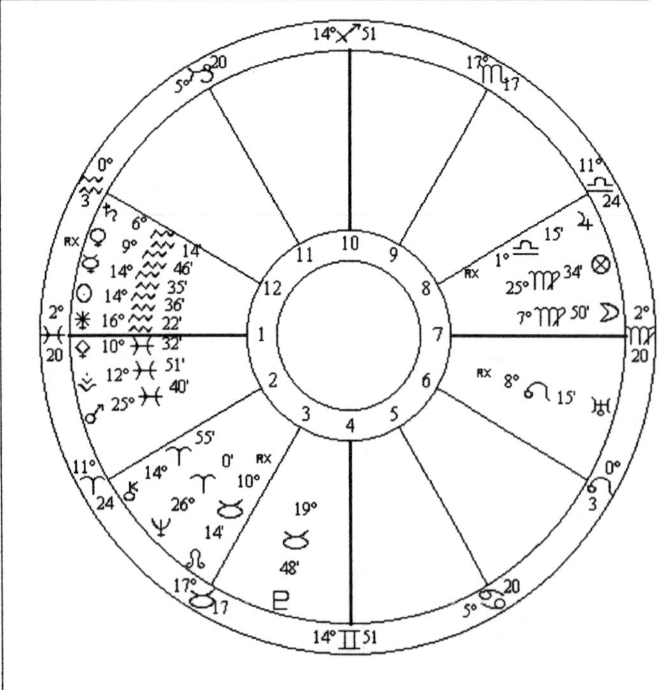

Within the 23-year orbit, Pallas has a repeating pattern of four to five years, returning after 23 and 46 years to the same degree on nearly the same day and month.

Pallas Athena was the Greek Goddess of Wisdom who presided over military strategies in wartime and over justice in peacetime. A pragmatist, Pallas Athena was known for her practical solutions during times of conflict. She sprang from Zeus' head fully grown and was pictured in golden armor. One aspect of Pallas women is that of being the "father's daughter" and the "motherless child." This definition should not be taken too literally, however, as what it really indicates is that the daughter embraces the values traditionally associated with the masculine rather than the feminine. An example is Hillary Clinton, born October 26, 1947, with Pallas stationing at 28°

Aquarius, ready to turn direct two days after her birth. She is a striking example of the Pallas woman who has achieved in law and politics and who is respected by men for her winning strategies and judgment. In October 1993 Pallas once more stationed at 23° Aquarius, three days before Hillary's 46th birthday. Hillary was close to both her parents who supported her ambitions and goals from early childhood. Pallas Athena, the goddess, had contempt for such feminine goddesses as Venus-Aphrodite and Juno-Hera, though she respected Ceres-Demeter, the Earth Mother goddess. Pallas women live in a man's world and embrace traditionally masculine values. Men come to her for advice and she has a strategic genius that takes her often into the world of politics, business or law. The asteroid is also strong in the charts of women who have achieved in the intellectual world as writers and thinkers.

Feminist writer Simone de Beauvoir had Pallas on her Mid heaven at 29° Virgo, opposite her Moon and Mars in the last degree of Pisces. She earned a degree in philosophy from the Sorbonne at age 21 and with Jean Paul Sartre, her lifelong friend and lover, she led the existentialist movement of young intellectuals in Paris after World War II. Beauvoir was a true daughter of Pallas Athena, never married and did not have children.

Actress Katherine Hepburn is another dramatic example of the Pallas Athena woman who was ambitious to achieve fame and recognition, and who played many Pallas type women on the screen, including the memorable Eleanor of Aquitaine in "The Lion in Winter." Her candid social conscience and independent spirit are typical of the Pallas Athena woman. Hepburn was born with Sun and Moon in Taurus, conjunct Pallas, as the clock struck noon, with Pallas and the Moon high on the midheaven. Her mother was also a Pallas type of woman, an active feminist and suffragette who served as a role model for the daughter. Hepburn had a 30-year relationship with Spencer Tracy whom she called a "man among men." Pallas Athena women admire heroic, godlike men, and have no use for victims.

Another notable Pallas Athena woman was the warrior queen Isabella of Spain, who drove the Moors back into Africa and sent Columbus on his voyage to the new world. Like the goddess Athena, Isabella presided over military strategy in wartime and domestic arts and justice in peacetime. She was the protector of cities, led armies in full armor even when pregnant, and men admired and respected her judgment. She and her husband Ferdinand were called the "Catholic Kings" and it was she who was the stronger partner. She united Spain and reformed the courts, administering justice and righting the wrongs of her country. Isabella's chart shows the asteroid Pallas conjunct Pluto in her 10th house.

Writer Gertrude Stein was born with Pallas rising in Pisces and was the center of intellectual life in Paris in the 1920s. A patron and friend of writers, artists and poets, such men as Hemingway, Fitzgerald, and Dos Passos gathered in her salon and valued her literary criticism.

Writer George Sand was also born with Pallas rising in Pisces as the focal point of a yod with Uranus and Venus. Her first novel attacked marriage and estab-

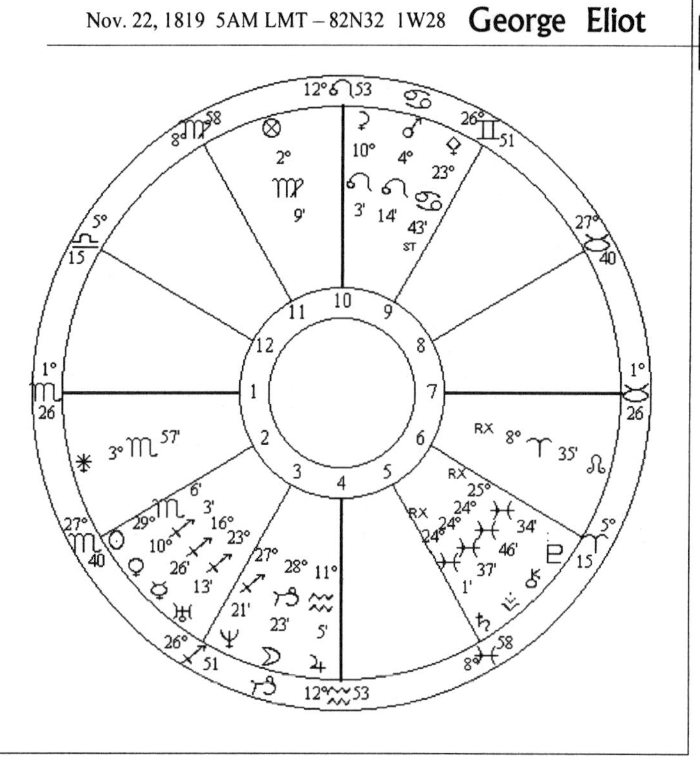

lished her at once as a "new woman," an image she embellished by wearing men's trousers, short jacket and top hat. She resembled a man in voice and manner, and the candor of her opinions. She had large black eyes *"like those you find in mystics."* Her lovers included Chopin, Liszt and de Musset. Her flamboyance and political causes and her free spirit made her a legend in her own time. Alfred de Vigney once wrote to Sand: *"O woman who makes yourself a man, you are lost."* Sand's salon, like Gertrude Stein's, was the literary center of Paris, and one admirer once wrote of her knowledge as *"knowledge that would seam our brow and turn our hair grey."* She armored herself in men's garb in order to compete in their world.

Novelist and non-Christian moralist George Eliot was born with Pallas stationary turning retrograde in her 9th house, inconjunct Mercury in Sagittarius. She was fluent in French, Italian, Latin and German and keen observation and moral concern mark her writing. A friend described her as having a *"large unprejudiced mind."* She lived openly with George Henry Lewes for 25 years, though he was never able to obtain a divorce. Their Sunday afternoon salons became a brilliant feature of Victorian literary life. Her novels developed the method of psychological analysis which distinguishes modern fiction.

Clara Barton, founder of the American Red Cross, had Pallas in Capricorn on the midheaven along with Moon, Sun, Uranus, Neptune and Ceres. Barton distributed supplies to soldiers during the Civil War and organized the bureau of records to aid in the search for missing men. She was the author of the amendment to the Constitution of the Red Cross which provided for the distribution of relief in war time as well as famines, floods, Earthquakes, cyclones and pestilence. Aviatrix Amelia Earhart was born with Pallas rising in Taurus and was the first woman to win a pilot's license, as well as the first woman to fly across the United States and back. *"Women must try to do things men have tried,"* she wrote. A social worker, feminist, and writer, Earhart took great interest in the development of commercial aviation. She disappeared in the Pacific Ocean while flying around the world. Pallas was on her ascendant at birth, square her Sun and lunar nodes.

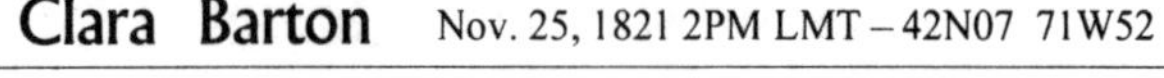

Clara Barton Nov. 25, 1821 2PM LMT – 42N07 71W52

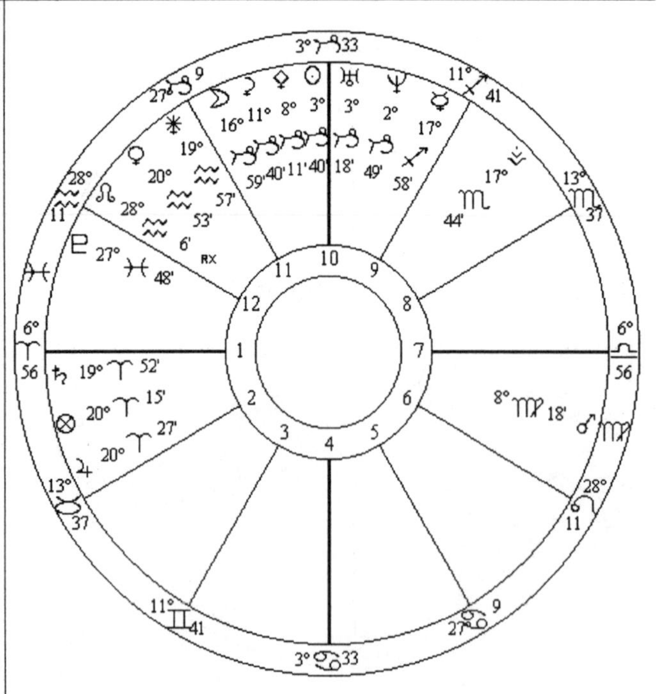

Senator Margaret Chase Smith had Pallas stationary turning direct in her 1st house in a grand trine with her Sagittarian Sun-Mars and her Moon in Leo. She succeeded her husband in Congress after his death and was the first woman elected to the Senate in her own right. She took a stand against the anti-communist activities of Sen. Joseph McCarthy and was the first woman ever placed in nomination for President at a major party convention.

Pallas women need fathers and husbands who will encourage them in careers of their own, as President Clinton has demonstrated by openly expressing his admiration for his wife's judgment and mind. Pallas women admire mothers who are professional or academic, or social activists, and are usually competitive with other women. Socially aware, often gifted in the arts as well as intellectually, Pallas women also have a good head for business. The late Jacqueline Kennedy Onassis was born with Pallas stationing in Aries, about to turn retrograde, conjunct a stationary Uranus in Aries, and

Stations During the Final Decade of the 20th Century

SR: January 1991, 25° Virgo	SD: April 1991, 6° Virgo
SR: April 1992, 7° Capricorn	SD: August 1992, 18° Sagittarius
SR: June 1993, 11° Pisces	SD: October 1993, 23° Aquarius
SR: September 1994, 24° Taurus	SD: December 1994, 5° Taurus
SR: March 1996, ° Scorpio	SD: June 1996, 19° Libra
SR: May 1997, 6° Aquarius	SD: September 1997, 17° Capricorn
SR: December 1999, 15 ° Leo	SD: March 2000, 18 ° Cancer

though she was also known for her roles as wife and mother, it was in the intellectual world that she chose to shine in her later years. President Kennedy admired her taste and judgment and often turned to her for advice in matters of state craft.

Pallas women are drawn to men of intellect or political talent, admire people in positions of power, and will not tolerate a marriage which does not support their own ambitions. Many of these women have chosen commitments outside marriage to men who shared their interests and work. They enjoy the companionship and confidence of men and seldom lose either their heads or their hearts. They prefer intellectual relationships to those based on emotional and sexual intimacy. Athena's bird was the wise owl, and her special gift to Athens was the olive tree.

Because of the eccentricity of its orbit, Pallas has an orbit that is harder to predict than that of the other major asteroids. Stations of the asteroid occur about every 15 to 18 months, and the retrograde period lasts about three to four months.

JUNO: FIRST LADY OF THE GODS

The fourth largest of the asteroids, Juno was the third to be found, after Ceres and Pallas, in the year 1804. Juno takes four to four and a half years to completely orbit around the zodiac, returning after 48 years to nearly the same degree on the same day. Within this larger cycle, Juno has a repeating cycle of 13-13-13-9-13-13-9 years when it stations in the same sign and turns retrograde, thus spending the greater part of a year in one sign. For instance, Juno entered the sign Scorpio in January 1994, stationed at 2° of that sign on February 19, moved retrograde back into Libra where it stationed at 17° of that sign on June 10. Reentering Scorpio at the end of August 1994, it moved quickly through that sign during the next three months, entering Sagittarius on December 1, 1994.

July 24, 1877 11:30 PM CST – 39N34 95W07 **Amelia Earhart**

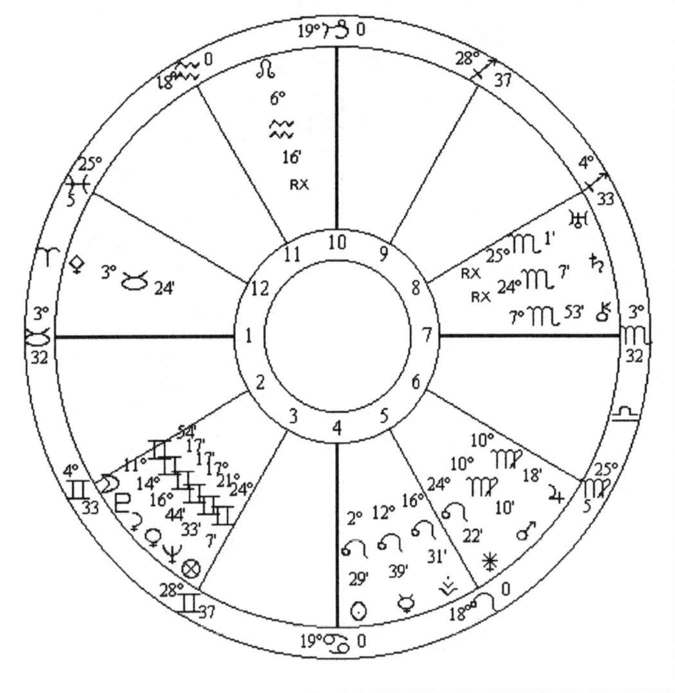

A planet or asteroid is always particularly strong in a chart when making a station. President Ronald Reagan was born with Juno stationary turning retrograde in Libra. According to Joan Quigley, Nancy Reagan was born with Libra rising, and her influence over her husband is well known. Nancy has Juno in Capricorn, retrograde, as the handle of her bucket chart, and opposite her powerful stellium in Cancer. President Lyndon Johnson was also born with Juno stationary, in his case turning direct in Capricorn. His wife, Lady Bird, had Sun in Capricorn conjunct his Juno.

The wives of US Presidents usually are born with a strongly placed Juno, rising near the ascendant or near the midheaven, or conjunct the Sun or a Node. Jacqueline Kennedy Onassis was born less than three weeks after Juno stationed and turned direct in Scorpio close to her South Node, and Juno fell near her ascendant. Her marriages to John Kennedy and Aristotle Onassis seemed particularly karmic but they brought her fame and fortune. She lost both husbands to death but most likely would not have achieved the legendary fame she did had she not married such successful men.

Jackie's mother-in-law, Rose Kennedy, also had Juno stationary in Scorpio, turning direct in her 10th house, close to the asteroid Ceres. As stated earlier Rose was the matriarch of the Kennedy family and noted for both her roles as wife and mother.

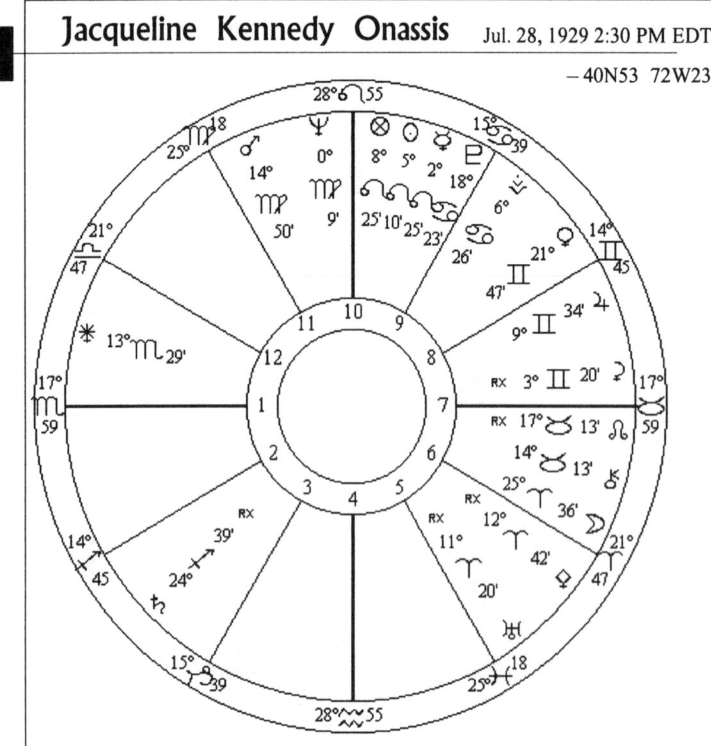

Juno, or Hera as the Greeks called her, was the wife of Jupiter (Zeus) and the only married woman on Mount Olympus. Homer wrote of her as a jealous, vindictive woman who was jealous not only of the other women in Zeus's life but of his children as well. Nancy Reagan has been depicted as jealous of Maureen Reagan, her husband's daughter by Jane Wyman. Juno's rage was directed at other women rather than at her unfaithful husband. Marriage was sacred to her and the role of wife was more important than that of mother. This is true of Nancy Reagan but not of Rose and Jackie Kennedy who also had strong Ceres placements.

Eleanor Roosevelt had Juno conjunct Mercury and Uranus in her 10th house which described her role in her husband's life. It was Eleanor who introduced Franklin to the plight of people born to poverty in the slums of New York, and she became his messenger and adviser after he became paralyzed from polio. A distinguished writer, lecturer and indefatigable traveler, she inspired her husband and influenced his liberal thinking. Uranus conjunct Juno also indicates the estrangement in their marriage after his love affair with Lucy Mercer.

Patricia Nixon was born with Juno rising in the sign Sagittarius, square her Pisces Sun and opposite Mars and Pluto in Gemini in her 7th house. She remained loyal to her husband throughout the Watergate ordeal. Barbara Bush also has Juno rising in Sagittarius, and in her case, it is opposite her Gemini Sun in the 7th. Barbara married the first man she ever kissed and appears to be as enamored of him after 50 years of marriage as she was then. It should not be surprising that so many First Ladies have Juno strong in their charts, as most of them would not have become famous but for their marriages.

President Jimmy Carter was born with Juno conjunct Saturn in the first degree of Scorpio, rising in his first house. His wife Rosalynn, known as the Steel Magnolia, was the

Stations in the the Last Half of This Decade

4° Cap R	Apr 25, 1995	—	18° Sag D	Aug 15,1995
17° Aries R	Aug 26, 1996	—	5° Aries D	Nov 16, 1996
6° Libra R	Jan 26, 1998	—	20° Virgo D	May 11, 1998
11° Sag R	Mar 31, 1999	—	25° Scorp D	July 23,1999
26° Aquar R	Jun 25, 2000	—	12° Aquar D	Oct 2,2000

first Presidential wife to sit in on cabinet meetings. Her Juno in Cancer is parallel her Sun and Neptune in Leo. These Juno women prove the saying that behind every famous man is a strong woman.

Queen Elizabeth of England also has Juno rising, conjunct Jupiter, opposite her Leo Moon, Neptune and Ceres. She, like Barbara Bush, married the first man she loved, and though she is the monarch, it is Philip who rules the domestic household and dominates the lives of their children.

Buckminster Fuller was born with Juno opposite his Sun-Jupiter conjunction and he died at his wife's bedside the day before her own death, and both were near ninety years of age.

Elizabeth Barrett Browning, who wrote the famous lines: *"How do I love thee? Let me count the ways,"* had Juno rising on her ascendant, opposite her Venus on the descendant. Her love and marriage to Robert Browning helped her to overcome ill health and she lived with him in Italy for 15 years before her death.

When Juno is in strong aspect to Pluto, the marriage is apt to involve some pain or loss, serious control issues and separation. Both Ted Kennedy and Elizabeth Taylor, born five days apart with Juno conjunct Pluto in Cancer, square Venus and Uranus in Aries have had traumatic marriages. They also were born just after Juno stationed and turned direct. Four of Elizabeth's six husbands have preceded her in death and Ted Kennedy is divorced from his wife Joan. Actress Debbie Reynolds also has Juno conjunct Pluto and square Uranus and suffered public humiliation and financial disaster from her marriages to Eddie Fisher and Harry Karl.

Juno can also indicate a long and happy marriage, as in the case of Will and Ariel Durant, famous writing team of historians. Will had Juno in Scorpio near his Sun and Mercury. Ariel had Juno in Sagittarius conjunct Saturn. Will was her high school teacher whom she married at age 15. They died a few days apart at ages 95 and 83.

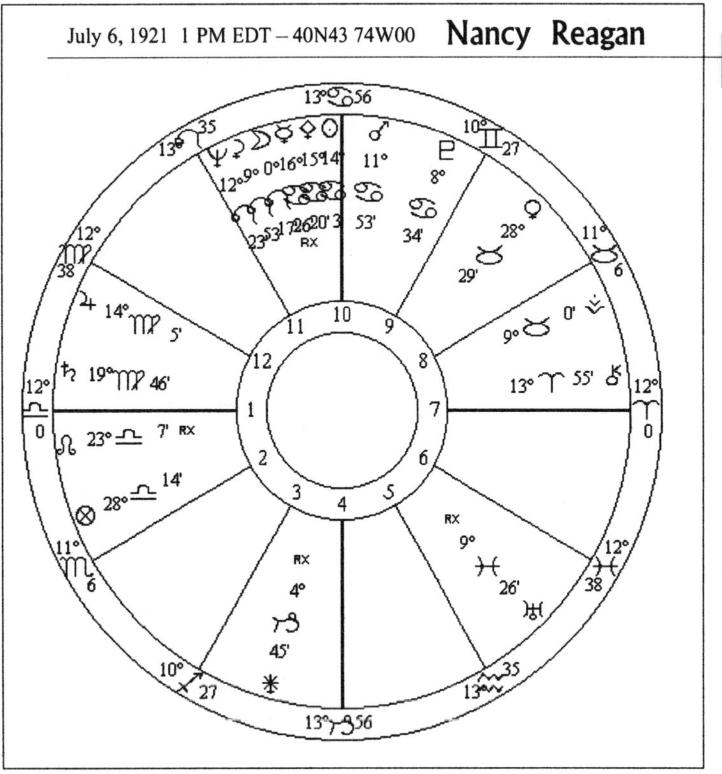

Writer Mary Shelley, wife of Percy, had Juno conjunct Venus and Mercury. She eloped with Shelley two years before his wife died and wrote her best work during her eight years with him. After his death she edited his letters and poems.

When Juno is conjunct the Moon's nodes, marriage seems particularly fated and the nature of the marriage is indicated by other planets in conjunction and opposition. Jackie Kennedy's Juno conjunct the South Node and ascendant has been noted. Psychic Jane Roberts was born during the solar eclipse of May 1929 with Juno conjunct the South Node in Scorpio, opposite her Sun and Jupiter on the North Node. Her books were actually written by her husband Robert Butts who took down all she said while in a trance state. Without him it is doubtful she would have been able to give tangible form to this material. She wrote *Seth Speaks* and other books.

This small asteroid can give more information than anything else in the chart about the importance of marriage to the native. Frequently a person marries someone whose Sun is in the same sign as his or her natal Juno. Or Juno's position by sign and aspect to other planets will describe the marriage partner. For instance Eleanor Roosevelt had Uranus conjunct Juno in Virgo, and she married an Aquarian with Uranus rising in Virgo.

VESTA: KEEPER OF THE FLAME

Vesta is the third largest asteroid and the fourth to be discovered. It has a 29-year cycle similar to that of Saturn. Within that 29-year cycle is a repeating cycle of 11-18-11-18 years, and at the end of 98 years it comes back to within 2° of the same degree on the same day and month. Vesta circles the entire zodiac every three to four years but is irregular because of retrograde motion.

In Roman mythology ,Vesta was the Goddess of the hearth, similar to the Greek Hestia whose job it was to keep the sacred fire burning in the home and temple. Vesta's hearth was round, and the public sanctuary or temple was a round building. The priestesses were originally the king's daughters and served for five years until they were old enough for marriage. Later they were chosen from respectable families and served 30 years under a vow of chastity. Letting the sacred fire go out was punished with a beating, and if they broke the vow of chastity they were buried alive. The life of a vestal virgin required transcendent self discipline and was not for the faint-hearted.

Patricia Nixon Mar. 16, 1912 11:50 PM PST – 39N15 114W53

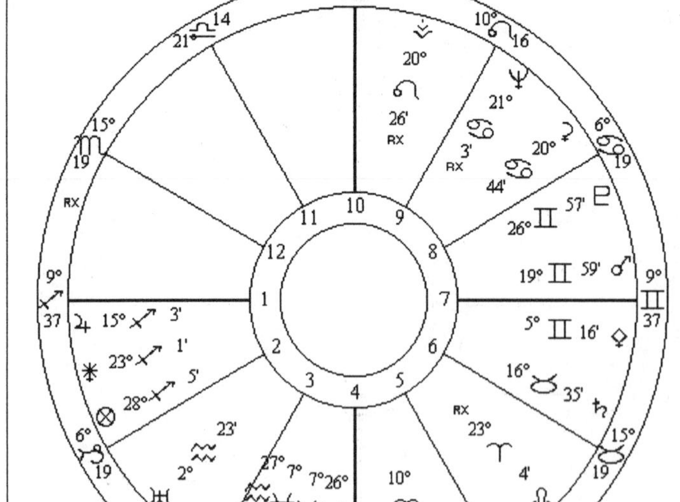

Vesta had a prominent place in worship both in the home and in the public place. The nuns of the Catholic church share the same archetypal role as the vestal virgins and key words are commitment, duty, purity, perfection, chastity and solitude. The vestal virgins, like monks and nuns, were protected by society, whereas today's examples of vestal energy may not always have the convent, the home or a secure place for their spirits to grow. Vesta natives are very private and seldom found in political, business or social circles.

Educator and scientist Maria Montessori, originator of the Montessori system of education, was born with Vesta stationary on her midheaven, in Taurus, trine her Virgo Sun. She was the first woman in Italy to graduate in medicine, and her educational methods were originally devised for working with deprived and underprivileged children. She was so successful that she tried the methods on normal children with equal success. She believed in simple tools and gave the child the freedom to move around and handle the materials in his or her own way. She taught botany, zoology, mathematics and geography to children from illiterate homes and worked at improving sense perception and coordination. In 1912 she wrote *The Montessori Method,* followed by many more books on developing human potential through direct experience. Under her method the teacher provides the materials and demonstrates their use, but the child is able to handle them in his own way.

Astrologer Zipporah Dobyns, who has suggested that Vesta is the true ruler of Virgo, has Vesta rising on her ascendant in Taurus. Indeed the asteroid seems to have much in common with the sign Virgo, including the concern for meaningful work, perfection, concentration and attention to detail. What does virginity mean here? Obviously all Virgos and people born with Vesta prominent in their charts are not virgins and yet these people demonstrate a need for solitude, purity and grace, and wish to preserve a part of themselves untouched. Former Governor Jerry Brown of California was born with Vesta stationary retrograde in Sagittarius trine his ascendant in Leo and Saturn in Aries, and exhibits a decidedly Vesta quality in his personality. After Jesuit training he graduated from Berkeley and Yale Law School and is known as a workaholic. He has never married and his ascetic appearance and style is more like that of a priest than a politician.

Scientist Marie Curie was born with Vesta conjunct her Uranus in Cancer, both in a grand trine with Sun in Scorpio and Moon in Pisces. Vesta was stationary in her chart, about to go retrograde, and she displayed the concentration and dedication typical of Vesta in her early interest in physics and chemistry. She married a fellow scientist and shared his work until his accidental death in 1906. After his death she held a chair in physics at the Sorbonne and won Nobel prizes in both chemistry and physics.

Vesta women are drawn to men who share their commitment to important work or a cause.

Researcher Michel Gauquelin was born with Vesta stationary in Aries trine his ascendant and Saturn, and also displayed Vesta qualities as a workaholic being totally committed to his research in astrological data through statistics. At the end of his life he was discouraged and depressed over the lack of response to his findings. Those who knew Michel remember his insistence on detail and perfection in research.

Chessmaster Bobby Fischer is another Vesta type, born with Vesta in Aries just past his midheaven and trine his ascendant. He won the US Chess Championship at age 14 and in 1972 defeated Russia's Boris Spassky to become the World Chess Champion. Solitude was so important to Fischer that he has lived much of his life as a hermit. His concentration and dedication to chess is typical of one born with a prominent Vesta.

Queen Victoria was born with Vesta conjunct Pluto and Saturn in Pisces, and following her husband's death she withdrew into solitude. Her letters to her

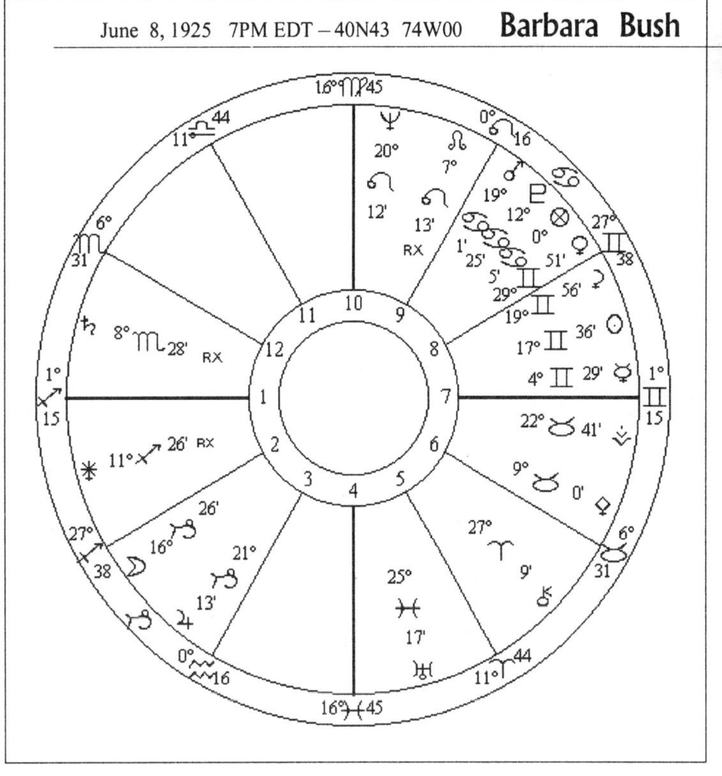

many children and grandchildren reveal her concern for education and moral development. Vesta often brings periods of isolation following loss, illness or demanding work. Victoria, unlike her royal ancestors and her own son, established a royal ideal of morality and commitment to public service. Another English Queen with a strong Vesta was Queen Mary, who married Victoria's grandson. She also had Vesta conjunct Pluto, in the sign Taurus, with both opposite Saturn and Ceres in Scorpio. Mary approached both motherhood and the monarchy with a sense of commitment and duty, and she never forgave her oldest son, the Duke of Windsor, for abandoning his throne to marry Wallis Simpson.

Another example of Vesta royalty is Grace Kelly who had the asteroid in Leo on her midheaven. We now know that Grace, a Scorpio native, was not sexually a puritan in her private life, but her public image, reflected by that elevated Vesta in Leo, was the essence of dignity and purity. She was devoted to her charities and brought dignity to the small principality of her husband Prince Ranier.

When Vesta is prominent there may be unchosen confinement and solitude as in the case of Anne Frank, the Jewish Dutch girl who died in a concentration camp at the end of World War II. Her diary was published after her death, describing her life during the two years of confinement in an attic when she was a young teenager. Frank had Vesta conjunct Mercury and Sun in Gemini.

Adolf Hitler was born with Vesta conjunct Mars and a retrograde Venus, with all square a stationary Saturn in Leo on his midheaven. His severe sexual inhibitions and repressions are described by this planetary picture. Perhaps it may also describe his obsession with ethnic purity.

Poet Emily Dickinson was born with Vesta conjunct Pluto and Mars in her 7th house, the point of a yod with Saturn in Virgo conjunct the North Node, and Moon in Scorpio. Following an unfortunate love affair with a married minister, she withdrew from the world and lived entirely at home with her books and writing. Vesta was stationary direct in the 7th house.

Vesta does not mean that one is necessarily conventional or conservative. A conjunction with Uranus can indicate a commitment to a radical life style, as in the case of Angela Davis, born with Vesta stationary turning direct conjunct both Uranus and Mars. Angela was born the day after a total eclipse of the Sun in Aquarius, opposite Pluto, and the Vesta-Uranus-Mars trio was part of a Grand Trine with Sun and Neptune. A Marxist, she also belonged to the Black Panthers. Another example of Vesta conjunct Uranus is Betty Friedan, founder of NOW who wrote *The Feminine Mystique.* Betty, who has Vesta-Uranus in Pisces, is concerned that women not be martyrs, but free and equal citizens.

Not surprisingly, Helen Keller had Vesta rising retrograde in Sagittarius, quincunx her Cancer Sun and Venus. Her inner centeredness and strength helped her to overcome both blindness and deafness, and she learned to communicate with a world she could neither see nor hear.

The religious life is a natural outlet for those born under Vesta. Mother Francesca Cabrini had Vesta rising in Leo, near her Venus and North Node, and her primary inter-

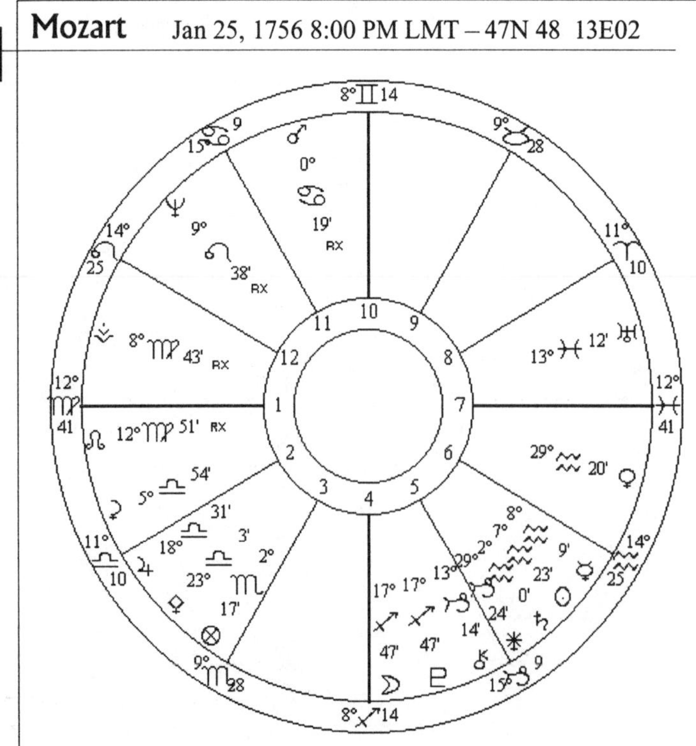

Mozart Jan 25, 1756 8:00 PM LMT – 47N 48 13E02

Vesta Stations Degrees During The Last Half of This Decade

Nov 7, 1994	10° Cancer R	—	Feb 12, 1995	25° Gemini D
Mar 29, 1996	24° Scorpio R	—	Jun 22, 1996	11° Scorpio D
Aug 30, 1997	1° Taurus R	—	Dec 3, 1997	16° Aries D
Dec 21, 1998	22° Leo R	—	Mar 25, 1999	7° Leo D
Jun 3, 2000	1° Aquarius R	—	Aug 29, 2000	18° Capricorn D

est was in helping needy and abandoned children. She founded orphanages and missions, and was canonized for her work in 1946. Another Vesta saint was Saint Therese de Lisieux, the Little Flower, born with Vesta on her South Node in Sagittarius. She was canonized for her devotion, simplicity and dedication.

Margaret Mead, a social anthropologist, was born with Vesta in Scorpio on her midheaven, square Moon in Aquarius. She was totally absorbed in her work, which she shared successively with three husbands. She demonstrated how Vesta women are attracted to men who share their work and dedication.

An example of a Vesta man is Supreme Court Justice David Souter, born with Vesta conjunct Saturn and the South Node. A bachelor, he lives an austere and monastic life style, totally dedicated to his work.

Vesta is often prominent in the charts of composers and musicians. Johann Sebastian Bach, perhaps the greatest musician of all time, was born with Vesta conjunct Venus and Mercury in Pisces. Mozart had Vesta in Virgo conjunct the North Node just above his ascendant. Franz Schubert had Vesta conjunct Venus in Capricorn, trine Uranus in Virgo. And Chopin had Vesta in Cancer in his 10th house trine his Pisces Sun. Leonard Bernstein had Vesta conjunct Jupiter and Pluto in Cancer. All these men were perfectionists about their work. The mystical writer, Antoine de St. Exupery, was born with Vesta conjunct Neptune in Gemini in the 10th house. His use of language was beautiful and even in translation it does not lose its poetry and magic.

When conjunct Pluto or Mars, Vesta has a different flavor. Yassar Arafat was born with Pluto conjunct Vesta in Cancer, right on his ascendant, and is known primarily as a terrorist, but now he has won the Nobel Peace Prize for his efforts to solve the problems of the Palestinians in Israel. And Oliver North has Mars conjunct Vesta in Gemini, trine his Libra Sun and quincunx his Moon in Capricorn. He came to public attention during the Iran Contra investigation, and recently ran for the US Senate.

Maurice Tempelsman, the faithful companion to Jacqueline Onassis, was born three days before Arafat,

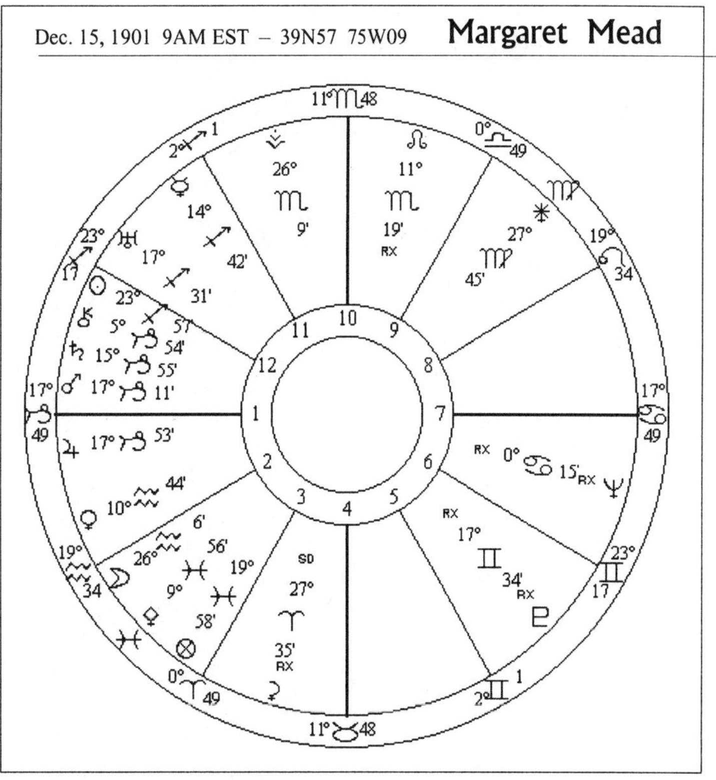

also with Cancer rising, and with Vesta conjunct Pluto in the first house. Tempelsman made his fortune as a diamond merchant and has been an adviser to presidents and kings. He also is a connoisseur of the arts and a man of refined aesthetic tastes.

Vesta natives do not ordinarily seek power or material reward. Commitment, dedication, perfection in their work is what they need. They may excel at their professions, and often do, but it is the quality and perfection of their work which drives them, not material reward, fame or power. Vesta has many of the qualities of the traditional woman, yet she does not need a man to feel complete. Her strength lies within herself, and she will share her life only with men who exhibit a similar dedication. As a mother she will be concerned more with her children's moral and mental development, their responsibility and commitment to tasks, than to social development. If she does not have a family to care for, she will turn her considerable talents to such social institutions as hospitals and schools. She relishes her privacy and may prefer to live alone. Rose Kennedy, who has Vesta conjunct Venus and Saturn in Virgo, is an example of the Vesta mother who was dedicated to instilling responsibility and a love of education in her children. It is she who encouraged them to give themselves to public service.

CHIRON: THE HOLISTIC TEACHER-HEALER

Although discovered in 1977, Chiron has only recently been classified as a comet. Meanwhile astrologers have been using this planetary body and are convinced it deserves planetary status and that it really does add a new dimension to chart interpretation.

Chiron has a 50-year cycle, but because of its extreme elliptical orbit, it spends a short time in the signs Virgo, Libra and Scorpio, and a very long time in Aries and Taurus.

The new planet was named for the mythological Chiron, a centaur of great wisdom, who was a kind of tribal medicine man to the Greek gods. The son of Saturn and a sea nymph, Chiron was born with the upper torso and head of a man, but the lower hind portions of a horse. He lived his life in the mountaintop cave where he was born and devoted his time to teaching music, mathematics, healing arts, martial arts, ethics and survival skills to the young Greek heroes.

Asclepius, Achilles and Jason were his prize pupils and to Asclepius and Achilles he taught the art of healing through medicinal herbs and surgery.

The word "surgery" comes from "chirurgery," and other Chiron words include chiropractor, chiromancy and chiropody. Chiron's approach to healing was definitely holistic and natural, and the name means "by hand," stressing the hands-on approach and the importance of working with nature.

Chiron had been given the gift of immortality but being half mortal, he was not immune to pain. When wounded by Heracles's poisoned arrow and condemned to eternal pain, he chose to give up his immortality to Prometheus. The late astrologer Tony Joseph, who was one of the first to study Chiron in depth, stated that Chiron taught us how to "die nobly." Tony, who was born in

David Souter Sept. 17, 1939 8:00 PM EDT – 42N27 71W04

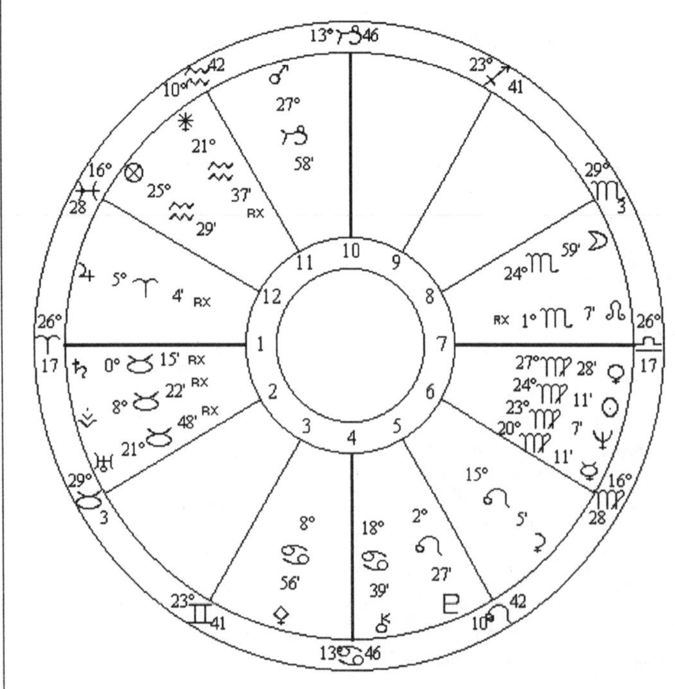

1946 with Chiron in Scorpio, died in 1986 with transiting Pluto on his natal Chiron.

The popular image of Chiron as the wounded healer is a distortion of the myth, as Chiron was famed as a great teacher and healer long before he was wounded and he ceased to teach and heal once he received the wound. He symbolizes the teacher-healer who is unable to heal himself. Many great physicians die of the very disease they have successfully treated in others.

The great mystic Yogananda was born in January 1893 with Chiron rising on the ascendant in Virgo. A lifelong celibate, Yogananda was founder of the self-realization movement. He taught and lectured all his life about Eastern philosophy and religion. Another mystic born with Chiron in Virgo was Sri Meher Baba, the "silent guru" who spent 13 years in complete silence.

Mother Teresa, the beloved nun who has devoted her life to nursing the sick and dying in the streets of Calcutta, has Chiron in the first degree of Pisces, retrograde, opposite her Virgo Sun. She won the Nobel Prize for Peace and recently she has worked to set up centers for AIDS victims all over the world. She has taken her healing arts to the homeless, the outcasts, the most vulnerable and helpless members of society. As Chiron moved to transit her Virgo Sun in 1993, she was hospitalized and her own health is now a concern.

Chiron is at its best when paired with Jupiter which brings out the holistic nature of both planets. Martin Luther King Jr. had this conjunction in Taurus on his ascendant and was a healing force with his people, winning the respect of persons from all races and walks of life. Another outstanding example of Jupiter-Chiron conjunct is Linus Pauling, eminent scientist and two-time Nobel-Prize-winning biochemist who has fought nuclear warfare. He became most controversial with his best seller *Vitamin C and the Common Cold.* More and more the medical world is beginning to recognize that certain vitamins are indeed preventatives of disease and decay. Pauling was born February 28, 1901 at 7:26 AM in Portland, Oregon with Chiron conjunct Jupiter in Capricorn in his 10th house. Distinguished in biochemistry, genetics, biology and physics, he won the Nobel Prize in 1954 for his chemical explanation of what holds atoms together. In 1962 he won the Nobel Prize for Peace for his efforts against nuclear warfare.

Romantic novelist Barbara Cartland was born July 9, 1901 with Chiron and Jupiter conjunct in Capricorn opposite her Cancer Sun. She is the president of the British National Health Association, which believes in vitamins and natural healing. Cartland has used ginseng root as a preventative against old age, and at age 92 is still writing every day. She began taking a wide variety of vitamins every day in 1951 as Chiron returned to its natal position when she was 50 years of age. She has a loyal fan in the Queen Mother who also is a firm believer in natural healing. The British government knighted Cartland with the title Dame for her work with nurses and midwives.

Controversial psychologist and behaviorist B. F. Skinner was born with Chiron rising just above his ascendant and he left a strong impact on 20th century psychology. His behavior modification work with rats

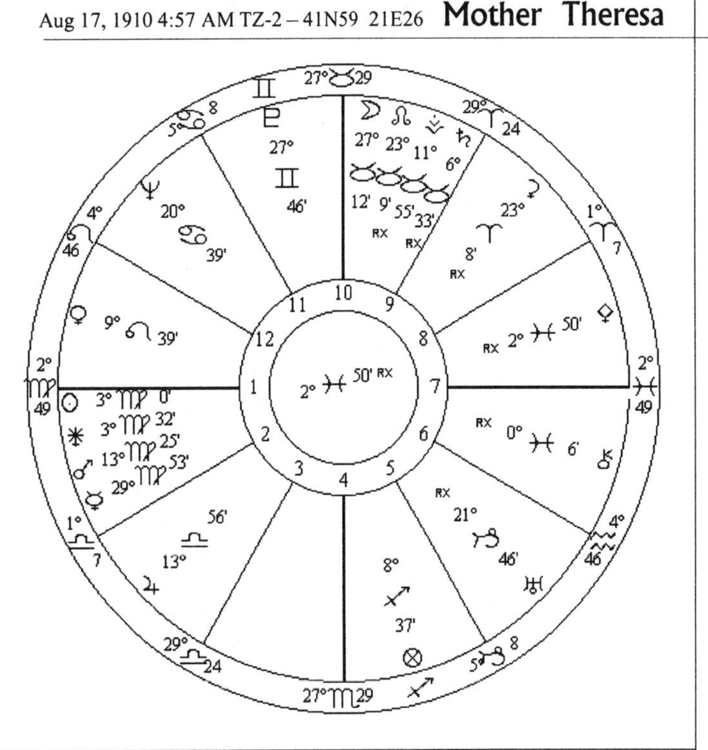

and birds won him both devoted followers and hostile detractors.

A distinguished crusader for holistic health was Norman Cousins, author of *Anatomy of an Illness,* who described how he overcame what doctors believed to be a fatal illness with vitamins and laughter. Cousins was born with Chiron conjunct Jupiter in Pisces as part of a grand water trine with Moon and Neptune.

Chiron had stationed and turned retrograde six days before Mary Baker Eddy was born. Chiron and Pluto were both stationary in her third house, and she founded the First Church of Christ Scientist based on the power of mental health. Clara Barton was born six months after Mary Baker Eddy, and also had Chiron stationing, turning direct. Chiron was conjunct Pluto in Miss Barton's chart and she almost single handedly founded the American Red Cross after serving on the battlefield of the American Civil War and the Franco Prussian War. Barton insisted that the Red Cross know no national boundaries and that it be allowed to administer to the injured and dying everywhere regardless of politics. Chiron is against politics and the system, and is always the maverick.

Alice Bailey, theosophist, was born with Chiron conjunct Neptune in Taurus, and she taught esoteric astrology, which she termed the "astrology of the soul." She was not interested in mundane events concerning physical survival and did not pay attention to the Moon, which is not a planet but a satellite of Earth. She concentrated on the Sun as the symbol of the eternal life of the soul.

Chiron was also conjunct Neptune in the chart of Helen Keller who was born blind and deaf. Keller communicated first by touch with people she could neither see nor hear. Norman Cousins wrote that Helen Keller taught us how the "human spirit is dimensionless and omnipresent."

The late great astrologer Dane Rudhyar was born with Chiron retrograde in Libra opposite his Aries Sun, and Chiron had just passed the midheaven into his 9th house. He was the wise, kindly, philosophical teacher who combined his interest in music, philosophy, medicine, education, ethics and nature with astrology. ✹

MAJOR FIXED STARS

Diana K. Rosenberg

Stars and constellations are the deepest sources of astrology.

As far back as records exist, we have evidence that civilizations all over the world formed pictures in the sky and gave names to them and their component stars. There is evidence that these sky figures, which seem arbitrary and strange to us today, were named for events that occurred when they rose, set, culminated, or were traversed by the Moon or planets. Astoundingly, these traditional patterns, which have survived from at least 8,000 years ago and probably much longer, *still function today as they did in prehistory!*

In astrology, stars are traditionally called "fixed" because in ancient times, amid constantly changing patterns of risings, settings, seasons, solstices, and the ever-weaving planets, the stars themselves seemed to hold consistently to their places in relation to one another (we now know that each star has its own "proper motion," but this movement is so slight that it would take several centuries to become apparent to an observer).

Because of this "fixity," star patterns were held to be eternal, sacred runes-in-the-sky within which ephemeral sky phenomena, including clouds, meteors, comets and planets, carried messages from the gods. The apparent stillness of the stars relative to each other, amidst other constantly changing phenomena, also made them the only "fixed" points from which other celestial motions could be measured.

Because the rotating Earth "wobbles" on its axis like a spinning top, each year the Vernal Equinox is 0°00'50.23" west of its position the year before; this adds up to 1° every 72 years. This movement, called "precession," has accumulated a span of approximately 24° (there is disagreement about the exact difference) between the figures of the ancient sidereal and the commonly used modern tropical zodiacs. *Precession **adds** an increment to birth chart positions as time progesses.*

In this chapter, longitudes are given in tropical degrees, for epoch 1980, along with Latitude (degrees N or S of ecliptic), Declination (degrees N or S of celestial equator), Right Ascension (degrees measured along the celestial equator, measured from 0° Aries) also given are Magnitude (visual brightness) and the Spectral Class of each star. It is frustrating to have to choose only a few fixed stars for this chapter there are innumerable others of great importance that had to be left out for lack of space. Nonetheless I trust that these few, for a start, will serve to whet the appetite of the student to learn more about the constellations and their component "fixed" stars.

BATEN KAITOS— Sea Monster's Belly, Whale's Belly

Nature (Ptolemy): Saturn; (Add): Neptune

	Long	*Lat*	*Dec*	*RA*	*Mag*	*Spec*
Zeta Ceti	21Ari40	-20 20	-10 26	1 50	3.73	K2

*Saturnian in both positive and negative aspects of the term

*Depth, hard work, renunciation

*Natural predeliction for solitude, study, creativity, poetry

*Inner sense of form and structure combined with powerful emotional expression

*Excellence in literature and the arts.

*Teachers, inventors, founders, innovators

*Ability to inspire others

*Deep sense of insecurity, alienation may lead them into lies, subterfuge to "keep the world at bay".

*Often feel trapped by their situation in life, yet are aware that they may have put themselves in that position

*Have ability to see past Saturnian boundaries

*May suffer enforced emigration, compulsory change, entrapment, misfortune, falls or blows through force or accident.

*Some are obsessed with religion, others with the monstrous may be drawn to the occult.

*This is the most frequently found star in shipwrecks, and many individuals may find themselves left "high and dry," broken on rocks of life yet after they pull through, have much to offer from the depths of their experiences

*Often develop strong sense of personal destiny.

Essentials of Intermediate Astrology

Throughout this chapter, key words for each star will be in 3 columns:

Positive:	Neutral:	Negative:
scholarly	inner-directed	melancholy
introspective	hyper-sensitive	death-obsessed
inspired	day-dreaming	self-limiting
sensitive	solitary	dishonest
brilliant	sexual fantasizing	abrasive
determined	feel humiliated	paranoid
hard-working	blunt, abrasive	selfish
inventive	insecure	assassination-prone

Mundane: Shipwreck, possibly with rescue; disease; assassination, massacres; "firsts"-first attempts, initiatives, first manifestations of new ideas, movements, inventions.

Sun

Raphael, *artist*
W. Booth, *Salvation Army Founder*
Cmdr. Matthew Perry, *Naval Officer*
Omar Sharif, *actor*
A. E. (G. W. Russell), *poet/mystic*
Baudelaire, Wordsworth, *poets*
Gen'l Ludendorf
Eruption of Tambora, 1815: *"largest explosive eruption of historical times-surpassed even Krakatau": 92,000 dead; atmospheric ash caused 1816 "year with no summer," famines*
Titanic *sailed on maiden voyage, 1912*
US drought's *"worst dust storm" 1935*
US Submarine Thresher *lost, 1963*

Moon

F. Valenzuela, *baseball player*
N. Leopold, *murderer*
Dr. F. Regardie, *occultist*
Sir Thomas More, *statesman (beheaded)*
Full Moon: Pope John Paul II *elected, 1979*
"Rainbow Warrior", *Greenpeace ship, sabotaged, sunk 1985*

Mercury

Catherine the Great *of Russia*
U. S. Grant, *US President*
Edward R. Murrow, *broadcast journalist*
Shakespeare, F. Garcia Lorca *(assassinated), poet/playwrights*
Start of 1912 Olympics, *1st to allow women*
First use of poison gas, *Ypres, Belgium, 1915*
Great 8.5 Alaska *quake/tsunami, 1964*

Venus

S. Hussein, *Iraqi dictator*
Z. Mehta, *conductor*
J. Swaggert, *discredited fundamentalist preacher*
Jim Jones, *cult leader (Guyana massacre)*
R. Baden-Powell, *w/sister, founder of Boy & Girl Guides (Scouts)*
J. Sorrentino, *started as hoodlum, became judge, author*
Jane Roberts, *author/channeler*
Miles Davis, *jazz trumpeter*
Dirigible Hindenberg *released, final voyage, 1937*
First man in space: *launch of Gagarin, Baikonur, 1961*
Tenerife air crash/fire *(worst in history), 1977: 2 jets collided in fog, 582 killed*
Launch of "Pride of Baltimore" *sailing ship-sank in squall*

Mars

A. Durer, *artist*
M. Maeterlinck, *author/occultist*
J. Campbell, *mythologist*
Rabbi M. Schneerson, *Lubavitcher leader*
O. Respighi, *composer*
Karen Kain, *ballerina*
H. Milk, *politician (assassinated)*
B. Cerf, *publisher/editor*
My Lai massacre, *Viet Nam, 1968*
SDI ("Star Wars") *announced by R. Reagan 1983*

Jupiter

Mary Wollstonecraft Shelley, *author ("Frankenstein")*
N. Leopold, *murderer*
M. Trudeau, *Canadian PM*
G. Flaubert *(pessimist), author*
R. Descartes, *philosopher/mathematician*
Clara Barton, *war nurse/founder American Red Cross*
J. Brahms, *composer*
Shirley Temple Black, *actress/diplomat*
Severe coastal storm, *S. California, 1988*

Saturn

Guy de Maupassant, G. Flaubert *(pessimist), authors*
W. Penn, *founder of Pennsylvania*
Burl Ives, *actor/folksinger*
R. F. Kennedy *assassinated, 1968*

Uranus

Dick Gregory *nutritionist, activist, comedian*

Baten Kaitos, cont.

Godfrey Cambridge, *comedian*
Yoko Ono, *artist*
B. Aquino, *Philippine politician (assassinated)*
FDR *assassination attempt, 1933*
Hitler *sworn in as German chancellor, 1933*

Neptune
Gandhi, *Indian leader (assassinated)*
Emma Goldman, *anarchist*
V. Lenin, *dictator*
E. Lee Masters, *poet*
German Empire, *1871*

Pluto
W. McKinley, *US President (assassinated)*
R. Koch, *scientist*
J. D. Rockefeller, *tycoon*
Massenet, Sullivan, Tschaikowsky, *composers*
Saint Bernadette
W. James, *philosopher/psychologist*
C. Flammarion, *astronomer/psychic researcher*
T. Hardy, *author*
S. Mallarmé, *symbolist poet*

N. Node
A. Schweitzer, *physician/musician/missionary*
Queen Victoria
D. Webster, *statesman*
D. W. Griffith, *filmmaker*
N. Tesla, inventor
1912 Olympics, *First to allow women*
Titanic *hit iceberg, sank, 1912*

S. Node
A. G. Bell, T. Edison, *inventors*
Michaelangelo, Rubens, *artists*
Paracelsus, *physician/occultist*
C. W. Leadbeater, *theosophist*
J. Glenn, *astronaut/US Senator*
Mario & Aldo Andretti (twins) , *auto racers (several severe injuries)*
Hawaii/San Francisco Pacific Cable *opened 1903*
Creation, "Operation Dynamo": *emergency rescue of British & French troops, using fleet of small boats, Dunkirk, 1940*
"Adm Nakhimov" *ship disaster, USSR, 1986*

ASC
R. Firebrace, *sidereal astrologer*
A.. Malraux, *author*
Brahms, *composer*
"Corky", *male autistic child*
Hakata Bay, New Moon 11/ 7 /1274 NS: *Khubilai Khan's 900-ship fleet w/40,000 troops invaded Japan. "Kamikaze" ("Divine Wind") storm arose, destroyed fleet: 200 ships sank, 13,500 perished (also Asc of Lunar Eclipse 7 /20/ 1274 visible at that area)*

MC
Buckminster Fuller, *engineer/designer*
Trotsky, *communist leader (assassinated)*
Dillinger, *gangster*
B. Harrison, *US President*
Sen. A. Gore, *US VP*
C. Steinmetz, *mathematician/electrical engineer/ inventor*

STELLA MIRA — "Wonderful Star" Nature: Saturn (Venus, Mars, Uranus, Pluto)

	Long	*Lat*	*Dec*	*RA*	*Mag*	*Spec*
MIRA Omicron Ceti	1Tau14	-15 57	-3 05	2 18	3.04v	Md

*Most famous variable; 6th strongest infra-red source in the sky; prototype for entire class of extreme & irregular variables.

*Diminishes to invisibility, then rises to 3rd magnitude or higher (averages 3rd to 9th magnitude—(the lower the magnitude number, the brighter the star) in variable cycle, about 330 days

*Not properly catalogued nor attributes noted until mid-1600's, no record of it in ancient texts.

*According to Ptolemy, all Cetus stars are like Saturn - for Mira, I would add Venus, Mars, Uranus, Pluto.

*Strong, arrogant, coldly royal nature; personal severity, persistence, boldness, endurance

*Care nothing for what others think

*When pressured, can display outbursts of demonic intensity.

*Artistic, literary, musical ability, poetic talent.

*Higher-than-average possibility of violent death, sometimes self-inflicted.

Essentials of Intermediate Astrology

Stella Mira, *cont.*

Positive:	Neutral:	Negative:
focussed	willful	arrogant
goal-oriented	intense	intolerant
persistent	conquering	dictatorial
multi-talented	enduring	domineering
imaginative	conservative	obsessive
courageous	outspoken	destructive
artistic	passionate	ruthless
musical	materialistic	cynical

Mundane: Freedom *vs* slavery; justice, human rights *vss* dogma; religion *vs.* atheism; entrapment; attacks; assassination; choking (dust storm, gas attacks), eye problems.

Sun
A.. Hitler, *dictator (suicide)*
Charlemagne, *King of Franks (1st Holy Roman Emperor)*
L. da Vinci, *artist/inventor*
Queen Elizabeth II *of England*
J. Miro, *artist*
T. Hobbes, *materialist philosopher*
Poison gas *first used in war, Ypres, Belgium, 1915.*

Moon
Robespierre, *French dictator (guillotined)*
Prince Charles *of England*
Imelda Marcos, *Philippine First Lady (deposed)*
Delibes, *composer*
J. Thurber, *author/cartoonist*
Jerry Lewis, *comedian*

Mercury
H. Fonda, *actor*
P. Curie, *chemist*
Mike Wallace, *TV News Correspondent*
J. P. Morgan, *financier*
Nazi book-burning *of "non-Aryan" authors, 1933, Berlin.*

Venus
Michaelangelo *(Venus ruled MC)*
Honegger, *composer*
A. Ginsberg, *poet*
Marjory S. Douglas, *environmentalist*
Arthur Shawcross, *cannibal/serial killer*
Joan Crawford, *actress*
US Supreme Court 1857 Dred Scott Decision *affirming slaveowners rights (w/Mira, this is also the degree of 45 Andromedae, in the constellation The Chained Woman).*

Mars
A. Eichmann, *Nazi Persecutor of Jews (executed)*
Ayatollah Khomeini, *Iranian leader*
J. Edgar Hoover, *Head of FBI*
Carl P. Tobey, *astrologer*
Battle of Marathon, *Greece, 490 BC*
Eruption of Vesuvius, *79 AD, buried Pompeii.*

Jupiter:
Sir Thomas More, *statesman (beheaded)*
Czarevitch Alexis, *hemophiliac/heir to Russian throne (assassinated)*
Martin L. King Jr, *civil rights leader (assassinated)*
C. Isherwood, *author/pacifist*
Start, Battle of the Somme, *1916 (1,100,000 killed)*
Poison gas attack *on Kurd villagers by Saddam Hussein's troops, Halabja, Iraq, 1988 (5,000+ dead)*

Saturn
R. Reagan, *actor/US President (assassination attempt)*
J. Genet, *playwright*

Uranus:
Andrew Jackson, *General/US President (assassination attempt)*
Van Dyck, *artist*
Van Cliburn, *pianist*
Guy de Maupassant *(became insane)*, LeRoi Jones, *authors*
(1930's) US drought's"Worst dust storm", 1935.

Neptune
Khubilai Khan, *Mongol Emperor of China*
Samuel Johnson, *author/critic*
J. London, G. K. Chesterton, *authors*
Robert Frost, Rainer Maria Rilke, *poets*
A. Schonberg, *composer*
K. Adenauer, *President of Germany*
Jinarajadasa, *Indian theosophist*

Pluto
Guy de Maupassant, *author (became insane)*
Miro, Van Gogh *(suicide), artists*
José Marti, *Cuban patriot*
Marshall Joffre, Gen Foch *of France, Commanders, Allied forces, WWI*
W. Lilly, *astrologer.*

N. Node
Spinoza, *philosopher*
H. Hoover, *US President*
J. Miro, *artist*
G. Foreman, *boxer*

Stella Mira, cont.

H. Ross Perot, *industrialist/politician*
D. Eisele, *astronaut*
Turgenev, *author*
Chet Huntley, *TV newsman.*
Lunar Eclipse 4/ 3 /33 AD OS, *possible date of Crucifixion of Christ*
Peace March *across US for nuclear ban, 1986.*

S. Node
J. Verne, *author*
C. Steinmetz, *mathematican/electrical engineer/ inventor*
M. Lanza, *tenor*
E. St-Hilaire, *naturalist, (blind at 68)*
Ulugh Beg's Star Catalogue *published, 1437, Samarkhand*
Nazis attacked Poland *1939, starting WWII.*

Asc:
Liza Minelli, *actress/singer*
Pearl Bailey, *singer*

MC
R. Murdoch, *newspaper tycoon*
M. Gauquelin, *researcher (suicide)*
A. Dumas, *author.*
Cocoanut Grove Night Club Fire, *1942, Boston, MA (491 killed)*

ALGOL— Medusa's Head - The Demon Star
Nature: Jupiter, Saturn (Mars, Venus, Uranus, Neptune, Pluto)

	Long	*Lat*	*Dec*	*RA*	*Mag*	*Spec*
Beta Persei	25Tau53	22 26	40 53	3 07	2.12v	B8

In Greek myth, Algol was the eye of the Gorgon Medusa, whose horrible snaky-haired head was cut off by Perseus; it has always been associated with beheadings. An eclipsing binary, every 68.818 hours (average) the eye "blinks" for about two hours. Manly Palmer Hall called Algol *"the most evil, violent, dangerous star in the heavens"*; some of the most horrible events in human history have occurred under this star; nonetheless, in a personal horoscope, it is not necessarily malevolent and may even bestow benefits.

Though often found in the charts of bigots and criminals, having Algol prominent on a nativity does not necessarily mean that one will commit or experience violence; rather, that one must come to terms with that level of human experience.

A young soldier might experience the horrors of war, a black child learn of the ordeals of slavery; a Jewish child might become aware that his grandparents perished in the holocaust. A police officer might assist victims of a disaster, a clergyman be called upon to comfort them, a journalist assigned to cover the story, a medical student assigned to a trauma center. An Algol placement insists upon confrontation and assimilation of such harsh aspects of human experience in this lifetime.

As for the personae of Algol natives, they are serious, strongly ambitious, patient people, driven to succeed and excel, needing to be in the spotlight. Unfortunately, if they cannot get attention in a positive manner, they might turn to spectacular crime. There is a strong artistic side to this star, and many of its natives are amiable and tolerant, though bigotry *vs* tolerance is an issue in these lives. Astronomers and astrologers often have placements here.

Mundane: Algol often marks great tragedies: war, mass murder, violence, mass disasters (earthquakes, fires, plagues, shipwrecks, mob violence), suffocation, hanging, beheading; especially any event in which a large number of people die or are killed brutally. The Chinese found this area extremely malevolent as well; to them Algol was part of a "Great Trench" (17-29 Taurus) of piled up, dishonored, dismembered corpses.

Positive:	**Neutral:**	**Negative**
ambitious	dogged	violent
spiritual	unyielding	dictatorial
serious	patient	harsh, cruel
verbal	macabre	win-at-all-costs
artistic	outré	intolerant
"figureheads"	inventive	murderous

Essentials of Intermediate Astrology

Algol, cont.

Sun
Ayatollah Khomeini, *Shiite Moslem leader*
P. Curie, *scientist*
Williamina Fleming, *astronomer*
W. Lilly, Garth Allen (Donald Bradley), *astrologers*
H. Fonda, J. Cotton, *actors*
Margot Fonteyn, *prima ballerina (husband shot in neck, paralyzed)*
Joan Benoit, *winner, first Olympic Women's Marathon*
G. Braque, E. Degas, *artists*
C. Linnaeus, *botanist*
J. Sorrentino, *started as hoodlum/became judge/ author*
Solar Eclipse 5/ 14 /1790: *French Revolution's "Reign of Terror"*
Egypt Plague *(80,000 dead)*
"Skull Famine," *India*
Slave revolts, *Haiti, Santo Domingo*
US Supreme Court *outlawed school segregation, 1954*
Gov Wallace *shot, paralyzed, 1972*
SLA- Los Angeles Police *shoot-out/fire, 1974*

Moon
Sen. H. Humphrey
W. Von Braun, *rocket scientist*
D. Eisele, *astronaut*
Calvin, *religious reformer*
J. Hoffa, *labor leader (murdered)*
A. Landers, A. Van Buren *(twins), advice columnists*
M. Jagger, *rock star*
R. Stroud, *murderer ("Birdman of Alcatraz"), healer of birds*
1902 Mt Pelée eruption: *29,000 killed-entire population of Martinique*
Lunar Eclipse 11 /17 /1910: *2.5 million died of bubonic plague, China*
Full Moon (cnj Uranus) 11/14-15, 1940: *Nazis bombed Coventry, 897-yr-old cathedral shattered*
New Moon 5 /15 /42: *Corregidor surrendered-Death March*
Russian Defense of Sevastopol *(previous seige of Sevastopol, 1855, followed solar eclipse at Algol)*
Battle of Coral Sea
Battle of Midway
Nazi Massacre *at Lidice, Czechslovakia*
Severe Chicago Flood *(water main collapse) 1992*

Mercury
D. Hume, philosopher
Z. Mehta, *conductor*
Susan Atkins, *murderer*
A. Durer, *artist*
O. Cromwell, *statesman/persecuter*
Maraquita Platov, *anti-war poet*
Cole Porter, *songwriter*
Spanish Armada *sailed, 1588*
1917 cnj. of Mercury/Mars/Jupiter: *virulent influenza pandemic killed 25-50 million worldwide (see Nostradamus' Centuries IX:55)*
Mercury/Venus/Jupiter/Uranus *conj. (square Mars), 1941: Nazis terror-bombed London: 3,000+ killed, House of Commons, Westminster Hall severely damaged*
Buddhist Monk Ngo Quang Duc *burned self to death protesting gov't persecution, 1963, Saigon*
Mt. Unzen eruption, *Japan, 1991*

Venus
Prince William *of England*
C. Steinmetz, *mathematician/engineer/inventor*
E. Rostand, *poet/playwright ("Cyrano de Bergerac")*
D. Kilgallen, *journalist (murdered?)*
Westley A. Dodd, *sexually tortured, killed children (hanged)*
V. Zhirinovsky, *Russian politician.*
Lincoln's & Garfield's *assassinations*
Nazi book-burning, *Berlin, 1933*
US 1930s drought's *"worst dust storm" 1935*

Mars
Andrew Jackson, *general/US President*
M. Bormann, *Nazi official*
F. Argelander, *astronomer*
G. Marconi, *inventor*
M. Cuomo, *politician*
R. De Niro, *actor*
C. Addams, *cartoonist*
George Sand, F. Kafka, *authors*
S. Dali, *artist*
Great earthquake/tsunami 365 AD *hit entire Mediterranean area, esp Knossos (Crete), & Alexandria, Egypt, toppled Pharos lighthouse, a wonder of the ancient world*
Sir Thomas More *beheaded 1535*
"Trinity"- *First atomic bomb tested, Alamagordo, NM, 1945*

Jupiter
Meher Baba, *mystic/religious leader*
A. Onassis, *financier*
Lenin, *revolutionary*

Algol, cont.

P. Picasso, *artist*
J-P. Sartre, *existentialist (became blind)*
Adm. Darlan, *French officer (assassinated)*
Edgar Guest, *poet*
A. de Musset, *poet/playwright*
S. Pepys, *diarist*
P. T. Barnum, *circus showman*
C. B. DeMille, *film director*
Harpo Marx, *comedian*
A. Fleming, *discoverer of penicillin*
Archbishop Laud *beheaded, 1645*
Jupiter transited Algol's degree 1905: *Plague ravaged India, 500,000 died+Jupiter st d 1906, 10 days before 8.9 Ecuador quake, 3 months before great San Francisco 8.3 quake/fire+(cnj Uranus) 1941, Stalin became Premier of Soviet Union and (same day) vicious Nazi decree "Regulating the Treatment of Inhabitants of Enemy countries" issued*
T'ang Shan Earthquake (8.0), *China, 1976: 250,000-750,000 dead*
Seveso, Italy *Dioxin chemical disaster 1976*
US ship shot down Iran airbus, *Persian Gulf, 1988*
Jupiter st d 1989:
Steinberg *child abuse trial*
Serial Killer *Ted Bundy executed*
French Revolution, 200th anniversary

Saturn

Joan of Arc, *warrior/martyr (burned at stake; Saturn ruled her 8th)*
J. Giraudoux, *playwright*
S. Goldwyn, *producer*
Lon Chaney, Bela Lugosi, *actors*
A. Garfunkel, *singer/songwriter*
R. Nixon, *US President*; *Saturn/Uranus cnj midpoint:*
R. Speck, *rapist/strangler*
J. Wayne Gacy, *serial killer (executed)*
Robespierre *guillotined, 1794*
London bombing *started, 1940*
German besieged Moscow, 1941; *desperate defense held: huge losses both sides*

Surrender of Bataan to Japanese: *Death March, 1942*

Uranus

Coleridge, *poet*
G. B. Shaw, *author/playwright*
Williamina Fleming, *astronomer*
N. Tesla, *inventor*
Ringo Starr,(*drummer),* John Lennon *(murdered),* Bob Dylan, *singers/songwriters/musicians.*
R. Valens, *singer (killed in plane crash)*
R. Speck, *murderer*
M. J. Kopechne, *secretary (drowned)*
Solar Eclipse 1 /15 /9 AD OS, *year Germanic tribes wiped out 3 Roman Legions*
Trotsky *assassinated, 1940*
"The Blitz" *Stationary Retrograd conj. 1940: massive air raids battered London*
Lascaux Discovery, *prehistoric cave paintings, 1940*
Wannsee Conference: *implementation of Hitler's " Final Solution" decision to exterminate Jews, 1942*

Neptune

Ezra Pound, *poet/virulent anti-semite*
B. Lugosi, *actor*
G. Patton, *US General, WWII*
N. Bohr, *physicist*
C. E. O. Carter, *astrologer*
A. Rubenstein, *pianist (blind)*
Hollywood *founded, 1887*
Sailing ship Annie C. McGuire *sank in storm, Portland Head, ME, 1886*

Pluto

Alexander the Great, *conqueror*
J. Stalin, *dictator*
D. MacArthur, *US General, WWII, Korea*
Mata Hari, *exotic dancer/spy (executed)*
M. Maimonides, *12th century philosopher/physician*
M. Buber, *Jewish theologian*
Isadora Duncan, *dancer (strangled in accident)*
S. Anderson, *playwright*
H. Hesse, C. Sandberg, E. Rice Burroughs *("Tarzan"),* E. M. Forster, *authors*
W. Hartley, *Titanic's bandleader (band continued playing -all went down with ship)*
W. C. Fields, *comedian*
L. Trotsky, *revolutionary leader (assassinated-pickax driven into head)*
A. Einstein, *physicist*
Lunar Eclipse 1/ 3 /641 OS/Solar, Eclipse 1 /17 /641 OS: *reputed final destruction of Alexandria Library by order of Caliph Omar: priceless scrolls burned to heat public baths*
Vesuvius *eruption, 1631*
Custer's Last Stand: *after attacks on Indian villages, Custer and troops annihilated by Sioux & Cheyenne warriors, 1876*
Yellow Fever *epidemic, Memphis, TN 1878*

Algol, cont.

N. Node

E. Rommel, *WWII German Field Marshal (forced suicide)*
Delibes, *composer*
B. Franklin, *publisher/statesman/diplomat*
Winslow Homer, *artist*
Stephen King *(horror stories), author*
Ramakrishna, *mystic/author*
Valentine's Day Massacre, *Chicago, 1929*
Bhopal Disaster, India, 1984 *(3,000 dead, 20,000 blinded, sickened, crippled)*

S. Node

Shah Reza Pahlevi *of Iran (deposed)*
M. Palmer Hall, *astrologer*
S. Goldwyn, *producer*
Natalie Wood, a*ctress (drowned)*
Aries ingress 1994: *massacres, Ruanda & Haiti*

Asc

G. Washington, U. S. Grant, *Generals/US Presidents*
W. Randolph Hearst, *publisher*
J. P. Morgan Jr, *financier*
Christa McAuliffe, *teacher (Challenger disaster)*
C. Sagan, *astronomer/anti-nuclear activist*
W. Reuther, *labor leader (died in plane crash)*
Cancer Ingress preceding 1201 quake *(Egypt/Syria): 1,300,000 dead*
Massacre of Huguenots *1572, Paris*
WWI - Britain's entry, *1914*
Hitler *sworn in as German Chancellor 1933*
First atomic reaction, *1942, Chicago*
Blackout, NE USA *powergrid 1965*
Biloxi, MS, tidal surge, *hurricane Camille, 1969: 400 dead, 400,000 homeless*
Guyana Massacre, 1978
Tiananmen Square Massacre, *Beijing, 1989*

MC

Jackie Robinson, *baseball player*
H. Ford, *manufacturer/ant-semite*
L. Bernstein, *conductor/composer*
A. Durer, *artist*
J. Lee Lehman, *astrologer*
Capricorn ingress New Delhi 1984 after Bhopal gas disaster; *assassination of Indira Gandhi*

IC

Titanic sank, 1912: *1503 died.*

ALCYONE— The Weeping One The Star of Sorrow: Brightest star of Pleiades Cluster

Nature: Moon, Jupiter (Neptune)

	Long	*Lat*	*Dec*	*RA*	*Mag*	*Spec*
Beta Tauri	29Tau43	4 03	24 03	3 46	2.87	B7

*Helps to prominence, especially in science, agriculture, military, government, (although not royal star, effect is very similar)

*Usually a high level of intelligence

*High-strung, quarrelsome, may be oversexed to an extreme degree.

*Great conflict between matter & spirit, science & spirit

*Usually many journeys; possible banishment, exile, (may feel like "outsiders" in their environment)

*Most experience sorrow in their lives, evacuation, imprisonment; wounding, shipwreck, disease are possibilities.

*Sorrows aside, they are generally active, optimistic and learn to cultivate the arts of peace.

*Alcyone, the major star of the Pleiades cluster, will reach 0° tropical Gemini (the world mind axis) by the year 2000; thus this star, which has been in tropical Taurus for 2,151 years, is entering a new tropical sign and triplicity, taking on a new energy matrix, bringing global awareness of human suffering.

*Tears, weeping, eye problems, blindness.

Mundane: pestilences, fires, wounding, shipwreck, attacks, invasions, forced evacuation, exile, banishment, refugees, imprisonment, torrential rain, floods; "something to weep about" (weeping & rain are a specific effects of the Pleiades)

Positive:	**Neutral:**	**Negative**
optimistic	ambitious	oversexed
highly intelligent	patriotic	wanton
energetic, capable	inquisitive	quarrelsome
multi-talented	alienated	manipulative
productive, cultured	act on beliefs	self-righteous
musical, artistic	eye problems	blindness

Alcyone, cont.

Sun

Marcus Aurelius, *Roman Emperor*
Czar Nicholas II *of Russia (assassinated)*
Machiavelli, *political theorist*
J. Norman Lockyer, *astronomer*
J. Tito, *Yugoslavian leader*
A. Sakharov, *physicist/activist*
Bertrand Russell, *mathematician/philosopher/activist*
Dr. J. Steinhardt, *biophysicist (cataracts, glaucoma)*
P. Hurkos, *psychic.*

Moon

J. P. Sousa, *composer*
E. Piaf, *singer*
Andrew Johnson, *US President*
Bob Crane, *actor (murdered)*
Lincoln's Emancipation Proclamation *took effect, 1/ 1/ 1863, 0 hour*
German invasion of USSR, *1941*

Mercury

Mary Wollstonecraft, *pioneer feminist/author (died in childbirth)*
J. Krishnamurti, *author/theosophist*
Dr. B. Spock, *pediatrician/author/activist*
T. H. Huxley, *scientist/Pres of Royal Society*
J. J. Audubon, *artist/ornithologist*
J.Y. Cousteau, *undersea explorer/environmentalist*
S. Freud, *psychiatrist*
G. Bush, *US President*
N. de Lacaille, *17th century astronomer*
Mt Pelée eruption, *1902, killed 29,000-entire population of Martinique*
Tiananmen Square Massacre, *Beijing. Mercury St d: 1989, tear gas used*

Venus

K. Marx, *social theorist*
R. Rodgers, *composer*
Richie Valens, *singer (killed in plane crash at 17- Venus ruled his 8th)*
N. Luboff, *choral conductor*
T. Hardy, *author*
J. Cocteau, *author/film director*
R. McKuen, *singer/poet*
A. Mesmer, *astrologer/physician/discoverer of hypnosis*
Lunar Eclipse, 6 /26 /1619, *2 months before 1st slaves brought to Virginia*
Japanese invaded China *1937*
N. Korea attacked S. Korea, *1950*
Chernobyl *nuclear disaster, 1986, USSR*

Mars

L. Mountbatten, *Sea Lord/diplomat (assassinated)*
Augustus Caesar, *Roman Emperor*
Bertrand Russell, *mathematician/philosopher*
Christopher Marlowe, *poet/dramatist*
Jackson Pollock, *artist*
Cyril Scott, *composer/author/occultist*
E. Bombeck, *humorist*
U.S. *Air Attack on Iraq, 1991*

Jupiter

L. Pasteur, *"father of bacteriology"*
Ann Frank, *diarist*
D. Bonhoeffer, *anti-Nazi minister (hanged by SS)*
Bob Dylan, *singer/songwriter*
L. Stokowski, *conductor*
J. McDivitt, *astronaut*
Charles Atlas, *strongman*
Howard Hughes, *billionaire recluse*
Maxine Yourman, *clairvoyant/astrologer/teacher of visually impaired children (two grandparents and mother became blind; as child, met Helen Keller)*
Solar Eclipse 2/ 23 /06, *2 months before 8.3 San Francisco earthquake/fire*
Tenerife *air crash disaster, 1977, (worst in history) in fog: 582 dead*
6.9 Armenian *quake, 1988, 25,000 dead*
Solar Eclipse 3 /7/ 89, *2 weeks before Exxon Valdez Alaskan oil tanker disaster*

Saturn

John Adams, *US President/diplomat*
Augustus Caesar, *Roman Emperor*
Mary McCarthy, *author*
B. Streisand, *actress/singer*
Worst collier explosion in history, *Manchuria, 1942, (1,549 killed)*
Battle of Coral Sea, *1942*
Babi Yar: *Nazi massacre of more than 100,000 Jews, USSR, 1941*

Uranus

F. Baily, *astronomer*
B. Streisand, *actress/singer/producer*
Helen Reddy, *singer*
Paul Simon, Art Garfunkel, *singer/songwriters*
German invasion of USSR, *1941*
Worst collier explosion in history *(w/Saturn)*
Battle of Coral Sea, *1942*

Neptune

Hadrian, *Roman Emperor*

Essentials of Intermediate Astrology

Alcyone, cont.

A. Rubenstein, *pianist (blind)*
J. Huxley, *biologist/philosopher*
I. Berlin, *songwriter*
M. Chagall, *artist*
Boris Karloff, *actor*
K. Rockne, *football coach*
Chiang Kai-Shek, *warlord*
Great NE US Blizzard of 1888: *4-day storm: more than 400 dead*

Pluto
Helen Keller, *blind/deaf author*
I. Stravinsky, *composer*
L. Stokowski, *conductor*
F. D. Roosevelt, *U.S. President*
Sir Christopher Wren, *Prof of Astronomy/architect*
Jean & Auguste Piccard *(twins), underwater explorers/baloonists*
Gen'l Umberto Nobile, *arctic explorer*
P. T. de Chardin, *Jesuit priest/scientist*
C. De Mille, M. Sennett, *filmmakers*
Spinoza, Keyserling, Locke, *philosophers*
Wallace Stevens, Edgar Guest, A. A. Milne, *poets*
Alice Bailey, *theosophist*
Cyril Scott, *occultist*
E. Benjamine (C. C. Zain), L. E. Johndro, *astrologers*
John & Ethel Barrymore, Lon Chaney, D. Fairbanks, *actors*
P. Picasso, *artist*
Virginia Woolf *(suicide by drowning)*, James Joyce, *authors*

N. Node
I. Kant, *philosopher*
E. Caruso, *tenor*
C. St. Saens, *composer*
J. Anouilh, *playwright*
Augustus Caesar, *Roman Emperor*
M. Gauquelin, *researcher (suicide)*
J.Y. Cousteau, *underwater explorer*
M. L. King Jr, *minister/activist (assassinated)*
National Negro Committee *became NAACP, 1910*

S. Node:
Beethoven, Stravinsky, *composers*
J. Heifetz, *violinist*
G. Santayana, *poet/philosopher*
R. Nureyev, *dancer*
Gov. Wallace *of Alabama (paralyzed in assassination attempt)*
Czar Alexander III *of Russia*
G. Hennard, *women-hating mass murderer/suicide (Killeen, TX massacre)*
Lunar Eclipse 4 /15/ 78 AD OS, *year Romans exterminated Druids, Isle of Mona (Anglesey), Wales*

Asc
Dr. C. Barnard, *heart surgeon*
Alexander the Great, *conqueror*
H. Hoover, *U.S. President*
W. Saroyan, *author*
Arthur Shawcross, *cannibal/serial killer*
Start, Battle of Flamborough Head, *1779, Serapis vs Bonhomme Richard (Capt J Paul Jones)*
A. Hitler *sworn in as German chancellor, 1933*

MC
Copernicus, *astronomer*
P. Yogananda, *mystic*
L. Walesa, *labor leader/President of Poland*
Cyril Fagan, *sidereal astrologer*
A. Copeland, *composer*
Lift-off of Apollo 11 *for Moon, 1969*

PRIMA HYADUM– Hyades cluster, Bull's face. (Saturn, Mercury, Venus, Mars, Uranus)

	Long	*Lat*	*Dec*	*RA*	*Mag*	*Spec*
Gamma Tauri	5Gem32	-5 44	15 35	4 19	3.63	KO

*Forces its natives to choose fame or infamy, good or evil, tolerance or intolerance

*Effect is extreme, intense and unrelenting.

*Many are "one- of-a-kind" individuals, able to "see with new eyes"

*Tend to make their own rules.

*Inner toughness: stubborn, formidable to deal with when confronted head-on.

*Have ability to tap into myth and/or create their own myth for others to follow

*Excellent placement for artists, musicians and writers: very original, often successful

*Confident in worldly matters, frequently rise to positions of leadership; some combine military & politics

*In many ways, Hyades are like royal Aldebaran, below. Torrential rain, storms, floods, shipwreck, air crashes, transportation disasters, mass movements, invasions (Chinese called the Pleiades/Hyades "The Announcer of the Invasion at the Border"), riots, murder, sedition, rebellion, revolution

Prima Hyadum, cont.

Positive:	**Neutral:**	**Negative:**
intense ambition	leadership drive	ferocity, violence
originality	active mentality	intense sexuality
inventiveness	focussed	brooding, resentful
artistic, musical	controversial	delusions of grandeur
vision	stubborn	"utter depravity"*
imagination	adventurous	extremism, sedition
strong intellect	sense of drama	persecuted/persecuter
daring	intensely energetic	insanity, murder
aggressive	revolutionary	eye problems, blindness

**Ptolemy*

Sun

H. Kissinger, *statesman*
H. Humphrey, *US senator*
Tito, *Yugoslav leader*
B. Cerf, *publisher/editor*
H. Wouk, E. Bulwer-Lytton, H. Ellison, *authors*
R. W. Emerson, *philosopher/author*
A. Mesmer, *astrologer/physician/discovered hypnotism*
V. Robson, *astrologer*
Sally Ride, *astronaut*
Isadora Duncan, *dance pioneer*
John Wayne, James Arness, Vincent Price, *actors*
Bob Dylan, *singer/songwriter*
First Anglo- Persian oil well, 1908, Iran
Dunkirk: *sea rescue of 338,226 British & French soldiers, 1940*

Moon

Queen Victoria
Frank L. Wright, *architect*
A. Garfunkel, *singer/songwriter*
California floods, 1986 *(Moon/Mars/Saturn)*

Mercury:

K. Marx, *social theorist*
W. B. Yeats, *poet/occultist*
Anne Baxter, S. Hayakawa, *actors/ authors*
Rennie Davis, *revolutionary*
Jeffrey Dahmer, *serial killer*
D. Kinsman, *strangler*
Napoleon's invasion of Russia, 1812
Race Riots, Detroit, 1943
Supreme Court outlawed segregation, 1954
Soweto uprising, S. Africa, 1976.

Venus:

P. Gauguin, *artist*
L. Hellman, *author/playwright*
Adm. Farragut, *naval hero*
H. Thoreau, S. Rushdie, A. Trollope, *authors*
Mary Wollstonecraft, *pioneer feminist/author*
O. Cromwell, *dictator*
Lunar Eclipse, 55 BC: *Caesar reconnoitred shores of England*
Beirut- *US Embassy bombing, 1983*
"Rainbow Warrior", Greenpeace ship, *sabotaged, sunk, 1985.*

Mars

Galileo *(became blind)*
G. Abell, *astronomers*
Massenet, Sir A. Sullivan, *composers*
Louis Armstrong, *trumpeter*
O. J. Simpson, *football star/actor/sportscaster*
Jack Abbott, *murderer/author*
John Wayne Gacy, *serial killer (executed)*
Kurosawa, C. De Mille, *filmmakers*
Mars, Solar Eclipse, 55 BC: *Caesar reconnoitred shores of England*
Confederates attacked Fort Sumter, *starting US Civil War*
Mars, Aries ingress 1910: King Edward VIII died, *devastating European floods,English constitutional crisis 6/22:*
Zeppelin "Deutchland" *1st Airship to transport passengers, wrecked in gale*
Violent typhoon *hit Japan-severe flooding (conj. Venus)*
Germany invaded Denmark, 1940
Allied invasion of Italy, 1943
Eisenhower given command of "D-Day" invasion, 1944
Reported UFO crash near Socorro, NM, 1947

Jupiter

Krushchev, *Russian leader*
Imelda Marcos, *Philippino dictator's wife*
G. Lincoln Rockwell, *American Nazi*
Degas, Whistler, *artists*
J. Smuts, *statesman/author*
A. Koestler, Arthur C. Clarke, *authors*
D. Berkowitz, "Son of Sam" *murderer*

Saturn

Jean, Auguste Piccard (twins), *scientists/baloonists/ deep-sea explorers*
M. Sennett, M. Antonioni, *filmmakers*
F. Kafka, author
Rube Goldberg, *sculptor/inventor/cartoonist*

Essentials of Intermediate Astrology

Prima Hyadum, cont.

Gene Kelly, *actor/dancer/choreographer*
P. McCartney, G Harrison, *singers/songwriters*
Mars-Saturn cnj 1883 *before great eruption of Krakatoa*
Saturn with Mercury, Detroit race riots, 1943
Attica, NY prison rebellion, 1971

Uranus:
T. Roosevelt, *US President*
J. Holdren, e*nvironmentalist*
Rembrandt, *artist*
P. Curie, scientist
S. Sirhan, assassin
Jane Austen, author
A. Chekov, J. M. Barrie, *authors/playwrights*
Jack Abbott, *murderer/author*
Sir A. Conan Doyle, Jane Austen, *authors*
Angela Davis, *revolutionary*
Uranus, Great Mutation (Jupiter/Saturn cnj) 1524: *Floods in Italy*; *volcanic eruption in Guatamala, Alvarado defeated last of Guatemalan Quiché Maya*; *Spain invaded France*
1st successful English colony established in America, Jamestown, VA, 1607
John Brown, *violent abolitionist, hanged, 1859*
Eisenhower *given command of European invasion, 1944*

Neptune
C. de Gaulle, D. Eisenhower, *generals/statesmen*
Earl Warren, *US Chief Justice*
V. Nijinsky, *dancer (insane)*
J. Cocteau, *author/film director*
V. Robson, *astrologer*
E. Rickenbacker, *aviator*
Lunar Eclipse 4 15 78 AD OS, *year Romans exterminated Druids, Isle of Mona, (Anglesey), Wales*
Coronation, *William the Conqueror, 1066*
Jack the Ripper murders, 1888*(w/Pluto:)*
US Cavalry massacred Sioux, *Wounded Knee, SD, 1890*

Pluto
A. Hitler, *fascist dictator (suicide)*
Louis XIV *of France*
Chiang Kai-Chek, *warlord/President of China*
D. Ben Gurion, *1st President of Israel*
T. S. Eliot, *poet*
M. Chagall, G. O'Keefe, *artists*
Wittgenstein, *philosopher*
Racine, Maxwell Anderson, G. Abbott, *playwrights*
C. Chaplin, *comedian*
B. Karloff, *actor*
A. Rubenstein, *blind pianist*
Irving Berlin, *songwriter*
Jack the Ripper murders, 1888
Solar Eclipse over Dakotas *2 years before 1890 Wounded Knee - US Cavalry massacre of Sioux*

N. Node
R. Varga, violinist *(blinded by exploding mine)*
Great Mutation, 7 BC, *preceding birth of Christ.*

S. Node
Henry Ford, *manufacturer/anti-semite*
Ian Brady, *torture/murderer of children*
A. Mesmer, *astrologer/physician/discoverer of hypnotism*
J. Barrymore, Helen Hayes, *actors*
J. Fonda, Pete Seeger, *performer/activists*
M. Fonteyn, *ballerina*
Liberace, *pianist*
Solar Eclipse 10 22 -2136 OS, *missed by (drunk) Imperial Astrologers Hsi & Ho*; *Emperor had them beheaded*
Racist draft riots, New York City, 1863
Andrea Doria *ship collision disaster, 1956*
AMTRAK train wreck/fire, *Big Bayou Canot, AL, 1993 (47 killed).*

Asc
A. Eichmann, *Nazi persecutor of Jews (hanged)*
G. Rossini, *composer*

MC
F. Chopin, I. Stravinsky, *composers*
R.M. Rilke, Baudelaire, *poets*
Prince Albert Victor, Duke of Clarence *(feeble-minded, dissipated, syphilitic)*
King Henry VIII
O. Wilde, *poet/playwright*
P. Gauguin, *artist*
G. Bush, *US President*
E. Hemingway, *author*

ALDEBARAN ROYAL STAR—Mars (Mercury, Jupiter, Sun)
Oculus Tauri, Bull's S. Eye, Watcher of the East, Infra-Red source

	Long	Lat	Dec	RA	Mag	Spec
Alpha Tauri	9Gem31	-5 28	16 28	4 35	0.85	K5 III

The Bull's red eye is one of four great Royal Stars, the "pillars of heaven" of ancient Persia (the others are Regulus, Antares, & Fomalhaut)

*Wealth, prominence, worldly honors, especially in politics, military, church

*Whatever profession chosen, native may find him/herself suddenly placed among the leaders in that field

*Popularity, extraordinary energy, eloquence, intelligence

*Instinctively place themselves in the line of fire, demonstrating an ability to perform under pressure

*Danger of fall from grace or power

*Danger of violent death, sometimes self-inflicted.

*Ambitious ferocity may overcome sense of honor, integrity

*May be losses, sickness, eye problems, blindness, fevers, prostate trouble, sexual or other physical abnormalities, violence

*Great perseverence, steadfastness, attention to detail

*Literature, music, art, law, astrology and science all benefit from the high level of ability associated with this star.

* Summit meetings, wars, sea battles, armadas, invasions, shipwreck, intense violence, nuclear events, natural disasters, destruction, assassination, murder, suicide, blindness, eye problems, wounds to head, beheadings.

Positive:	**Neutral:**	**Negative:**
intelligent	popular	ferocious
courageous	energetic	violent
responsible	powerful	self-destructive
persevering	thinks boldly	murderous
eloquent	striving	seditious
leadership ability	goal-oriented	manipulative
inventive, original	competitive	contentious
incisive	committed	need to dominate
multi-talented	aggressive	law unto themselves
confident	imaginative	eye, ear problems

Sun

J. F. Kennedy, *US President (assassinated)*
Prince Rainier *of Monaco*
T. Mann, *author*
Dr P. Ehrlich, *population expert*
Keir Dullea, Marilyn Monroe (suicide?), Clint Eastwood, Clint Walker, *actors*
Benny Goodman, *jazz musician*
D. Kinman, *sex murderer*
Titanic *launched, 1911*
Sea-Battle of Jutland (Skaggerak), 1916
Solar Eclipse 5 30 1984, *(path across US, Mexico): Mexico City earthquake, Hurricane Gloria, Bhopal industrial disaster (eclipse path ran thru area of original Union Carbide Corp; degree was same as Bhopal's Sun)*
Bush-Gorbachev *summit, 1990*

Moon

J. Kepler, *astronomer/astrologer*
B. Mussolini, *dictator (assassinated)*
L. Mountbatten, *First Lord of Admiralty/statesman (assassinated)*
J. deLorean, *inventor/designer/business executive*
M. C. Escher, Grandma Moses, *artists*
Anne Boleyn *beheaded, 1536*
Abolitionist John Brown's *raid on Harper's Ferry, 1859*
(New Moon:) Sea-battle of Jutland, 1916
Take-off from Frankfurt-Am-Main of sabotaged Pan Am 103, 1988
San Francisco quake, 1989

Mercury

Toussaint L'Ouverture, *slave/revolutionary ruler of Haiti*
Prince William *of England*
J. Anouilh, *playwright*
J. Dillinger, *gangster*
Savonarola, *Dominican reformer, tortured, burned, 1498*

Essentials of Intermediate Astrology

Aldebaran, cont.

1st telegraph message *"What hath God wrought?", 1844*
Pope John Paul II shot, 1981

Venus:
J. Massenet, *composer*
C. Guevara, *revolutionary*
J. Glenn, *astronaut/US Senator*
M. Yourman, *clairvoyant/teacher of visually impaired children*
E. St Hilaire, *naturalist, blind at 68*
Solar Eclipse 6 /17/ 139 BC (-138) OS: *astrologers driven out of Rome*
End of Battle of Solferino, 1859, *watched by Henri Dunant, who, horrified by wounded left to die, was inspired to found Red Cross*
D-Day- *invasion of Normandy, 1944- "greatest amphibious landing in history"*
"Trinity"-*1st atomic bomb explosion, Alamogordo, NM, 1945*
R. F. Kennedy *assassinated, 1968*
Apollo 11 launch to Moon, 1969

Mars
M. Maimonides, *12th century philosopher/physician*
A. Sakharov, *physicist/activist*
Graf von Zeppelin, *aeronautical engineer*
H. Melville, *author (manic depressive)*
Henry Moore, *artist/sculptor*
Charles Jayne, *astrologer (nearly blind)*
G. Lombardo, *bandleader*
Spanish Armada sailed, 1588
Confederate attack, *Fort Sumter, SC, 1861, start of US Civil War*
Atomic bomb dropped on Hiroshima, 1945

Jupiter
A. Graham Bell *(teacher of deaf)*, T. Edison, *inventors*
A. Armstrong-Jones, *photographer*
Bart Bok, *astronomer*
Robert/Roberta Cowell, *racing driver/fighter pilot/ transsexual*
Jaqueline Kennedy Onassis, Betty Ford, *US first ladies*
C. W Leadbeater, *theosophist*
H. de Balzac, *author*
USSR founded, 1917

Saturn
A. Bruckner, *composer*
B. Cellini, *designer/artisan*
A. Durer, *artist*
T. H. Huxley, *scientist/President of Royal Society*
Mussolini, *fascist dictator (assassinated)*
Eruption of Krakatoa, 1883
Cocoanut Grove *nightclub fire, 1942, Boston, MA: 491 dead*
1st controlled release of atomic energy, Chiago, 1942

Uranus
L. Walesa, *union leader/President of Poland*
R. Taney, *US Chief Justice, presided in Dred Scott decision that retained slavery despite relocation (but freed own slaves)*
O. North, *gov't official/perjurer*
Confederate States, *US Civil War*
World's 1st oil well, *Titusville, PA 1859*
D-Day *invasion of Normandy, 1944*
Refugee ship Wilhelm Gustloff torpedoed, 1945: *5,348 dead*
(Uranus st d:) Dresden firebombed, 1945
Buchenwald *(Concentration Camp) liberated, 1945*

Neptune
Rommel, Goering, *Nazi officers (suicides)*
J. P. Getty, *billionaire*
J. Miro, *artist*
P. Yogananda, *yogi*
A. MacLeish, Christopher Marlowe, *poet/dramatists*
R. Steiner, *occultist*
Eruption of Vesuvius, 79 AD: *buried Pompeii*
Lunar Eclipse 7 16 1562 OS, *the month Mayan codices were destroyed by Spanish priests*

Pluto
Mao Tse-Tung, *revolutionary/dictator*
N. Kruschchev, *Russian leader*
D. D. Eisenhower, *General/US President*
I. Newton, *physicist*
F. Franco, *Spanish dictator*
Rommel *(forced suicide)*, Goering *(suicide), Nazi officers*
D. Rudhyar, *astrologer/composer*
P. Yogananda, M. Baba, K Singh, *mystics*
Jimmy Durante, Jack Benny, Groucho Marx, *comedians*
J. Miro, N. Rockwell, *artists*
J. P. Getty, *billionaire*
E. Rickenbacker, *aviator*
Archbishop Laud *beheaded, 1645, London*
Vaillant, *bomb-throwing anarchist, guillotined, 1894, Paris*

Aldebaran, cont.

N. Node:
King Henri II *of France (died after jousting opponent's lance split, driving splinters into his eye-transiting Saturn here at event)*
Earl Warren - *US Chief Justice*
Sen Dan Quayle, *US VP (classic example of Royal Star's effect: premature power)*
Bob Crane, *actor (murdered)*
A. Beardsley, *artist*
1st performance of Handel's Messiah, *1742, Dublin*

S. Node:
King Henry VIII *of England*
Lord Mountbatten, *First Sea Lord/diplomat (assassinated)*
St. Exupery, *aviator/author*
Nietzche, *philosopher (became insane)*
A. A. Milne, *children's author/poet*
Virginia Woolf, *author (suicide)*
Ernie Pyle, *war correspondent (killed, Okinawa, 1945)*

Asc:
Sen D. Quayle, *US vice-President*
Gov M. Dukakis *of Massachusetts*
R. Hayworth, *actress/dancer (Alzheimer's)*
Respighi, *composer*
Nazi invasion of USSR, 1941
US Declaration of War *against Japan, 1941*
Ships began firing, *D-Day invasion of Normandy, 1944*
"Twilight Zone" *filming disaster, 1982*

Dsc:
Start of Battle of Hastings, 1066

MC:
W. A. Mozart, *composer*
Mary Downing, *artist/astrologer*
Modigliani, *artist*
Helen Hayes, *actress*
Columbus *discovered America, 10 12 1492, 2 AM*

SIRIUS—The Dog Star, The Scorching One Nature: Jupiter, Mars (Neptune),

	Long	*Lat*	*Dec*	*RA*	*Mag*	*Spec*
Alpha Canis Majoris	13Can48	-39 36	-16 42	6 44	-1.46	A1

Sirius, the 2nd nearest star to us, is the brightest star in the sky, visible from virtually every portion of the globe. Sirius is the calendar star—throughout history all major calendar changes have been accompanied by eclipses, outer planet transits, or stations at the longitude of Sirius.

*Intense word & visual imagery; entranced by their internal world

*Must "own themselves," dare to be different, not worry what others may think; surprised when criticized.

*Sense the underlying magic in the humdrum of everyday existence

*Conjure passionate inner visions of what the outer world might become, try to make them manifest

*Quirky originality that is sensually, visually based.

*Highly inventive, put a strongly personal stamp upon their work

*May behave in a dictatorial manner without necessarily meaning to.

*Fierce, fiery temper

*Don't usually play by the rules; would rather make their own, sometimes skirting the edges of law, propriety.

*Issues of imprisonment, entrapment, slavery. heat waves -"dog days"; disease, fires, floods, storms, dog bites, rabies; torture.

Positive:	**Neutral:**	**Negative:**
original	take chances	easily enraged
visionary	improvise	hot-tempered
inventive	hyper-sensitive	selfish
magical	make their own rules	dictatorial
literary ability	self-involved	rebellious

Essentials of Intermediate Astrology

Sirius, cont.

Sun
G. Garibaldi, *Italian nationalist leader*
Rube Goldberg, *sculptor/cartoonist*
C. Whitman, *murderer*
Leona Helmsley, *hotel executive (jailed for tax evasion)*

Moon
Maraquita Platov, *anti-war poet*
W. Booth, *Salvation Army founder*
Savonarola tortured, *hung, burned 1498, Florence (noon position)*

Mercury
Prince Philip *of England*
Mitch Miller, *conductor*
Pearl Buck, I. Velikovsky, *authors*
J. Corot, *artist*

Venus
M. Begin, *Israeli PM*
N. Rockefeller, *US Vice President*
Leona Helmsley, *hotel executive*
Ulugh Beg *published star catalogue, 1437, Samarkhand*
(Venus Rx:) Infantry attack, *start of Battle of the Somme, WWI, 1916 (1,100,000 died)*
(Venus) Solar Eclipse 6/ 30/ 92 *preceding Hurricanes Andrew, Iniki, Typhoon Omar, Windsor Castle fire*

Mars
Shakespeare, *playwright/poet*
P. Picasso, *artist*
Isadora Duncan, *dancer/choreographer*
Odette Sansom, *WWII spy, withstood Gestapo torture*
Savonarola tortured, *hung, burned, 1498, Florence*
(Aries ingress)) 1914, *year WWI began*
Chicago hotel fire, 1993, *14 dead, 30 injured*
(Aries ingress)) 1993*: Waco cult fire, great Mississippi flood, Bangladesh flood, China floods, Japan quake*

Jupiter
A. Sadat, *Egyptian President (assassinated)*
Kafka, K. Hamsun, J. K. Huysmans, *authors*

Saturn
John Wayne, Sean Connery, Ben Gazzara, *actors*
L. Sullivan, *architect*

Uranus
Bob Geldof, *rock star/humanitarian*
D. Gibson, *artist*
J. P. Morgan, Jr, *financier (used astrology)*
Isabelle Pagan, *astrologer*
Montgolfier Balloon, *1st manned untethered flight, 1783, Paris*

Neptune
Toussaint L'Ouverture, *slave/revolutionary General/ ruler of Haiti*
J. W. Silver, *fighter for racial equality*
Oskar Schindler, *Nazi businessman/spy/rescuer of Jews*
Ian Fleming, *author*
Eddie Albert, *actor/environmentalist*
First Anglo-Persian *oil well came in, 1908, Iran*

Pluto
W. Rehnquist, *Chief Justice, US Supreme Court*
G. Rostropovitch, *cellist/conductor*
Miles Davis, *jazz trumpeter*
Truman Capote, James Baldwin, John Fowles, William Styron, Harper Lee, James Clavell, Leon Uris, *authors*
R. Serling, *TV writer/playwright*
Rev R. Abernathy, *civil rights activist*
Queen Elizabeth II
V. Grissom, *astronaut*
J. de Lorean , *inventor/businessman*

N. Node
Prince William *of England*
J. Corot, *artist*
J. Cocteau, *artist/filmmaker*
Great Johnstown, PA *flood, 1889: 2,200 killed*
Buchenwald Concentration Camp *liberated, 1945*
1963 eruption of Surtsey, *new volcanic island off Iceland*
Unification Church *mass wedding, NY, 1982: 2,075 couples*
"Twilight Zone" *filming disaster, 1982*

S. Node
Woody Allen, *filmmaker*
L. da Vinci, *artist/inventor*
Marie La Laurie, *sadist/murderer*
Hill/Thomas *Congressional Hearings, 1991*
Oakland Hills *fire, 1991: 25 killed, 3,000 homes burned*

Asc
H. S. Truman, *US President*
H. Cabot Lodge II
Burl Ives, *folksinger/actor*
Jack Lemmon, *actor*
W. Backhaus, *pianist*

Sirius, cont.

MC
Cat Stevens, *musician/convert to Islam/recluse*
D. Bowie, *rock star*
Arthur Ashe, *tennis champion*
Antivertex:
Tunguska event, *huge explosion over Siberia, 1908*

CASTOR – Apollo, Nature: Mercury (Mars)

	Long	*Lat*	*Dec*	*RA*	*Mag*	*Spec*
Alpha Geminorum	19Can58	10 06	31 56	7 33	1.58	A1 V

Castor (with Pollux, just 2°56' later), represent the famous inseparable twins of the Greek myths

*Impulsive, hungry rush at life

*Some forced out into the world early, must fend for themselves

*Tend to be willful, headstrong, very ambitious, controlling, intemperate

*Usually inventive ability, keen intellect

*Possible evolution towards humanitarian ideals, worldly distinction.

*Siblings are often important

*Often a connection, direct or indirect, with murder & assassination: Assassinated US President Garfield's MC is here; Eleanor Roosevelt, whose uncle Theodore and husband Franklin, both US Presidents, were targets of assassination attempts, had the Moon here; it is Ronald Reagan's Neptune (assassination attempt); Ted Kennedy, (Two brothers assassinated) has Pluto here, as did J. F. Kennedy's wife; John Wilkes Booth, Lincoln's assassin, had Mars at Castor, as did Marie Antoinette, who was sent to the guillotine; L. B. Johnson (Venus) became President as result of JFK's assassination; Mussolini (Jupiter) was killed by partisans; Lenin (Uranus) ordered the Russian royal family killed; Trotsky (SNode) was assassinated on orders of Stalin. G. Moscone, assassinated Mayor of SF, had Pluto at Castor.

*Racial, religious, brotherhood issues; assassination, murder, shipwreck.

Positive:	**Neutral:**	**Negative:**
adventurous	impulsive	dictatorial
talented, inventive	willful	show-off
ambitious	headstrong	over-aggressive
leadership ability	controlling	intemperate
humanitarian	mischievous	violent

Sun
A. Wyeth, J. McNeil Whistler, *artists*
V. Cliburn, *pianist*
M. Proust, *author*
N. Tesla, *scientist/inventor*

Moon
Charles Atlas, *body builder*
E. Roosevelt, *US first lady/humanitarian*
Dr Tom Dooley, *Navy MD/humanitarian/author*
Liza Minelli, *actress*
Steve Cauthen, *jockey*
Grant Lewi, *astrologer*

Mercury
G. B. Shaw, *author/playwright*
A. Wyeth, A. Modigliani, *artists*

Venus
L. B. Johnson, *US President*
D. Brinkley, *news commentator*
Annie Oakley, *sharpshooter*
Louis Armstrong, *trumpet player*
Judy Garland, *singer/actress*
Mary Cassatt, *artist*

Mars
Toscanini, *conductor*
Marie Antoinette, *Queen of France (guillotined)*
W. Wilberforce, *English politician/philanthropist/ fought for abolition of slave trade*
Susan B. Anthony, *pioneer feminist*
John Glenn, *astronaut/US senator*
J. Wilkes Booth, *actor/assassin*
Lisbon *earthquake/tsunami/fire, 1755*
Galveston *hurricane, September 1911*

Jupiter
B. Mussolini, *dictator (Castor & Pollux were the patrons of ancient Rome. Mussolini had Jupiter at Castor, Venus at Pollux)*
O. Cromwell, *Lord Protector of England*
Orville Wright, *aviation pioneer*

Essentials of Intermediate Astrology

Castor, cont.

Saturn
V. Zhirinovsky, *Russian politician*
Battle of the Somme, 1916,*(w/Moon) start of Infantry attack, (1,100,000 died)*
Uranus
N. Culpepper, *physician/astrologer/herbalist*
Wilhelm Grimm, *(w/brother Jakob,) collector of folk tales*
N. Lenin, *Russian dictator*
Jan Smuts, *S. African statesman/author*
Patricia Hearst, *kidnapped heiress.*
Kubilai Khan's *2nd attempt to invade Japan, 1281: 4,000 ships, 100,000 men lost*
Neptune
H. Humphrey, *US Senator*
R. Reagan, *actor/US President*
F. Goya, *artist*
Al Capp, *cartoonist*
P. Hurkos, *psychic*
Elia Kazan, *director*
E. G. Marshall, Burgess Meredith, Douglas Fairbanks Jr, Vincent Price, *actors*
J. Agee, *author*
J. Anouilh, *playwright*
Titanic *launched, 1911*
Pluto
E. Kennedy, *US Senator*
G. Moscone, *San Francisco Mayor (assassinated)*
Queen Elizabeth II *of England*
Jim Jones, *cult leader/mass murderer*
D. Eisele, "Buzz" Aldrin, *astronauts*
Jacqueline Kennedy Onassis, *US first lady*
Clint Eastwood, William Shatner, Leonard Nimoy, *actors*
Odetta, Johnny Cash, *singers*
Sean Connery, Ed Asner, Rip Torn, James Earl Jones, James Dean, Anthony Perkins, Omar Sharif, Elizabeth Taylor, Debbie Reynolds, *actors*
Colin Wilson, John Updike, *authors*
Tom Wolfe, *journalist*
M. Gauquelin, researcher *(suicide)*
N. Node
M. Tilson-Thomas, *pianist/conductor*
Queen Elizabeth II *of England*
Marshall Joffre, *Allied commander, WWI.*
S. Node
L. Trotsky, *revolutionary leader (assassinated)*
N. Vincent Peale, *clergyman/author*
Will Rogers, *humorist*
Lunar Eclipse 6/26 & Solar Eclipse 7/11/1619, *just before 1st slaves arrived in Virginia*
Mt. Unzen & Mt. Pinatubo *eruptions, 1991.*
Asc.
A. Schwarzenegger, *body builder/actor*
Kaiser Wilhelm II *of Germany*
Eclipse, *18th century champion racehorse born on total solar eclipse*; *never beaten*
New York City, *Lunar Eclipse 2 days before Great December Nor'easter, 1992*
Davenport, IA, Solar Eclipse 5 21 93, *preceding great Mississippi floods*
MC:
J. A. Garfield, *US President (assassinated)*
Universal Declaration of Human Rights *adopted by UN General Assembly, 1948*

PRAESEPE—"Beehive" (Open Cluster) Nature: Mars, Moon (Neptune)

	Long	*Lat*	*Dec*	*RA*	*Mag*	*Spec*
M44 Cancri	6Leo55	1 34	20 03	8 39	3.1	AO

NORTH ASCELLUS—Northern Ass or Donkey Nature: Mars, Sun

	Long	*Lat*	*Dec*	*RA*	*Mag*	*Spec*
Gamma Cancri	7Leo16	3 11	21 32	8 42	4.66	A1

SOUTH ASCELLUS—Southern Ass or Donkey Nature: Mars, Sun

	Long	*Lat*	*Dec*	*RA*	*Mag*	*Spec*
Delta Cancri	8Leo27	0 05	18 14	8 44	3.94	KO

Praesepe, No. Ascellus, So. Ascellus cont.

In Platonist and Orphic philosophy, the Crab was the "Gate of Men", the point of entry for reincarnating souls; in China, it was a "Ghost Carriage". Two stars in the Crab, North & South Ascellus, are called the Two Asses or the Manger; along with nebulous cluster Praesepe, the Beehive,(also "Little Cloud, Mist, Crib or Manger") they produce people who tend to be:

*Single-minded, aggressive, ambitious, hungry for recognition

*Fascinated by myths and glories of the past

*Ready to die (or to commit aggression) to serve an imagined "glorious cause."

*Idealism, mysticism, and/or violently intolerant fundamentalist passions

*Physical and/or spiritual blindness

*Attract antagonism and controversy

*Struggle with a conflict between lewdness and purity, hard cold facts vs mystic beliefs

*May suffer from eye problems, mental problems, suffer disappointments and sudden downfalls. Battles, fires, fevers, epidemics, volcanoes, ghosts, UFO's; rain, storms, violent & severe accidents, shipwreck, murder and/or a violent death, assassination.

Positive:	**Neutral:**	**Negative:**
energetic,	conquering	fanatic,
ambitious	aristocratic	intolerant,
productive	critical	bigoted
hard-working	aggressive use	dictatorial, cold
analytical	of power	possible mental
musical, artistic	single-minded	problems
natural leaders	into mysticism	commit or
detail oriented	strongly Neptunian	draw violence
		addiction prone
		eye problems,
		blindness

Sun

Rembrandt, *artist*
D. Hammarskjold, *statesman*
Mussolini, *dictator (killed by partisans)*
A. Schwarzenegger, *bodybuilder/actor*
A. de Toqueville, *statesman/author*
Emily Bronte, *author*
Henry Moore, *sculptor*
Y. St Laurent, *couturier*
H. Ford, *manufacturer/anti-semite*
Lunar Eclipse 7/16/1562 OS: *Spanish priests destroyed Mayan codices*
Solar Eclipse 7/30/35; *one month before Nuremberg racial laws promulgated in Nazi Germany*

Moon

R. Waldo Emerson, *philosopher/author*
A. Vivaldi, *violinist/composer/priest*
H. Hoover, *US President*
Gloria Steinem, *feminist*
Sir E. Halley, *scientist/astronomer*
Mary Cassatt, *artist*
Battle of Vienna I: *1529. Turks beseige Vienna (unsuccessful)*
Spanish Armada *sailed, 1588*

Mercury

Napoleon I, *conqueror*
Bill Clinton, *US President*
B. Mussolini, *dictator (captured, killed)*
Dorothy Kilgallen, *journalist (murdered?)*
M. Begin, *Israeli PM*
Ernie Pyle, *war correspondent (killed at Okinawa)*
David Koresh, *cult leader (suicide)*
Leona Helmsley, *hotel mgr/real estate tycoon*
Charles Emerson, *astrologer*
James Randi, *magician/debunker*
Ulugh Beg *published Star Catalogue, 1437, Samarkhand*

Venus

Sir Walter Scott, L. Tolstoy, G. B. Shaw, *authors*
J. Wilkes Booth, *actor/assassin*
A. Bremer, *psychotic/attempted assassin*
L. Bernstein, *composer/conductor*
A. Gaudi, *architect*
I. Semmelweis, *surgical antisepsis pioneer (ideas rejected- became insane)*
Amy Fisher, *teen prostitute/attempted murderess*
Roncevaux: *Basques ambushed, killed Charlemagne's knight Roland, 778 AD (inspired "Chanson de Roland")*
Spanish *royal treasure fleet sailed from Havana 1622, 8 ships lost in hurricane*
Battle of Waterloo, 1815

Mars

P. Rubens, *artist*
Duke Ellington, *musician*
Patrick Stewart, Helen Hayes, *actors*
Charles Emerson, *astrologer*
Joe Louis, Jack Dempsey, *boxers*

Praesepe, No. Ascellus, So. Ascellus cont.

H. Himmler, *head of Nazi SS (suicide)*
Pompey the Great, *Roman conqueror (murdered)*
Matteo Ricci, *Jesuit missionary/author*
H. Hoover, G. Cleveland, *US Presidents*
Giordano Bruno burned at stake for heresy, *1600, Rome*
D-Day, *WWII Allied invasion of Normandy, 1944- "greatest amphibious landing in history"*

Jupiter
W. Shakespeare, *playwright*
T. H. Huxley, *scientist*
Hong Xiuquan, *Christian fanatic/leader of Taiping rebellion, 1851-64*
J. Peron, *President of Argentina*
Battle of Teutoburger Forest, *9 AD: Germanic tribes destroyed 3 Roman legions*
Handel's Messiah, *(1st performance) 1742, Dublin*
First Anglo-Persian *oil well 1908, Iran*
Guyana Massacre: *Jim Jones forced 909 members of his "People's Temple" cult, incl children, to drink poison, shot himself, 1978*
Mt. Unzen *eruption 1991, Japan*

Saturn
Chiang Kai-Shek, *warlord*
John Brown, *violent anti-slavery abolitionist (hanged)*
O. J. Simpson, *football star/actor/sportscaster*
B. Karloff, *actor*
Salmon Rushdie, Sir A. Conan Doyle, ("Sherlock Holmes"), *authors*
S. Spielberg, *filmmaker*
B. Pascal, *philosopher/mathematician*
P. Curie, *scientist*
Ted Bundy, *serial killer (executed)*
Kaiser Wilhelm *of Germany*
Betty Ford, *US First Lady*

Reported UFO crash *near Socorro, NM, 1947*

Uranus
G. Savonarola, *Dominican preacher/reformer (tortured, burned)*
G. Hennard, *mass murderer/suicide*
Gertrude Stein, *author*
H. Houdini, *magician*
Marconi, *physicist/inventor*
Algol Solar Eclipse 5 /14 /1790, 4:32 UT:
-French Revolution
-Egypt plague killed 80,000
-"Skull Famine" in India
-Slave rebellions, Haiti, Santo Domingo

Neptune
Ingmar Bergman, *director*
A. Schlesinger, *historian*
N. Mandela, *President of S. Africa*
G. A. Nasser, *President of Egypt*
Henry Ford II, *manufacturer*
Margot Fonteyn, *prima ballerina*
Liberace, *entertainer*
F. Marcos, *Philippine President*
Oral Roberts, *preacher*
L. Bernstein, *conductor/composer*
Indira Gandhi, *President of India (assassinated)*
James Lovelock, *scientist (Gaia hypothesis)*
Pope John Paul II *(assassination attempt)*
A. Sadat, *President of Egypt (assassinated)*
"Miracle of the Sun" *at Fatima, Portugal: Sun appeared to whirl, then seemed to fall toward onlookers, 1917*

Pluto
Voltaire, *satirist/skeptic*
Janis Joplin, Jimi Hendrix, Diana Ross, Mick Jagger, *singers*
Arthur Ashe, *tennis champion*
L. Walesa, *union leader/President of Poland*
Angela Davis, *revolutionary*
W. Strieber, *author/UFO abductee*
Jack Henry Abbott, *murderer/author*
Larry Flynt, *porn publisher (shot, paralyzed)*
Arthur Shawcross, *cannibal/serial killer*
Refugee ship Wilhelm Gustloff, torpedoed 1945: 5,348 died, 1,252 rescued
Dresden *firebombed, 1945*
Buchenwald Concentration Camp *liberated, 1945*
Cocoanut Grove *nightclub fire, 1942, Boston, MA: 491 dead*
D-Day, WWII *Allied invasion of Normandy, 1944, more than 5,000 ships - "greatest amphibious landing in history"*

N. Node
J. Kepler, *astronomer/mathematician*
M. Gandhi, *Indian leader (assassinated)*
Angela Davis, *revolutionary*
J. Henry Abbott, *murderer/author*
Joe Frazier, *boxer*
William Blake, *artist/poet/mystic*
Battle of Teutoburger Forest, *9 AD: Germanic tribes destroyed 3 Roman legions*
Great Fire of Rome, *64 AD*

Praesepe, No. Ascellus, So. Ascellus cont.

Solar Eclipse, 1/ 9/ 772 AD OS, *year Charlemagne cut down Irminsul tree, sacred to Odin, in Westphalia*
Battle of Vienna II: *2nd attempt by Mohammedans in 154 years to invade Europe: seige lifted Sept 1683*
Rachel Carson's *"Silent Spring" published, 1962*

S. Node
T. Herzl, *Zionist leader*
Amelia Earhart, *aviator*
L. Pasteur, *biologist*
W. Masters, *sex researcher*
E. Renan, *historian/religious scholar/ancient languages expert*

Asc
M. Heindel, *Rosicrucian*
P. Picasso, *artist*
King George III *of England (intermittent insanity)*
John Dee, Aleister Crowley, *occultists*
H. Daumier, *lithographer/caricaturist*
Irving Berlin, *songwriter*
Trotsky, *revolutionary (assassinated)*
Tambora *eruption (1815)*
Titanic *,Departure of 1912*
Washington DC, for Solar Eclipse 6/ 30/ 92 preceding 3 storms: Andrew (Florida, 8/24), Iniki (Hawaii, 9/11) and Omar (Guam, 8/28)
Hurricane Andrew hits Miami 8/ 24/ 92
AMTRAK Sunset Ltd *train wreck/fire, 1993, Mobile, AL: 47 dead*
Mustard gas/cyanide attack *on Kurd villagers by troops of Saddam Hussein, Halabja, Iraq, 1988: more than 5,000 dead*
Tanker "Braer", *off Shetlands, sent "Mayday," 1993*

MC
D. Berkowitz, *"Son of Sam" murderer*
A. Bronson Alcott, *transcendental philosopher*
Lunar Eclipse visible in Egypt, 1/ 18 /-47 OS: *Caesar & Cleopatra: 40,000 scrolls accidentally burned when Egyptian fleet set afire*
Eruption of Helgafell *volcano, Heimaey Isl. off S. Iceland, 1973*
"We are the World" *recording session of superstars, 1985, LA (USA for Africa)*
Los Angeles *riots/burning/looting after Rodney King verdict, 1992*

Vertex
Chernobyl *atomic disaster, 1986*

REGULUS—Lion's Heart, ROYAL STAR "Watcher of the North" Nature: Mars, Jupiter

	Long	*Lat*	*Dec*	*RA*	*Mag*	*Spec*
Alpha Leonis	29Leo33	0 28	12 04	10 07	1.35	B7

*Extremely fond of power - willing to take great chances in pursuit of high positions

*Prominence usually achieved, especially in military, religion, medicine, astrology

*Like the other royal stars, fall may follow successful rise

*"Larger than life" quality in everything they do: any mistakes are BIG mistakes

*Strong character, courage of their convictions; great daring and elan.

*May be violent, refuse to accept criticism, search for victims to blame for failures, rather than looking at their own dark image in the mirror.

*The courage conferred by the Lion's heart is legendary, but will not protect them from the consequences of their follies. Murder, assassination, fall from power, abdication, storms, fire, shipwreck, astrology

Positive:	**Neutral:**	**Negative:**
courageous	daring, dramatic	heedless
magnanimous	energetic	arrogant
idealistic	independent	destructive
generous	risk-taking	violent, murderous
high-spirited	authoritarian	scandalous

Essentials of Intermediate Astrology

Regulus, cont.

Sun

H. Norman Schwarzkopf, *American general*
Meriwether Lewis, *explorer*
Deng Xiaoping, *Chinese leader*
Princess Margaret *of England*
B. Disraeli, *PM of England*
Dr D. Cooley, *heart surgeon*
H. Cartier-Bresson, *photographer*
Amy Fisher, *teen prostitute/attempted murderess*
1834 horary query *"What will be the Destiny of Astrology?" from Zadkiel's Introduction to Astrology, 1852*
Solar Eclipse 8 /22 /70: *Hurricanes David & Frederick hit Gulf of Mexico*
-Mountbatten *assassinated*
-S. Korean President Park Chung Hee *murdered*
-Afghanistan President Taraki *killed in coup*
-Deposed Shah of Iran, Tito of Yugoslavia & Supreme Court Justice Douglas *died*
-President Romero *(San Salvador)*& Emperor Bokassa *(Central African Empire)deposed*
- Queen Juliana *of Netherlands abdicated*
-Islamic *revolutionaries seized US Embassy, Tehran*
-Grand Mosque in Medina *seized by Shiite Moslems, held 5 days*
Attica, NY *prison rebellion, 1971*

Moon

F. Pierce, *US President*
M. Thatcher, *PM of England*
Robert Graves, *author*
Jane Fonda, *actress*

Mercury

Goethe, *author/poet*
Crown Heights, Brooklyn; *Black-Jewish race riots, 1991*

Venus

Joseph Montgolfier, *w/brother Jacques, invented 1st hot-air balloons*
H. Himmler, *head of Nazi SS (suicide)*
Czarevich Alexis *of Russia, (assassinated)*
Pope Paul VI
"Objections to Astrology," *signed by 186 leading scientists, featured on front page of NY Times and Boston Globe, 1975*

Mars

H. Ford, *manufacturer*
Imelda Marcos, *Philippine First Lady*
Royal Spanish treasure fleet left Havana 1622: *8 ships, $250 million cargo lost in hurricane, 550 dead*

Jupiter:

Drs D. Cooley, M. de Bakey, *heart surgeons*
Eleanor Roosevelt, *US First Lady*
Voltaire, *skeptic*
US Navy Tailhook *sex attack scandal, Las Vegas, NV, 1991*

Saturn

A. Sadat, *President of Egypt (assassinated)*
S. Hayakawa, *actor/author*
A. Solzhenitzyn, *author*

Uranus

St John of the Cross, *poet/mystic*
M. Buber, *Jewish theologian*
Samuel Johnson, *author/critic*
Inquisition *officially established, Rome, 1542*

Neptune

W. Mondale, *US VP*
Anne Frank, *child diarist*
Imelda Marcos, *Philippine First Lady*
Joan Sutherland, *soprano*
Jane Roberts, *author/channeler*
Eclipse, *18th century champion English racehorse*

Pluto

G. Hennard, *mass murderer/suicide*

N. Node

C. E. O. Carter, *astrologer*
Princess Diana *of England*
A. Rubenstein, *blind pianist*
SS Lt Col A. Eichmann, *Jew-hunting Nazi*
Cocoanut Grove *nightclub fire, 1942, Boston, MA: 491 victims*

S. Node

J. Paul Jones, *naval officer*
R. Waldo Emerson, *philosopher/author*
Elias Ashmole, *astrologer/alchemist/collector/historian of heraldry*
Sir E. Bulwer-Lytton, *author/MP ("Last Days of Pompeii")*
Kaiser Wilhelm II
Huge cyclone/tidal wave *hit Ganges Delta, 1970: 300-500,000 dead, thousands more died weeks later from typhoid, cholera ("worst disaster of the century")*

Asc

Gauguin, *artist*
L. G. Cooper, *USAF Major/astronaut*

Regulus, cont.

Frank Augustyn, *premier danseur*
P. Yogananda, *mystic*
G. Hennard, *mass murderer/suicide*

MC
Jacqueline Kennedy Onassis, *US First Lady*
Dr Tom Dooley, *Navy MD/humanitarian*

VINDEMIATRIX—Almuredin, Virgin's N. Wing Nature: Saturn, Mercury

	Long	*Lat*	*Dec*	*RA*	*Mag*	*Spec*
Epsilon Virg	9Lib40	16 12	11 04	13 01	2.83	G9

*"Star of Widowhood"

*Religious issues are part of their lives

*Perpetrators or victims of vicious persecutions

*Gift for imagery, wit

*Elegant and/or sophisticated use of words.

*Some involved in either the preservation or destruction of ancient knowledge, traditions. "Witch hunts", persecutions, disasters, shipwrecks, tuberculosis

Positive:	**Neutral:**	**Negative:**
love of words	angry	sarcastic, sardonic
leadership	headstrong	hypocritical
multi-talented	aggressive	fanatic, intolerant
scholarly	materialistic	depressive
religious		

Sun
M. Gandhi, *India religious/social leader (assassinated)*
Horatio Nelson, *naval hero (killed in action)*
Samuel Johnson, *lexicographer*
W. Rehnquist, *Chief Justice, US Supreme Court*
W. Stevens, *poet*
Graham Greene, Faith Baldwin, Gore Vidal, *authors*
Marc Edmund Jones, *astrologer*
A. Besant, *theosophist*
Society of Jesus (Jesuits) *officially recognized by Pope Paul III, Rome, 1540*

Moon
Pope Paul VI
R. Nureyev, *dancer*
W. Disney, *cartoonist*
"Stonewall" Jackson, *Confederate general*
Matthias & companions burned alive for sedition on Herod's order, 4 BC, Jerusalem (Moon at noon)
Pentagon cornerstone, 1941

Mercury
Noah Webster, *lexicographer*
J. Fenimore Cooper, O. Henry, *authors*
Elia Kazan, *director*

Venus
Elizabeth I *of England*
Louis XVI *of France (beheaded)*
e. e. cummings, *poet*
O. Wilde, *poet/playwright*
Solar Eclipse 10 /23/60 AD OS, *preceding Roman drive to exterminate Druids, Isle of Mona (Anglesey), Wales, 61 AD*

Mars
G. Orwell, *author*
Bill Gates, *Microsoft (MS-DOS) founder*
M. Thatcher, *UK PM*
Solar Eclipse 1/ 15 /009 AD OS, *year Germanic tribes wiped out 3 Roman Legions*
Kristallnacht: *Nazi-organized anti-Jewish riots, Germany & Austria, 1938*

Jupiter
Raphael, *artist*
Marie Antoinette *of France (beheaded)*
James Agee, James Jones, *authors*
Massive Lisbon quake/tsunami/fire *1755: 85% of city destroyed, including all libraries & museums w/rare ancient manuscripts, art. 100,000 dead: Inquisition accused some survivors of heresy, hanged them on the spot "for angering God"*

Essentials of Intermediate Astrology

Vindamiatrix, cont.

Hindu fanatics *demolished 464-yr-old Babri Mosque, Ayodhya, India 1992*

Saturn

1834 horary question *"What will be the Destiny of Astrology?" 8 21 1834, 3:28 PM LMT, 53N25-from Zadkiel's Introduction to Astrology, 1852*

Uranus

M. Chagall, *artist*
R. Waldo Emerson, *author/philosopher*
E. Bulwer-Lytton, *author/MP ("Last Days of Pompeii")*
Ben-Gurion, *PM of Israel*
A. Borodin, *composer*

Neptune

Savonarola, *Dominican reformer (tortured, burned)*
Daniel Webster, *statesman*
S. Bolivar, *S. American liberator*
N. Culpepper, *astrologer/herbalist*
Stephen King, *author*
O. J. Simpson, *football star/actor/sportscaster*
Ted Bundy, *serial murderer*
Clarence Thomas, *Assoc .Justice, US Supreme Court*
Aries ingress, 1947: *Dead Sea Scrolls discovered, Israel*
Huge explosion/inferno *devastated Texas City, TX, 1947: 752 killed, 3,000 injured, "biggest Red Cross operation in history"*

Pluto

SS Edmund Fitzgerald *sank in Lake Superior storm, 1975*
8.0 T'ang Shan, China quake *1976, 500,000-750,000 dead, entire province devastated*

N. Node

Carl Reiner, *comedy writer/producer*
Elmer Bernstein, *composer/conductor*

S. Node

Aleister Crowley, *occultist*
Agrippina, *Roman Empress/poisoner (killed by son Nero)*
D. Hammett, *author*
Matthias & companions burned alive for sedition on orders of Herod, 4BC, Jerusalem

Asc

P. Foster Case, *occultist*
Dr Felix Jay, *scholar/astrologer/author*
Ringo Starr, *drummer*
Cat Stevens, *singer/songwriter/convert-Islam/recluse*
Asc at 0 hour, Washington DC 1/ 1/ 1863: *Emancipation Proclamation took effect*

MC

J. Milton, poet *(became blind)*
MC at Lunar Eclipse 1/ 3/641 OS, Alexandria, Egypt: *reputed final destruction of Great Library of Alexandria on orders of Caliph Omar, priceless scrolls used as fuel to heat public baths*

SPICA— "spike"of wheat, left hand Nature: Venus, Mars

	Long	*Lat*	*Dec*	*RA*	*Mag*	*Spec*
Alpha Virginis	23Lib34	- 2 03	-11 03	13 24	0.98	B1

ARCTURUS— In left leg, or hem of tunic, or between legs, 4th brightest star Nature: Jupiter, Mars

	Long	*Lat*	*Dec*	*RA*	*Mag*	*Spec*
Alpha Bootis	23Lib57	30 44	19 17	14 15	0.04	K2

Spica and Arcturus, two of the brightest stars in northern hemisphere, marked the Autumnal Equinox in the 3rd century AD, the beginning of the Age of Pisces.

*Reknown, self-determination, prosperity

*Success in religion, victory in war

*Possibility of murder, assassination.

Spica, Arcturus, cont.

Positive:	**Neutral:**	**Negative:**
drawn to religion, philosophy	self-willed	belligerent
artistic, musical	popular	quarrelsome
literary	extravagant	stubborn
productive	voluptuous	promiscuous
	persistent	

Sun

St Francis *of Assisi*
D. Ben-Gurion, *1st Israeli PM*
Pope John Paul I
W. Douglas, *Assoc Justice, US Supreme Court*
F. Nietzche, *philosopher*Great dust storm, *Texas, 1935*

Moon

E. Manet, *artist*
H. Kissinger, *statesman*
Montgolfier Balloon, *first manned, untethered flight, 1783, Paris*
Lunar Eclipse 4/ 11/ 1865, *4 days before Lincoln assassinated*

Mercury

L. Flynt, *pornography publisher*
J. Millet, *artist*
Start of Hill/Thomas *Congressional Hearings, 1991*

Venus

Woody Allen, *comedian/writer/filmmaker*
Agrippina, *Roman Empress/poisoner/patron of literature/fiscal expert (Nero's mother, murdered on his order)*
M. de Falla, *composer*

Mars

Pope John Paul II
Cardinal J. O'Connor, *of New York City.*
R. Chaffee, *astronaut*
"Twilight Zone" *filming disaster, 1982, three killed*

Jupiter

W. Churchill, *PM of England*
Bill Clinton, *US President*
Henri II *of France*
T. Mann, *author*
R. Nader, *consumer activist*
Shari Lewis, *ventriloquist/puppeteer*
Ed Wynn, *comedian*
Lunar Eclipse 12/ 19 /45, *month ancient Gnostic gospels discovered, Naj Hammadi, Egypt*

Saturn

J. Paul Jones, *naval officer*
J. B. Priestley, *author*
N. Krushchev, *Soviet leader*
Solar Eclipse 7/ 10/ 9 AD OS, *two months before Germanic tribes wiped out 3 Roman legions at Teutoburger Forest*
London killer fog *1952 (w/Neptune)*

Uranus

E. Rickenbacker, *aviator/war hero*
Battle of Trafalgar, *last great action fought by sailing ships, 1805: England's sea superiority established for 100 years*
Solar Eclipse (path over Dakotas) 1/ 1/ 1889, two years before massacre of Sioux at Wounded Knee, SD by US Cavalry
Roe *v.* Wade, *US Supreme Court decision affirming women's right to abortion, 1973*
Eruption of Helgafell *volcano, Heimaey Isl, Iceland 1973*

Neptune

A. Schopenhauer, *philosopher/pessimist*
Lord Byron, *poet*
London killer fog, *1952(w/Saturn,)*
US Supreme Court *decision against school segregation 1954*

Pluto

Prince William *of England*
Unification Church *mass wedding, NY, 1982: 2,075 couples*
"Twilight Zone" *filming disaster 1982, 3 killed*

N. Node

J. Glenn, *astronaut/senator*
Madonna, *singer*
Michael Jackson, *rock star*

S. Node

S. Pepys, *diarist*
A. Schweitzer, *physician/missionary/musician*
A. Warhol, *artist*

Asc

Noel Coward, *playwright/songwriter*
G. Puccini, Sir A. Sullivan, *composers*
J. F. Kennedy, *US President (assassinated)*
Eruption of Helgafell *volcano, Heimaey Isl, Iceland, 1973 (cnj Uranus)*

MC

Princess Diana *of England*

Spica, Arcturus, cont.

Michaelangelo, *artist*

Danny Kaye, *comedian*

IC

1947 Aries ingress, Khirbet Qumran, Israel: *Dead Sea Scrolls discovered.*

ZUBENELGENUBI— South Scale, (was S. Claw of Scorpion) Nature: Jupiter, Mercury

	Long	*Lat*	*Dec*	*RA*	*Mag*	*Spec*
Alpha Librae	14Sco48	0 20	-15 58	14 50	2.75	A

*Quietly competitive, capable, intelligent

*Uncanny abilty to overcome setbacks & disappointments which they often encounter.

*Have to deal with attempts to dominate them, their own need to dominate others

*May encounter or perpetrate betrayals.

*Some are unforgiving, deliberately dishonest.

*May be loss of relatives &/or possessions, often in war or natural disasters.

*Religious and sexual issues

*May be an interest in the occult disciplines.

*Military leaders often born under this star-there is strategic ability and a longing to be a "figurehead" to others.

*Earthquakes, volcanoes, fires, head injuries.

Positive:	**Neutral:**	**Negative:**
intelligent	competitive	untruthful
musical	survival skills	unforgiving
strategic genius	psychic ability	manipulative
occult ability		dominating
		intense interest in sex, violence

Sun

A. Camus, *author*
R. Coniff, *conductor*
Billy Graham, *evangelist*
J. P. Souza, *composer*
Al Hirt, *trumpeter*
Patti Page, Johnny Rivers, Joni Mitchell, *singers*
Solar Eclipse, 10/ 23 /60 AD OS *preceding first Roman attempt to exterminate last Druid stronghold, Isle of Mona (Anglesey), Wales, 61 AD*
Surtsey, *new volcanic island, appeared off Iceland, 1963*

Moon

Ernie Pyle, *war correspondent (killed at Okinawa)*
J. Mitchell, *discredited US Att'y General (Watergate Scandal)*
Mario Andretti, *auto racer (twin), broke ribs, face scorched in flame-out*
Full Moon (Nissan 15) 4/ 10/ 73 AD OS: *defenders of fortress of Masada, last Jewish resistance against Rome, chose suicide rather than surrender, slavery*

Mercury

A. Carnegie, *steel tycoon/philanthropist*
A. Crowley, *occultist*
Oscar Wilde, *poet/playwright*
Bruce Lee, *martial arts actor*
Battle of Hastings, 1066
Montgolfier Balloon, *1st manned untethered flight, Paris, 1783*

Venus

Al Capp, *cartoonist*
H. G. Wells, *science fiction author*
E. Fermi, *nuclear physicist*

Mars

T. E. Lawrence *("of Arabia")*
Goebbels, *Nazi propaganda minister (poisoned wife,children; shot himself)*
Horatio Nelson, *naval hero, became blind in right eye after wound at 36-when his Sun progressed to this Mars*
A. Schweitzer, *physician/musician/missionary*

Jupiter

R. Reagan, *actor/US President*
Messalina, *Roman Empress/nymphomaniac (executed)*
J. Verne, J. Heller, *authors*
H. Ibsen, *playwright*
Chaing Kai-Shek, *warlord*
Tschaikowsky, *composer*
Triangle Factory *fire, 1911, 146 dead*

Zubenelgenubi, cont.

Tokyo/Yokohama 8.3 quake/tsunami/fire 1923: *143,000 dead, 200,000 injured, 1/2 million homeless*
Hebron massacre: *fanatic Jewish settler slaughtered Muslim worshippers at prayer: 50-60 dead*

Saturn
Anna Freud, *psychotherapist*
Virginia E. Johnson, *sex researcher*
Tamerlane, *conqueror*
A. Artaud, *morbid poet/playwright, became insane*
Jackie Cavalero-Slevin, *astrologer*
S. Peckinpah, *director of violent films*

Uranus
Mao Tse-Tung, N Krushchev, *communist leaders*
Neptune
S. Pepys, *diarist*
H. de Balzac, *author*
A. Pushkin, *poet (killed in duel)*
Surtsey, *new volcanic island off Iceland, appeared, 1963*

Pluto
Paracelsus, *alchemist/physician*
Battle of Teutoburger Forest: *Germanic tribes wiped out 3 Roman Legions, 9 AD*
Crash/fire *of sabotaged Pan Am 103, Lockerbie, Scotland, 1988*
7.1 San Francisco *quake, 1989*

N. Node
S. Mineo, *actor (murdered)*
E. Fermi, *nuclear physicist*
Columbus *sailed from Spain, 1492*
Battle of Vienna I, 1529: *100,000 Turks under Sulieman the Magnificent besieged Vienna, failed*

S. Node
A. Lavoisier, *chemist (guillotined)*
R. Reagan, *actor/US President*

Asc
G. Abell, *astronomer*

MC
Duke of Wellington *general/PM of England*
Tennessee Williams, *playwright*
Clark Gable, *actor*
N. Machiavelli, *political theorist*
1835 New York City fire ,(start) 650 buildings destroyed

ANTARES—Scorpion's Heart, ROYAL STAR The Watcher of the West

Nature: Mars, Jupiter

	Long	*Lat*	*Dec*	*RA*	*Mag*	*Spec*
alpha Scorpii	9Sag29	-4 34	-26 23	16 28	0.96v	M1

The fiery red heart of the Scorpion is exactly opposite Aldebaran. Like Aldebaran, it is an infra-red source, and one of the four great "royal stars" of ancient Persia.

*Possibility of great power, authority, wealth

*Courage, intelligence, prominence, honors and riches, but can fall from high position

*Tendency to violence, suspicion, self-destructiveness

*Talent for writing, the military, politics, sports, occult

*Quarrels with friends and relatives, who may not understand the native

*Domestic life may be unhappy, may be more than one marriage

*Great strategic ability; if chart warrants, may be prominence through war; otherwise war will bring loss, death, disgrace

*According to Watters, when Antares is directed to an angle, there is severe stress; I have found this to be true.

Mundane: War, destruction; issues of race, slavery, civil rights, human rights; issues of tolerance and/or intolerance; summit meetings, nuclear events, disasters; fires; assassinations; eye problems, blindness, heart attacks, heart surgery; astronomers, astrologers.

Positive:	**Neutral:**	**Negative:**
courage	tough	exaggerates
intelligence	energetic	hypocritical
eloquence	impulsive	belligerent
humor	glory-seeking	obstinate
hard worker		malevolent
strategic ability		destructive,
quick-witted		violent
imaginative		makes wrongful accusations

Essentials of Intermediate Astrology

Antares, cont.

Sun

W. Churchill, *PM of England*
William Blake, *poet/artist/mystic*
Woody Allen, *playwright/filmmaker/comedian*
Mark Twain, L. May Alcott, *authors*
Solar Eclipse 10/ 21/37 BC OS, *missed by (drunk) Chinese Imperial Astrologers Hsi & Ho Emperor had them beheaded (in China, Antares was "The Heart" of the great Blue Dragon, associated with the Imperial Family, & "The Great Fire" of Spring renewal; no wonder the Emperor was not amused!)*
US Navy *founded by Congress, 1775, Phila., PA*
Solar Eclipse 11/ 30/ 1834, *path over southern US: rise of abolitionist movements to end slavery*
President Andrew Jackson, assassination attempt
John Brown, *radical abolitionist, hanged, 1859*
Atomic reaction, *1st controlled , Chicago, 1942*
Montgomery, AL 1955: *Rosa Parks refused to move to back of bus , sparking civil rights movement*
School fire, *Chicago, 1958, 95 children killed*
First heart *transplant, 12/3/ 67*
First artificial heart *implant, 1982*

Moon

P. Picasso, *artist*
T. H. Huxley, *scientist/President of Royal Society*
Dr. Denton Cooley, *heart surgeon*
Copernicus, *astronomer*
Nietzsche, *philosopher*
G. Armstrong Custer, *military officer*
G. Borglum, *sculptor*
Moon, *final & strongest of New Madrid, MO, quake series, 1812*
Himmler *announcement to German generals of Hitler's "Final Solution" plan to exterminate Jews, 1943*
Full Moon 5 /31/ 88, *Moscow Reagan-Gorbachev summit*

Mercury

Bram Stoker *("Dracula")*, Jane Austen, *authors*
N. Leopold, *murderer*
Japanese *attacked Pearl Harbor, 1941*
President J. F. Kennedy *assassinated, 1963*

Venus

J. Racine, *playwright*
K. Vonnegut, *author*
M. Van Buren, *US President*
Capt. James Cook, *explorer/scientific navigator/geographer (killed by natives)*
Dick Francis, *jockey/author*
Dr C. Barnard, *heart surgeon*
Cocoanut Grove *nightclub fire, Boston, MA, 1942: 491 victims*
7.1 San Francisco *quake, 1989*

Mars

D. Ben Gurion, *PM of Israel*
A. Koestler, *author*
Dr M. deBakey, *heart surgeon*
W. Cronkite, *newsman*
Battle of Teutoburger Forest - *9 AD: Three Roman Legions wiped out by Germanic Tribes*
Great Chicago, IL & Peshtigo, WI *fires (same night) w/ high winds, 1871*
Surtsey, *new volcanic island, appeared off Iceland, 1963*

Jupiter

Karl Krafft, *astrologer (killed at Buchenwald)*
Helen Hayes, *actress*
1st live televised heart surgery *(w/Uranus) 1983, Phoenix, AZ*

Saturn

P. Cezanne, *artist*
First man in space (Gagarin), 1957
Start of "Great Peace March" *across US (LA-DC) for nuclear ban, 1986*

Uranus

Maria Sibylla Merian, *artist/naturalist*
Ada Byron, *mathematician/inventor (w/Babbage) of first mechanical calculator*
Bismarck, *German Chancellor*
H. Himmler, *Chief of Nazi SS (suicide)*
Ernie Pyle, *war correspondent (killed at Okinawa, 1945)*
Sen C. Pepper, *US Sen., advocate for seniors*
Great Galveston, TX hurricane, *1900: city totalled, 6,000 dead, "one of the worst recorded natural disasters ever to hit N. American continent"*
First televised heart surgery *(w/Jupiter), 1983*
Great Eruption of Tambora, *1815*

Neptune

A. Lincoln, *US President*
C. Darwin, *scientist*
Matthias *& companions burned alive for sedition, on orders of Herod, 4BC, Jerusalem*
Archbishop Laud *beheaded, 1645, London*
Patty Hearst *kidnapped, 1974*
"Objections to Astrology" *signed by 186 scientists, on front page of NY Times, Boston Globe, 1975*

Antares, cont.

President Ford, *two attempts to assassinate, Sept 1975*
Union Carbide *granted license to make deadly MIC gas in Bhopal, India, 1975*

Pluto
Nostradamus, *physician/astrologer/poet/seer*
J. Madison, *US President*

N. Node
W. Wordsworth, *poet*
A. A. Milne, *author/poet/playwright*
Ernie Pyle, *war correspondent (killed at Okinawa, 1945)*

S. Node
E. Warren, *Chief Justice, US Supreme Court*
Henri II *of France (killed in tournament)*

Asc
C. Lindbergh, *aviator*
John Glenn, *astronaut/US Senator*
R. Chaffee, *astronaut*
Start, Battle of Hastings, *10 /14 /1066 OS, approx. 9:30 AM*
Cornwallis *flag of truce, Yorktown, 1781*
Oakland Hills, CA *fire, 1991, 25 dead, 3,000 homes burned*

MC:
A. Lincoln, J. Monroe, *US Presidents*

FOMALHAUT— Royal Star, Watcher of the South, Nature: Venus, Mercury

	Long	*Lat*	*Dec*	*RA*	*Mag*	*Spec*
Alpha Piscis Aust	3Psc35	-21 08	-29 44	22 57	1.16	M2

*Struggle with cynicism, pessimism, fear, despair brought about by losses and disappointments

*Are carriers of secrets; tend to shut themselves off from social contacts

*Delve deeply into religious/philosophical waters, trying to make sense of life.

*A few give way to their weaknesses and sink into apathy, but those who acquire a strong foundation of faith rise above their fears and failures to become the teachers of succeeding generations.

*Battle for rights of minorities, outsiders, "underdogs"; fanaticism.

Positive:	**Neutral:**	**Negative:**
honorable	easily influenced	dissipated
intelligent	longing for utopia,	unfocussed
analytical	social justice	cynical,
feeling for	fearful, depressed	pessimistic
the underdog		angry, vengeful

Sun
Prince Naruhito *of Japan*
S. O'Faolain, *playwright*
Sir Thomas More, *philosopher/humanist/saint (beheaded)*
Robert Young, *actor*
S. Peckinpah, *film director*
Giordano Bruno *burned at stake for heresy, 1600, Rome*

Moon
G. Roddenberry, *writer/producer/creator of "Star Trek"*
Robert/Roberta Cowell, *transexual racing driver/ fighter pilot*

Mercury
P. Melanchthon, *theologian/reformer/educator*
Robert Burton, *mathematician/ astrologer/minister/ author ("Anatomy of Melancholy") (suicide)*
Charles Lindbergh, *aviator*
Patty Hearst *kidnapping, 1974*

Venus
R. Nixon, *US President (resigned)*
K. Singh, *mystic*

Mars
Benny Goodman, *bandleader*
Nell Gwyn, *fishmonger/mistress of Charles II of England*

Jupiter
Earl Warren, *Chief Justice, US Supreme Court*
L. Trotsky, *revolutionary leader (assassinated)*
A. Bremer, *psychotic/attempted assassin*

Formalhaut, cont.

Saturn
D. Bonhoeffer, *anti-Nazi minister (imprisoned, hanged)*
T. Edison, *inventor*
J.-P. Sartre, *existentialist philosopher (became blind)*
Schopenhauer, *philosopher/pessimist*
C. Leadbeater, *theosophist*
Battle of Tsushima Strait- *Russian vs Japanese fleet 1905 Russia lost 33 ships: total Japanese victory stunned world*
Van carrying Hasidic students attacked, *1994, Brooklyn, NY*

Uranus
Bret Harte, *author*
19th Amendment *(Women's Suffrage) ratified, 1920*

Neptune
P. Gauguin, *artist*
J. Whitcombe Riley, *poet*
First Women's Rights Convention, *Seneca Falls, NY, 1848*

Pluto
Amos Bronson Alcott, *transcendentalist philosopher*
M. Fillmore, *US President*

N. Node
F. Dostoievsky, H. Hesse, *authors*
W. Landowska, *harpsichordist*
Capt. James Cook, *explorer/scientific navigator & geographer (killed by natives)*

S. Node
J. Whitcombe Riley, *poet*
Archbishop Laud *beheaded, 1645, London*

Asc
Gertrude Stein, *author*
Vincent Price, *actor/art collector*

Sen. Edmund Muskie, *US Senator*

MC
F. Schubert, *composer*

SCHEAT— (conjunct Black Hole NGC7457 Pegasi) one of four stars of the "Great Square of Pegasus" Nature: Mars, Mercury

	Long	*Lat*	*Dec*	*RA*	*Mag*	*Spec*
Beta Pegasi	29Psc06	31 08	27 58	23 03	2.42v	M2

*Potential for a high level of artistic, musical, literary expression

*Imaginative, inventive

*Enjoy position or feelings of power, influence, control

*May experience difficult family environment, abuse

*Cause their own problems through headstrong, erratic behavior. ften refuse to listen to advice

*May have difficulty focusing, concentrating on goals

*Run gamut from high ideals, sensitivity to suffering of others to uncaring, selfish self-gratification

*Subject to criticism, loss of friends, persecutions

*Vacillating, erratic, accident-prone

*May suffer sorrow, misfortune, grief

*Sorrows, suffering, extreme misfortune, sadism, sadistic pederasty, eye problems, murder, insanity, imprisonment, floods, drowning, earthquakes, tsunamis, aggression.

Postive:	**Neutral:**	**Negative:**
artistic	psychic	unreliable
musical	sensitive	headstrong
literary	stubborn	erratic, lazy
creative	charming	sadistic
inventive	—	deceitful

Sun
J. Madison, G. Cleveland, *US Presidents*
S. Mallarmé, *symbolist poet*
Irving Wallace, Philip Roth, *authors*
Edgar Cayce, *psychic/photographer*
A. Speer, *Nazi architect/Armaments, War Production Minister (20-year imprisonment)*

Moon
Hillary Clinton, *US First Lady/lawyer/spokesperson for children's issues, health care*

Scheat, cont.

H. Hesse, *author*
R. Rodgers, *composer*
John Wayne Gacy, *serial sexual torture-murderer of young men (executed)*
Moon at noon, *1st US Thanksgiving proclaimed, 1789*
Silent Spring published, 1962
Titanic *sank, 1912*
Wreck of Titanic *discovered, 1985*

Mercury
Baudelaire, *poet/critic*
Dinah Shore, *singer*
Fort Sumter *fired on by Confederates , SC, 1861, start of US Civil War*
Great Chicago flood, *4/ 6/ 92 (with Venus)*

Venus
V. Van Gogh, *artist (became insane)*
F. Mendelssohn, *composer*
Hans C. Anderson, *author*
Maj. Gen. Orde Wingate, *commando genius (died in plane crash)*

Mars
Spencer Tracy, Burgess Meredith, Stewart Granger, Debbie Reynolds, *actors*
Simone de Beauvoir, *author*
Titanic *launched, 1911, Belfast (Mars ruled 8th)*
Massive 8.5 Alaska quake/tsunami, *1964: huge upheaval of earth "10 million times stronger than Hiroshima bomb"*

Jupiter
W. von Goethe, *poet*
W. L. Shirer, S. Bellow, *authors*
Mary Cassatt, *artist-nearly blind in old age*
Yul Brynner *(died of lung cancer)*, Peter Falk *(lost one eye), actors*

Saturn
Lionel Barrymore, Rex Harrison, *actors*
Ian Brady, *sadistic torturer/murderer of children*
Noah-Jiro Greenfeld, *autistic child*
NOW *(Nat'l Organization of Women), 1966, Washington, DC*

Uranus
F. Castro, *communist dictator*
Miles Davis, *jazz trumpeter*
Marilyn Monroe, *actress*
John Burr Fairchild, *fashion editor*
St. Bernadette *(Bernadette Soubirous) (asthma, died of bone TB)*

Neptune
Ivan the Terrible, *Tzar*
R. Steiner, *occultist/educator*

Pluto
H. Melville *(manic depression)*, G. Flaubert, *authors*
F. Engels, *socialist*
W. Whitman, *poet*
Queen Victoria *& consort Prince Albert of Saxe-Coburg*
H. Schliemann, *banker/amateur archeologist (discovered site of ancient Troy)*
Clara Barton, *nurse/founder of American Red Cross*
G. Coubert, *artist (imprisoned for political activities)*
Massacre of the Huguenots, *1572, Paris*

N. Node
J. Thurber, *cartoonist/humorist*
Arthur Bremer, *psychotic, attempted assassin*

S. Node
Kurt Vonnegut, *author*
Dr C. Barnard, *heart surgeon (First heart transplant)*
Charles Bronson, *actor (started as coal miner)*

Asc
Robert Redford, *actor (claustrophobic)*
Confederates *fired upon Fort Sumter, SC, 1861, start of US Civil War*

MC:
William Blake, *artist/poet/mystic*
O. Hammerstein II, *lyricist*
Marie Curie, *scientist*
Isaac Stern, *violinist*
Jerry Lewis, *comedian*
Keith Emerson, *rock musician*
Charles Jayne, *astrologer (almost blind)*
Henri II *of France, died after shattered lance pierced eyes in tournament)*
MC at London, *Aries Ingress 1910: King Edward VII died one months later, veto power of House of Lords ended within year*
MC at Berlin, *Aries ingress 1914, year WWI started*
Great 8.0 T'ang Shan, China quake *1976, 1/2-3/4 million dead, entire province devastated*
MC at Davenport, IA, Solar Eclipse 5/21/ 93, *preceding great Mississippi flood*

Essentials of Intermediate Astrology

Learning astrology, and developing proficiency in its techniques, is a demanding, time-consuming process.

Why, then, return to the ancient sky figures and their component stars? Quite simply, because this is where astrology began, where it still resides in its purest form, and because these ancient stars manifest distinct energies. One chapter cannot begin to cover all that is known about these forces, but will serve as a beginning and introduction to the roots of our discipline.

Because time and space are limited, very many important stars had to be left out of this chapter. I hope each student, when time allows, will delve more deeply into these extremely powerful elements in the sky.

QUESTIONS

1. Why are the stars, in astrology, called "fixed"? (Give two reasons)
2. Do stars have their own individual motion? What is it called?
3. What is precession? Is a precession correction subtracted or added to a natal chart as time progresses?
4. Which is brighter: Aldebaran, magnitude 0.85, or Fomalhaut, magnitude 1.16?
5. How do you measure a star's

   (a) latitude

   (b) declination?

   (c) Right Ascension?
6. What is the preeminent shipwreck star?
7. What is the effect of a royal star on one's nativity?
8. What star is connected to both nuclear events and fires?
9. What characteristics might be manifested by a person with Mars at Prima Hyadum, Saturn at South Assellus, Neptune at Vindemiatrix, and the Sun-Mercury midpoint at Castor?
10. What might be the fate of a ship launched with Sun (ruling the 12th) culminating at Aldebaran, Mars (ruling the 8th house) at Scheat, and Neptune at Castor?

ANSWERS:

1. a) In ancient times, stars seemed to hold their relative positions eternally, while other sky phenomena shifted and changed.

   b) They were the only "fixed" points from which other celestial motions could be measured.

2. a) Yes.

   b) It is called "proper motion."

3. a) Because the Earth "wobbles" on its axis as it rotates, each year the Vernal Equinox is 0°00'50.23" west of its position the year before this adds up to 1° every 72 years.

   b) Precession is added to natal positions as time progresses.

4. Aldebaran is brighter.

5. a) A star's latitude is measured in degrees North or South of the Eclipseiptic.

   b) declination is measured in degrees North or South of the Celestial Equator.

   c) Right Ascension is measured in degrees along the Celestial Equator, starting from 0° Aries.

6. Baten Kaitos, Zeta Ceti, is the star most often found in shipwrecks.

7. A royal star in one's nativity may bring wealth, prominence, honors, but the possibility of a fall from grace. It enables one to associate with prominent people in one's chosen field. There is danger of illness, eye problems, violent death.

8. Antares is associated with both fires and nuclear events.

9. Since all four of these stars manifest great talent, leadership ability, and aggressiveness, these will most likely be prominent in this person's life. There is considerable energy (Prima Hyadum, S. Asselus), a tendency to be headstrong (Castor, Vindemiatrix), daring and adventurous (Prima Hyadum, Castor). With Saturn at S. Asselus and both Sun, Mercury at Castor; there is a tendency to be dictatorial, and he will either exhibit or suffer (or both) fanaticism and intolerance. Neptune at Vindemiatrix (the "Star of Widowhood") shows that he might sustain the loss of a partner. Three of these stars (Prima Hyadum, S Asselus, Castor) show a possible violent streak, and since Mars and Saturn are both represented at these violent stars, this, combined with his aggressiveness, show a person with great abilities, but a dictatorial personality, and the grave danger of the loss of control. (O. J. Simpson)

10. Aldebaran and Castor are associated with shipwreck, and Scheat with drowning. Not auspicious for a launch! (Titanic)

Bibliography:---------------------------------

Allen, Richard Hinckley. 1899. Reprint. *Star Names: Their Lore & Meaning.* Mineola, NY: Dover Publications, Inc., 1963.

Daniel, Clifton, *ed. Chronicle of the 20th Century.* Chronicle Publications, Inc., Mt Kisco, NY, 1987.

Eggenberger, David. *An Encyclopedia of Battles.* Mineola, NY: Dover Publications, Inc. 1985.

Hirshfeld, A., Sinnott, R.W., eds. *Sky Catalogue 2000.*: Sky Publishing Corporation, Cambridge, MA, 1982.

Manilius, Marcus. *ca.* 10 AD. *Astronomica.* Trans by G. P. Goold. Cambridge, MA: Harvard University Press, 1977.

Nash, Jay Robert. *Darkest Hours.* Nelson-Hall, Chicago, IL, 1976.

Pottenger, Mark. *CCRS Horoscope Program.* Orleans, MA: AGS Software, 1988.

Ptolemy, Claudius. *ca.* 150 AD. *Tetrabiblos.* Trans by W. G. Waddell & F. F. Robbins. Cambridge, MA: Harvard University Press, 1940.

Robson, Vivian E.. *The Fixed Stars & Constellations in Astrology.* The Aquarian Press, 1969.

Rosenberg, Diana K.. *Correspondence Course in Fixed Stars & Constellations.* New York, 1989.

Contributors

Contributors

Alphee Lavoie

Alphee began his astrological career in 1962, abandoning a lucrative engineering business. He is founder-director of the Astrological Institute of Research in Connecticut. He has been consulting clients on a full time basis for 30 years. He has combined his engineering and astrological backgrounds to create popular AIR Software programs including chart calculation, research, horary, electional and financial programs. Author of *Horary Lectures* and *Lose this Book... and then find it with Horary.* Member of the NCGR Advisory Board, he serves as Fund-raising Director.

Diana Rosenberg

Rob Hand has called Diana Rosenberg *"the leading authority on fixed stars."* She is also the NCGR Journal's Copy and Charts Editor, and vice president of NCGR's Uranian Society (Uranian / Cosmobiology SIG). A faculty member of NCGR and UAC,, she has written articles for the *NCGR Journal, Astrological Quarterly, Traditional Astrology, Mountain Astrologer, Dell Horoscope, American Astrology* and numerous other astrological journals and magazines. She is the author of *Fixed Stars Workbook* and a *Correspondence Course in Fixed Stars and Constellations*, and has co-authored *Asteroid Names and Nodes* and *Ephemeris of the Asteroid Diana.* Llewellyn's *The Astrology of the Macrocosm* includes her chapter in earthquake prediction.

Susan Manuel

A professional astrologer since 1973, Susan has taught natal and mundane astrology for many years. As a researcher, writer, speaker and consultant, she specializes in forecasts based on traditional methods enhanced by innovative heliocentric techniques. Susan is on the board of Project Focus, is the editor of the *NCGR Memberletter* and is a member of AFAN, ISAR and NCGR. She has a degree in anthropology from the University of Michigan, and much of her work in astrology is focused on cultural change and sociological trends in historic and contemporary American culture.

Frances McEvoy

Began the study of astrology in 1948 with Grant Lewis in Arizona where she grew up. In 1951, she moved to Boston and continued her studies with Isabel Hickey and, later, with Dane Rudhyar. She worked as a newspaper reporter and as a portrait painter. Frances has particular interest in retrograde planets, planetary patterns including the yod, and planetary cycles. She has been president of the Boston Chapter of NCGR for 16 years and a member of the National Board since 1981. She is editor of the NCGR *Geocosmic Magazine.*

Essentials of Intermediate Astrology

Joyce Levine

Joyce Levine is an astrological consultant, lecturer, and metaphysical teacher with over 20 years experience. She is an Advisory Board Member of NCGR and its Boston Chapter, a certified professional by the AFA, and a Past President of the New England Astrological Association. She is the author of *A Beginner's Guide to Astrological Interpretation* and the text for *Starscope,* astrological delineation software by A.I.R. Software. In 1994, Joyce founded Visualizations, a metaphysical publishing company specializing in meditation tapes.

J. Lee Lehman Ph.D.

Lee is NCGR Research Director, Chair of the Executive Committee, and served as Program Co-Chair for UAC '95. Her publications include *The Ultimate Asteroids Book, Essential Dignities,* and *The Book of Rulerships.* Her numerous articles bridge the gap between classical and modern astrology. She is Corporate Treasurer for UAC, Inc.

Ken Negus, Ph.D.

Ken is from Princeton, N.J. He is a member of the NCGR's National Education Committee, and the National Board representative for the NCGR Special Interest Groups. He has been president of the Astrological Society of Princeton since 1972, and a professor Emeritus of German at Rutgers University since 1986. His publications include writings on astrology and literature, harmonics, Chiron, astrology at the university, the validation of astrology, Johann Kepler, the Cyclic Index, four volumes of his own astrological and esoteric poetry, and numerous translations of poetry and astrological texts.

Maria K. Simms

Maria is an alumna of Illinois Wesleyan University with a B.F.A. in art. She is Director of ACS Publications and Astro Computing Services. Maria has been a consultant, teacher and lecturer in astrology for over 21 years. She is a certified as a professional consultant by National Council for the Geocosmic Research and by American Federation of Astrologers (AFA). Author of *Twelve Wings of the Eagle, The Dial Detective* and *The Magical Child.*

Michael Munkassey
Michael has been active in astrology and astrological research for over 25 years. He developed his astrological interests when efforts to forecast movements in financial markets exposed him to cycles. Michael is a member of the executive committee and NCGR Clerk. He has lectured internationally on astrology and has appeared on numerous radio and television shows. He is the author of *Midpoint: Unleashing the Power of the Planets, Concept Dictionary* and *The Astrology Thesaurus: House Keywords.* He has contributed chapters to Llewellyn's *Financial Astrology* and *The Houses.*

Warren Kinsman
Warren is president of the Washington, DC NCGR Metro Chapter. He serves on the national NCGR board as Director of Chapters Affairs. Warren is a graduate of Syracuse University where he studied religion. He joined the peace corps during Kennedy Administration and served two years in Turkey. In 1988 he volunteered for Project 2000, a program designed to bring adult male role-models into the classroom to serve as mentors to inner-city boys, through their college years.. It was through this program he meet the boys described in this article.

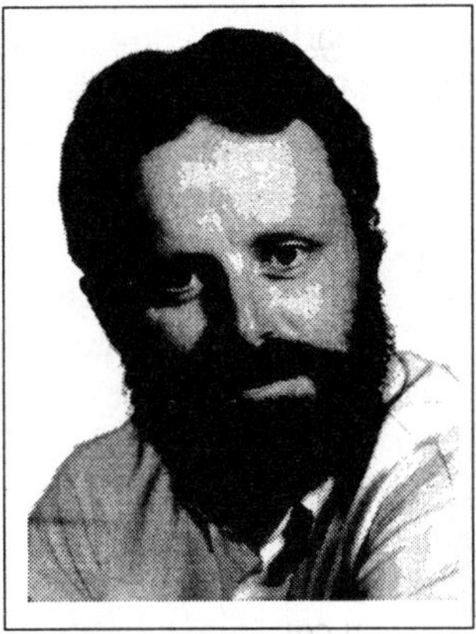

Steve Cozzi
Steve Cozzi began his study of astrology in 1968. He has a Bachelor of Arts in Psychology and minor in Biology from Metro-State, Denver. His lectures and workshop have helped hundreds of people gain new insights. Teaching both basic building blocks and advanced concepts, Steve has continually provided fresh ideas and sound methods. He is President of the South Florida Chapter of NCGR and a past Vice President of Rocky Mountain Chapter. He is the author of *Generations and Outer Planet Cycles* and *Planet in Locality.*

Robert Hand
Has been an astrologer since 1960 and a full-time professional since 1972. His books include Planets in Composite, Planets in Transit, Planets in Youth, Horoscope Symbols, and Essays on Astrology. He is one of the founders of Astrolabe, Inc. and currently is involved with the Association for the Retrieval of Historical Astrological Tests and is the general editor for Project Hindsight. He is the chairman of NCGR and a patron of the Faculty of Astrological Studies.

Essentials of Intermediate Astrology

Lorraine Welsh
Is a Director of NCGR and editor in chief of the NCGR Journal. She is vice president of her local chapter (Boston) and editor of its monthly publication, *The Astrologers' Newsletter.* Lorraine is also vice president of NCGR's ASTSIG (special interest group on Asteroids), for which she edits the occasional publication *GAIA*. Although she uses many astrological techniques in her personal work, she relies very heavily on transits.

Bill Meridian
Obtained his MBA in 1972 and began to study astrology and psychotherapy. He worked on Wall Street for Merrill Lynch as an analyst. He began applying computers to financial astrology in 1983, and eventually designed the *AstroAnalyst* and *Financial Trader* programs. He is currently a fund manager in the Middle East. His most recent publication is *Planetary Stock Trading.*

Mary Downing
Is Executive Director of NCGR, has served on the AFAN steering committee, and participated in planning the past four UACs. She is a graphics designer who produces many of NCGR's publications and advertising materials. Mary has written for many publications, and contributed to *Financial Astrology in the '90s.*

Gary Christen
Holds a Bachelor in Arts Degree in Astrology through Livingston College, Rutgers University (1974). He is president of Astrolabe, Inc. and has been lecturing since 1970, counseling since 1969. Although noted as an Uranian astrologer, he is involved in many other forms of our art and science.

Notes